S0-BRO-222

917.303
D39s

74707

DATE DUE			

GAYLORD M-2   PRINTED IN U.S.A.

WITHDRAWN

Supergrow

by Benjamin DeMott

Supergrow

ESSAYS AND REPORTS ON

IMAGINATION IN AMERICA

BY **Benjamin DeMott**

E. P. DUTTON & CO., INC.

NEW YORK   1969

CARL A. RUDISILL LIBRARY
LENOIR RHYNE COLLEGE

917.303
D39s
74707
July, 1971

Copyright © 1969, 1968, 1967, 1966, by Benjamin DeMott
All rights reserved. Printed in the U.S.A.
First Edition

No part of this publication may be reproduced or transmitted in any form
or by any means, electronic or mechanical, including photocopy, recording,
or any information storage and retrieval system now known or to be invented,
without permission in writing from the publisher, except by a reviewer
who wishes to quote brief passages in connection with a review written
for inclusion in a magazine, newspaper or broadcast.

Published simultaneously in Canada by Clarke, Irwin & Company
Limited, Toronto and Vancouver

Library of Congress Catalog Card Number: 71–82042

A 31975   [01]

NOTE: The essays in this book appeared originally (in some instances under
different titles or in different form) in *The American Scholar, Antioch Review, Book World, Educational Record, Esquire, New American Review, The New York Times, Saturday Review,* and *The Urban Review.*

How to Raise a Brighter Child (excerpt): © 1967 by Joan Beck. Reprinted by permission of Simon & Schuster, Inc.

Give Your Child a Superior Mind (excerpt): © 1966 by Siegfried and Therese Engelmann. Reprinted by permission of Simon & Schuster, Inc.

Excerpt from poetry of Joel Oppenheimer: The Love Bit. © 1962, Joel Oppenheimer. Published by Corinth Books, New York.

Excerpt from Understanding Media by Marshall McLuhan: From Understanding Media by Marshall McLuhan. © 1964 by Marshall McLuhan. Used with permission of McGraw-Hill Book Company.

Excerpt from W. H. Auden's *Lullaby:* © 1940 and renewed 1968 by W. H. Auden. Reprinted from Collected Shorter Poems 1927–1957 by W. H. Auden by permission of Random House, Inc.

Florida Road Workers by Langston Hughes: From The Panther and the Lash by Langston Hughes. © 1967 by Arna Bontemps and George Houston Bass. Reprinted by permission of Alfred A. Knopf, Inc.

Life Story by Tennessee Williams: Tennessee Williams, In the Winter of Cities. © 1956 by Tennessee Williams. Reprinted by permission of New Directions Publishing Corporation.

Merritt Parkway by Denise Levertov: Denise Levertov, The Jacob's Ladder. © 1958 by Denise Levertov Goodman. Reprinted by permission of New Directions Publishing Corporation.

To Joey
Tom
Benj
&
Megan
Love from the old man—

Contents

Contents

Foreword

The essays collected in this book are about everything under the sun—rock music, improving your sex, the Hollywood life, the uses of poetry, Marshall McLuhan, violence in Mississippi, group-grope theater, student revolts at home and abroad. . . . And there isn't a unified tone and manner. Now the writer looks detached or even invisible; now he steps onstage and mugs a little; one minute he's in slippers in a study with fire and wine and cat (a relaxing ramble), and the next he's pressing an idea, selling something, obviously out to convince.

Still, there is one kind of unity: most of the pieces keep turning a single simple idea, namely, that people ought to use their imaginations more. For revolutionary sensibilities, this idea lacks charm. Using the imagination is felt to mean working for a sense of what it would be like to be Over There, on the other side, with the enemy. And revolutionaries consider that such work complicates passion, weakens the lust for confrontation, and leads as often as not to bargaining and other accredited mendacity. An example: The Black Panther Chairman abuses the black Supreme Court Justice (the latter having just denied a Cleaver plea) as an "Uncle Tom, a bootlicker, a nigger pig, a Tonto, and a punk." And at that moment I decide to undertake to "use my imagination." Why bother? asks the revolutionary. What will come of it, except some brooding to no purpose on intricacies and counter-pressures within the Supreme Court Justice's feelings? Why smooth out jaggedness and fury? Why fuzz up issues? We've

11

been "imagining the other side of the question" for generations in this country: Why hang ourselves up, forever pondering the "true nature" of our Hitlers, Wallaces, Daleys, and the rest?

My belief is that this line is mistaken: the country hasn't arrived where it is because it's overpopulated with orgiasts of the personal imagination. Its problems are traceable largely to obliviousness, habitual refusal to harry private imaginations into constructing the innerness of other lives—both the life of the Supreme Court Justice and that of the Panther Chairman. Long ago, William James remarked that Americans refuse to see that foreigners "have insides of their own." This blindness has had clear consequences for recent American foreign policy, and if it were replaced with a measure of imaginative flexibility, it's doubtful that the sequel would be nothing but political blur. The claim of this book isn't, in short, that the reason for more reliance on the resources of the constructive imagination is that radical energies need dissipating; it is that the right use of the constructive imagination increases the effectiveness of those energies, enables people to anticipate moves and countermoves, prevents them from becoming frozen into postures of intransigence or martyrdom which, though possessing a "terrible beauty," have as their main consequence the stiffening of resistance and the slowing of change.

Two more words. The idea of imagining-from-within has vitality in numberless contexts unmentioned here. Nothing in these pages, for instance, about phenomenology or Husserl—and what post-Heglian wouldn't chuckle at the picture of somebody running on about the personal idea, or being-for-itself, or the *Umwelt*, without touching that body of thought? Nothing here either about the psychological or developmental ramifications of the themes, and they are fascinating in themselves, as a hundred passages in Piaget attest:

> In verbal intercourse it would seem that children do not understand each other any better than they understand us. The same phenomenon occurs between them as between them and us: the words spoken are not thought of from the point of view of the person

spoken to, and the latter, instead of taking them at their face value, selects them according to his own interest, and distorts them in favor of previously formed conceptions. . . . This phenomenon occurs, it is true, among adults. But these have had at least some practice in argument or conversation, and they know their faults. They make an effort to understand and be understood, unless indeed distrust or anger reduces them to a childish state, because experience has shown them the appalling density of the human mind. Children have no suspicion of this. They think that they both understand and are understood.

[*Language and Thought of the Child*]

—But the subject launched is, after all, endless, and these collected glances around the culture scene weren't in my mind means of situating a theme solidly in a system of thought or inquiry: they were simply chances to bring an old idea into sight again and put some claims for it in passing.

Finally, there's the matter of how to judge my implied argument or cause as a whole—and I admit I'm defensive about this. Is the fair test, for someone who's on about the marvels of the imagination, how well he uses his own? Do we say: Has this writer earned the right to puff the imagination in general by showing that his own in particular is swell? Now and then I act as though I believed that test were fair—but it is an act. My failures or successes at seeing what was going on in the mind, say, of an adversary teacher in Mississippi or in the minds of a homosexual's neighbors at an eastern watering place—these determine the "quality of a piece," but little more than that. The case is that the arena in which to judge the worth of the sort of imagining most often spoken of in this book isn't literary (Jack is a better writer than Jim, etc.). The testing arena is dailiness, ordinary human encounter, family life experience, the supper table. And about the value of the imagination on that turf there really isn't any arguing: take the stuff away, and none of us, tads or dads, can live.

AMHERST, MASSACHUSETTS
January 9, 1969

Supergrow

Superflow

"But He's a Homosexual...."

What is a homosexual artist? A devil and a liar, says the current noisy indictment—a desecrater, a self-server, a character nobody on earth should trust. Sly and sulky, he poisons hope and idealism with the mean flow of his resentment. Sick and exhibitionistic, he jams the media with neuroses, teaching that Women are destroyers and heterosexual domestic life is hell. Worse by far, the man is power-mad. Skinnying his way onto established grant committees, prize panels, editorial boards, and other seats of authority, he spurns aspirants not of his clique, thereby creating a tyranny of taste that soon will have every center of imaginative expression—theater, opera, symphony hall, publishing house, museum, gallery—under its cheesy thrall. In sum: The homosexual artist is an enemy of the people, a threat to the quality of American life.

As every magazine reader knows, indictments like the foregoing have for some time been highly salable. For a representative sample, consider an article about Messrs. Albee, Warhol, et al.—the title was "Who's Afraid of Aunt Fanny?"—that appeared a while back in *Ramparts*. The initial stance of this piece was one of tolerant sophistication; the author, Gene Marine, gave assurances that he was no scandalmonger, no keyhole inquirer into celebrities' private lives, no naïf eager to set up equations between, say, "long-haired hippies" and homosexuality:

Let me put things straight [he wrote], for you and the libel lawyers. I don't absolutely know for certain the names of any famous homo-

17

sexuals, though I probably make the same guesses you do, and if I did know any for certain, I wouldn't tell you. As far as I know, Edward Albee is a square family man, Andy Warhol is afflicted with satyriasis and California has no homosexuality south of the Santa Ynez river. I couldn't care less.

But having given these assurances, Marine went on to prove them spurious. Employing the tricks of an innuendo-cutie and a manner of sleazy downrightness, he developed an ever more expansive series of charges, and ended by dealing damnation round the entire American cultural landscape. Here are some steps in the progress:

> The point is that homosexual playwrights and homosexual directors and homosexual producers are having more and more to say about what can and can't be done in an American theater.

> People who know more about it than I do . . . tell me that it's even worse in the world of art—by which I mean painting and sculpture. The galleries take what the decorators want them to take, and the decorators want them to take their gay friends.

> I'm getting damned tired of all the art being campy and all the plays being queer and all the clothes being West Fourth Street and the whole bit. *Some* I don't mind, but it's getting too close to *all*, and I have the feeling that there are healthier bases for a culture.

> You can take almost any part of the world of culture, and there it is, in bold lavender. Dance and interior design, fashions (women's *and* men's), music—especially outside the relatively virile jazz and rock fields—and music promotion, novels and poetry, little theater and magazines.

The ploy in question is, predictably, more or less standard throughout the contemporary muckraking press. (*Fact* enlarged the area of presumed "domination" by printing a "study" of homosexuals in TV.) And hints of the influence of this ploy— more about them in a minute—have been visible in journals of a quite different character: the Sunday drama section of *The New York Times*, highbrow periodicals like the *New York Review of Books* and the *Drama Review*.

That the subject of homosexual influence in the arts should engage attention at this moment isn't mysterious. American interest in matters cultural and aesthetic is on the rise. New levels of candor about sexual behavior seem to be achieved every other week. And, most important, the national reserves of credulity have not diminished much over the years. If this were not so, baiters of homosexual art probably would pull smaller audiences. For their charges are rooted in the belief that centralized control of the arts can be achieved by a nonpolitical, essentially nonideological nonorganization—and only the credulous can rest comfortably in such faith. Tyrannies of taste do occur, to be sure— they are inevitable whenever a professionally practiced art lacks multiple centers of power. (Serious music is the sector of the arts that most nearly meets the latter description at this moment. Outlets for the work of living American composers are extremely few, which means that homosexual cliquishness could—some informed people say it does—throttle free musical expression.) And homosexual centers of power do exist—a cluster of art galleries here, a group of experimental moviemakers there. (One famous Fifty-seventh Street gallery has even been, in fairly recent days, a center of homosexual poetry as well as of painting and sculpture.)

But countless other galleries flourish that are nothing of the sort, and a half-dozen low-budget cinematic experimenters continue to produce—and exhibit—films untouched by what is called "homosexual fantasy." And in other sectors of the arts mixed situations seem generally the rule. The financial backers of one newly founded off-Broadway production firm are homosexuals; those of several other newish producing firms are not. A few trade publishing houses appear to be particularly well disposed to homosexual writers; the majority have no clear policy save the pursuit of profit. Given present complications and uncertainties of taste and prejudice, and given the continued emergence from time to time of new centers of activity (the American Place Theatre is an example), the danger of total domination will remain slight. Cliquishness cannot be abolished, and, as just indicated, it can cause damage in fields of artistic endeavor where opportunities for professional hearing are subject to autocratic control. But, while complacency about these fields is inexcusable, they are less numerous then scourgers of "homosexual tyranny"—and the more gullible of their readers—profess to believe. And the heralded culture explosion should reduce their number, not increase it, in the future.

But if the homosexual himself isn't a serious threat to cultural vigor and variety, the same can't be said of those who harass him in print. The point at issue here isn't, true enough, easy to grasp. A piece writer who beats up "the fairies" for a few thousand words would seem, on the face of it, only another harmless canny profiteer. It's plain, after all, that complaints about "homosexual art" will never mobilize hostility and frustration at the destructive levels sustained in yesteryear by the Red-baiters.* And conceivably "frank talk" in this area, no matter how woolly and superstitious, can have beneficial effects. (The public needs to be reminded, some say, that reputations in the arts are made things, not miracles: edifices built by the continuous effort not simply of a single artist but of friends who sometimes praise a man's work when what they actually value is his personal charm. And the public needs the experience, others say, of *talking* about homosexuality—because such talk fosters the growth of tolerance: when homosexuality in one quarter of the community is freely and openly assessed, responses to homosexuality in the community at large should become less hysterical.) Why turn hypercritical toward characters who, whatever their own personal cynicism, may function as nourishers of American sophistication?

The answer is simple: At the center of most talk about "homosexual art" lies the assumption that books, pictures, poems created by homosexuals are private documents, narrow in range,

* Two mythy items that figure in "thinking" about the coming homosexualization of America are the concept of a nation asleep at the switch, as it were, too absorbed in business to notice its sex is changing, and the concept of a doomsday recognition scene, a moment at which people discover to their horror that they have frittered away their birthrate and are the last generation of their kind. Both concepts figured, in slightly different form, in Senator McCarthy's speeches on the Commie conspiracy a decade ago.

incapable of speaking truly to anyone not himself a homosexual. The prime effect of this already widely disseminated idea has been to neutralize or denature several of the most provocative critical images of contemporary life to win mass audiences since World War II. And from this it follows that the self-appointed enemy of "homosexual art" isn't just a nuisance: he is a pernicious waster of an invaluable cultural resource.

As might be guessed, the ways of waste—the means by which commentators cheat the work of homosexuals and torture it out of strength—are nothing if not ingenious. Chief among them is a trick of medical inside-dopesterism that transforms texts clear enough on their surface into complex codes or allegories—productions whose deepest truths yield themselves only to psychoanalytic exegesis. Consider, for instance, the operations of clinical exegetes on Edward Albee's *Who's Afraid of Virginia Woolf?* In both the stage and film versions, the ending of this work seems a moment of poignance. Weary beyond fury, blasted (almost) into kindness, George and Martha have arrived at a nowhere world in which combat is pointless. The audience knows that cozy murmurs about reconciliation, forgiveness, happiness ahead would be puerile, but is nevertheless aware of a passage into an atmosphere of feeling less ridden by fantasy, more open, more yielding. Nobody has "won," but a loss has been suffered jointly: pity is in the room.

Enter the clinical exegete, and every "simplistic" reading of the play is laved in scorn. (Exegetes of this brand are printed in psychoanalytic journals as well as in magazines of art.) *Virginia Woolf*, wrote Dr. Donald M. Kaplan (a psychoanalyst) in the *Drama Review*, is in its essence a predictable homosexual claim that "genitality is . . . an unnecessary burden"; the closing scene is a moment of triumph, it signifies that a married man "can prevail through the tactics of pregenital perversity" and need not grow up to his role:

> The sexuality of the parental bedroom [Nick and Martha offstage] is no match for the multifarious derivatives of George's oral aggression, anality, voyeurism, masochism and procreative reluctance. In

the end, Martha returns to George, as she so often has in the past. The enfant terrible again triumphs over the cocksmen of the outside world, and the nursery is preserved. . . .

Fitted into this pattern of homosexual aggression and glee, Albee's play is easily dismissed as a projection of dementia—a set of remarks about Rorschach cards, a collection of symptoms, nothing a "straight" could even begin to take straight.

Clinical exegesis isn't, of course, the harshest line of critique found in discussion of so-called homosexual art. Traditional American manliness makes itself heard in *Fact* and *Ramparts* ("I *like* women," Gene Marine said stoutly) and even in tonier periodicals—witness Philip Roth's attack on Albee's "pansy prose" that appeared in the *New York Review* following the opening of *Tiny Alice*. But the survival of tough-guyism is less interesting—and less regrettable—than the nearly universal acceptance of the central assumption just mentioned, namely, that art produced by homosexuals is irrelevant to life as lived by nonhomosexuals. A year or two ago the Sunday theater section of *The New York Times* printed a pair of articles by Stanley Kauffmann, then the newspaper's drama critic, on the "subject of the homosexual dramatist." A liberal, humane man, Kauffmann clearly had no terror of "perverts," no desire to suppress the work of the artists he was discussing. His articles, seen by many as another heroic breakthrough for frankness, dealt in passing with the matter of "homosexual style," and with the supposed tendency of the homosexual writer to treat theme and subject as immaterial and surface as all-important. They were partly conceived as defenses of the homosexual's right to freedom of expression, and they offered several telling observations about uses and abuses of that right.

Yet everywhere in his comments this critic signified his conviction that plays by homosexual dramatists should be regarded as codes to be deciphered, disguises to be seen through, private languages requiring continuous acts of translation by the audience:

In society the homosexual's life must be discreetly concealed. If he is to write of his experience, he must invent a two-sex version of the one-sex experience that he really has.

Kauffmann blamed this situation upon society—not upon the homosexual writer. And he argued forcibly for an end to the repression and inhibition that harries these writers into deceit:

If we object to the distortion that homosexual disguises entail, and if, as civilized people, we do not want to gag these artists, then there seems only one conclusion. The conditions that force the dissembling must change.

But, like the psychoanalyst quoted earlier, Kauffmann was committed to the notion that a homosexual's image of life is necessarily an expression of "homosexual truth"; the man has no choice except to "transform [what he knows] to a life he does not know, to the detriment of his truth and ours."

Even those critics whose avowed purpose is to make a case *for* "homosexual art"—as it is—to rescue it from vulgar attack and place it in a dignified light—fall into modes of discourse that are reductive and evasive in discussing its meaning. Consider the approach adopted in Susan Sontag's "Notes on Camp." This critic announces herself to be "strongly drawn" to the kind of art she is setting out to describe; yet throughout her essay she speaks of that art always as a phenomenon of style alone; the worth of its statement, the nature of its view of life, even its cultural associations and origins are passed off as boring matters. ("One feels," says the critic, "if homosexuals hadn't more or less invented Camp, some one else would.") What counts about this art is its *tonality*, not the total experience offered and the meanings created through that experience:

Camp and tragedy are antitheses. There is seriousness in Camp (seriousness in the degree of the artist's involvement), and, very often, pathos. The excruciating is also one of the tonalities of Camp; it is the quality of excruciation in much of Henry James . . . that is responsible for the large element of Camp in his writings. But there is never, never tragedy.

The obvious question is: Given the nature of the life represented in a so-called "Camp novel," is the quality of excruciation tendentious or appropriate? Can a man learn or confirm any truth of experience through a confrontation with Camp? When such questions aren't asked, much less answered, the implication is that this art may truly be empty of substance.

The point at stake bears restating. Dumb-ox or tough-guy or Philistine versions of works of art produced by homosexuals tend to be crudely dismissive—too crudely dismissive, often, for educated audiences to accept. But other dismissive lines have now become available. There is chic psychoanalytical chatter that evades the truth of a scene by seeing the scene as a symptom. There is a liberal critique that evades the truth of a scene by tolerantly viewing the scene, not as an image of life, but as a product of indirect censorship. And there is a brand of aesthetic criticism that evades the truth of a scene by focusing solely on matters of form. None of the approaches mentioned appears hostile to the so-called homosexual artist; each embodies different values and assumptions. But all are alike in espousing, or else in refusing to challenge, the dogma that the homosexual's representation of life can be only an expression of homosexual truth— "his truth" as opposed to "ours," as Kauffmann put it. And that dogma, while comforting to the majority, is quite without foundation.

It is probable that most readers and theatergoers—save for the scandalmongers who shriek about homosexual tyranny—will accept the claim that the most intense accounts of domestic life and problems in recent years, as well as the few unembarrassedly passionate love poems, have been the work of writers who are not heterosexual. The problem of compulsive promiscuity, or Don Juanism—one that Jose Ortega y Gasset described as the most delicate and abstruse in contemporary human relations— has been examined with extraordinary force and directness by

Tennessee Williams in several plays. And that intensity has time and time over proved to be an illumination of a kind. Some of the writers in question can be overpraised, to be sure. There is phony elegance and needless obfuscation in Albee's current manner, total dishevelment in the bulk of Ginsberg, too much self-indulgence in Williams, who seems bent on writing the same play four hundred times.

Yet a fair assessment of these writers, or of any of their relevant superiors—Genêt and Auden for two—can hardly be wholly negative. With a few other poets and dramatists, they are the only compelling writers of the postwar period who seem to know anything beyond the level of cliché about human connectedness, whose minds break through the stereotypes of existential violence or Nietzschean extravagance into recognizable truths and intricacies of contemporary feeling. They are not purveyors of situation comedy or Bond banalities or *Playboy* virility or musical-marital bliss (*I Do! I Do!*) or mate-murders. A steady consciousness of a dark side of love that is neither homo- nor hetero-sexual but simply human pervades much of their work; they are in touch with facts of feeling that most men do not or cannot admit to thought. They know what Catullus knew about *odi et amo*—simultaneities of hatred and its opposite—and they know the special terms and strains of these simultaneities in modern experience, wherein prohibitions against self-indulgence have lost force. They know that love and suffering are near allied and that love ought not to be confused with the slumbrous affection or habitual exploitation that is the rule in numberless households. They know that the lover's demand for exclusive possession has vanity as one of its roots.

They have in mind, not as aphorisms but as potential behavior and gesture, knowledge of the kind compressed in Mme. de Staël's remark that love equals self-love *à deux*, or in Proust's claim that there are people for whom there is no such thing as reciprocated love, and that these people are by no means the most insensitive among us. They know that instability is a fact of love, as of human personality generally. And the tensions and furies arising from contradictory desires and impulses seem to them proper subjects for intelligence to probe.

As good an exhibit as any, perhaps, is Auden's much celebrated "Lullaby":

> Lay your sleeping head, my love,
> Human on my faithless arm;
> Time and fevers burn away
> Individual beauty from
> Thoughtful children, and the grave
> Proves the child ephemeral:
> But in my arms till break of day
> Let the living creature lie,
> Mortal, guilty, but to me
> The entirely beautiful.
>
> Soul and body have no bounds:
> To lovers as they lie upon
> Her tolerant enchanted slope
> In their ordinary swoon,
> Grave the vision Venus sends
> Of supernatural sympathy,
> Universal love and hope;
> While an abstract insight wakes
> Among the glaciers and the rocks
> The hermit's sensual ecstasy.
>
> Certainty, fidelity
> On the stroke of midnight pass
> Like vibrations of a bell,
> And fashionable madmen raise
> Their pedantic boring cry:
> Every farthing of the cost,
> All the dreaded cards foretell,
> Shall be paid, but from this night
> Not a whisper, not a thought,
> Not a kiss nor look be lost.
>
> Beauty, midnight, vision dies.
> Let the winds of dawn that blow

Softly round your dreamng head
Such a day of sweetness show
Eye and knockng heart may bless,
Find the mortal world enough;
Noons of dryness see you fed
By the involuntary powers,
Nights of insult let you pass
Watched by every human love.

Reductions of this poem to homily or "general truth" play into the hands of Auden's detractors—those given to abusing the poet for being overchic. But that risk can be run. Some of the distinction of the "Lullaby" lies in the steadiness of its refusal to exclude the narrative consciousness from the lyric consciousness; joy, love, enchantment are placed, in this poem as in life, in immediate, living, indismissible adjacency to their opposites. Another part of the poem's distinction lies in the capacity of the singer at once to inhabit the lullaby-trance of union, to experience it in its fullness and uniqueness, and to look on from outside, acknowledging, neither merely pityingly nor merely knowingly, the replicability (in an age of indulgence) of this "ordinary swoon." And everywhere in the poem there is an alertness to contrarieties and puzzles of response—the murderously brief and beautiful sense of moral being perfected in sensual delight.

Grave the vision Venus sends
Of supernatural sympathy,
Universal love and hope . . .

In this small poem a densely instructive world of feeling is created, a world that is proof against the simplicities of desiccation (the typist in *The Waste Land*), as well as against those of romantic melancholy (Frederick Henry in *A Farewell to Arms*). And in Auden's *Collected Poems* there are a number of songs—see for instance the matchless lyric "Warm are the still and lucky miles"—worth equal praise.

Does the knowledge embodied in such poems qualify as unique? Is it in itself a guarantee of "profundity"? Of course not:

most reflective men know what these poems know—namely, that love is the only human entrance into an ideal world, and that life, a teaser and mocker, lets few men through to stay. Why then is such knowledge more vivid in homosexual art than elsewhere? Again quick answers are unsatisfactory. Heroicizing the "homosexual artist" is, certainly, as senseless as condescending to him as a case. It does need to be said, though, that the homosexual artist's aptitude for the presentation of certain human (not homosexual or heterosexual) complications of feeling can't be understood by people oblivious to the features of his situation that lend it a measure of dignity. "To be free is to have one's freedom perpetually on trial." It isn't necessary to endorse every line of existential scripture to see the application of this text from Sartre to the intelligent, responsive homosexual who has a gift for the formed re-creation of experience. The latter gift is, as everyone knows, distributed according to no visible plan; sexuality conceived as a pure and separable essence is not its determinant. But the homosexual who possesses it does have special occasion to exercise and refine it in fundamental, as well as in craft or professional, areas of life, owing to the peculiarities of his situation in the general culture. If I am a Citizen, Husband, Straight-Arrow, I easily can put myself on trial. I can speak for a troubling cause, enter upon a bout of promiscuity, teach in a turtleneck, grow my hair long in back. But I cannot escape the promise of ease, the possibility of subsiding into the accepted and the respectable; always an oasis of habitual, unexamined, unjudged life awaits me.

The intelligent homosexual, however, is in another situation. A tide of suspicion flows toward him, perpetually demanding that he justify his difference; relaxation into unthinking self-acceptance in the presence of other eyes is prohibited. If he is rich and shrewd, he may manage to create for himself the illusion of a life unexposed to antipathetic scrutiny—but sustaining that illusion is hard work. If he isn't rich and shrewd, his immediate confrontations with hostility—the interruptions of his taken-for-granted daily existence—will be numberless. And these interruptions will induce in him a heightened awareness of the feelings and assumptions of others—an immediate living consciousness of the fragility of the shields that hide human cruelty from general view.

To say this isn't for a moment to suggest that lives can, by any system of categorization, be precisely compared in terms of their remoteness from challenge: we measure with inklings and intuitions here, and confidence isn't in the equation. Neither is it to suggest that the intelligent and sensitive homosexual is the only man who is ever thrust into tasking encounters with himself and others. It is to say that these encounters are probably more difficult for the homosexual to avoid than for other men. And the encounters do have "excruciating" value to anyone whose art depends finally upon his ability to experience dailiness rather than simply pass through it, to inhabit moment-to-moment reality, to be aware of present time and know it not as something between yesterday and tomorrow but as the edge of his life. Admittedly a man of strong mind can close himself off from the coarseness that teases the homosexual in his round of errands in any town or suburb other than a gay colony—schoolchildren mincing behind his back as their elders have more or less instructed them to do, overheartiness or dropped eyes among tradesmen, slyness and lubricity in the cleaning woman. And the danger of sentimentalizing experience of this kind, assigning more value and meaning to embarrassment than it possesses, is real. Everyone knows about homosexual arrogance; everyone knows that aristocratic poses fend off "nights of insult"; everyone knows that flights of defensive scorn or resentment—the familiar gestures of mediocrity—are common in homosexual conversation.

But self-deception and mediocrity are, after all, everywhere the rule—and the writers and artists spoken of publicly as homosexuals, and thus looked down upon, are by and large not mediocrities. They are men who have been *provoked* into dwelling on the relative emptiness and unthinkingness of most men's commitments to the terms of their own lives. They are people whom we put on endless trial, because our manner declares that no condition of moral being except our own can be approved, because our explicit claim is that love can only be a permanent attachment, and because we dare not detach ourselves from our "institutions" even though we know they derive in great part from superstition. They are people forced to face up to the arbitrariness of cultural patterns—arbitrariness that we insist on regarding as altogether unarbitrary, a logical bidding of nature, a sane, wholly explicable pattern, like the movement of the earth. The fury that lifts James Baldwin's prose to eloquence, when that writer has before him the cruelty of cultural arbitrariness, stems not alone from Baldwin's experience as a Negro. And the racking power of those moments in Genêt, when this writer has the same spectacle in sight, arises not only from a career as thief. The usefulness of the instruction offered through this eloquence and power doesn't vary in accordance with the condition of the reader's sexuality. We need not be "perverts" to see into the life of that moment when Genêt's Divine enters the café, smiles round the room in "her" crazy aloneness, tests the blade of hate:

> She smiled all around, and each one answered only by turning away, but that was a way of answering. The whole café thought that the smile of (for the colonel: the invert; for the shopkeepers: the fairy; for the banker and the waiters: the fag; for the gigolos: "*that* one"; etc.) was despicable. Divine did not press the point. From a tiny black satin purse she took a few coins which she laid noiselessly on the marble table. The café disappeared, and Divine was metamorphosed into one of those monsters that are painted on walls—chimeras or griffins—for a customer, in spite of himself, murmured a magic word as he thought of her:
> "Homoseckshual."   [*Our Lady of the Flowers*]

The making of a monster—a demon fabricated by simple habitual acts of *learned* disgust—is the theme momentarily in view here. And the reader who regards his imperviousness to it as a badge of moral distinction is at best a pious fool.

The case I am urging is, needless to say, open to a hundred misunderstandings. Someone says: You pretend that you aren't claiming that the homosexual is more sensitive to certain aspects of human relations than the heterosexual. But haven't you just been saying that homosexuals have insights that are denied to heterosexuals? Answer: Not quite. The notion of denial over-simplifies the issue, leaves out important parts of the full context. The difference between what the homosexual sees and what the heterosexual sees can't be explained in narrow physiological terms. Neither kind of sexuality can be separated from the culture and regarded as a physical or neurological thing-in-itself determining degrees of insight. Homosexuality, like heterosexuality, is a situation, a complex set of relations between self and society: the nature of these relations determines to some extent the special quality of the perceptions that each perceptive man can have. The relations vary with time and place; surely there are few significant likenesses between the situations of homosexuals in the arts in New York City now and the situations of their counterparts in, say, Paris in 1815 or London in 1600. There isn't, in short, any abstract entity properly called "homosexual insight" or "heterosexual insight"; there are only differences in the kinds of life situations in which intelligence tests itself. And these are the differences that shape the artist's vision.

Again, another query: You seem almost to imply that someone reading a poem or play dealing directly with homosexual experience could nevertheless achieve—through his encounter with this work of art—deeper understanding of aspects of strictly hetero-sexual relationships. Do you really mean this? Answer: Yes. Look for a minute at the poem by Tennessee Williams called "Life Story."

> After you've been to bed together for the first time,
> without the advantage or disadvantage of any prior
>   acquaintance,
> the other party very often says to you,
> Tell me about yourself, I want to know all about you,
> what's your story? And you think maybe they really
>   and truly do

sincerely want to know your life story, and so you light up
a cigarette and begin to tell it to them, the two of you
lying together in completely relaxed positions
like a pair of rag dolls a bored child dropped on a bed.

You tell them your story, or as much of your story
as time or a fair degree of prudence allows, and they say,
                    Oh, oh, oh, oh, oh,
each time a little more faintly, until the oh
is just an audible breath, and then of course

there's some interruption. Slow room service comes up
with a bowl of melting ice cubes, or one of you rises to pee
and gaze at himself with mild astonishment in the bath-
        room mirror.
And then, the first thing you know, before you've had time
to pick up where you left off with your enthralling life story,
they're telling you *their* life story, exactly as they'd intended
        to all along,

and you're saying, Oh, oh, oh, oh, oh,
each time a little more faintly, the vowel at last becoming
no more than an audible sigh,
as the elevator, halfway down the corridor and a turn to
        the left,
draws one last, long, deep breath of exhaustion
and stops breathing forever. Then?

Well, one of you falls asleep
and the other one does likewise with a lighted cigarette in
        his mouth
and that's how people burn to death in hotel rooms.

Not a masterwork to be sure, much too easily and sardonically
knowing a poem, too pleased by its own blackishness, and
perhaps also too needlessly "daring" in its sequence of third-
person masculine pronouns. But "Life Story" is a sharp perception of relations between promiscuity and the self-regard and self-
absorption of an age gone mad for Identity—and the sense of

this relatedness is as much an illumination for the straight world as for the queer.

And one more hostile question: You ask for pity, understanding, admiration for homosexual artists—thus suggesting that these are badly mistreated people of this day. Are they? Aren't they in reality all the cry just now? If we put them under pressure, they, for their part, do find excellent means of freeing themselves. And, finally: Suppose it *is* granted that the best "homosexual art" is indeed art—art without modifier; are we obliged to be decent to the worst? When we go off for a night at the theater and encounter something amounting simply to a play in drag, must we smother resentment?

The answer is that of course homosexual artists, like other ones, can be inferior, and that of course these artists have invented ways of easing the pressure we put them under. They do on occasion compose fantasies. They do on occasion express *their* resentment. They do on occasion revenge themselves through sexual disguises in plays and poems. They mock our solemnities with Happenings and joke pictures and weirdo flicks. They parody the ceaseless commercial agitation of "straight" sexual appetites. They create an art heavily dependent (see Genêt) on magic and metamorphosis, an art usually thin in political content, relatively unconcerned with what are called "public issues." And they can give themselves over to glee at the thought that whatever we think of them, few among us match them in brio or brilliance.

But these satisfactions can scarcely outweigh all torments— and, in any event, the fact that an achievement has earned a reward usually is not thought of as ground for discounting the achievement. And there are achievements here—this is the point of moment. A portrait of a man exacerbated by a woman need not be only a thrust at a generalized Enemy; in at least one American play such a portrait faced a mass audience with truths about the new world of sexual equality and universal self-absorption quite inexpressible either in Ibsen or Bernard Shaw. An image of egos dependent upon a fantasy child can be more than a faggish leer: in one American play such an image showed mean uses of the family and, in addition, the vapidities of the doctrine that procreation in itself equals fulfillment. And, by the same token, artists with extensive experience of respectable marriage and child rearing may write with seeming authority about subjects the homosexual can "never know," and yet be worthless—because they are blind to the truth that the acceptable life, the embrace of heterosexuality, can become a cliché, an automatized rather than freely created value.

The canard that negation is not necessarily stupidity and affirmation not necessarily illumination does, in fine, need summoning once more—in discussion of "homosexual art." Nobody is obliged to accept Nietzsche's claim that "every good thing, even a good book which is against life, is a powerful stimulant to life." But the sort of mind that seeks to place all hostility to established institutions as proof of disease does dirt on the revolution of candor that we claim to prize. Failure to hear out the homosexual artist with a seriousness matching his own, overeagerness to dismiss him as ignorant or perverse, assurance that we know what we are—this behavior at a time when Don Juans by the thousand jam the week-night motels and divorce rates soar and children everywhere are flogged into meaningless ambition—this is worse than senseless. It is a mockery not only of art and of the suffering that art rises out of and seeks to comprehend: it is a mockery of our famous, preening new liberation as well.

Against McLuhan

A marvy year for Marshall McLuhan, take it all in all. Tom Wolfe compared him with Darwin, Freud, and Einstein; Susan Sontag said in public she thought he was swell. London saw him as an epoch maker and intellectual frontiersman (*Encounter* and the *Times Lit Supp*), and *The New Yorker* reviewed him rapt. What is more, Academe—after a period of sitting tall but silent on his bandwagon—began talking out loud about his work. (One example: a recent international convocation of savants at Southern Illinois University spent days discussing the "communications revolution" in open session—mainly in McLuhanian terms.) Success being what it is, wasps and carpers were doubtless waiting for the man a piece or two up the road. But no amount of carping could obscure the facts of his rise. Overnight the author of *Understanding Media* had emerged as Midcult's Mr. Big. And ahead of him lay a shot at mass adulation and the title of Everyman's Favorite Brain.

The secret of this ascent isn't instantly visible to casual reportorial eyes. Marshall McLuhan is no literary old pro blessed with a power base and a rich experience at name-making. An English professor for most of his working life (Wisconsin, Assumption, St. Louis), he moved on from teaching only quite recently to his present post as director of Toronto University's Center for Culture and Technology. And despite long years in the classroom, he has no credit reserves in the trade—no stretch of unheralded, scholarly labor of the kind fellow professionals pant to puff. McLuhan avoided book writing until he was forty. His first work, *The Mechanical Bride* (1951), was an analysis of the sex-power–horsepower ploy by which two generations of ad men have sold us our annual car. (Not much there for the Modern Language Association.) And after the *Bride* appeared, the author resumed his silence as a bookman and maintained it for another full decade and more.

Nor can it be said—still on the mystery of the McLuhanian boom—that here is a case of a late-blooming stylist, somebody who had to turn fifty to turn a slick phrase. In terms of style, this flower has yet to bud. Marshall McLuhan's present reputation rests on two books—*The Gutenberg Galaxy* (1962) and *Understanding Media* (1964); both are sometimes stimulating, but neither is pretty prose. One problem is that of opacity (McLuhan's pages are dense with stoppers like "sense ratios," "interiorizations of alphabetic technology," and the like). Another is that the favored method of organization has a bit too much in common with that of an impresario squirrel. *The Gutenberg Galaxy* looks gathered, not written: a paste-up from a hundred histories of math, political theology, nationalism, and fur trading, and from a thousand "other authorities." (Walt Whitman and Walt Whitman Rostow, Cicero and Father Ong, de Chardin and de Beauvoir, Rabelais, Riesman, and Shakespeare, the Opies, Powys, and Poe—name your hero, he surely is here.) The man's work reads for pages at a stretch like a Marboro clearance ad:

> Clagett [author of *The Science of Mechanics in the Middle Ages*] presents the treatise of Nicholas of Oresme *On the Configurations of Qualities* in which Oresme says: "Every measurable thing except numbers is concieved in the manner of continuous quantity." This recalls us to the Greek world in which as Tobias D. Dantzig points out in his *Number: The Language of Science* (pp. 141–2): "The attempt to apply rational arithmetic to a problem in geometry resulted in the first crisis in the history of mathematics. . . ." Number is the dimension of tactility, as Ivins explained in *Art and Geometry* (p. 7) [etc.].

Furthermore, the two leading articles of this thinker's gospel can't be called easy to grasp. The first is a theory of culture which contends that communications media impose a wide range of assumptions "subliminally." (The form of the media, not the content, structures men's values, according to McLuhan; the form also determines the content of the senses and the very look of the world.) The second is an interpretation of history which claims that revolutionary transformations of media occur periodically through the ages, and that one such transformation is in progress right now. (A five-hundred-year-old "typographic and mechanical" era is ending and an "electric galaxy of events" has begun; the new "galaxy" offers experiences of simultaneity and heightened interdependence in which traditional values—privacy, independence, and so on—are engulfed.) Neither of these items is wholly lacking in interest, and McLuhan's historical chapters are often enlivened by canny, comprehensible remarks. But the key idea, to repeat—that of the centrality of *form* in the media as the determinant of social structure and individual minds—is to most men unfamiliar and abstract. An author who makes it into his dogma would ordinarily be ill-advised to brood overmuch about fame.

That Marshall McLuhan is now in position (if he chooses) to brood about nothing else owes a little to his skill with the magic of the modern. "Baby, it's what's happening" is a regularly sounded ground theme in his work. The basic language is video-mesh, circuits and data processing. Injunctions to *Think Modern!* appear on page after page. ("We still have our eyes fixed on the rearview mirror looking firmly and squarely at the job that is receding into the nineteenth-century past.") The right names—Cage, Camp, Bond, Van Der Beek, the whole of the switched-on mob—are fingered throughout like sacred medals. The Farthest-Out Art—electric landscapes, pop Happenings or whatever—is treated either as classic or already passé, and idols of the hour are probed intensely, like important neglected codes:

"The Beatles stare at us with eloquent messages of changed sensory modes for our whole population, and yet people merely think how whimsical, how bizarre, how grotesque. The Beatles are trying to tell us by the antienvironment they present just how we have changed and in what ways."

Old times and old-timers do turn up, as indicated—especially in *The Gutenberg Galaxy*. But even they swim into the reader's ken to a definite R-and-R beat. (Who was Christopher Marlowe? The man, says McLuhan, turning dead Kit hummingly on, who "set up a national P.A. system of blank verse." Who was Heidegger? A cat who "surfboards along on the electronic wave." What were the Middle Ages? *"The Late Show* for the Renaissance.")

Among other crowd-pleasing elements in the McLuhanian equation, the author's literary persona rates a word. At some moments this writer plays Inside Dopester (I called the Kennedy-Nixon election, he announces; I knew exactly why Jack would win). At others he's simply a Scrappy Little Professorial Guy. Enemies as various as George Bernard Shaw ("he lost his nerve") and General Sarnoff ("the voice of the current somnambulism") are worked over in his books; Lewis Mumford, Arnold Toynbee, and dozens more are patronized, and English profs ("literary brahmins") come off naturally as jerks. The author also does a turn as Kitsch Cynic, mocker of goodie-good types—and it is here that he shows his best stuff, speaking again and again with the clarity of last night's knowing cabby or this week's issue of *Time*. People who are easily shocked give him the laughing fits. ("The historian Daniel Boorstin was scandalized by the fact that celebrity in our information age was not due to a person's having done anything but simply to his being known for being well-known. Professor Parkinson is scandalized that the structure of human work now seems to be quite independent of any job to be done.") And he likes interrupting the argument to defend the innocent guilty and to lean on moralizing twerps:

> So great was the audience participation in the quiz shows that the directors of the show were prosecuted as con men. Moreover, press and radio ad interests, bitter about the success of the new TV medium, were delighted to lacerate the flesh of their rivals. Of course,

the riggers had been blithely unaware of the nature of their medium, and had given it the movie treatment of intense realism, instead of the softer mythic focus proper to TV. Charles Van Doren merely got clobbered as an innocent bystander, and the whole investigation elicited no insight into the nature or effects of the TV medium. Regrettably, it simply provided a field day for the earnest moralizers. A moral point of view too often serves as a substitute for understanding in technological matters.

A literary self that amounts to an amalgam of Bogie and Dr. Huer might not seem everybody's dish; but the thing obviously meets a felt need.*

And the same can be said about McLuhan's gamesmanly ploys as a historian. A specialist in unnoticed causes, this scholar never delves into a historical situation without emerging with "major factors" nobody quite hit on before. The handling in *Understanding Media* of the advent of philanthropy a century ago is typical of his cunning moves. Why did "even the hardiest of the rich dwindle into modest ways of timid service to mankind"? Because of the invention of the telegraph, McLuhan explains—and does not stop for questions. What is the key factor in the southern civil-rights struggle? The internal-combustion engine. ("The real integrator or leveler of white and Negro in the South was the private car and the truck, not the expression of moral points of view.") Why were the Jews murdered by the million? Because radio came before TV. ("Had TV come first there would have been no Hitler at all.") The talent in question isn't the kind treasured by trad historians, but it is what is called provocative and universally pleasing to wits.

In the end it won't do, though, to pretend that Marshall

* There are occasional bad breakdowns or inconsistencies in this public literary mask. McLuhan stands forth usually as a man quite unafflicted by any sense of inferiority. "I am in the position of Louis Pasteur," he tells his reader repeatedly. Yet the word "humility" comes not infrequently to his lips. For example: his address at Southern Illinois, which began with a summary of likenesses between Marshall McLuhan and Plato, ended with the assertion that "I really feel shatteringly humble." It was a sequel that left some alert listeners confused.

McLuhan's secret is a matter either of mere wit or mere newsiness or mere literary self-creation. The truth is more complicated —and more painful—than that. Grasping it means facing up to the dozen different kinds of stratagem by which this author empties facts and agonies from the world he thinks of as "Now." Some of these stratagems depend on tricks of futuristic projection, displacements of present-day reality which treat desperate hopes as facts. (Write that "the real integrator of the white and Negro *was*," and you imply that the struggle has already been won.) Other tricks include sudden weird tonal abstractions—see the flip comment about TV and Hitler—deadenings of feeling and sympathy that distance holocaust and shame. Still others con the reader into a frankly theatrical view of experience, a vision that insulates him from immediacies and shows forth all life as a production or stunt. Taken singly, needless to say, none of the stratagems would rank as original, amazing, or troubling; taken in concert they have powerful and obnoxious effect. The complaint isn't that Professor McLuhan puts together a thoroughly fantastic account of the situation of contemporary man; it is that he sets himself up, speaking bluntly, as the constituted pardoner of this age—a purveyor of perfect absolution for every genuine kind of modern guilt.

Do I chide myself for trivial failings—my laxness as a parent, my sins of permissiveness, my failure to exact respect from the kids? Do I worry about rearing layabouts incapable of work or thought?—Oh, but come *on*, says Marshall McLuhan, a benign, forgiving face, the truth is your children are grand:

> Some people have estimated that the young person, the infant and the small child, growing up in our world today works harder than any child ever did in any previous human environment—only the work he has to perform is that of data processing. The small child in twentieth-century America does more data processing—more work —than any child in any previous culture in the history of the world. . . . We haven't really cottoned on to the fact that our children work furiously, processing data in an electrically structured world. . . .

Do I feel bad about my *own* laziness, say—my own unending belt of mindlessness in front of TV? Situation comedy, secret agents, mean mockeries of domestic life . . . Has my intellectual appetite gone dead? My mind turned slush?—Forget it, says this Constant Comforter. The medium is the message, and whatever you think you are doing in front of the box, the fact is you're being expanded-extended-improved. "TV has opened the doors of audile-tactile perception to the nonvisual world of spoken languages and food and the plastic arts. . . ." TV has trans- formed "American innocence into depth sophistication, indepen- dently of 'content'. . . ." TV has "changed our sense-lives and our mental processes. It has created a taste for all experience in *depth*. . . . And oddly enough, with the demand for the depth, goes the demand for crash-programming [in education]. Not only deeper, but further, into all knowledge has become the normal popular demand since TV."

Or am I bugged by my pointless affluence, my guilt about having fat on my hide at a time when sores of starvation are the rule for hundreds of millions elsewhere?—But don't be *silly*, says my adviser; you're being ridiculous again. You're mired in out- moded thinking; you're the victim of moldy figs. Oh, yes, we've all heard about the underdeveloped nations, the "ascent into history," the necessity of hard labor, the problems of locating resources, building factories, educating work forces, creating credit systems, and the like. But *we* know, don't we now, *we* know that we have it within us practically at this instant to do the miracle of our choice whenever we choose:

> The computer will be in a position to carry out orchestrated pro-
> gramming for the sensory life of entire populations. It can be pro-
> grammed in terms of their total needs, not just in terms of the
> messages they should be hearing, but in terms of the total experi-
> ence as picked up and patterned by all the senses at once. For
> example, if you were to write an ideal sensory program for
> Indonesia or some area of the world that you wanted to leapfrog
> across a lot of old technology, this would be possible if you knew
> in the first place its present sensory thresholds, and, second, if you

had established what kind of sensory effect a given technology like radio or literacy had upon sensory life as a whole.

Or suppose I am simply worried about my *natural* self, my condition as part of the creation, my indecencies to the life around me that is coextensive with mine. I deface the garden, Earth, with cigarette butts, billboards, beer cans. I pollute the streams with uncycled wastes from my factory. Should I not then despise myself as a rapist?

Well, do what you like, answers Marshall McLuhan sniffishly, but you are a bit of a wag. Men may have been a bit hard on the planet in the past—but full amends are about to be made. If you'll just be patient a minute or two, you'll see us doing a kind of honor to this Little Old Earth that will more than make up for the past:

> If the planet itself has thus become the content of a new space created by its satellites, and its electronic extensions, if the planet has become the content and not the environment, then we can confidently expect to see the next few decades devoted to turning the planet into an art form. We will caress and shape and pattern every facet, every contour of this planet as if it were a work of art, just as surely as we put a new environment around it.

In sum: give it all over, is the message. Give over self-doubt, self-torment, self-hatred. Give over politics. Give over conscience. Relax, go soft and complacent, accept your subliminal perfectibility. Before us, almost at hand, is a moment of revelation when it shall be shown that "we are living in a period richer" than that of Shakespeare, that our time is properly thought of as "the greatest of all human ages, whether in the arts or in the sciences." And while we are waiting, there are worthy acts to be done. We can cut ourselves off from our depressions. We can look beyond the trivia of daily life—beyond entanglements with wives and children and employers, beyond neighbors, bond issues, tax bills, and the rest. We can overcome the tired sense that there are urgent local and international issues, and learn to see the dropout, the teach-in, even the casualty himself as part of The Greater Showbiz:

> . . . we now experience simultaneously the dropout and the teach-in. The two forms are correlative. They belong together. The teach-in represents an attempt to shift education from instruction to discovery, from brainwashing students to brainwashing instructors. It is a big dramatic reversal. Vietnam, as the content of the teach-in, is a very small, misleading Red Herring. It really has nothing to do with the teach-in as such any more than with the dropout. The dropout represents a rejection of nineteenth-century technology as manifested in our educational establishments. The teach-in represents a creative effort to switch the educational process to discovery, from package to prove.

Thus will we rise to the certainty that Style and Method are all, that the visible—Vietnam or wherever—is not in any real sense *there*. And having done this, we can take off absolutely, fly up from the nonworld of consciousness into the broad sanctuaries of ecstasy and hope. ("The computer, in short, promises by technology a Pentecostal condition of universal understanding and unity . . . a perpetuity of collective harmony and peace.")

It is here, of course, precisely here—in the gift of oblivion—that the heart of the McLuhanian munificence is found. This writer does bestow on his reader a welcome grant of hip modernity. He stimulates in addition a voluptuous sense of mastery (to say "The Middle Ages were *The Late Show* for the Renaissance" is rather like cornering a Corvette). And whether or not the basis of his sunniness is sheer terror, his work does rank as the strongest incitement to optimism yet produced in this age. But the great gift offered is, ultimately, the release from consciousness itself. Those who accept it have clearly won a deliverance, a free way up and out.

Are they so reprehensible? it is asked. Poor men, the ignorant, the hopeless, have to buy *their* release from pushers. The Professor's enthusiasts spend less and get more. They buy a guarantee that the disorder, chaos, and misery around them are but veils and shadows, lies told by the stupid conscious mind—yet they make no sacrifice whatever of their ability to function in the workaday world. In the act of discounting their own senses and anxieties, they rise up to form an elite—men dignified by their access to the knowledge that nobody knows what's what. If they are at bottom blind devotees of the subliminal dogma, they have at least kept their self-respect.

—And in any case what *is* the compulsion to Gloomsville that makes it shameful to smile with a Happy Prof? By what laws are we obliged to speak and act always as though tragedy, endless tragedy, were the perpetual human lot? Is it really a badge of reason to hold at every hour of day and night that—as Santayana claimed—"the only true dignity of man is his capacity to despise himself"?

The frustration that breathes in these questions, the boredom with canting pessimism, the thirst for a freshening of life, the longing for an inward sense of courage—these are doubtless the deepest secrets known by our new King of Popthink, the deepest needs his elixir is designed to meet. And making light of the needs is no less inhuman than exploiting them. The best that can be done is to repeat the questions that consciousness—were there any of it left around—would probably feel bound to raise, viz.:

How much can be said for an intellectual vision whose effect is to encourage abdication from all responsibility of mind?

Or: What good is this famous McLuhanacy if it makes men drunk as it makes them bold?

Rock Saves?

All at once "they"—the opinion-makers, tastemakers, types who Know and Know—were hailing rock music as a high road to cultural and even spiritual salvation: should sane folk buy that jazz?

They're not likely to tomorrow, certainly. For most people pop music is one thing; intellectual or spiritual transformation is another; closing the gap between the two means rearranging a whole cluster of assumptions about art, order, and values. And while such rearrangements have occurred in the past, just at the moment some barriers exist. The most obvious barrier to grown-up, middle-class receptivity to rock is the disquieting life style of rock groups and audiences—the hair, the costumes, the volume, frightening hints of sexual liberation, etc. But there are others. One is the tendency of a number of preachers of rock as Revelation to shock rather than argue or explain—witness Allen Ginsberg's comparison of the Fugs with Jesus Christ: "The Bible says that when Christ comes back, 'every eye shall see.' . . . When the Fugs break thru . . . every eye shall see." Another is that rock lyrics are often, speaking gently, hard to fathom—witness the Lemon Pipers' "Jelly Jungle":

In the jelly jungle of orange marmalade
There are tangerine dreams waiting for you in orange marmalade
In the jelly jungle of orange marmalade.

Still another problem: rock seems at moments only a footnote to the pot or drug experience, not an independent meditative

45

engagement in its own right. (William Kloman recently reported, in *The New York Times,* on the marked increase in rock records designed for use as background music for pot parties—"intricate harmonies, gently orchestrated melodies, and abrupt shifts in tempo which would strike the normal listener as pointless and distracting.")

And then beyond all this—a further obstacle to acceptance of rock as a vision—stands the seeming faddishness of the phenomenon. Lengthy picture and text rock stories in *Look* and *Life* and *Time,* rock commentary added to *The New Yorker*'s regular cultural coverage, the commissioning, by the *New York Review of Books,* of essays on this or that rock group, the emergence of rock magazines like *Crawdaddy,* the density of rock pieces in pow periodicals along the spectrum from *Village Voice* to *Cheetah* to *Eye,* the rock interests of scenely figures like Marshall McLuhan, John Cage, and Susan Sontag, the apparent impossibility of contriving a radio or TV commercial without a rock beat—none of these can simply be laid at the door of a nasty music-biz flackdom. Yet together they encourage belief that rock is "merely" a fashion—part of the famous swinging Now-culture that is bound to age and may already be passing away. How can serious thought and feeling flourish amid such ephemerality?—so runs the inevitable squarish question.

That the idea of the new pop music as a religious force is so far credible only to With-Its doesn't signify, however, that it will never gain credibility for others. As already indicated, rock is now being taken seriously in many quarters usually thought to be proof against chichi or frivolity—the upper echelons of the United Presbyterian Church, for one. (The leadership of this institution recently retained a rock group called the Astrakhan Sleeve to produce religious records; a spokesman explained that rock is a "forum for serious messages far removed from the moon-June variety.") And there are signs that secular organs of opinion which, in the past, have exerted powerful, if trickle-down, influence on majority thought are moving in a comparable direction. On the appearance of the Beatles' last LP, *Partisan Review* carried a long tribute by Professor Richard Poirier, Chairman of English at Rutgers and a *PR* editor—an essay that invoked Shakespeare and T. S. Eliot in characterizing the Beatles' gifts, saw a likeness between their "knowledge" and that of contemporary writers like Beckett and Borges, and, at its climax, argued that the Beatles speak with an intensity of philosophical-aesthetic insight matched only by titans of the past:

> "And the time will come," it is promised in one of [the Beatles'] songs, "when you will see we're all one, and life flows on within you and without you." As an apprehension of artistic, and perhaps of any other kind of placement within living endeavor, this idea is allowable only to the very great.

And the Beatles are by no means the only group that has inspired writing at this pitch of awe. The third issue of *New American Review* carried a discussion of rock music by Professor Albert Goldman of Columbia in which a rock composition was compared to *King Lear,* and the group called The Doors was said to "achieve their purpose as gurus, which is to confront their audience with the most basic unbearable truths." In course of this essay Professor Goldman laid down numerous other claims for rock music:

> [Rock] has acted like a magnet, drawing into its field a host of heterogeneous materials that has fallen quickly into patterns. No other cultural force in modern times has possessed its power of synthesis.

> [Rock] has cleared a channel from the lowest and most archaic to the highest and most recent, and through that conduit is now flowing a revitalizing current of energy and of ideas. The result has been the elevation of rock to the summit of popular culture and the accelerating expansion of its interests and resources.

> By pushing toward higher levels of imaginative excellence, rock has begun to realize one of the most cherished dreams of mass culture; to cultivate from the vigorous but crude growth of the popular arts a new serious art that would combine the strength of native roots with the beauty flowering from the highest art.

Claims are just that, needless to say—claims. Some eyes confronting the ones just quoted may find vexing resemblances between them and youth cult paroxysms on the same subject—effusions like those of Mr. Gene Youngblood of the Los Angeles *Free Press:* "There is only one word for [Jimi] Hendrix: inspiring. He's an electric religion. . . . After he hurled his guitar at the screen in a cataclysmic-volcanic-orgasmic finale we fell back limp in our seats, stunned and numbed." But a resemblance of any sort between low-cult and high-cult accounts of the rock experience demands to be taken as evidence in itself that that experience is indeed no negligible "cultural force." The questions arising are: Why is rock making it, in the graceful phrase, so big? What specific qualities of this musical experience explain its attractiveness to rude youth, thoughtful youth, literary intellectuals, "cultivated minds"? Finally: Who among the mass of listeners can rock truly "save"—or truly harm—and how?

As may or may not go without saying, rock fans hold that the success of the movement is best understood in musical, not metaphysical, terms. And that argument isn't wholly absurd on its face. The movement has produced several inventions in the field of singing style (Ray Charles is the most gifted of the inventors). The performers in the "mainstream soul" division—in particular Aretha Franklin and the late Otis Redding—are not much inferior in freedom, exuberance, range of color, and individuality of phrasing to the best singers in jazz and blues history. A dozen Beatle songs can be played with delight by any amateur musician who relishes tunes with surprising changes, structural inventiveness, and melodic lines of uncommon length and sweetness. There are passages of genuine musical excitement—who is unaware of this?—throughout "Rubber Soul," "Revolver," and "The Magical Mystery Tour" (the entrance into "Blue Jay Way" is especially lovely). A fine fragment of music drama—the poised ironical stiff-arm called "Lady Jane"—turns up in a Rolling Stones album. (The Beatles best the stony Stones when the latter imitate them but not invariably otherwise; no third group can compete with either—even after so many years.) Several groups possess able instrumentalists (slightly overrated by rock fans)— the guitarists Mike Bloomfield and Eric Clapton, for two examples. And, viewed as a disaster epic, a Hendrix concert is only a shade less terrorizing—though there are no dancers and much less blackness—than the much-praised Merce Cunningham–La Monte Young "Winterbranch."

Moreover—still in the area of musical accomplishment—there are some feats of assimilation in the development of rock that have few parallels in the history of pop music. Over the past two decades, a long list of performers contributed directly and indirectly to the development in question. (Rock "began," in a sense, with a Cleveland disc jockey's decision, in 1954, to feature some obscure rhythm and blues records made by Negro record companies in the South.) Some names on the list are still familiar, either because the performers were superstars in their time or ours or because they remain active now—Elvis Presley, Chuck Berry, Ray Charles, the Everly Brothers, the Beatles, Bob Dylan. Others, who were in their way not less important, haven't quite become household words—Frankie Lymon, for instance, Bo Diddely, Little Richard, B. B. King, several more.

But the roster of names testifies that rock came to its eminence by mixing into the basic rhythm and blues texture other musical elements and traditions—materials that hitherto had had separate publics of their own. The audience for rhythm and blues records of the early fifties lay mainly in the black ghettoes of the North. But new vocal sounds that were added in the mid-fifties— the gospel sound (Little Richard), country and western (Presley), an unprecedented crossing of gospel and blues (Charles)— widened the audience geographically and socially. And there were comparable developments in instrumental sound and in rock lyrics. B. B. King, the guitarist, moved the rock band on from the scrappy haphazard sound of R & B, and other major contributions came from the eclectic Beatles, from the inventors of the supergorgeous Mantovanian Motown Sound, and from the pioneers of progressive or art rock. (As for rock lyrics: California surf and drag rock superimposed the "contented" experience of middle-class white youths upon the original blues-based shouts; Bob Dylan and the school of folk rock complicated the blend with political and social commentary; the works of the Stones and the Fugs steadily sharpened the ironical edge or fury of the commentary.) As Professor Goldman puts it:

> The Rock Age has assimilated everything in sight, commencing with the whole of American music: urban and country blues, gospel, hill-billy, Western "goodtime" (the ricky-tick of the twenties), and Tin Pan Alley. It has reached across the oceans for the sounds and rhythms of Africa, the Middle East and India. It has reached back in time for the baroque trumpet, the madrigal, and the Gregorian chant; and forward into the future for electronic music and the noise collages of *musique concrète*.

But while all this is true, the new musical possibility supposed to have been created by rock's assimilating power—the possibility of a "new serious art that would combine the strength of native roots with the beauty flowering from the highest art"—still looks frail and remote.* Market pressures touch rock no less directly than they have touched every other kind of music in the American pop past. As there were crashing mindless set pieces in the Swing Era to excite the go-go-go Saints! Saints! big-tipper mob ("One O'clock Jump," Sing Sing Sing"), so there are a hundred versions of Jimi Hendrix's "Wild Thing" and "Purple Haze" now (wilder and louder, naturally, than in Olden Times). As the dance bands of the late thirties "advanced" toward fancy charts, with cathedral voicings of reed sections (Glenn Miller) and few opportunities for individual musical creativity, so the

---

* Some jazz lovers claim that, for aesthetic reasons, it will ever be thus. But several rock groups—Cream, The Jefferson Airplane—have lately taken tentative steps toward meeting the flatly dismissive objections of the jazz buff. (The objections are that the high volume and blocky pounding monotonous 4/4 beat rule out rhythmic intricacy and pliancy, as well as subtlety in dynamics, and that, while there is a jazz and blues foundation to the music, improvisation has never become a prime feature of the form.)

famous Motown rock rises to a comparable glossiness at a comparable musical cost and commercial profit.

Again and again, in truth, the listener to rock records is haunted by echoes of the kitsch sounds of the thirties—not to mention echoes of the old anxieties about integrity vs. sellout. Martha and the Vandellas singing "My Baby Loves Me"—the background here is pure Big Sky music, appropriate for Joel McCrea's Arizona or for a De Mille epic or even (at a pinch) for backing some footage of the Olivier-Oberon *Wuthering Heights*. Diana Ross, that wispy lead singer heard on The Supremes' "Stop in the Name of Love"—her timbre (or no-timbre) is straight out of "Oh Johnny"-ville, is it not? And where, oh, where, in schlock rock like Tommy James and the Shondells, is there even so much as a memory of the authentic gritty joyousness of Otis Redding singing:

> On a cold, rainy, windy night
> She shut all the doors
> She cut off all the lights
> She holds me and squeezes me tight
> She tells me Big O everything's all right . . .
> Come on now
> Bring my breakfast to the table
> When I go to work she know's I'm able
> Do my job, I come back in
> You oughta see my baby's face
>
> She just grins, grins, grins

The progressive or art rock school does, to be sure, continue to experiment, and newish groups like The Doors conceive unusual ambitions and are more venturesome in pattern and theme than most of their American competitors. And there are the Beatles and the Stones. The Beatles, though, are in full flight from rock to a kind of show music—and it must be said, furthermore, that their smoothie, nice-lad manner never much engaged lovers of mainstream soul. As for art rockers like Van Dyke Parks, they don't sell. And while The Doors do, their trade appears to depend, not upon musical freshness, but upon exploitation of the sexiness of the singer Jim Morrison. (On one recent occasion Mr. Morrison began a public performance by recounting his latest sexual adventure; it had taken place five minutes before curtain time.)

The point of this glance at economics is that the subject has important bearing on the matter of the nature of the rock triumph. If the rock world were conscious of the junk, kitsch, and exploitative sexuality that litters the present scene, if alertness to differences of musical quality in rock material were the rule, the argument that the success of rock is essentially musical would be less implausible. As it is, the suspicion lingers that the rock experience is as impure, by musical criteria, as most of the pop experiences that have preceded it.

The jazz intelligentsia of the thirties tended to embrace the entire jazz enterprise, avoiding musical discriminations, invoking few standards save the one that permitted chuckles at the Lombardo brothers or Horace Heidt, excluding little that called itself jazz, regardless of how pretentious and incompetent the stuff might be. And the rock intelligentsia of the present day behaves similarly. (Professor Goldman avoids musical assessments entirely. Professor Poirier speaks of the Rolling Stones, the Left Banke, and the Bee Gees as equals—all are "exceptionally good"; a counterpart statement in the nonrock world would find Al Hirt and Liberace to be as interesting as Miles Davis and Thelonious Monk.) Three decades ago such refusals of judgment signified that the experience of listening to jazz was less musical than political in nature—an occasion on which a longed-for relationship (one of solidarity) between self and underdog or underadvantaged could be achieved. Nowadays the refusals signify that the experience of listening to rock is less musical than—

Well, than what? What exactly is the rock audience hankering after? We are back, if not at the theme of rock as salvation, then at a restatement of the truth that the key to the success of rock music appears to lie elsewhere than in the music itself—perhaps in an adjustment or harmony between certain extramusical features of the rock experience and certain extramusical needs or desires characteristic of the rock audience. But the questions remain: What needs? What desires? What precise means of gratification?

The familiar moral line—rock thrives among the educated because modern man thinks the test of an education is how far it enables you to spit at gentility—offers a way into the problem. Throughout the postwar decades popular culture has repeatedly been used by teacher and student alike as a weapon in a war against "liberal," "humane," or "highbrow" values of the past. Publicity is better than craft for an artist, murder is a means of self-improvement for everybody, says the novelist (Norman Mailer)—and the Sayings are instantly enshrined by university professors as mighty challenges to the "trad." TV is life, books are death, says the pundit (Marshall McLuhan)—and is hailed by whole congresses of teachers for smashing the venial-lineal past. "The Mona Lisa is crap," says the pop singer (John Lennon)— and intellectual reviews snap him salutes.

And the salutes aren't mysterious. Some are traceable, no doubt, to the self-contempt and desperate fantasy of academic men who, unnerved by the library life, mock those who are nourished by it, and dream of a golden world of organic illiterate pimps and pugs. Others, though, bespeak a determination to call the bluff of the older culture; they attest people's belief that the older culture has been "found out." Keep your voice down, don't bother the people next door, said that culture, counseling self-restraint, moderation, and sequential reasoning (as opposed to harrowing shrieks and groans). But when the people next door turned out to be Dachau people, Hiroshima people, Johannesburg and Selma people, the counsel was known at once to stink. What better counsel was available? Any advice, any sound free of complicity, had a superior claim. Any assertion that outraged the Establishment. For it was the governors, not the guitarists, who did the killing, while solid citizens looked impassively on. From which it followed, did it not, that virtue lies precisely in that which the governors find vile?

One use of rock, in short, was to *occasion* scorn—to stimulate the hypocrite to display his nature. Turn it down! Good Folk cry, in love with their own complacency. And that gesture against "being disturbed" reenacts (some say) a hundred hideous obliviousnesses of the past.

But there are other uses, for—peace to the moralist—rock fans don't wholly exempt themselves from sin. Their chief need, in fact (no sense, incidentally, pretending that only rock types share this need), their chief need is relief from significant life quandaries and guilt. And first among the quandaries is one that comes down roughly to this: I, an educated man (or adolescent), thoughtful, concerned, liberal, informed, have a fair and rational grasp of the realities of my age—domestic and international problems, public injustices, inward strains that give birth to acts of human meanness. But although I know the problems and even perhaps the "correct" solutions, I also know that this knowledge of mine lacks potency. My stored head, this kingdom—my pride, my liberalism, my feeling for human complexity—none of this alters the world; it only exhausts me with constant naggings about powerlessness. What can I do?

Pop tunes that begin "I'll Build a Stairway to the Stars" don't help much with that problem—which is to say, thirties' pop lyrics didn't link up very directly with "reality." Rock lyrics of the sixties, on the other hand, do link up—many of them. The world of the rock lyric encompasses war protest (The Fugs: "Kill for Peace"), overdue social justice (Bob Dylan: "Blowin' in the Wind"), black hippies' fury (Jimi Hendrix: "If 6 Was 9"). That world includes, in addition, intricate human relationships in which people press themselves to define their feelings precisely (The Beatles: "She Said She Said"). And it blinks neither at sexual hypocrisies (The Rolling Stones: "Back Street Girl") nor at depressing or disgusting visual details or urban scenes (John Hartford: "Shiny Rails of Steel"). Boosters of one or another rock lyric, true enough, often lose their cool. " 'Learn to forget,' " a writer says in *Crawdaddy*, quoting a snippet of a rock tune. "—what power that phrase has! It's possible to get stoned for days by listening to this song. For a while it will seem the one truth available to us . . . a catalyst with more potential for generating truth . . . than anything since middle Faulkner.")

But learn to forget boosters: rock lyrics *are* in closer touch with contemporary life than pop used to be. And it's plain that contemporary minds and rock "groove" together partly because many rock songs take cognizance of the ills that exacerbate such minds. Partly—but not wholly. The complex case is that, if one phase of the rock experience is confirmation of what a man knows, the other phase, equally telling, is escape from the knowledge. —Bring along all your views, says the rock invitation. Your liberal opinions. Your knowledge of the atrocities committed by numberless power structures of the past. Your analyst's ideas about today's oedipal hangup. Your own manipulative, categorizing, classifying, SAT braininess. You can not only cross the rock threshold bearing this paraphernalia; you can retreat to it, consult it, any time you want—by tuning back in to the lyrics. No obligation, in this pop world, to mindlessness . . . —But now if you'd *like* something else . . . If you want your freedom, if you'd care to blow your mind, shed those opinions, plunge into selflessness, into a liberating perception of the uselessness, the unavailingness, the futility of the very notion of opinionated personhood, well, it so happens to happen there's something, dig, real helpful here. . . . What is being said is that the rock invitation offers the audience a momentary chance to have it both ways: if I accept the invitation, I can simultaneously be political and beyond politics, intellectual and beyond intellectuality, independent and beyond personal independence.

I can be these contrary things because the rock experience at its most intense is an intimation of engulfment and merger, a route to a flowing, ego-transcending oneness. As fans and enemies alike know, rock sound overwhelms separateness, the mental operations that discern and define here and there, me and not-me. (Many of the lyrics work symbolically or subliminally toward the same end.) Pounded by volume, riddled by light, the listener slides free from the restraining self and from the pretenses of a private, "unique" rationality. Preparation for the descent is of various sorts. One man may have given houseroom in his head to a desire for connection with the unconscious roots of life—D. H. Lawrence's blood being. Another, unbookish, has experienced frustration in the public world of objective laws, ethnic or money interests—learned his impatience with the procedural and the discrete outdoors, as it were. Another despises the tyranny of his "family self" or his student role. All are alike, though, in their relish for a thunderous, enveloping, self-shattering moment wherein the capacity for evaluating an otherness is itself rocked and shaken, and the mob of the senses cries out: What we feel, we are!

That this half-real, half-metaphorical self-shattering lies at the tumultuous center of the rock experience is an observation made verbally (the music itself makes it to anyone who listens) over and over, by low-cult and high-cult critics alike. Mr. Paul Williams in *Crawdaddy* remarks that "the direct appeal to the mind made by 'folk' (straightforward words, guitar, voice) cannot compare . . . to the abilities of rock to move people's goddam muscles, bodies, caught up and swaying and moving so that a phrase . . . can actually become your whole body, can sink into your soul on a more-than-cognitive level. Rock, because of the number of senses it can get to (on a dance floor, eyes, ears, nose, mouth and tactile) and the extent to which it can pervade those senses, is really the most advanced art form we have." Professor Goldman comments that, "like the effect of LSD, that of rock . . . is to spotlight [things] in a field of high concentration and merge them with the spectator in a union that is almost mystical."

And, as indicated, the rock lyricist is himself hip to the phenomenon of the "mystical union." The truth "allowable only to the very great" which Professor Poirier heard in a Beatles' song is an explicit assertion of the arbitrariness of ego separations, and of the desirability of soaring free from the mind-ridden world of subjects and objects. "I am within you and without you," these sirens call. "I am he as you are he as you are me and we are all together. . . ." The kitsch version of this "truth"—it emerges as

an endorsement of a kind of universal group-gropeism—appears
in a hundred lesser songs:

> I think it's so groovy now
> That people are finally getting together
> I think it's so wonderful—and how!—that people are finally
> getting together
> Reach out in the darkness
> Reach out in the darkness, etc.

[Friend and Lover: "Reach Out in the Darkness"]

And its mate is a crude symbolic vision of the nonhuman world—
the hard-edged manifold of objects, landscapes, nameable locations—as capable of losing its own stiff substance and flowing
into a dislocating unassemblable gooeyness:

> MacArthur Park is melting in the dark,
> All the sweet, green icing flowing down.
> Someone left the cake out in the rain,
> And I don't think that I can take it,
> 'Cause it took so long to bake it.
> And I'll never have the recipe again,
> Oh no.

[Richard Harris:
"MacArthur Park," composer, Jim Webb]

Admittedly, the point of substance here is itself slippery—hard to
keep in sight. Speak in expository prose about a mind-blowing
moment, and you tame the sensations—the obliterating seizures
of sound at a Hendrix concert or at the Electric Circus or any
multimedia discothèque—by turning them into "evidence." Speak
the rock writer's flaky, half-literate idiom, and you either over-
heat the Ineffable or identify the rock experience too directly
with the drug experience, obscuring the specific features of both
that rockers value most. (" 'The End' [a Doors' composition] is
great to listen to when you're high . . . but 'Soul Kitchen' will
get you high, which is obviously much . . . more important":
Crawdaddy.) But if the point is tricky, it isn't trivial. That rock is

a mixed experience, appealing at once to my sense of my sophistication and my sense of the unavailingness of sophistication; that
rock lifts from me the burden of knowing the good and yet
believing my knowledge to be useless; that rock permits me to be
part of others, not a mere resentful conscious self, not a perceiver
harried on every side by multitudes of other conscious selves
pressing their "distinct" values, opinions, interests, greeds forward into my space and notice: all these truths matter considerably. They establish that rock can possess quasi-religious force. It
leads me past my self, beyond my separateness and difference
into a world of continuous blinding sameness. For a bit, it
stoneth me out of my mind.

Judging that trip, like judging any vision, isn't work for a
journalist. But certain strengths and weaknesses stand forth in
plain sight. Grown men of mind can benefit from access to an
experience that shakes the grip of mentalism, allows the being to
sense the world again, restores a feeling of continuity with "out
there"; through it they can preserve an idea of human solidarity,
as well as some consciousness of intellectual limits and a seemly
general humility. For youngsters, too, as may be added, there is
value in an escape from the narrow worlds of schoolhouse or
family dining room into a sense of power, physicality, roughness,
openness. (The prepubescent middle-class kid who sings mimeti-
cally along with Hendrix or Percy Sledge as he listens to a record
is behaving much like Penrod imitating Rube in Tarkington's
wonderful story. Such behavior recovers potentialities of being
that are too rigidly excluded by "nice" families in the name of an
arid politesse.)

At pubescent and postpubescent levels, though, overindul-
gence in mystical I-am-you-you-are-the-tree-the-tree-is-me self-
transcendence isn't all plus signs and roses. The schooling of
a maturing mind—*pace* now to self-hating academic revolutionaries—is often at its most intense, most interesting and most
life-enhancing when its business is to toughen the concept of
Difference, or when it is occupied with hierarchies of aesthetic,

political, moral experience, or when the classroom or library effort is that of refining the imaginative power to comprehend a difficult otherness. And aptness for such studies can be weakened. Once upon a time it was weakened by what was called class prejudice —or by inherited or inculcated religious or political self-righteousness. The Mormon or the Catholic or the Grottlesex boy couldn't break out of himself, couldn't enter the "other point of view." So it was that teachers then complained about their pupils' inflexibility, incapacity to stand one place while imaginatively penetrating another. So it was that twenty years ago the great historian of science and teacher Herbert Butterfield was writing about troubles dealing with people who were so convinced that one or another historical position or figure—Oliver Cromwell, say—was "right," that they couldn't stir themselves to fathom the innerness of King Charles' head:

> [Someone] who is so much the prisoner of his ideas that he [is] forever unable to summon the imaginative sympathy to enter into the mentality of men who are not like-minded with himself—is the very antithesis of what is required in history. He is no more an historian than that man is an actor who cannot play Othello as well as King Lear—in fact, he is only like that bogus kind of actor who . . . is always the same, always only himself.

The problem for the future, perhaps, will be the appearance of a generation so rich in experience of merger and self-transcendence that to its mind Cromwell and Charles and early twenty-first century Harvard sophomores will seem all one, why so much fuss, man? A generation of characters whose problem won't be that they're always the same but that they're never the same . . . Because the self, like, man, the self is, like, an individuality, dependent on consciousness, and, like consciousness,—man, that's the trap we jumped. That was a nightmare . . . Consciousness. Like, *ugh*.

Future-mongering and solemnity are handmaids: proper to shoo them off and turn on the phonograph again—Paul singing "Here There and Everywhere"—to temper the profundum, and charm the mind back to pleasure and ease. You think as you listen: Perhaps in a way rock's too good a stuff to be wasted on youth. Or: Ridiculous, the idea that speaking a warm word for such attractive lyric inventiveness could ever corrupt a youth . . . Then you think: have to turn the volume controls all the way up for an hour before a person could even begin to approximate the whirly amiable slow-up available from two or three back-to-back joints of pot.

And then you think: sound judgment is quite impossible anyway, for it must wait until we know what's to come of us, what the next human beings will be like, what qualities will be saved and lost, what "our" future is to be. A long wait.

—But this flurry of *gentilesse* and tolerance is, as a final word, too soft. People who like the tunes but reject the salvation— moldy figs who play the music at the old sound levels and hunt for the old musical pleasures and go on making the traditional musical discriminations and persist in thinking that chaps are dotty who claim they am I and I am they—these senior types, never blowing their minds, aren't fools and may still preserve a civilized value now beleaguered on many fronts.

What value, exactly?

Just conceivably, nothing less than that of the self itself.

Mississippi Learning

In its first summer the Tougaloo Enrichment Program at Mary Holmes Junior College in West Point, Mississippi, enrolled two hundred black students from the delta counties of the state. The students were either already enrolled or about to enroll in integrated high schools. The faculty was drawn chiefly from high schools and colleges in the South; the tutorial staff, responsible for most of the teaching, consisted of undergraduates from two Massachusetts colleges (Smith and Amherst), plus several students from Negro colleges in the South. The following is from a journal kept during a short visit.

Is it any good? Are we doing anything that matters? There are troubles, speaking mildly. We have a thousand ways of naming them, but everything comes down to this: The air in the classroom is too dense—more obstacles, more currents of feeling, more contrarieties of response, more "irrelevant" emotion between student and teacher and the public than I've known before. These are not simply schoolchildren. They are always more and less than "students." Their innerness is different.

These children at most moments are exercising an extraordinary amount of self-control and are by no means unconscious of that fact themselves. Many of them are Purple Hearts now—bomb fragments from McComb, concussed heads from the baseball bats that beat people up on the first day of integrated school

61

in Grenada. Girls and boys alike have been set on, and they expect to be set on again. They may run and get away alive, or they may not. Yet they are functioning. They're put down here amid a new community—strangers, "white oppressors"—and they go on functioning. And they know that to function in these circumstances is an accomplishment. They know that there is ground for pride in what they are, and there is some pride and even arrogance in them. The Grenada crowd, for instance—they had told their tutors they would just as soon be home this summer, because home is where the action is, more exciting and dangerous than sleepy old West Point.

A longing to provoke violence and a terror of violence and a pride in having endured it and a sullenness at seeming dependent on people who haven't endured it—all these feelings coexist in many of these heads. And the feelings don't stay out of the classroom. They come and go and thicken the air, and while you are working you suddenly feel the tightness of God knows how many membranes holding the order and calm together. The tightness—and the *thinness*.

There is a mixture of pugnacity and fear—but there's more to it than that. The tutors complain that while there are reservoirs of disaffection in their students, they—the tutors—can't tap them in class. "How is your life?" the tutor asks. "Nice," the students answer, for at school life *is* nice. It has to be. Something somewhere has to be nice. What do you think of this enrichment program? Nice, the students answer. What does it mean to be an American? Your rights are protected and you can buy more nice things, they reply. Reality is excluded by convention from the classroom; the negative spirit is kept out of this desperately needed nice place. The notion that Teacher wants to permit that negating, cynical, mocking, back-alley nature to assert itself during class, wants to bring reality—things as they are—into the school, is in some way crazy; bad manners; dumb. It's like interrupting a beautiful hymn on Sunday morning with a discussion of your old man's Saturday-night drunk. Let's keep the few clean worlds we know inviolate.

And there's no stopping even here. There is a more painful truth: Frustration among teachers and students is being fostered, purposefully exacerbated. The center of the student-teacher community at West Point isn't the administration or the white majority among the tutors; it is a nascent black-power subculture solidifying among the Negro tutors and several of the older, sharper Negro students. There is an effort to use the white tutors; to make them look foolish; to harass them for money, special privileges, and the like; to heighten suspicion of them among the students; to turn their whiteness into the Enemy. A great deal of the time, the effort amounts only to competitive ploys, acts of pettishness not thought out in advance. But at other moments private wars—open contests between whites and blacks—actually break out. And these wars are obstacles or barriers that, once again, can't be thought of as having a place in the normal transactions called "teaching" and "learning."

How can I make the point less abstract? There is no choice except to talk about my own brief, private war—and about the feelings I thought were engaged in it. (I believe that war had a lot in common with others being waged at West Point.)

Who was my opponent? Calver Jackson, I'll call him—Negro tutor, intelligent, twenty-two, chief SNCC organizer in ———— County, Alabama. How far can I go in offering the character of C.J.? How much do I know? I've spent time brooding about him, I'll say that—my black challenge. The day I arrived voice after voice seemed to be talking about C.J.: "That's C.J."; "C.J.'s just plain marvelous." Another voice I remember said: "C.J. just hates us. You never know where you are with him. Sometimes he's awfully nice. But that's rare, really. He hates us, really. It's terrible. He makes them all hate us."

C.J. is about five foot eleven, rather chubby, light on his feet, very black, with very quick eyes—more menace than humor in them—handsome features tending toward sulkiness, movements suggesting reluctance to waste any physical energy, and a faint swagger in his walk. According to C.J. you lose your figure when you go to work for SNCC—too sedentary. The kids say C.J. was quarterback of his high school football team for three years, star basketball player in college, etc. I watched him play basketball. He gave away five years and more to the other players, and the game is played hard. C.J. is a playmaker, court general, brilliant passer, sizer-up of situations, etc. His shooting eye has gone, but I record, for the truth of it, that he sank—surprising everyone—a fine outside jumper that iced the game for his team. It was Skins vs. Shirts, and C.J. played in a weird, slickerish jacket that he wore to sweat off blubber. There was constant communication with him from the sidelines; the kids ceaselessly called out to him: "Hey, C.J. C.J., how about this, how about that . . . ?"

He looks past you when you are introduced. He nods at you when he comes into your party. He doesn't stay long. He talks a good deal, outdoors, to the other Negro tutors and to the tutorial groups. He is said to be irresponsible, and there's something to this. He drives wildly with a dozen kids in the back of the project's rented station wagons, taking them to the swimming pool in Starkville. (West Point had a pool, but when an integration move was made, the town simply filled it with sand. So you drive fifteen miles over back roads to Starkville where there's money, hence an integrated pool—meaning open to Negroes and whites, but whites don't come, having access to private pools.) C.J. drives wildly and is admired as a hero by the younger lads, as he is admired as a daring lover by the girls.

What placed C.J. in a private contest with me? The professors who preceded me at West Point, the white ones, apparently were badly briefed and ill-informed about the audience. They gave abstract talks about economic determinism. They explained NATO and the Common Market, etc., at a level that implied that all two hundred children were subscribers to *The New York Times*. Maybe they were worried about seeming to condescend. In any case, their deficiencies provoked the Negro tutors into taunting the white tutors about the irrelevance and fatuity of their instructors. The white tutors who knew me retaliated by puffing me as a white hope. Maybe the other professors were abstract or irrelevant, but I wouldn't be. I was this; I was that.

They could speak with great confidence because they planned to get to me the minute I arrived, fill me in, tell me what to do and say. They did just that the night I came in.

How did it work out? If it was a contest, who won? As always in life, nobody won: Death and pain and accident interfered—turned the whole idea of a contest into an ugly joke. I record in passing—a stroke of vanity—that I gave the best performance of my life in a public lecture, doing the history of a blues note, moving from weary blues and boogie-woogie through to Langston Hughes and on to Ralph Ellison, telling what the blues expressed and why the thing expressed is a mass feeling, talking about the Negro writer's struggle to create a language capable of expressing more than a mass feeling, more than the blues sense that nobody can win, capable of articulating an individual response. It was an antiblues talk; it invoked Ellison's hero, Louis Armstrong, as expander and transcender of the blues; it was rabble-rousing and self-dramatizing and funny.

I shouted some blues and played some on the auditorium piano, and they shouted with me. They wanted more, and I taunted them by saying that it's all too imitable; the world is full of blues-doers, people white and black and Japanese. We want a man to inhabit his own skin, name his own feelings, have his own response to the world. Having your own responses is being free. Pure blues is a jail to be broken, etc.

It was damned good. And at the very moment I was thinking how damned good, one of our station wagons was piling up on a back road: one student was killed and several were badly injured. Possibly the wagon had been tailgated; that had happened often—revenge by rednecks against Negroes driving shiny cars with a white girl aboard. It was an ambiguous accident and a bad moment for the program. I am not speaking about the poor torn-up kids—who in my position can say anything here? The director came out of the hospital with personal belongings to be returned to the dead lad's parents—in exchange for fostering his ambition, they got a pencil box (the thing was so dear to the boy that he took it everywhere with him, even to the swimming pool), unbroken glasses, and a swim suit. The project hung on the edge of hysteria that night.

I taught the next morning, and I didn't think much about the dead lad (I didn't know him, if that's an excuse) once the memorial service was over. Why was this so? Partly because C.J. was in my class. I had by now taught the whole cycle—eight English classes—gradually improving as I went because I had learned how to start closer to where they seemed to be. During this class, C.J. and I were in a running wordless dialogue. C.J. sat in the back row—not with the three other tutors but by himself. Everyone was suppressed and edgy in the aftermath of the accident. C.J. sat in back and spoke not a word. He opened a comic book and stared down at it—an expression of contempt. Whenever I looked his way quickly during that class, I caught his eye. Instantly, he looked down angrily, pretending he had not been listening and would not dream of listening, that he was bored.

At the end of the hour, when I had the ritual conversation with the tutors, asking them what they would be doing in English hour that afternoon and giving them suggestions, C.J. said abruptly, "We ain't meetin', my group." I felt the resistance, the wall, the antipathy, and I was with the sweet-faced Smith girl who said they hate us. But, of course, my mind wouldn't cut out altogether. It thought by habit, as the younger people's minds probably didn't. It told me first, repetitiously and piously, that exactly this militancy and intransigence were what was desperately needed.

Then habit went further. It said there was personal jealousy in the equation. C.J. was charismatic in his community, and my students presented me as charismatic in mine. My blues lecture the day before did impinge, did move onto his turf. Two little girls from the newspaper had interviewed me. They asked if I would play afterward (nobody yet knew of the accident). There was cheering, applause, etc. So here was a stranger on C.J.'s turf who wasn't quite as easily put down, because fortunately he had been warned about being abstract before he opened his mouth.

And then my mind said to consider the class, too. Consider the

feelings that must have been there in the room as I worked—not
just the standard continuum of pride, fear, shame, etc., or guilt
and anger about the little boy killed. But look at what this time
must have been like for C.J.—and for several others in the class. I
had been talking about a poem called "Florida Road Workers" by
Langston Hughes. My opening ploy had been to change the
meaning of a word by changing the way it was said—the little
idea being to help them see the need to act out poems, act
through the words. A word changes meaning according to the
music you play it in with your voice. We began by going up and
down a row of kids asking for five different hellos, and I got some
funny ones—a wary telephone hello, a chaser's hello, salesman's
greeting, etc. The little idea was that to say the right hello, you
have to know the situation: who's speaking, when, why, and so
on. Similarly, reading a poem means knowing not just words but
events and people and how human beings feel—in particular, the
human being saying the poem—in various circumstances.

I said there were some words the Florida road worker says that
are like hello in the sense that you have to hear the music that
goes with the word. But I suggested that we read and enjoy it,
and then we could worry about that:

Florida Road Workers

> I'm makin' a road
> For the cars to fly by on,
> Makin' a road
> Through the palmetto thicket
> For light and civilization
> To travel on.
>
> I'm makin' a road
> For the rich to sweep over
> In their big cars
> And leave me standin' here.
>
> Sure,
> A road helps everybody!
> Rich folks ride—
> And I get to see 'em ride.

I ain't never seen nobody
Ride so fine before.
Hey, Buddy! Look!
I'm makin' a road!

I asked for some readers, and all the readings were straight. The
taunting, ironic thing in the worker's voice—"Hey, Buddy!" or
"Sure"—wasn't in the room. So I started on a lad in the front and
asked if he means what he's saying, this worker, when he says a
road helps everybody. Usual moment: Will the school-church
never-never-land be opened to reality or won't it? C.J.'s head was
up, listening. I didn't show that I knew this. Yes, the youngster
said, he means it. He does? I said incredulously. How so? Why?
What do you mean? Well, the boy said, it's just true, that's all.
The road is good for the white man to ride on, and it's good for
the Negro to look at him. I was stopped momentarily. Was the
boy putting me on? No, clearly not. I looked up; C.J.'s eyes were
down again, but I thought I touched some fury in him.

Now the class started. I tried to get somebody to feel that the
man is not in love with his job or with the world. It took time and
teacherly moves and hints and leads and lots of lousy stuff and
some breaks, and I felt everybody holding his temper and
patience, including me. We were all relieved as hell when at last
a student said that the worker is mad: It's not the same to ride as
to watch; he's making a mad joke; you could make "Sure" pretty
fierce and sneering—"really hot"—and be right. And when all
this came, it came with a lovely breaking surge. When they saw,
they *saw!* They turned around and looked at each other, absolutely delighted; they were in the game, impressed—very up. I
felt exhilarated in their exhilaration. It mattered.

But, I told myself, think what obstacles to the teaching job
could have been in that room. Cross over into C.J.'s head. What
an exacerbation, what a humiliation, what an infuriation those
moments must have been. Here's the white man; see him trying
to "explain"—to the Negro—a Negro's helpless self-mocking rage
at the exploitation of the Negro. See the friendly white man

taking up the black man's cause and trying to be patient about getting the nature of this complaint across. And no doubt thinking, somewhere in him, My God, they really are dumb, aren't they, the niggers? They don't get anything.

So C.J. had to watch this—a white man scratching at this job, and all the while sapping the potential and necessary energies of hatred in the blacks before him. Maybe—if he were just a shade less self-absorbed than I thought he was—maybe C.J. suffered, watching the soul brothers stumble around, missing the point, having to be shown it.

Then I had another feeling. Why should a white man be there at all at this spectacle, claiming to understand a pain he never shared? Why should he understand, interpret, carry over—every part of it involving placing himself in a superior position, standing forth as their superior, the man with magic.

You have no right to see yourself standing there in the role of the teacher, they say to themselves. You have nothing to teach us. What does it matter what some trick of irony comes to in a poem? We know the beating beyond the words. We watched the cars. We were there. Our fathers were beaten and exploited. We were beaten. Things, not words. And if we can't master the symbols, the black marks, we have felt the clubs and the knives and the pickax and the heat.

So, man, get out of my way, we ain't going to meet.

And here I am, aware of this sullen fury bent on me, and not just aware of it but educated by it. By everything that's right, by everything these kids have endured as children, by all they stand to endure next week, month, their whole lives, they possess an inherent claim to dignity and value that surpasses Teacher's, no matter how smart or good he says he is. In absolute moral terms, in terms of balance and courage and patience and humor—God knows they are better creatures than I am, with more substance, more truth in them.

And the point is that these strains—these seeings and counter-seeings and tensions of self-assessment—are going on *in a class-room*. I am not only teaching—I see over to the far side of the moon and grasp for a moment the absurdity of this kind of "leading out"—leading out into the white world of invented agonies, invented tranquilizers, invented puzzles. I saw my puerility, my helplessness. I saw that the culture I lead them toward knows less than it claims to. Our "grading them up" is a kind of minor epicicular correction, not a fundamental offering of light. The world stopped for that second, I was on edge. I even knew at that instant that part of C.J.'s feeling was a kind of shame at himself, for being mean to us when we can't know any better, when we are at least trying to understand, trying to care as many do not. Listen to me, listen, I forgive you, you white bastard, but just get out, will you?

And, finally, what did I want to do when I saw all this? I wanted to *say* I saw it; I wanted to turn it into talk, into a discovery, into something to note down in a journal. Marvelous! Hey, buddy, I get it! Jesus Christ, look at me, I'm building a piece of prose! I get it! *Can* I possibly get anything? I'm leaving. I'm white and I'm always going to be leaving. I'm always going to be thinking it into a set of complexities, naming them off, feeling better for the names, and then clearing out and forgetting the experience. Hey, buddy! White man! Leave us alone; *we ain't going to meet.*

All right, a bit overheated. C.J. and I never traded blows, after all. The day I left he said a sulky good-bye (he spoke first, I noted childishly in my pride) from behind half a pickup truck. The main point—I repeat it—is that these classrooms and these situations were crowded. Every kind of human tide crossing and meeting, buzzing, a thousand kinds of feeling. I would say the teaching, as teaching, went much slower than usual. I would also say that there is more in it for the teacher. He feels himself being read as he reads. The light comes and goes in his students. Apathy and stoniness put it out. There are fantasies and longing. Then it comes to life again. People are sometimes unbelievably quick. There was a lot in this for us, and our kids knew it. They tended to want to hang around there. A white Alabaman on the faculty said to me, "Listen, if I didn't have kids like these on the weekend to work with during the year, I don't know where I'd get my strength."

And that's what I got, too: strength. It wasn't from some cliché about Negro vitality. And it wasn't from some self-inflating sense of *noblesse oblige;* if I have quadratics and alphabet skills, I share them because I am "nice." No, the strength comes from the infusion of certainty. And that's my last "observation." It is about the gift of certainty—knowing where you are, knowing what's right and wrong—that is an amazing experience.

You go there and you understand for the first time—clearly, if you're like me—that there are some things on earth that must be changed. They simply must and simply will. You are rich in the understanding of necessity and potency and rightness. (Beatings are wrong. Ignorance of exploitation is wrong.) You know for the first time that certain events must occur and that you and others are going to make them occur, or at least are going to work to make them occur. You see that revolution is not a word but a pointing toward what obviously, absolutely must happen, and you are lifted up by this sight, by the freshening awareness of how criminally wrong a wrong can be *known* to be by a mere human being—namely, yourself. And knowing all this, knowing that the real "success" for the white teacher is to end up for a while on the receiving end of hate, you plan to work out a way to come back.

The Age of Overkill

The Spirit of Overkill was everywhere in this period. Drifting sluggishly over the land from the international power struggle, a dense, polluting wave, it penetrated the very marrow of the culture. Journalism, conversation, manners, the arts—the innermost thoughts and feelings of men—all were touched or tainted.

At first the influence appeared only in certain small changes of accent and idiom, hints of the habitual irascibility to come. The emergence of anger as the normal Anglo-American tone of voice was scarcely noticed. But in the sequel the whole age was caught up in verbal ferocity, and at the climax, in the late sixties, the fury turned compulsive. In speech and song, poem and proclamation, fiercely, ceaselessly, a weird, inexplicable "assault" was pressed—not at new "enemies" but at old ones already in tatters. There was no breaking out of the mindless cycle of supertaunts; long after the target institutions lay in lifeless ruin at their feet, men continued to rain down abuse upon them, locked in the rage to rage. And at the end, crazed by hatred that could find no standing object to destroy, they beat and tore at themselves.

As might be guessed, the movement at its height was marked by episodes of uncommon vulgarity and tastelessness. One periodical of the day—its motto was "Irreverence is our only sacred cow"—published a "report" on President Lyndon Johnson's behavior on the Air Force plane that bore him back to Washington from Dallas after the assassination of President Kennedy; it asserted that the President, before taking the oath, had mounted the casket and reached sexual climax in the throat wound of his dead predecessor (*The Realist*, 1967). Another—a Methodist church magazine, which lusted, like the secular organs of the time, after new modes of mockery—another invented a news-story framework for the nineteenth-century Nietzschean cry that "God is dead," and "quoted" the reactions of the crude and witless great to the "item." The Pope: ". . . it is difficult to imagine how we shall proceed without Him." De Gaulle: "God is dead! Long live France!" President Truman: "I'm always sorry to hear somebody is dead. It's a damn shame." President Eisenhower: "He will be missed" (*Motive*, 1966).

More interesting than the vulgarity at full tide, however, was the power of Overkill throughout its span to draw together ill-sorted minds. The decade's steady hounding of people "over thirty" was led, for the most part, by public entertainers, "rock groups," and the like. Beatle Harrison spoke against "all these old fools who are governing us and . . . bombing us and doin' all that. . . ." Stone Jagger laid it down: "Politics, like the legal system, is dominated by old men. Old men who are also bugged by religion." Leary of Milbrook, a guru, told undergraduates at Yale: "Your legislators, your President, and your Defense Department are for the most part impotent old men who are riding on youth. They don't want you to be free. Laws are made by old people who don't want young people to do exactly those things young people were meant to do—to make love, turn on, and have a good time" (*Friday*, 1968).

But in the very season that Stones and Beatles and gurus were thus baying the aged, a respected Nobel Prize winner himself elected to run with the pack. At the time I did my best work, said Dr. James Watson to an undergraduate audience of hundreds at Harvard (the time was the spring of 1968), "I thought of people over forty as at the end of their lives . . . and that was the right attitude to take—not too much reverence for the big boys. If they knew what to do, they'd be doing it."

And Professor Watson was but one of hundreds of distinguished figures from the world of mind who lent weight to the

Overkill cause. From the first, indeed, that cause was a favorite with artists as well as intellectuals. James Baldwin, the novelist and essayist, spoke authentic Overkill whenever he appeared in public. (The author of *Another Country* was given to describing his country as "the Fourth Reich": *New York Times*, 1968.) Susan Sontag, a writer well known in that day, was no less fiercely ignorant in her essays on history and race: "The white race is the cancer of history," she said flatly. "It is the white race and it alone—its ideologies and inventions—which eradicates autonomous civilization wherever it spreads, which has upset the ecological balance of the planet, which now threatens the very existence of life itself" (*Partisan Review*, 1967).

Given leadership of this order, youth inevitably responded with explosions of its own—student editorials calling for guerrilla bands to roar through "college campuses burning books, burning degrees and exams, burning school records, busting up classrooms, and freeing our brothers from the prison of the university . . ." The Berkeley *Barb* continued: "The universities cannot be reformed. They must be abandoned or closed down. They should be used as bases for actions against society, but never taken seriously. The professors have nothing to teach. . . . We can learn more from any jail than we can from any university." And the result was, to repeat, that by the end of the sixties the entire articulate Anglo-American community—young, middle-aged, and aged people alike—was transformed into a monster-chorus of damnation-dealers, its single voice pitched ever at hysterical level, its prime aim to transform every form of discourse into a blast.

There were Overkill aphorisms in that period ("The world belongs to politics, which is to say the world belongs to death": Theodore Roszak), and Overkill definitions ("The family is the American fascism": Paul Goodman). There were Overkill toppers, comebacks, and sneers. (When a television interviewer in England told the novelist Mary McCarthy that she appeared to be "accusing [the American] people of stupidity, not wickedness," the author stoutly replied, "I think they are wicked, too.")

There were Overkill critical assessments (Thomas Wolfe was a "professional hillbilly": Alfred Kazin), and Overkill letters to the editor, especially in the Manhattan weeklies of the day. "We are rats in a laboratory maze," the letter writers regularly wrote in. "The Government is feeding us frustration, bringing us to the verge of madness." (Replies to these letters were themselves similarly tinged. One columnist for a suburban paper called *Newsday* answered his mail by stamping the letters with an obscenity—special oversized rubber stamp—and returning them straight to their senders.) There was Overkill in public speaking, sometimes in rhetorical questions ("You call yourselves revolutionaries?" shouted Rap Brown. "How many white folks you killed today?"), sometimes in hymns of praise ("All the people at the Pentagon!" shouted the poet Allen Ginsberg, honoring the turned-on tastes of a group of peace marchers. "They were all heads!"), sometimes in historical analogies ("Reading a speech of Andrew Jackson's . . . the other day," said Robert Bly, declining a prize at the 1968 National Book Awards, "I realized he was the Westmoreland of 1830").

And there were reams—floods—oceans of Overkill poetry. New chants were reported in newspapers. ("Dean Rusk is a murderer!" shouted four hundred in unison outside a West Coast hotel.) Simple Overkill refrains were "socko" Off Broadway. ("The middle class/ Are just like pigs . . . The middle class/ Are just like pigs": Jacques Brel.) Old-style blues underwent sea changes: "My Baby Done Left Me and I Feel Like Homemade Shit": The Fugs.

And prose poems of immeasurable putridity took art straight to its borders—witness the garbage epic by a Mrs. Hentoff, columnist for a paper called *The Village Voice*. The theme of the work—New York *as* garbage—was a response to a lengthy strike by city garbage collectors early in 1968. The opening strains sang softly and with satisfaction of Manhattan sans sanitation. (". . . almost as if [the city] had become what we knew it was all along. There was garbage on the sidewalks, garbage in the gutters, garbage lining the walls of buildings, garbage blowing in the wind . . .") Then, to a moving ripe air, the voice rose in a plea that the strike never be ended, that it go "on and on until the garbage fill[s] the canyons and the rats leap from mound to mound." And finally, at the close, a gentle self-loving cadence celebrated the poet's "truthful image" of the town.*

Contemporary observers who maintained critical detachment from the new fashion, and sought to define its relations with the past, turned up several notions that still possess interest. One writer theorized that Overkill was an extension of the American tall-tale tradition. Another traced its genesis to the post-nineteenth-century expansion of literacy and general education, developments that intensified a threat to the elite. (According to this view, men who considered themselves to belong to the elite were obliged to speak and write in extravagant terms in order to establish their position. In ages of limited literacy, this was unnecessary; a man possessing the ability to order his thoughts cogently on paper was an aristocrat by virtue of that ability. But once cogency was brought within Everyman's reach, it ceased to be a distinction: wildness had to come in.)

Still other theorists sought to connect the advent of Overkill with the new educational theories of the time. "Think," wrote one observer, "think of the uphill fifty-year struggle waged by educators on behalf of 'immediacy' and 'relevance' as against knowledge and the sense of the past. Is no measure of credit owing here? Suppose for a moment that, in place of new-style utter now-sense, children were still immersed in the dreary stuff of history:

---

* Another Overkill salute, by an American poet, to New York filth can be found in the Russian poet Yevgeny Yevtushenko's poem "Smog," which detailed a trip to America in the 1960s. Yevtushenko quoted Robert Lowell as having explained city soot as "a vengeance from heaven for depravity and moral collapse." It is worth nothing, perhaps, as a curiosity, that the Russian poet appears to have picked up a taste for Overkill idiom during the trip in question. In the same poem he saw a likeness between his accommodations at the Chelsea Hotel on Eighth Avenue and Twenty-third Street and a concentration camp. ("In the cell-like room," he wrote, "there is a smell of Dachau.")

could the thrust of a story of Western Civilization like Miss Sontag's [see above] ever then have been felt?"

But though a few contemporary theses or "explanations" retain an edge of usefulness, most were error-strewn. It was usual, for instance, to date abuse-escalation in the late sixties, coincident with the Southeast Asian wars, and to ignore the embryonic states, as well as sudden prophetic outbursts like Lord Russell's against Macmillan and Kennedy:

> We used to call Hitler wicked for killing off the Jews, but Kennedy and Macmillan are much more wicked than Hitler. . . . We cannot obey these murderers. They are wicked. They are abominable. They are the wickedest people who ever lived in the history of man and it is our duty to do what we can against them.*

Again: a standard practice was to associate verbal extravagance and apocalyptic expression primarily with the political left—new militants, student activists, Filthy Speech chiefs, and the rest. It was an understandable mistake: many public events that attracted notice were reported in ways that nourished acceptance of the equation. A writer for *The New Yorker* magazine attending a young people's political convention in Chicago in 1967 observed that, for a whole week, the word *revolution* was used "for every nuance of dissent."

Yet even so it must remain mystifying that, on the basis of slim evidence like this, men could conclude that Overkill was an identifying mark of the left. Before Berkeley there were the so-called Birchers, radical rightists apt at every form of verbal excess. ("The whole country is one vast insane asylum and they're letting the worst patients run the place": Robert Welch, founder of the Birch Society.) And could it really have been believed that, say, Norman Mailer (another writer well regarded

---

* In 1961. Lord Russell's name is another reminder of a point worth stressing: many foreigners learned to speak Overkill with ease. Not least notable of them was Fidel Castro, who produced much classic work—including a jibe (at the 1968 International Cultural Congress at Havana) at population-control programs. Such programs, the Cuban premier asserted, were proof of "imperialism's lack of faith in the future."

in this period) on the American narcosis was in any significant sense different from the 1967 Christian Crusade's Dean Noebel, who held forth as follows on the "Commie-Beatle Pact"? ". . . the Communists have contrived an elaborate, calculating and scientific technique directed at rendering a generation of American youth useless through nerve-jamming, mental deterioration and retardation. . . . The destructive music of the Beatles . . . reinforces . . . mental breakdown. . . ."

The truth that should have been plain even then was that Overkill was larger than politics: Overkill masters cared far more for style than for views. The issue of *The Realist* that carried the report on the behavior of President Johnson also contained an account—equally slanderous—of President Kennedy as a client of Dallas call girls. And there was the celebrated Kopkind case, involving a correspondent in Washington for an English leftist weekly. Though yielding to no man in his detestation of President Johnson, the correspondent Kopkind was haunted (apparently) by an even deeper passion—that for Overkill—and he spoke the tongue continually, even when no one hateful was by. ("Senator [Eugene] McCarthy is one of the Senate's few intellectuals," wrote this pundit, "and . . . one of its most obvious hypocrites: the two go hand in hand.")

And if the movement was larger than politics, it was also—dare we say?—more complex than the conventional wisdom of our own day even yet allows. "Despondent over their inability to alter the course of national affairs, men turned in helpless fury to a vocabulary of imprecation which they themselves knew to be useless, but that at least permitted an expression of agony, of fierce frustration, of certainty that apocalypse was near." Here is the genetic thesis in favor just now; it is attractive, and when pressed in connection with certain literary heroes of that time—rare men whose integrity matched their intensity—it may be held to contain a piece of the truth.

But surely we oversimplify if we consider impotence to be the single key. The route to satisfactory accounts of broad cultural movements passes invariably through thickets of complication.

And in travelling that path, there is some point always in attending to primary meanings. In the time of which we speak, the term *Overkill* referred to surplus obliterative power—mega-weapons capable of killing ten times the human population and turning the earth to ashes thrice. And implicit in the surplus, as in certain usages of the word, was the assumption that lives destroyed still await destruction and are thus in some inexpressible sense unreal. (A man's third death can be counted as well as his first.) Putting it another way: When obliterative power is adjusted to the sum of the obliterable, that adjustment constitutes an acknowledgment of the reality of existence. But when there is no such adjustment, when men ignore the sum of the obliterable, when men manufacture destruction beyond what is "needed," it is a sign of a weakened sense of the hard, substantial, objective world.

And precisely that weakness figured, as we must now recognize, in Overkill as a *cultural* phenomenon. It is in fact possible that this element alone—the loss of belief in a substantive outer reality—separated the Overkillers of the sixties from premodern titans of abuse. The heroic scorners of earlier times—Dante on to Swift—had no more energy of contempt than late twentieth-century man. But they did have a far stronger conviction that beyond them lay living targets, villains whose substance words could touch and wound. ("Vilify! Vilify!" went Beaumarchais's famous aphorism. "At least some of the dirt *will stick*.") Even the cooler arguefiers of the pre-Overkill past dwelt on the substantiality of the world inhabited by their enemies, and upon the necessity of imaginatively penetrating that world in order to hurt. William James, for one, never tired of quoting a contemporary who insisted that the first duty of men with the pacifist conscience was to "enter the point of view of the militarist and seek to move the point." Everywhere in former days the clearly held assumption was that the "opponent" did exist.

But in the sixties—to say it once again—a frail sense of outer reality had become the rule: a disbelief in counterunderstandings of events that pit themselves over against mine. The disbelief showed itself not only in Overkill spectaculars—the notorious fits of fury that plucked out eyes from severed heads. It appeared also in the frequency of theatrical metaphor in Overkill masters' chat. All England is an empty music hall, cried the playwright John Osborne, as the curtain rose on the Overkill age. "On the Vietnam stage," said the editor of the *New Statesman* at the end of the decade, "the West enacts a travesty of itself, spoken in Newspeak, performed by fake heroes and real buffoons. . . ." And these writers only echoed the common American line. "The stars of Vietnam," wrote a critic on *The Village Voice*, "are LBJ and Ho, Westmoreland and Giap . . . they are all playing the parts. . . . Senator Eugene McCarthy, waiting in the wings for a piece of scenery to fall on the actor he is understudying . . . Senator Robert F. Kennedy . . . in his dressing room . . . this multi-billion dollar superproduction . . ." Ceaselessly the Voice of Overkill chanted to itself that there was nothing substantial Out There. The bad men were shadows, not substances; mere actors, figures in shows, not penetrable, imaginable bodies, not men who thought and felt their way into their mistakes. The likelihood is, in sum, that the Overkill phenomenon is best thought of as part of a seamless cultural whole embracing even the astrophysics of that day—that incredible world view wherein, as one critical contemporary (Hannah Arendt) wrote, "instead of objective qualities . . . we find instruments, and instead of nature or the universe . . . [the investigator] encounters only himself."

But, as must be added, the latter is of course only "a likelihood"—not a certainty. The historian's voice speaks confidently, bent on establishing once more that no corridor of the past is beyond reach, no puzzle beyond solution. But questions nag. Mysteries remain. The age we study was not, after all, composed of innocents. Scholars then were no less aware than ourselves that in periods of strife violence is done upon language. Then, as now, sober heads could read Thucydides on the confusions of meaning and the transformation of terms during social upheavals. (During the Corcyrean Revolution, said the great man, "reckless audacity became courage . . . prudent hesitation, specious cowardice, ability to see all sides of a question inaptness to act on any. Frantic violence became the attribute of manliness; safe plotting, a justifiable means of self-defense.") And there were writers closer to the sixties in time—the Englishman Orwell, for one—who insisted on the obligation of men of mind to guard against pollution of meaning traceable either to political flatulence or intensity.

Yet in the sixties men of mind were heedless. Why so? Can any of our confidently advanced explanations finally tell us much? What were the sacred texts that misled thinkers in that day? Was it that they believed, perhaps, with the aesthete Cyril Connolly, that henceforth there would be no means of judging a man save by "the quality of his despair"? Did they therefore drive themselves into fury because fury—however abstract, frustrating, unfocused—seemed a possible substitute for moral clarity and worth? Or are we simply to conclude that verbal dementia was only the other side of the coin of physical violence—a mere necessitous counterpart to assassination, riot, arson?

If we cannot know the answers—history has cunning passages —we can at least pause to ponder our ignorance. And it will not be amiss if, as we do so, we turn again, with a freshly grateful eye, to those never sufficiently praised architects of the Great Disengagement at the century's end. But for their genius, their determination to negotiate a defusing of The Words as well as of The Bombs, what would our future now be? Who among us, reader or writer, can doubt—given the truth of what nearly happened in the sixties—that it is to their decision to lay down the lash of language that we today owe the breath of our life?

Tickle-Touch Theater:
A Reservation

"It was so wonderful," said our hostess happily—the bright-eyed girl, in the yellow velvet hostess skirt, near the punch bowl. She'd been to a performance by the Becks' Living Theater that afternoon. "The girls were scared but it only took a minute. He spoke to them twice and right away they were up on their feet and out in the aisles. Completely into it—free, being what they wanted to be. It's the future, really. They adored it!"

The Becks were in the provinces again, bringing the drama of participation to our neighbor college (Smith), exciting the entire valley. And though the idea of fencing with their rooters came to mind, it didn't stick. *Why so combative?* says the inner voice. *Can't relax and share somebody else's pleasures? Twenty years a prof and still lusting to set people straight? You actually think the Becks are far out?* For longer than a decade, after all, most of the shows that have pulled people from Snowville to the city—*The Connection* was first—have *used* the spectator, set him in a highly self-conscious relation to events "onstage," even threatened to bust or devour him.

What's more, the mod plays that turn up on litry reading lists—the ones about which it seems decent to say Something Important Started Here—invariably invented new tricks of anti-illusion, teased a picture-frame convention or tromped on spectator space. ("Those lady musicians sitting onstage in the Berliner Ensemble production of *The Caucasian Chalk Circle*—you do see the Milestone there, don't you, Student? —When they

come out, sit down and then *smile* at the audience, completely
aware of us and cozily reminding us we are at a show?")

And then, beyond these items of firsthand knowledge, there
are a hundred more known through rumor or gossip about games
insiders play, Off-Off-Off bits, radical theater and dance-theater
materials and attitudes. During a visit here last fall, the Polish
Theater Lab director, Jerzy Grotowski, kept telling New York
interviewers about a production of Marlowe's *Dr. Faustus* in
which the spectators sat around a long table with Faustus
(impromptu questions were addressed to them), and about
another, odder pre-*Marat/Sade* production of *Kordian* (1960):
"We transformed the [theater] space into an insane asylum. The
entire room became a hospital with beds and so on. The actors
were on the beds along with the spectators. The actors were
either doctors or patients, the most interesting cases. The doctors
treated the spectators as also sick. Those spectators who were
treated as patients were furious—the others were very proud
because they had been judged 'sane.' "

On a different front there are the famous Ann Halprin "myths"
as performed in the San Francisco Dancers Workshop Company studios by dancers and audiences. Consider "Myth Seven:
Carry":

> People—not, for this performance, defined as audience—entered
> the performance area and sat on high levels. Drums were playing
> and they sat facing each other and looked at one another for a long
> time.
>
> The director then asked, "Would anyone volunteer to choose a
> person and carry him through this passage?" After a pause, a man
> jumped down, selected a girl, and very simply carried her, and the
> drumming rhythm, the lights, and the carry action began to work
> together. This kind of activity continued very simply and began to
> include "Will two people carry one person?" "Will five people carry
> two people?" etc.
>
> New direction was added on the spot as a result of what was hap-
> pening. "Will those of you who want to be carried stand in the
> passage and wait?" After much waiting: "Will those who volunteer

carry those who want to be carried?" People realized the primitive, archetypal connotations of this act (carried in the womb, bride carried across threshold, pope carried to alter [*sic*], corpse carried to grave, etc.) and the scene, especially when it seemed to resemble a Bacchanalia, was suffused with a ritualistic quality. The event concluded with an action that involved everyone either carrying or being carried. . . .

Or (yet more exotica), consider theater on the model of Allen Kaprow's *Self-Sacrifice*, advertised as "a piece without spectators," but in reality a list of "activities" to be performed by the likes of you and me, amidst the other business of our "normal lives." Activities proposed for Boston and roundabouts included these:

> For a few moments at night, shouts, words, calls, all through bullhorns. Voices moving on the streets, from windows, around corners, in hallways, alleys.
> Cars drive into filling station, erupt with white foam pouring from windows.
> People tie tar paper around many cars in supermarket lot.
> On another day, twenty or more flash-gun cameras shoot off at same time all over supermarket; shopping resumed.

Think of all this, repeat, and then come back to the Becks and the velvet hostess celebrating them, and ask yourself, Why so chuckly, chum? Whence that scratchiness, that impulse to frown and squirm?

The answer isn't that the impulse is rooted in the comic sense, though it must be said that hilarious passages do occur in some descriptions of these projects. (One Halprin dancer, for instance, has been quoted as saying that "at first it was beautiful when I was carried, but it went on and on, and I felt I was being used." Another said, "I find it hard to be really open with guys from the outside. They were kind of horny. They got me up tight." Miss Halprin's answer to the first dancer was, "Well, they didn't understand the body." To the second, she said, "They usually get horny when the lights go off.") Neither is the answer that the notion of an exchange of space and roles between performers and audience is inherently ridiculous, or that it's a Demeaning Thing when some god from the machine is lowered onto the stage—as in the Firehouse Theater's *Iphigenia Transformed* (1966)— bringing four cases of beer for an actor-spectator blast. The effort of the so-called environmental theater to dynamize theatrical interiors is fascinating as often as it is loony, and the whole tickle-touch body-contact school of dramatic production induces a kind of anxiety that's conceivably stimulating to certain types of self-bound heads.

No, the reservations come simply because the assumptions built into the rhetoric or ecstasy of enthusiasts of the new troupes and inventors—assumptions about spectator life in the old-style theater—often seen tendentious at best and at worst libelous, woolly, and dumb. What are these assumptions? One (see the velvet lady) is that the trad playgoer is a passive blob—a standing or sitting vessel that doesn't "do" but merely "receives," is blown upon or poured into. Another assumption (see Richard Schechner's "Six Axioms" for experimental theater in the Spring 1968 *TDR*) is that the central truth about the trad audience is a truth of inhibition: "they bring to the theater a decorum that has been learned elsewhere but which is nevertheless scrupulously applied here," with the result that the main audience occupation in a theater is the maintenance of Proper Tone.

Yet another assumption—more famous but not less simplistic— can be summoned by reference to Brecht's postscript to *The Rise and Fall of the City of Mahagonny*, wherein this genius distinguishes his theater, which presses the spectator to "make decisions," from the traditional theater, which asks the spectator to enlarge his empathic responses. (In the *Little Organon for the Theater*, Brecht asks, "How long are our souls going to have to leave our 'gross' bodies under cover of darkness to penetrate into those dream figures up on the rostrum . . . ?")

Spelling out persuasively, in a paragraph, what's wrong with such formulations is, needless to say, no job for a party fencer— no matter how combative-portentous his nature. It demands intuitive knowledge of the mystery of collaborative creation, the process by which the spectator himself becomes a maker and inventor and unfolder of character, an intelligence engaged in simultaneities of sympathy and judgment, one who penetrates (by quickness of mind and feeling) the actor's dream of a character, and constructs, out of gestures and shadings and restraints and inflections, a clear "imagination of an imagination," a firm map of another human being's inwardness. Great men have sat to the task of describing this process—Whitman and Tolstoy, for example, are superb on the *reader's* act of creation. And at least one uncommon mind—Péguy—has gone on to point to the palpable truth, namely, that exact counterparts to a reader's activity exist everywhere in the arts, whether in the rendering of a dramatic scene or painting or piece of sculpture or song. A "reading of a poem," says Péguy, is a joint act—call it the act of reading and being read—performed by the work and the reader, and a play is a joint act or common operation of dramatic work and spectator. And passivity is never in question, for the spectator or reader is ceaselessly "entering into" the source of the work, bending himself with sympathy and complaisance and love toward its innerness, yet ever retaining clarity of contemplation.

In a word, we don't make out Masha or Richard II by behaving well, by maintaining decorum, by not sneezing or wandering in the aisles, or by relaxing in our limply sensitive receiving souls. We create them with the actor, by a labor of constructive imagination—arduous, deep, testing. And just as there are good readings of poems, fine "audience work," so, in Péguy's words, there are excellent seeings of plays, harmonious, rhythmic representations on the stage of the mind, attendings as honest, clear, and innocent as a flower blossom or a peach.

Ah, says a voice, you claim this activity has been banished from tickle-touch theater? Certainly it hasn't much of a place there. Absorption, attentiveness, concentration on otherness— these are hard for a playgoer to sustain in a situation in which the immediate urgent question inside him is: Does that actor heading my way mean to hit (kiss, fondle, solicit) me? Security vanishes, and, with it, guarantees of continuous outward focus. It's not all loss, naturally. Challenge and interruption are values, when sparingly, pointedly used; they can awaken the mind to action. But are there not limits to this action? Could a man write a chapter of a novel amid the uncertainty thus aroused, amid such promptings to nervous self-regard? Yet the good playgoer is, for the length of *his* performance, like a novelist: he is an interpreter, a provider, filler-in, reader-creator of motives, an active, strenuous, comprehensive intelligence.

Ah, says another voice, how comes it that an occupation so noble no longer turns people on? —You could say in answer that the trouble stems from the virus, Skepticism; people hate thinking of themselves as illusion-prone, connable by playactors. Or you could say the trouble is that people reared in a cave of self-hyphenation (self-this, self-that, self-realization, self-encounter, self-involvement, etc.) can't bear the prospect of self-diminution, and despise the notion of laboring over any character not their own. Or you could speak flatly of imaginative incompetence: in ages when men knew each other, when turpitude and virtue took the form of visible, trackable, right-or-wrong relations between one man and his neighbor, people were sharp at fathoming each other. Now they're clumsier, and embarrassed at their clumsiness.

But all this chatter scarcely fits the situation. What was wanted there by the punch bowl was just a way to say—lightly, quickly, provocatively—that, Yes, sure, it's wonderful to like something. Lovely to hear the Becks praised. But . . . It's not quite true that in Olden Times, before this Revelation, audiences "just sat there," locked up, locked in, mere blobs. I remember (for the record, "I" is a mid-fortyish lad) being loose-limbed and easy in a theater not on demand but in delight. I remember a disciplined freedom that nevertheless seemed every instant limitless. I remember whole hours in which, through constant steady inventings and piecings-out at once decorous and wild, I and neighbors roundabout were becoming—uninterruptedly becoming, for only our imaginations touched—everything *we* wanted to be. . . .

America the Unimagining

A man in his early fifties, vigorous, strong-faced, well liked in his town; family man, business success (small-city merchandising operation). No reader but a great keeper-up—business papers, hard news, world events, facts that matter. Pleasures? He "gets a kick out of" gadgets and machines—wild stereo layout in the cathedral living room, complicated ship-to-shore gear on his boat, a genuine systems approach for stock control in the stores. Further pleasures: he's outdoorsy, handy at home, a Dartmouth man, skier, active in business and community clubs, nonchurchgoer, nonpolitical argufier. . . .

At parties he doesn't talk much to women. Also, he stands back a little from his kids. Pleasant-tentative with his bright daughter, straight-arrowish "Dad" with his teen-aged boys. Stands back, too, from the "creative" phases of the business—buying, advertising, display, and so on—leaving this to a younger brother. (Let something "real sticky" turn up anywhere, though, and nobody but himself can cope. Who else, for instance, would be up to a face-off with the old family friend, one of his store managers, when the detective service reports the man is robbing them blind?) As for a personality profile:

"I am more interested in a man's behavior than in his inner life." Check. "In shaping character, externals are more important than inner tendencies." Check. "I sometimes have trouble figuring out the behavior of people who are emotionally unstable." Check. "Math is one of my best subjects." Check. "I think I'm practical and efficient when there's something that has to be done." Check. "I don't have the temperament for the 'romantic' point of view." Check. "I have few emotional problems." Check. "A first principle with me is that it's a man's duty to adjust himself to his environment." Check. "I am a fairly conventional person." Check. "My relations with other people are usually uncomplicated." Check. "My ideas are more often sound and sensible than unusual or imaginative." Check. "I say what I have to say in a few simple words so that I'm easily understood." Check. "There's a lot in the economic interpretation of history." Check. "I find it easier to deal with concrete facts in one special field than with general ideas about man or nature." Check. "I think science offers as good a guide as any to the future." Check. "When I'm working out a problem I try to stick as close as possible to the facts." Check. "I enjoy an intimate conversation with one person more than general conversation with several." No. "When I hear a person talk, I think more about his personality than I do about what he's saying." No. "I think I have a good understanding of women." No. "I love to talk about my innermost feelings to a sympathetic friend." Nah. "I often think I can feel my way into the innermost being of another person." No. "It takes a good deal to make me angry." Check. "Unselfishness and sympathy are more desirable than high ideals and ambitions." False. "I'm apt to make up stories by myself about the private thoughts and experiences of the people I meet." No. "I believe the world may be well lost for love." No. "I live in my imagination as much as I do in the external world." No. "I dislike everything that has to do with money—buying, selling, bargaining." Oh, sure. "I like being in the thick of the action." Yes, emphatically. "I like to have people about me most of the time." Yes, emphatically. . . .

Other items (not on the Harvard clinic test) worth noting about this man? One: Inclined to treat characters as functions, he regularly "explains" people by telling you what they do (a parenthetical phrase—Harry's a doctor, Hank's a cop, Lucille's had a pair of twins). Another point: The fellow is good to tie up by on a sloppy night at Southwest Harbor, and makes, in general, a fine summer neighbor—fun outings to the island, family picnics, softball on the sand, sun's over the yardarm, and so on. Further point: When you step away from him, sit in judgment, dwell on his limits, you feel like a heel. You discover again that one of the several reasons for not judging is that the minute it's done, the judge is judged, stands fully visible in his own fatuity and self-congratulation, beyond sympathy, ripe for sentence himself. Yet another item: The man "beheld" is representative. Tens of millions are excluded from his place, just at this moment; going up from the middle in society is where you're likely to find him, not from the middle down. But the excluded millions can't forever escape; even now they are being graded "up" on his curve. Every year the movement of economic life shoots tens of thousands toward him—into his set of mind, his style, his inward truth. He is no "middle-class stereotype," in short: he is an American destination or finish line, the possible end of the race.

Finally, last point about the man: He is in trouble. There's a withering in him, a metaphorical arm gone, some limb, some key part missing, something stunted or ungrown. The present judge speaks quickly, on the run, hoping to hide himself from the next judge: The man just described is, in one flat word, *unfulfilled.*

To say as much is, by instant extension, to discount the seriousness of the famous American commitment to the ideal of individual self-fulfillment. And while such discounting is standard practice among the knowing, it isn't at first glance easy to defend. Granted, the language in which national commitments and values are usually spelled out—the language of civics classes and Scouting Award nights—does beg to be mocked. "The social organization of America is compatible with its free political institutions. . . . America is a society in which equality of opportunity is supported by specific social mechanisms, including classlessness, a wide spectrum of inviolable and equal individual rights guaranteed to all individuals, guarantees of minimum welfare for all and special assistance to any that are at unusual economic disadvantage. . . . Enhancing the dignity of the individual citizen, developing his capabilities for self-fulfillment, is a prime concern of the American government. . . . The environments which help to shape the character of the individual—his home life, education, religious training, occupation, etc.—are in varying degrees matters of public concern. The object of this concern is to develop typical traits of character—independence of spirit, respect for the rights of others, cooperativeness, sense of civic responsibility—and others which will make the individual a better, more constructive citizen." Formulations like these cry out for qualification, amendment, hints of stylish self-restraint. Some humility, please.

But the cry for humility can itself become cant. Spells of living abroad in middle-class communities—leafy Edgbaston in England, say, or a Costa village in Portugal—offer only ambiguous testimony on the matter of the American versus European sense of civic responsibility. But in the area of attitudes and policies concerning education, those ambiguities disappear. The cause of "trained excellence" is Everyman's cause in America; my right to as much education as I can bear goes relatively unchallenged. No events, no crisis, seemingly, can interrupt the national dream of self-realization through mental strife. And no taxpayer protest ever badly smutches this piety. Two years ago, after the peace demonstration at the Pentagon, President Johnson, meeting with a group of teachers at the White House, turned eloquent—some might have said moving—on the subject of self-realization and the school. Appointments this morning, he explained, with the National Security Council and with the President of Mexico—but you, you teachers, you're more important. Whatever else they said about him, the President went on, they would have to say that because of programs he instituted, a million people were in college this year who would not otherwise have had a chance to go. And how much more remained to be done! Four men out of ten on earth could not read or write! He himself was returning to teaching when his political career was over.

The books on the Cabinet Room shelf suggested an absence of

a passion for the higher literary culture—O. Henry, a high school physics text, a high school chemistry text, and the like. (There has been no report that President Nixon has replaced them.) The few educational institutions in the country where the idea of standards is well rooted are meritocratic in assumption—which means not only antiaristocratic but antidemocratic as well. By far the larger part of the huge federal expenditures in the field of education supports phases of the defense program. And, more important than any of this, profound inequities still exist in the American system of public education. But from none of this does it follow that the cause or dream in question was a sham. The old programs and the new—Head Start, the regional educational laboratories, the tuition loan bank—have flaws, cannot meet every need. But the motive behind them is, in essence, no more suspect than the motive behind the foundation of the first free public education system on earth. That motive is the nurture of a citizen useful to the community at large but also decently developed for himself—gifts realized, mind awake, wholeness intact. An unmockable aim, in sum: dignity for man.

And yet, and yet: the Product of It All looks out from the mirror and reveals himself to be—stunted. Somewhere—not simply in the stereotype of himself but in his actuality—he is locked in himself; somewhere he is fixed in an inhuman rigidity; somewhere there is a "malfunction." How to account for this? Has the nation from the start been the captive of theories about the formation and nurture of individual selfhood that are wrongheaded—theories that are obstacles in themselves to self-realization? Is there a uniquely American muddle about fulfillment? If so, what is its nature? How is it to be solved?

Stupidity alone answers confidently—but several relevant observations come to mind. Chief among them is that, for complex social, historical, and cultural reasons, the nature of human growth—in particular, the central role of the imagination in determining its rate and quality—has not often been placed clearly before the national view.

Commentators by the hundreds score the country off for garishness, gross materialism, unspirituality; few focus on the poverty of its conception of personal growth. Yet that is the fairer target. The nation prates of self-realization, and rests in near obliviousness that my humanness depends upon my capacity and my desire to make real to myself the inward life, the subjective reality, of the lives that are lived beyond me. The nation feeds itself on rhetoric about "individual rates of progress"—and yet possesses little knowledge, if any, of the steps by which the human being becomes itself, the separate, private acts of the imagination on which the achievement of personhood depends.

And, to repeat, this ignorance or obliviousness is no mystery. Human growth stems from the exercise of our power to grasp another being's difference from within. How can that truism maintain itself among a people convinced of the fundamental sameness of men? As Tocqueville long ago pointed out, the myth of sameness is a keystone in the deep structure of American belief. (Tocqueville's specific point was that the American protest on behalf of "the individual" was rooted in the assumption that all individuals, once free "to be themselves," would desire the same things and feel in the same ways.) And it is a fact that the moral imperative of the imaginative act is rarely proclaimed in American public or cultural life. A Negro singer invited to a White House conference bursts out in condemnation of the guests for the unreality of their proposals, their abstractness when seen in the light of her experience. The First Lady's eyes moisten. Shaken but proud she responds that she "cannot understand" the outburst; she has not had the same experience. And in the morning the country's best newspaper, *The New York Times*, editorially salutes the First Lady for her "candor," agrees that the feelings and sense of life of the black community are beyond our imagining, and consigns all whites to blank, useless, uncomprehending pity.

And the story is not different on the contemporary intellectual scene. It is a French voice—Jean-Paul Sartre's—not an American voice, that is heard urging men to more intelligent conceptions of human growth, demanding that they break free of the notion that others have no life except that which they exhibit when serving as the material out of which we fashion our experience. (". . . there are men who die without—save for brief and terrifying flashes of illumination—ever having suspected what the *Other* is. The horizons of my life are infinitely shrunk.") And among recent philosophers it is a German voice—Max Scheler's—not that of an American, which dares to formulate an equation setting out relations of identity between individual growth, the perfection of love, and a grasp of the full distinctness and separateness of another human being. ("Love calls explicitly for an understanding entry into the individuality of *another* person *distinct in character* from the entering self . . . a warm and wholehearted endorsement of 'his' reality as an individual, and 'his' being what he is. . . . In love . . . there is built up, within the phenomenon itself, a clear-cut consciousness of two *distinct* persons. This consciousness is not merely a starting point; it reaches full maturity only as love pursues its course.")

What is more, a backward glance at the American cultural heritage confirms that the most powerful voices of American literary culture have been precisely those which, in one manner or another, have been most committedly hostile to the enterprise of attentive imaginative concentration on the fathoming of individual differences. D. H. Lawrence, in his *Studies*, broods hard on the stunted quality of the selves created in the writing of Poe and Whitman, and attributes it in the end to their incapacity to imagine and value a *separate* otherness. Love was a theme for both, but for neither was it a possibility; each man was drawn by fantasies of merging, total engrossment, loss of awareness of the other as separate—fantasies that teased him into confusing "understanding" with the act of sinking one's soul in another.* And wherever the engrosser or merger disappears from American letters, an even more frightening figure—the self-bound man (Captain Ahab is the Prince)—stands forth in his place. In

---

* A version of this now turns up in Love Generation mystic-union gabble (You-am-I and I-am-you, etc.).

Emerson, for example, self-fulfillment appears to require an absolute denial of others, a massive, unrelenting independence, a readiness for isolation. Responding to a culture of conformity, this sage declared that a man bent on realizing himself must learn to carry himself in separation from otherness—"as if everything were titular and ephemeral but he." Widen the gulf, Emerson cries:

> We must go alone. I like the silent church before the service begins, better than any preaching. How far off, how cool, how chaste the persons look, begirt each with a precinct or sanctuary! So let us always sit.

Or again:

> At times the whole world seems to be in conspiracy to importune you with emphatic trifles. Friend, client, child, sickness, fear, want, charity, all knock at once at thy closet door, and say, "Come out unto us." But keep thy state; come not unto their confusion.

Or yet again:

> Live no longer to the expectation of these deceived and deceiving people with whom we converse. Say to them, O father, O mother, O wife, O brother, O friend, I have lived with you after appearances hitherto. Henceforward I am the truth's. . . . If you are noble, I will love you; if you are not, I will not hurt you and myself by hypocritical attention.

Emerson does allow that he could love another, if the person were noble; and every Emersonian knows how risky it is to fix the man in a single attitude. But separateness, far more often than involvement, is the theme that rouses him to lyricism; the poetry in him inclines strongly to the view, saying it once more, that becoming a fulfilled man means drawing oneself more tightly, consciously, firmly back within the limits of the primal existent self.

And that view or stance turns up repeatedly in American literature, in popular culture (the art Western), everywhere in American society. (It may even whisper to us in the writings of David

Riesman and Nathan Glazer; the utopian archetype of self-realized man described by them as "autonomous" has a definite taste for Emersonian gestures against otherness.) Over and over we are enjoined to find "our own thing," "our own bag," in the hippie phrase. And again and again the success of our search is presumed to depend upon our power to cut ourselves off, to harden the wall around us, not only to march to the beat of our own drum, but seemingly to hear no other sound.

There are, of course, countervoices here and there. Though his message did not cut through, smothered in clichés of life adjustment, John Dewey frequently dwelt on connections between human growth and sound education of the imagination—that instrument by which people gain in "flexibility, in scope, and in sympathy, till the life which the individual lives is informed with the life of nature and society." More than one American research psychologist has convinced himself of the centrality of imagination in the course of human development, and has attempted inquiries into the nurture of the imaginative man—witness the labors of Henry Murray and his associates at Harvard in the late 1930's. "Self-Other" theories of growth, which stress self-dramatization and imaginative role-playing, have a place in the history of American philosophy, owing chiefly to the writings of George Herbert Mead. ("The self by its reflexive form announces itself as a conscious organism which is what it is only so far as it can pass from its own system into those of others, and can thus, in passing, occupy both its own system and that into which it is passing. . . . Shut up within his own world . . . he would have no entrance into possibilities other than those which his own organized act involved. . . . It is here that mental life arises.")

And there is one great, seldom-studied American who put the case for fulfillment as dependent upon imaginative growth in utterly unambiguous terms—I speak of Charles Horton Cooley, a founder of American sociology. In *Human Nature and the Social Order* (1929), Cooley laid it down that:

. . . the imaginations which people have of one another are the *solid facts* of society. . . . I do not mean merely that society must

be studied *by* the imagination—that is true of all investigations in
their higher reaches—but that the *object* of study is primarily an
imaginative idea or group of ideas in the mind, that we have to
imagine imaginations. The intimate grasp of any social fact will be
found to require that we divine what men think of one another.
Charity, for instance, is not understood without imagining what ideas
the giver and recipient have of each other; to grasp homicide we
must, for one thing, conceive how the offender thinks of his victim
and of the administrators of the law; the relation between the employing and hand-laboring classes is first of all a matter of personal
attitude which we must apprehend by sympathy with both, and
so on. . . .

Nor did Cooley stop here—with a mere definition of an appropriate area of inquiry for his field. He went on to assert that the
quality of imaginative sympathies is the surest measure of the
degree of human growth and fulfillment:

> One's range of sympathy is a measure of his personality, indicating
> how much or how little of a man he is.

And he was certain beyond doubt that those who deprecated this
sympathy, shrugged it off with prattle about *sensitivity*, missed
its richly complicated nature and meaning:

> [Sympathy] is in no way a special faculty but a function of the whole
> mind to which every special faculty contributes, so that what a
> person is and what he can understand or enter into through the life
> of others are very much the same thing. We often hear people de-
> scribed as sympathetic who have little mental power, but are of a
> sensitive, impressionable, quickly responsive type of mind. The sym-
> pathy of such a mind always has some defect corresponding to its
> lack of character and of constructive force. A strong, deep under-
> standing of other people implies mental energy and stability; it is a
> work of persistent, cumulative imagination. . . .

But if there is a native tradition which understands the nurture
of the imagination to be a key to general human growth, it is, by
all odds, a minority tradition, far away from the center of
popular belief. The weight of the general culture presses continually toward feats of objectification—objectification of labor

(the assembly line, time study), of love (sex research), of desire (image-making, consumer research). At the center stands the conviction that fulfillment is deliverance into a function—a job, a title, a carpet, an income, a pool, somebody else's respect. I, the free American, am free to "find my own place," my "social niche," my "professional slot." I go forth from myself, I *go places*, ranch house to White House, dropout to Ph.D., twelve dollars weekly to a hundred dollars a day. And up the line, where I have it made: I "am more interested in a man's behavior than in his inner life"; I believe man's first duty is to "adjust himself to his environment"; I doubt that anyone can "feel his way into the innermost being of another person"; I don't seek inward truths. . . .

Is mockery in order? The objectifying American culture can be damned for having only once in its history concerned itself intensely with the matter of precisely what this or that individual man felt in this or that instant of time (the occasion was the period of witch trials in the seventeenth century, where it was found useful to know the inward workings of the devil). It can be damned as well for having consistently refused to introduce into its elementary educational system those "studies"—improvisation, mime, dance, dramatics—that elsewhere in the West are accepted as the basic human efforts at developing an imagination of otherness. It can be damned, more fiercely, for its incalculable failures of imagination—for example, its incapacity to make real to itself the inward life, man by man, woman by woman, child by child, of its black people.

But there are, here as always in life, qualifications to be entered: If there is no imagination of deprivation among us, there is at least guilt at good fortune, and this has sufficed to rebuild a world or feed a dozen famines. And in any event, it is not seemly for a professing humanist to lay down accusations here, for the American humanist—the teacher and scholar whose texts and knowledge should have been the greatest resources of those in pursuit of the truth of "the other subject"—has himself been a cop-out, an objectifier, a character madly eager to turn art itself into a "body of objective knowledge" to be "mastered" for "career examinations."

The point of substance, in fine, lies beyond accusations or "cultural critiques." It is a matter simply of a general, culture-wide dimming of the lights of inward life, a matter of failed encounters, missed meetings, hands that do not reach out, minds that hear the lock turn in their prison doors.

It is nighttime, the Maine harbor again. A lantern in the rain, motion of shore waters, a welcome, a beginning . . . But we don't go on, neither he nor she nor I. "My ideas are more often sound and sensible. . . ." "I say what I have to say in a few simple words. . . ." No hardrock, an occasional pot putterer, we would nevertheless prefer that people "not get ideas about us." And as for the famous still sad music of humanity, "we" don't hear it much. We don't flow; we hold on tight inside; we do the generous thing over and over, and invariably do it ungenerously; we see and feel and imagine ourselves to be highly responsible, competent, the solid people of the earth, the independents, the resilients, the unwhiners.

And for that idea or vision of self, some among us pay a lot—gouge out their innerness—become less than men.

Supergrow

At first glance they look downright insignificant—the kid fixers, the Supergrow brainfood crowd. Their product says what it is on the package, witness such hard-selling titles as these: *How to Double Your Child's Grades in School, How to Raise a Brighter Child, Give Your Child a Superior Mind, College Begins at Two*, etc. None of the authors is famous. (The big sellers are Eugene M. Schwartz, Isabelle P. Buckley, Siegfried and Therese Engelmann, and Joan Beck.) None holds a top establishment job. (Mrs. Beck's perch is the Chicago *Trib*, Schwartz is "in" Executive Training Techniques, Mrs. Buckley taught school in Hollywood and has some stars for fans, and Mr. and Mrs. Engelmann, the comers of the lot, fill a "research associates" slot in education at a making-it midwestern state U.) And as for the group's moral as opposed to pedagogical assumptions, they're as old as the Protestant Ethic—no ties with tricky New Thought—and rouse smiles as well as pain.

Humor doesn't, to be sure, get a conscious play in Supergrow books. A typical page of this writing—see Mrs. Buckley's *College Begins at Two*—quotes J. Edgar Hoover as a "spiritual authority," plumps, stiff-lipped, for a school-as-war metaphor ("the more disciplined the troops the fewer the casualties"), and cries up infant heroes like "Peter," whose "first college courses commenced" when he was two ("No wonder he was an enthusiastic little boy, for he knew where he was going")—all without a trace of a grin.

But here as elsewhere the straighter the face, the funnier the turn. Supergrow texts often favor sock-it-to-'em chapter heads ("How to Power Read," "How to Burn Facts into Your Mind"), and other belt-em and butt-em ploys:

> Teach [your child] to read aggressively. Actively. Tearing the ideas out of the pages with the techniques we are showing him in this book. [Schwartz, *How to Double Your Child's Grades*]

They print pinpoint schedules of development suitable for nurseries in sci-fi-flicks:

> By the time the child is 34 months old, he should know his capital letters perfectly. . . . The child should learn to count to ten by the time he is 30 months. . . . By the time the child is 3, he should know all the position words. . . . Point at these [geometric] shapes when the child is 28 months old. . . . [Engelmann and Engelmann, *Give Your Child a Superior Mind*]

They offer countless "Shut up, he explained" situations:

> Go over the [planet] chart at least once a week, beginning when the child is about 3 and ¾. Tell him what these balls on the chart are. "These are the planets in the solar system." Then explain what that means. [Engelmann and Engelmann, *A Superior Mind*]

And everywhere in their pages you run into the playpen polymaths of the future, characters it'll be criminal to deprive of the vote:

> Before the child enters kindergarten he can learn the basic rules of language, learn the alphabet, learn the names of the geometric shapes and begin counting, learn to spell, tell time, add, subtract, multiply, divide, understand fractions and basic algebra, learn to read, learn to deal with such complex mathematical problems as the squares of numbers, equations, factors and exponents. . . . [*A Superior Mind*]

Many a Supergrow writer, furthermore, has a gift for barkerese from which comic excesses regularly flow:

CARL A. RUDISILL LIBRARY
LENOIR RHYNE COLLEGE

Let me be perfectly clear on this point. Your child's grades—if he
applies these techniques—will actually double. If your child is graded
by a percentage point system rather than letters, this doubling process will result in an improvement of about ten to fifteen points. . . .
Where he had 70 before he may now reach 80. [Schwartz, *How to
Double* . . .]

And some are given to fits of italics which, though seriously, even
fiercely, intended, read like cartoon balloons. (*"It is too late!"*
shrills Grandma Buckley at the parents of some kid let go till he
was six. "You must *push him!"* shout the Engelmanns, banging
their crop on a crib.)

There are, of course, bad moments—times when Supergrow
edges off into pathos or mystery, moments when it's hard to work
up a grin. These occur often in the miracle or testimonial parts of
the books, wherein one or another hurt baby held ineducable is
hustled grimly into the joys of the mind:

In Florida, a fragile, dark-haired girl of forty-five months was reading
a third-grade book to her father, a surgeon. Severely brain-damaged
from birth and still unable to sit up or walk, Debbie had repeatedly
been diagnosed as mentally retarded. At two well-known medical
centers, her father had been advised to place her in an institution as
a "human vegetable." Yet now, although she was not yet four,
Debbie had a reading vocabulary that exceeded 1000 words. [Joan
Beck, *How to Raise a Brighter Child*]

And abrupt changes of subject tend to bring on grossness, as
when the Supergrow writer interrupts a math lesson for a chat on
charm:

Help the child to develop desirable personality characteristics.
Harold charges into the kitchen. "I want a cookie," he announces.
"Sorry," his mother says, "that's not the way to ask for it." "Please!"
Harold says. "No, not in that tone of voice." Harold flashes a frozen
grin. "May I please have a cookie?" She hands him a cookie. "I can
do a trick," he says. He motions for her to bend over. Then he hugs
her and kisses her on the cheek. She gives him another cookie, and
he runs outside.

Harold's mother has a rule: only one cookie in the afternoon. But this rule is not like the one about taking a nap or crossing the street. This rule is made to be broken. Harold's mother uses it to encourage Harold to develop desirable personality characteristics. She is showing him that *some* rules (and only *some*) can be broken with "charm." [*A Superior Mind*]

But despite the grossness, and the comedy, and the apparent general mockableness of kid-fixing in the large, Supergrow does possess cultural interest. Its testimony isn't unique in all areas, admittedly. Head Start, the revitalized Montessori movement, Omar Moore and his Responsive Environment Machine, the Carl Bereiter projects at the Illinois Institute for Research on Exceptional Children, and many other developments testify to the impact, on popular and professional minds, of the so-called revolution in theories of early childhood learning—that high-fashion, possibly unwholesome blend of Bruner and Piaget now on every lip. Supergrow texts add but a footnote to this evidence. And since teacher-critics like Herndon, Holt, Kozol, and Kohl, and writers like Goodman, Leonard, and Friedenberg have already richly documented the charge that America is too preoccupied with "cognitive learning," the new evidence implicit in Supergrow—no place in these books for the "affective"—is more or less *déjà vu*.

On other themes, though, Supergrow provides fresh perspectives. On the matter, for instance, of contemporary Horatio Algerism, or the bootstrap myth. The Supergrow audience is, as would go without saying, concerned about upward mobility. And at its coarsest and grubbiest—the work of Eugene M. Schwartz—Supergrow exploits the concern directly, pressing the connection between college degrees and lifetime earnings, stimulating anxieties about "falling behind," speaking in traditional Algerist idiom.

But elsewhere subtle new mutants appear. In Mrs. Beck's *How to Raise a Brighter Child* there are signs that some American Algerists are currently in the market for masks. The ideal reader of Mrs. Beck's book has a lot in common with the old-style Dad-on-the-make-for-his-kid; he's a worrier, his competitive nerves are a-jangle, he's tormented about his boy's prospects of getting ahead. Yet when this man worries, he's ashamed of it, and eager to ease the shame, and Mrs. Beck helps him ingeniously. She takes up a carefully judged position about overambitiousness that lets him confront his pushiness—and dissociate himself from it:

> Early learning doesn't mean that you should try to teach your three year old to read or make him a status symbol, or because your neighbor's child can read, or because you want to be sure he gets into Harvard fifteen years from now. You aren't trying to make a six year old out of a four year old, or turn a nursery school into a first grade, or deprive your moppet of the chance to be a child.

And after thus showing him who he isn't, she shows her reader who he is—a chap interested in home-teaching not for the sake of the rat race, but because at bottom he's a "pure science" type, an explorer, a voyager, a taster of life's joys:

> Early learning does mean that you try to understand your youngster's innate drive to learn, to explore, to fill his developing brain's urgent needs for sensory stimuli and satisfying learning experiences, just as you try to understand and fill the needs of his body for nourishing foods. You aren't stuffing his brain with facts so he'll make Phi Beta Kappa, any more than you give him vitamins to force his growth so he'll make the Chicago Bears' backfield. . . .

The easy-rider stance adds gentility to trad Algerist competitiveness and envy. And while the result may not qualify as moral progress—except in the eyes of cynics who associate moral progress with higher hypocrisies—it does constitute (at the minimum) a tonal break with the past.

And the same can be said, for different reasons, about another style of Algerism found in Supergrow texts—most notably in the Engelmanns' *Give Your Child a Superior Mind*. On its face *Superior Mind* is a work of standard design. The package contains strategies for teaching a child to tell time, point at an object, creep up on concepts—fast-slow, tall-short, and the like. And the promises made are of normal extravagance. (The authors claim to have a surefire method of teaching reading, "a program with the confusion, doubt, and uncertainty removed.")

But the Engelmanns address a reader who, no less distant from the Algerist norm that Mrs. Beck's reader, is nevertheless significantly different from hers. The Engelmanns' reader has no social pretensions, no need for masks—is in fact a reluctant Algerist at best. He's a doubter, a cynic, a disbeliever in the gospel of Work-Your-Way-Up, a person whose prime problem as a teacher would be defeatism born of a conviction that the child he's teaching isn't fated to learn. This defeatism belongs, speaking bluntly, to the ghetto, and the Engelmanns deal with it in the same curt, authoritarian way that they deal with most other attitudes and subjects. (People who have watched Mr. Engelmann at work in a classroom with young children say he puts his pupils "through the wringer"; his writings indicate he would regard that account of him as praise. See Maya Pines, *Revolution in Learning, The Years from Three to Six*, Chapter 4.)

Still, these authors do deal with defeatism. They know other people exist besides university lab-school parents, spawners of suburban SAT sharks. (Siegfried Engelmann collaborated with Carl Bereiter three years ago on a book called *Teaching Disadvantaged Children in the Preschool*. The hard-driving, skill-centered Bereiter-Engelmann methods are now being tried out on five thousand students in twelve American school systems. The systems are among eighty participating in Follow Through, a program for first-graders who've been through Head Start; Ocean Hill-Brownsville is among them.) And the principle aim of their effort appears to be to seed belief in upward mobility in just the areas wherein pessimism and self-hatred have for decades smothered it. Again and again the Engelmanns hammer at their doctrine: Nobody is beyond help; moment-to-moment encouragement and unremitting reenforcement must be the rule; every child can earn a chance to rise. Again and again a swift registering eye focuses on the damage done by parental or teacherly negativism and despondence:

> A trained observer can quickly spot a child who has been led to believe that he is stupid. The child will manage to give the wrong

response even if the task is relatively easy for him. When he is asked a question he tenses up because he *knows* what is going to happen. He knows that the wrong answer will slip out, and that he won't be able to hold it back. He pauses and his eyes dart. He fights down several words; then he says the wrong answer and he seems almost relieved. "I don't know that," he says. "I keep forgetting."

And, as indicated, the interest of the focus is that, like Mrs. Beck's, it marks a movement of cultural feeling. Mrs. Beck's book hints that, at social levels where overambitiousness was invariably self-righteous, self-criticism has begun to appear; the Engelmanns' book suggests that, at levels where defeatism was once too deep to know itself, there's now hope of stimulating consciousness of defeatism's destructive ways. On the one hand determined energy is bent on striking sparks of ambition, pricking the competitive nerve; on the other, it attempts to refine or subtleize the overambitious. And the contrasting efforts are an index—not a wholly depressing one, at that—of the mixed character of the present cultural hour.

Nor is Supergrow relevant only to Algerism and ambition. It has bearings on themes as large as that of Individualism and the Family. The emergence of the latter theme in history is—digressing a moment, for a purpose—a complex tale. The central strand, according to Philippe Ariès, was an achievement of privacy centuries in the making. And the achievement was bought at a price: forms of connectedness preceding the sealed-off private family vanished from the West. (No more open communication among generations and classes; an end to broad-scale human solidarity arising out of Everyman's solid knowledge of his betters and inferiors.) But in the exchange middle-class society gained the right to create a space for uniqueness for each new being brought to birth. The business of life became that of nourishing, within private walls, a sense of self, of difference, of special identity. No human unit was freer than the nuclear family to encourage the growth of separate egos; none better placed to sustain self-absorption or to keep off The Others—the endless parade of elders, rulers, owners, coworkers, the crowd that once allowed nobody a room of his own. ("All freedom," wrote Lord

Acton, "consists *in radice* in the preservation of an inner sphere exempt from state power.") And, in public rhetoric, the nuclear family continues to savor this freedom.

Maintaining it intact, however, has lately grown more difficult. Standardized food, clothing, and shelter, standardized working conditions, standardized public education and entertainment—these and other features of modern industrial civilization narrow the distance between the crowd world and the world of the private individual (the separate household, the sanctuary). As that distance narrows, the sense of family separateness and personal uniqueness weakens, and the family's ability to perform its newish function of developing significant differences among its members declines.

It's questionable, perhaps, whether that ability ever was equal to the task. The nuclear family as an institution may not have been capable, in the best of circumstances, of discharging the obligations laid on it by a culture of Individualism and Self-Realization. Nurturing separate wholenesses, ordering family life in a fashion that creates manageable distances between children and adults and among siblings, is, as every grown-up knows, a demanding job. Parent and child compete for space, are disposed to exact total capitulation from each other, and forget that, while safe separateness, serene private being, are the goals, the entire family seeks them, and none can be satisfied save through compromise, sacrifice, endless, amusing, exacerbating tradings-off.

Furthermore, the complexity and delicacy of the pursuit, seldom fairly rendered by artists or by social scientists, are often denied outright, opportunistically, in popular parents' manuals—see, most recently, Haim Ginott's *Between Parent and Child, New Solutions to Old Problems.** Everywhere in such texts the

---

* Dr. Ginott claims, plausibly, that children's separate being must be recognized and respected by parents, and that the only route toward genuine recognition lies through the imagination:

The first step in the long-term program is a determination to become interested in what children are thinking and feeling inwardly, and not just in their outward compliance or rebellion. . . . All we need is an ear

language favored is that of "problems" and "solutions"; seldom is there an attempt to locate growing points for private egos. Everywhere the friendly guides give assurances that the combination of objectification and sympathy necessary to functioning parents can be attained by formula; nowhere do they glance at the evidence proving these assurances false. Nor is this because the evidence is in short supply. Most grown-ups, to repeat, could contribute lavishly from their experience. Few can have found the task of helping individuality to breathe and occupy its own space less than arduous, frustrating, contradictory; many have run from it back into the authoritarian "role models" of their own or their grandparents' bad dreams.

Or else back into the simplicity of the classroom. The advent of Supergrow—returning to the point—is a sign of the lure of that flight, and, as such, it's a telling symptom of the vulnerability of family to "community." When parents take upon themselves responsibility for school learning, when they announce that their account of their child's strengths, weaknesses, feelings, correct temper, and occupation precisely jibes with that of the school, when in short they behave in a manner implying that the home is

---

to listen, an eye to behold, a heart to feel. Our inner motto is: Let me understand. Let me show that I understand. Let me show in words that do not automatically criticize or condemn.

But the purpose of this recognition appears throughout Ginott's book as that of cooling kids, mediating fights. And, still worse, the body of the work—here, incidentally, is the major reason for its enormous success—the body of the work aims to persuade parents that the task is easy, all I need is a "heart to feel" and a bag of "effective four-step sequences" like the following:

1. The parent recognizes the child's wish and puts it in simple words; "You wish you could go to the movies tonight."

2. He states clearly the limits on a specific act: "But the rule in our house is 'no movies on school nights.' "

3. He points out ways in which the wish can be at least partially fulfilled: "You may go to the movies on Friday or Saturday night."

4. He helps the child to express some of the resentment that is likely to arise when restrictions are imposed: "It is obvious that you don't like the rule." Etc. Etc.

but an adjunct of the school, yet another subtle erosion of the imagination of difference occurs. The child takes the cultural wind straight on his bow and hangs defenseless, unable to set courses of his own. He perceives that his father, when most intentionally concerned with him, is in fact a mere extension of school people who have no private involvement of feeling with him; he perceives, as his father runs through the drill of letters, number, planets, that the world "beyond" privacy is the one Real World; he perceives (or will at length perceive) that the serious acts of life, the challenges, the major uses of mind and imagination, occur out there, in stock, standard-brand, public situations, not within private walls. Astonishing indeed if such perceptions didn't induce a depressed sense of the possibility of a private individuality.

—From which it follows: *à bas* Supergrow?* You do not come out here, I think, if you've worked in ghetto classrooms, K-3, or for that matter in any setting where children kill time at assignments they can't do. The relevant sight is a row of children "doing" commercial seatwork, unable to read—sitting at a table, being "good," copying a word now and then into a blank, moving their pencils and their lips. "We had —— to drink at Christmas." A little girl chews her eraser, and, dutiful and serious, fills in the first word from the word list: "We had *overcoat* to drink at Christmas." Next desk: "Do not *kitchen* at the party." . . . With this sight in mind, as I say, you don't instantly scoff at early-education schemes, at any prekindergarten step that creates alternatives to victimization and waste.

But it's one thing not to scoff, and another to endorse. Most days after teaching black classes in "my" project, an hour or so of story-talk, acting out, easy back-and-forth, laughter, inquiry, animation, I go over the District of Columbia line and teach white suburban children the same age. And there's something to

* That line is taken by Eda Le Shan in *The Conspiracy Against Childhood*, a ferocious assault on early learning by a writer who aligns herself with John Holt, and appears to have little feeling for the comparative chances of rich and poor to learn to work their minds.

the sentimental or pastoral—or self-hating—claim that teaching is a flatter occupation Over There—more wariness, less response, sadness in the lucky middle-class eyes. Everybody reads, everybody's bright, boffo SATs lie ahead. No commercial seatwork. Yet the impression persists that participatory energies are greater in the ghetto—more appetite, more ease with the idea of breathing.

And you have only to admit this for a moment to be lost in the famous quandaries, viz.: Don't bug the kids:, they breathe better if left alone. . . . Why should the "disadvantaged" recapitulate the experience of the middle class? What've they done to deserve that? —Ah, but rejecting the middle-class experience means denying the powerful awakening satisfactions of consecutive thought. —Ah, but embracing that experience means (sooner or later) declining into wanness, pallor, contempt for the very cause, Individuation, that nourished the middle-class rise. . . . Etc.

That the quandaries can't be straightened in a phrase doesn't signify that the only end of brooding about Supergrow—or about Supergrow vs. Innergrow—is ambiguity. For one thing, reading the books at hand does freshen the sense of the foolishness of pedagogical priorities fixed in ignorance of the areas of life (worlds of knowledge and feeling) over- and under-taught by the relevant nonschool environments. And, more important, it touches up belief in the notion that in some situations the young may need training in truancy as well as in application. "You teach your daughters the diameters of the planets," said Dr. Johnson, "and wonder when you have done that they do not delight in your company." And while it's wrong to press that button too hard—the great man isn't claiming that planets are boring, he's saying that parents shouldn't be—it's worse to wind the education dialectic (Supergrow vs. Innergrow) so tight that all the homely proportioning truths disappear.

We need to remember, that is to say, that we seek something more than proficiency or privacy or preparation for next year's objective tests. We want appetites and responsiveness, a feeling of personal unity and togetherness, belief in the possibility of meeting a problem by using the mind, openness to pleasures that can spring as easily from a "shocking" dirty word shared at age forty around the supper table, as from a thousand-word vocabulary picked up at three. We want a competency and self-reliance which, while not unrelated to manipulative skills, derive less directly from them than from the habit of inquiry into connections among visible bits of experience, keen practice at exploring "the working of each part on every part of the common life of men." We want children exhilarated by the onset of such competence and teachers absorbed in nurturing its increase. We want, in short, not doubled grades or "superior minds" or better "early education techniques," but a life-college good enough to begin at two. And if we miss the difference between the former and the latter, if we go on whoring after Supergrow slyness and Ivy SATs, like "realistic" deans of admission in the empty colleges of this day, we'll never make a start toward getting it.

How We Lost
the Sex Lab War

The world of mind divides itself, the halves berating each other in extravagances, competing destructively in situations that cry out for harmonious collaboration—where can a student find models of humane, wholistic concern?

The world of mind, building on foundations laid in the nineteenth century, develops detailed new knowledge with significance for the inward well-being of millions, and then allows reductionism, timidity, and vanity to deflect the passage of this knowledge to the public—how much can be said for contemporary intellectual life?

A story with bearings on these questions begins in 1954 with a decision of a young associate professor of obstetrics and gynecology at the Washington University Medical School to enter a field he'd been preparing for years: the laboratory study of human sexual response. The story ends with the announcement not many weeks ago by the same professor, Dr. William Masters, that the project's hugely publicized piece of equipment—a plastic artificial phallus—had been "disassembled," no plans in mind "for reconstruction." In the decade and a half between the decision and the disassembling, scores of sages, sexmongers, poets, and culture critics held forth in print on sex research, confusing issues or inventing them, distracting attention from significant realities of the subject. And, going at once to the matter of responsibility, the researchers themselves bore part of the blame, since they poured out a series of charges and simplistic rationales which obscured (and still obscure) the best uses and meanings of their undertaking.

The most tendentious of these charges was that the so-called literary or general-cultural view of human sex—every view, in short, that underemphasizes sex as physical activity pointed toward orgasmic release—is a lie that urgently requires scientific straightening out. The Washington University scientists didn't take this aggressive line publicly at the inception of their research; they took no line, for their chief concern at that time was to avoid a break in the voluntary press blackout which, as it developed, the St. Louis newspapers and wire services maintained about the sex lab into the sixties. But once they felt safe, they hit hard. Dr. Masters' earliest paper on sex research, a 1960 report appearing in the *Western Journal of Surgery*, lashed out at "literary fiction and fantasy" on the ground that it perpetuates an "unbelievable hodgepodge of conjecture and falsehood" in the area of sexual relations. The full-scale formal report of Masters' Reproductive Biology Research Foundation, brought forth in 1964 under the title *Human Sexual Response*, was presented, jaw out, as a compendium of "physiologic truth as opposed to cultural fiction." And even at the present late hour, the sex researchers are still pressing an attack, in interviews and essays, against bookish "traditionalists" whose chat about love and "mystery" foists (they say) "an incredible amount of misconception, fantasy and fallacy" upon people, nourishing "superstition and myth," weakening the sense of fact.

Predictably, literary types took unkindly to this abuse, and counterattacked even before publication of *Human Sexual Response*. A characteristic salvo was Leslie Farber's "I'm Sorry, Dear," printed in *Commentary* in 1964. Since the author was himself a psychiatrist and a former chairman of the Association of Existential Psychology and Psychiatry, the assault looked at first glance more internecine than two-cultural. The manner and matter of the piece, however, together with the circumstances of its publication, established that Farber spoke as a humanist. "I'm

Sorry, Dear" came decorated with a multitude of literary epigraphs and allusions (C. S. Lewis, Herman Melville, the Marquis de Sade, Lionel Trilling, and Eleanor of Aquitaine figured in one way or another). The essay opened, moreover, with a page of invented dialogue, novelistically notated (the conversation of lovers just following an unsatisfactory episode of lovemaking), and was composed in a fashionable literary tone (stern, Sartrian, sniffish).*

The minor charges in Farber's critique of Masters and Johnson were that their sexology (1) made "both the brothel and pornography less exciting dwellings for our erotic investigation," (2) removed the erotic life from "the traditional disciplines, such as religion, philosophy, literature, which had always concerned themselves with sex as human experience," (3) was overabsorbed with gadgetry "at the expense of any imaginative grasp of the occasion" of love, and (4) was sick with democratic zeal (Masters believes that "the more minute physiological developments [in lovemaking] should belong to every citizen," and he increases "the political clamor for equal rights for women"). The major charges were, first, that the new sexology had in effect "invented" the orgasm as the essential part of woman's—and man's—whole sexual experience (in olden days "the moment of orgasm was not abstracted . . . and idealized," and was only an "occasional" part of the experience); and, second, that the sexologists denied Original Sin, encouraged lovers "to will the perfection on earth which cannot be willed," and thereby brought upon men "the pathos which follows all such strivings toward heaven on earth."

Important as the charges were, though, and frequent as their reiteration soon became, neither Farber's nor any subsequent literary response to the sexological crusade against "myth" was, in

* In explaining his belief that "sex for the most part has lost its viability as a human experience," Farber cited modern man's self-conscious, willful alienation from his own physicality, and rehearsed an argument about knowing and being known through sex that was taken directly, without acknowledgment, from Jean-Paul Sartre's *Being and Nothingness.*

a decisive sense, a matter of specific charges. The literary mind built its case more through tone, nuance, implication, than through discrete, answerable arguments. The impression conveyed was that sex research was merely an aspect of the decline or collapse of Western culture. Farber and other littérateurs adopted a voice of ironic resignation which spoke at every moment—regardless of the ostensible subject—of the "inevitability" in a dying culture of an endless succession of corruptions. They presented themselves as yearners for transcendence, people with a fastidious, half-*spirituelle* distaste for physicality and sensuality. And they constantly played off ideals and glories of past (imaginary) worlds of love against the base actualities of the modern sex research lab.

Farber himself concentrated on the central figures of Arthurian romance (Queen Guinevere, Sir Galahad), and on the intense, delicate doctrines of Courtly Love, in setting up the contrast. Others ranged farther. The English poet and novelist David Holbrook, for example, writing about "The Delusions of Sexology" in the *Cambridge Review*, invoked Duns Scotus, the medieval philosopher who scorned "imperfect love . . . 'love of concupiscence' . . . because it seeks the other for advantage." And the American novelist George P. Elliott, for another, harked back, in the *Hudson Review*, to heroic love affairs in Proust, reminding his reader of the refinement of Swann's feelings "as the phrase from Vinteuil's sonata is evoking tender memories of the days when Odette was in love with him."

All, however, used these models of elegance, decorum, discipline, and superhuman grace from the cultural past for a similar purpose, that of dramatizing the slobbishness of sex research science. Think of Guinevere, think of Galahad, Farber told his audience, and then think of people tasteless enough to welcome the "prospect of arriving at the laboratory at 10:00 A.M., disrobing, stretching out on the table and going to work in a somewhat businesslike manner while being measured and photographed. . . . (Thank you, Miss Brown, see you same time next week.)" Think, said the novelist Elliott, think of marvelous Swann and

Odette, and then think of a "sane, taxpaying, tenured professor solemnly copulating with his wife on a cot in [the] laboratory, their arms strapped for blood-pressure readings, cathodes at their temples, cardio-tachographs zigging, their anuses wired, 'My bunny, my love, O sweetest joy!' Well, every man has the right to make himself look like a fool."

Imagine, said Holbrook, imagine the dignity and restraint of Scotus' mind engaged on its analysis of love, and then:

> Imagine . . . a group of scientists making the Masters-Johnson color film of a female masturbating: the faceless torso, the arm, the moving fingers, the erotic flush on the thighs, the moistening organ, the stiffening nipples, the physical contractions of orgasm, the fine film of sweat covering the whole body afterwards. Or imagine for that matter the group of overalled scientists observing dials, with a camera team working on a man and woman who have coition (having never met before) on the laboratory couch for a research fee. Sometimes the scientists stop them to make adjustments or measurements: then when they get going again the instruments are all set to time the physical features of orgasm: How often? How long? How many sperms? How acid or alkali? How strong is the ejaculation? Where did it go? Do the sperms survive?—Do the participants punch one another in their final ecstasy?

On both sides of the Atlantic dozens of other writers—panelists, reviewers of the Masters-Johnson volume, letters-to-the-editor men—echoed the literary complaint that a monstrous new vulgarity was poisoning the land.

As should be said, Masters and Johnson were not the only sexologists of the period who provided materials for abuse. The earlier, Kinsey or pollster school of research was still active in the mid-sixties, and produced several mockably formulaic statements of its findings—witness the following passage from a paper of a San Diego psychologist:

> Both men and women engage in the more serious types of sex play as the type of dating involvement increases. The men, however, are significantly more liberal in their actual conduct particularly for the

first few dates (NoK, N, PAWPBW, SI, $X^2 = 16.22$ 3df, p < 1 percent), frequent and continuous dating (NoK, N, PAWPBW, SI, $X^2 = 14.62$ 3df, p < 1 percent), and going steady (KN, PAW, PBW, SI, $X^2 = 15.62$, 3df, p < 1 percent) . . . [R. L. Karen, "Some Variables Affecting Sexual Attitudes, Behavior and Inconsistency." The paper included a key to symbols: N = nothing. K = kissing. PAW = petting above waist. PBW = petting below waist, etc.]

And as also should be said, there were occasions throughout the sixties when the ranks of literary antisexologists were swelled by writers who were cruder than the crudity they damned. The commonest offender was the novelist—a cluster of sex research novels appeared in the late sixties—and the reason for this was simple. Novels on the subject tsk-tsked and looked grave about the laboratory experiments, delivering short essays at key moments on lubricity, dehumanization, and such. Yet commercial exigency dictated that events inside the labs be depicted with seemly fullness, and this requirement set up counterstrains.

Consider, for instance, Robert Kyle's *Venus Examined* (1968). The implied argument of the book is that the ordinary stuff of life (and of novelese)—personal relations—cannot be kept out of the sex lab, despite the avowals and high intentions of the researchers. (In Kyle's sex lab, the volunteers fall in and out of love with each other, arrange secret meetings, seek to seduce their scientist-observers, etc. etc.) The overt argument—its spokesman is an English prof at Barnard who sits on the board of a foundation asked to fund the (electrical) phallus—echoes the standard charges:

Your laboratory isn't the only place in the modern world where numbers have replaced names, where a machine is substituted for a living person, where action is separated from feeling and no act has any consequences. But somehow your modernity is a little more vivid! To me your copulation machine stands as a symbol of the other evil things that are being done to us in the name of science. It's too perfect! How skillfully it gives a woman her orgasmic relief, carrying

her out of the frustrations and compromises of ordinary life into a
condition of perpetual spasm—

And the conclusion of the book is a wild passage of new Luddite-
ism that might have been—in the hands, say, of Nathanael
West—a compelling bit of contemporary terror. (A discharged
volunteer returns in bitterness to the sex lab, smashes the copulation machine, and is herself electrocuted in the act.)

But, to repeat, the various novelistic indictments of tastelessness, crudity, and vulgarity lacked force because of the density of
vulgarity surrounding them in their own pages. In *Venus Examined* there are interminable discussions—not comically intended
—about whether a lady who's *lost* her orgasmic capacity after
participating in the project should sue the projectors. ("'You
never had trouble having orgasms before, and we can prove that
from Prescott's own records. . . . You could . . . sue him,'
Anne said. . . . 'Would you turn down half a million bucks?
They give that much for a leg.'") And a leering clumsiness marks
nearly every episode of intercourse observed. (One gamey episode details the attempt of a Dr. Masters-type to teach a timid,
previously "ineffective" husband named Hallinan to pleasure his
lady via cunnilingus.)

Pots calling kettles black weren't the only factor adding to the
confusion. A dozen conflicting unconscious attitudes and preju-
dices figured in the arguefying between sex scientist and littéra-
teur from the start—elitism vs. egalitarianism, love of the past vs.
optimism about the future, the sense of style vs. the relish of
freedom, nostalgia for religious passion vs. delight in the "end" of
superstition. And stock responses were everywhere the rule. The
literary man told his audience that the scientist operated under
the delusion that the isolatable, observable, physiological act was
the "only" act of love—a delusion betraying irremediable inward
coarseness. The scientist told his audience that if his idea of sex
was limited, at least he believed sex existed. Nobody on his side
ever claimed, he said, as the poet Holbrook claimed, that "there
is really no such thing as sex." ("There is only," Holbrook added,

"the use of the sexual capacities of individuals to express potentialities of being.") Nor had anybody on his side ever denied, as
Farber denied, that sexual frustration was real. (Until recently,
Farber maintained, the unorgasmic woman had been "content
with the mystery and variety of her difference from man, and in
fact would not have had it otherwise.")

Inside the rhetorical exchanges, smothered, choking, there
were a few genuine and discussible differences of assumption
and value. But these were seldom in direct view. The antagonists
spoke as though convinced that the proper aim for each was the
complete discrediting, if not destruction, of the other. Not only
did they show small consciousness of the root causes of the furies
to which they were giving utterance; they appeared not even to
have considered asking the most pertinent question: What in this
instance will victory or defeat for either of us mean to everyone
else?

[2]

On both sides the root causes of the furies just mentioned are, of
course, various. Jealousy is in the equation, as well as snobbish-
ness, and resentment about lost eminence and power, and scorn
for private metaphor allowed to go public and pass itself off for
ages as truth. But there are other, less frequently noted items as
well. Not the least of these, on the literary side, is the humanist's
custom of abstracting science from general cultural history—
treating particular scientific enterprises as unique phenomena,
assuming that while this or that "controversial" experiment may
conceivably "belong" to some special field of science, such work
has no natural or logical place in the mainstream of liberal
humane inquiry. Again and again the assumption has proved
false, and the present episode is no exception. The case is that sex
lab research is a direct result (others are beyond counting) of a
long struggle waged by scientific *and* literary minds on behalf of
the Cause of intellectual inclusiveness—a struggle begun in the

nineteenth century, and still unfinished. Had the struggle not been waged, neither the Masters and Johnson investigation nor that of Kinsey over a decade ago could have been imagined, much less conducted. And both probes will probably soon impress more as markers of the progress of that Cause than for their particular findings.

To say this isn't to imply that Dr. Masters is a major intellect or that the cause of inclusiveness flourished because those who created it worked together in conscious coalition. Marx in the Manchester factories, Darwin gazing at a gang of Fijians, Frazer teasing out the meaning of the sacred grove at Nemi in *The Golden Bough,* Freud interpreting dreams and explaining displacement in the *Introductory Lectures on Psychoanalysis,* Lawrence creating Mellors in *Lady Chatterley's Lover*—these aren't thinkers in league. But a unity of effect can be felt in their work.*
The effect was to put men in touch with a range of material (behavior, values, symbolic acts, words, modes of feeling, thinking and perceiving) lying outside the official culture of the day—materials establishing that human reality, present or historic, wasn't fully represented in official images. And the demand for fuller representation has grown ever more insistent throughout this century. Comparative study of cultures and value systems, inquiry into the parallel evolution of man and animal, the development of psychoanalysis, new models of social and economic history, genetical research in the fields of art and literature—these and numberless other undertakings are directly traceable to the whetted appetite for news of the prefatory, disorderly, just possibly basic states of being which established culture ignored.

* A favored trick of the antisexologist was to deny this unity and dissociate literary men from the great changes of attitude and understanding brought about in the last century. Farber, for instance, claimed that literary artists who dealt with sex in their works thought of it in terms of "qualities such as modesty, privacy, reticence, abstinence, chastity, fidelity, shame." (Blake? Strindberg? Yeats?) Nowhere did he acknowledge that the accepted meanings of these terms have changed markedly in the last century and a half or that literary men were themselves responsible in large measure for the redefinitions.

—From which it follows that treating the original Masters and Johnson concept as a running down of intellectual energy, a symptom of contemporary irrationalism or decline of mind, is senseless. The project had honorable links with a dignified intellectual past, and, depending on the quality of its execution, it could have become an embodiment, minor but useful, of the best intellectual taste of the age. The current habit of culture is either to turn away from sexual intercourse, accounting it a private act, or to exploit it in public entertainment for commercial profit; both practices worsen social and moral problems, and contribute nothing to knowledge. Well enough, let us gaze straight at sexual intercourse, take it in as a definable, separable, natural phenomenon among phenomena—an act or event whose characteristics can be discerned, measured, and compared. And let us maintain that same perspective over the entire "field" of sexual behavior—masturbatory orgasms, homosexual experience, the experience of the prostitute, physiological response to pornography. Let us seek "truth of a sort," on the ground that it has value in itself, and has occasionally proved of use in encounters with "social problems."

Granted the Masters-Johnson project had comical as well as "shocking" aspects. The researchers shared the Yankee preoccupation with know-how; the passages in *Human Sexual Response* in which a personal voice (a hint of scoffing) cuts through the neutralism are usually those critical of false know-how:

> Most marriage manuals advocate the technique of finding the clitoris and remaining in direct manual contact with it during attempts to stimulate female sexual tensions. In direct manipulation of the clitoris there is a narrow margin between stimulation and irritation. If the unsuspecting male partner adheres strictly to marriage manual dictum, he is placed in a most disadvantageous position. He is attempting proficiency with a technique that most women reject during their own automanipulative experience.

Granted, too, Masters and Johnson, like many other scientists, exemplified the national relish of technological gimmickry; the culture of charcoal filters and poptops was perhaps reflected in the copulation machine:

> The artificial coital equipment was created by radiophysicists. The penises are plastic and were developed with the same optics as plate glass. Cold-light illumination allows observation and recording without distortion. The equipment can be adjusted for physical variations in size, weight, and vaginal development. The rate and depth of penile thrust is initiated and controlled completely by the responding individual. As tension elevates, rapidity and depth of thrust are increased voluntarily, paralleling subject demand. The equipment is powered electrically.

But America isn't through and through a joke, not even in the St. Louis project. There are some notable national elements in the research that only the most priggish literary aristocrat could take as ludicrous; they're especially vivid in the passages of *Human Sexual Response* recounting the life history and sexual experience of some participants in the project—passages that chronicle a movement from emptiness to light.

Consider the case of Subject D, a "34-year-old male, married 6 years and the father of two children." An only child, a minister's son, father now dead, mother a receptionist for a doctor. Profession: draftsman. College: two years. Reason for dropout: death of the father. "There is a history of strict parental control during the teenage years, and an excessive concern for social mores." No "automanipulative history" (meaning masturbation) until freshman year in college, and this single experimental episode was followed for a full year by a "severe guilt residual." Sophomore year an episode of petting leads once to "involuntary ejaculation, with the experience followed for several months by residual guilt feelings." Afterward for four or five years: prostitutes and masturbation, prostitutes and masturbation. Then Subject D marries. His bride is a business-school graduate. There is a record of relative failure in coition, though neither partner is lacking in desire. Years pass, the couple hears of the Masters and Johnson research; husband and wife make inquiry:

For orientation, five episodes were necessary after team interrogation. The first exposure was to background and equipment; during the second, coition was attempted without ejaculatory success. The third episode developed as successful coition for Subject D, but his wife was not orgasmic. During the fourth session both husband and wife were successful in individual automanipulative episodes, and in the fifth episode no difficulty was encountered by either partner in response to coital or manipulative stimuli. This pattern of freedom from restraint has been the rule in subsequent program exposure, much to the surprise of both husband and wife. The family has cooperated with long-range response-evaluation and male physiology programs. . . .

. . . Subject D was concerned with his own overcontrolled background, lack of sexual experience, and a considered degree of sexual response to coital or manipulative stimuli. This pattern of freedom incidence was reported as rare with coital exposure but consistent with manipulation. Subsequent to working in the program her orgasmic achievement during coition has risen to the 80 percent frequency level. She has not been multiorgasmic either during coition or automanipulation.

Subject D's wife has stated repeatedly that subsequent to program participation her husband has been infinitely more effective both in stimulating and in satisfying her sexual tensions. He in turn finds her sexually responsive without reservation. Her freedom and security of response are particularly pleasing to him. Together they maintain that they have gotten a great deal more out of cooperation with the program than they have contributed, and they wish to continue on a long-term basis.

The literary mind, the figure of style and breeding, may smile at such a recital, shaking his head at the cozy cure brought off with *Reader's Digest* ease—"The latest democratic dream: not guaranteed annual wages but guaranteed 'success' in bed." But the laughter is too easy. Everywhere in the West men and women by the millions burn, helplessly, within and without marriage, finger themselves off, torment themselves with guilt, belabor each other in silent, killing war—and that which helps them, that which lifts them momentarily beyond the meanness of their losing lives, can't really be despised. The Washington University study didn't aim at improving people's sex lives—but the directors knew that in a neutral setting homely words could be said that might effect change. A sense, in fact, of meanness conquered and ordinary life freshened here and there, surprised by joy, can be made out in the closing pages of the Masters and Johnson report by anyone as yet unfrozen in postures of *de haut en bas*. Doubtless connections exist between this new American fantasy—joyous sex for the masses—and others of the past: salvation through community colleges, salvation through Beethoven LPs. But there is dignity in the fantasy nevertheless, as in all humane egalitarianism, and beauty as well—the beauty of decency, generosity, and hope. With this in mind, and remembering the continuity of the project with intellectual tradition, the idea of abusing Masters and Johnson as sin and deviltry looks cheap.

[3]

But those who delivered the abuse *were* provoked to do so—which is to say that, when the full context of the sex lab war is studied, there's blame for everybody, not just for literary men. If the world of science has a right to be embarrassed for poets who miss the unity of rational inquiry in the immediate past, the world of letters has the right to be embarrassed in turn for scientists who persist in hawking superstitions of the kind implicit in Masters-Johnson chatter about "physiologic truth as opposed to cultural fiction." A major lesson of the sharpest contemporary thought, after all, stresses the mutuality of mythical and scientific understanding of "fact"; the pretense that "subjective" and "objective" realities can be crisply disentangled by any bright chap with a white coat, a stopwatch, and a mind unviolated by poetry is disingenuous if not dumb. Masters and Johnson learned that there is a sense in which coital and masturbatory orgasms, when compared in strict physiological terms, can be described as "the same." But the manner in which they reported this and a dozen other "challenges to myth" indicated that they had excluded attitudinal considerations, and were persuading themselves that the purely physiological man they posited wasn't a conceptual model, or abstraction, but a genuine human being. And the literary men who scored off this delusion did indeed have a point.

What is more, the sex researchers look to have been, on balance, a rather fearful lot. A striking portion of their evidence bore on the comparative intensity of male and female sexuality; the evidence suggested the edge belongs to the female. Yet the researchers never faced the findings directly: they trimmed in the presence of them or shyly turned aside. As might have been expected, fellow professionals called them out for their reticence. Writing in the *Journal of the American Psychoanalytic Association*, Dr. Mary J. Shurfey remarked, on the basis of the Masters-Johnson research, that "to all intents and purposes, *the human female is sexually insatiable in the presence of the highest degrees of sexual satiation*," and went on not only to draw attention to the possible social consequences of dissemination of findings in this area, but to chide the researchers for their evasiveness and self-censorship: *

* Dr. Shurfey commented first on the likeness between the sexual responsivity of the human female and that of certain higher primates: "having no cultural restrictions, these primate females will perform coitus from twenty to fifty times a day during the peak week of estrus, usually with several series of copulations in rapid succession. If necessary, they flirt, solicit, present, and stimulate the male in order to obtain successive coitions." After observing that "our myth of the female's relative asexuality is a biological absurdity," she noted that the satiation-in-insatiation state of the primate and human females parallels "the behavior ascribed to women during the prepatriarchal, Mesolithic period—and well into the Neolithic Bronze Age—of history. . . ." Her argument was that womankind's sexuality has been ruthlessly suppressed in the name of monogamy, and in service of a man-centered civilization. Since that suppression seems now to be easing ("a decided lifting of the ancient social injunctions against the free expression of female sexuality has occurred"), the present moment, Dr. Shurfey speculated, could well become one of cultural reorganization:

". . . one thing is certain: if women's sexual drive has not abated, and they prove incapable of controlling it, thereby jeopardizing family life and

The most provocative gesture of the sex researchers, however, wasn't finally a matter either of trimming or superstition. It was, instead, the rejection of imaginative flexibility—a gesture that smutched the very ideal of inclusiveness that brought the project to life. Brainy men can indeed stand to know everything, the nineteenth-century idealists had implicitly insisted. Not only can the full truth of human smallness, as well as of human nobility, be endured; it perhaps can be used for the betterment of this world. And those who use it, the argument ran, will become men of humor, blitheness, unarrogant skepticism. They will learn to take pleasure in their own deflation; they will become even-handed acceptors of the general human humiliation, steady riders, sound hearts. Thomas Mann spelled out the vision once in a famous address on "Freud and the Future," claiming that with the analytic revelation "a blithe skepticism has come into the world, a mistrust that unmasks all schemes and subterfuges of our own souls. Once roused and on the alert, it cannot be put to sleep again. It infiltrates life, undermines its raw naivete, takes from it the strain of its own ignorance . . . inculcates the taste for understatement . . . for the deflated rather than for the inflated words, for the cult which exerts its influence by modera- tion, by modesty. Modesty—what a beautiful word!"

But however valuable the Masters-Johnson documents are for the improvement of the national sex life, they don't incarnate the beautiful vision. The problem isn't that the projectors should have acknowledged that, as the literary men charged, the Sub- jects were "making fools of themselves," or were without taste or

---

child care, a return to the rigid, enforced suppression will be inevitable and mandatory. Otherwise the biological family will disappear and what other patterns of infant care and adult relationships could adequately substitute cannot now be imagined."

Speculation in this vein might have been inappropriate in the Masters- Johnson report. But that report was needlessly inhibited about underscoring findings with direct bearing on central domestic institutions. For a further discussion of Dr. Shurfey's interpretation of these findings, see the *Journal of the American Psychoanalytic Association* for July 1968.

reticence, or were having their sexual needs catered for too lavishly. The problem is that, when at length the researchers undertook to deal with the *innerness* of their subjects, they offered up a false account of feelings, one whose omissions were as substantial as any found in the "cultural fiction" against which they inveighed.

Consider the passages about "Subject D" quoted above. The authors are speaking here, by their own claim, not about physiological reactions but about what it was like, in human terms, to be a Subject in this study. Yet their words leave the impression that the entire sequence of feeling can be expressed as a straight line progression from doggedness to surprise to gratitude. Understandable, perhaps, not to allude directly to courage, desperation, presumed humiliations, frowns of impatience and self-disgust (as when "coition [was] attempted without ejaculatory success"). Forgivable, owing to the need for sustaining a neutral tone, for the authors to translate the comments of Subject D and his wife into bureaucratese. (Subject D's wife probably didn't *state* that "subsequent to program participation my husband has been infinitely more effective both in stimulating and in satisfying my sexual tensions." And Subject D himself probably did not *say* that "I, in turn, find her wholly responsive without reservation.")

But unforgivable, and utterly unscientific, to pass out adman or testimonial simplicities as a substitute for an account of the whole psychological process of improving a sexual relationship— the subtleties and intricacies of self-perception in such a venture, the details of inward change, shadings, and redefinitions of trust and confidence, and subsequent characterological transformation. "Together they maintain that they have gotten a great deal more out of cooperation with the program than they have contributed, and they wish to continue on a long-term basis"—as a summary of the emotional and intellectual realities known by human beings in course of such a project, is this statement not as deceitful as the claim that "there is no such thing as sex?" Was it not unprofessional—not to say "fictional" or "mythical"—to set forth patches of backpatting uplift as a substitute for the full story?

How is the ordinary reader—hundreds of thousands of copies of
Masters and Johnson have been bought by ordinary readers—to
know, given these deeply censored case studies, together with the
five years of silence that have followed them, that a full story has
been withheld?

Again a cautionary word is necessary. Asking such questions
doesn't mean lining up with the literary antisexologist, the critic
whose hostility to the scientists' practice of expunging psychological contingencies from the records leads him to vilify sex
research as sin. Neither does it mean ignoring the probability that
the sex researchers included their uplift case studies in the hope
of justifying their project and quieting criticism. It does mean
asserting that the sex researchers' determination to praise themselves as courageous debunkers was obnoxious, and that the
alternative to myth that they have thus far presented isn't much
more adequate to truth than the myth itself. They do have an
achievement to their credit. The sex lab proved that, in physiological terms, no significant relation exists between the size of the
penis and coital satisfaction, nor any necessary connection between masturbatory orgasm and "frustration." The special physiological language it developed can be helpful to men, and does
provide relief from the voguish porno puerilities of an "age of
sexual liberation." Say it straight out: The laboratory situation
creates a possibility of teaching people *what to do*. If participation by the scientific and literary intellects in each other's ac-
countings of "facts" were the rule, as it ought to be not only here
but in a dozen other critical areas of contemporary intellectual
inquiry, the "achievement" would rouse more positive feelings
than depression.

But as matters stand that feeling is appropriate. Founded as
yet another venture on behalf of inclusiveness, the sex lab and
attendant controversies testify that, for poet and methodologist
alike, the whole human story is too much to face up to, too
complex, contradictory, dense in variables to be touched in
professional words. We are led out from a valley of deprivation
into a valley of abstraction. We understand that the latter could

be furnished, could be made comfortable for humanness. Sensitive men from both letters and science—call them scientific humanists—could do the job, provided they were committed to direct, patient, collaborative survey of problems, provided they were prepared to determine in continuous partnership when and where the methods of detachment can be productive, and when and where sympathy with contrarieties and delicacies of moment-to-moment personal response must not be foregone. But where are these men? They haven't come forth as of this moment, and until they appear abstraction rules unchallenged. We are offered no choice save to avert our eyes from full inward intricacy, comedy, dignity—full human nakedness—that which the great thinkers of the relevant past imagined men would someday learn to relish, not just endure. And our deep need—stupid ever to make light of it—for a sense of an ideal possibility, a ground from which sane minds can feel forward, tentatively, in the direction of a more habitable future, continues to go unmet.

Exactly What One Means

Expecting your arrival tomorrow, I find myself thinking I love You: then comes the thought—I should like to write a poem which would express exactly what I mean when I think these words.
—W. H. Auden

Why so, friend? mutters a voice like mine. With deepest respect, why this Thing about exactitude? Don't misunderstand me, as they say in Russian novels. I'm not intolerant. Poetry's good stuff; terrible what they did to Cinna, don't shoot the nightingale, doing the best he can, etc. But seriously: this endless yammer about accuracy can become waffle, can't it? And abusing the millions who settle for "I love you" and get on with the job is a shade priggish, right? And it does on occasion happen, doesn't it, that songbirds preoccupied with the one right word lose touch with the Not-Me, with the world at large, a place never more exciting than now, never richer for seeing, learning, wondering?

Oh, and one last point before being hanged for frankness: it isn't only Philistia that finds the stuff produced by some of the birds in question quite hard to read, *n'est-ce pas?* Might not the sacred rage to express "exactly-what-I-mean" be at least part of the problem?

As every schoolboy knows, the approved current answer to such badgering neither trims nor hems. It declares roundly that precision of meaning stands among the brightest causes of civilization, and that the true heroes of any age are those bent most intensely and faithfully in service of the cause. And there's obviously something to the claim. A sense of heroic struggle often is communicated by poets in the act of refining a statement, qualifying, doubling back, complicating pat formulations, teasing out terms that connect fully and freshly with dailiness.

And the resulting experience is by no means invariably grim. Consider, for instance—one instance among a thousand—Kingsley Amis' "A Bookshop Idyll," a poem whose steps toward "accuracy" lead also toward a charming human view. A browsing poet stands in a shop thumbing the pages of an anthology of verse. The poems by men, he notices, are stony, all about foreign landscapes, Rilke and Buddha, the double vortex. Whereas the lady poets in the book tend to drown in love. Dwelling on the contrast, the browser first produced a smug notion about masculine imperviousness ("We men have got love well weighed up; our stuff/Can get by without it") and feminine unprotectedness (". . . the awful way their poems lay them open/Just doesn't strike them"). He advances from smugness to cozy sentiment:

> Women are really much nicer than men.
> No wonder we like them.

Neat, cute, huggable—but rather more thought up than felt. Impatient, he presses on another inch—and now a pretty payoff comes. The part about women being nicer than men was, the poet avers, evasive. I said it only to bury what those poems by lady poets brought embarrassingly to mind—memories of my own softness, my own vulnerability, time and time again, when:

> We sat up half the night
> Chockful of love, crammed with
>   bright thoughts, names, rhymes.
> And couldn't write.

Nothing momentous here, maybe, but nothing tiresome or useless either: a commonplace ("Man's love is of man's life a thing apart") complicated by remembrance; wit melting toward truth.

Or for another instance, consider the famous unwritten poem in prose that provides the epigraph—Mr. Auden's "Dichtung und Wahrheit," fifty paragraphs on *I love You,* fifty tries at clarifying relations between words and feelings, lyric and life. In theory a wearing project, in practice nothing of the sort. For this is a poet's pursuit of exactitude, not a pedant's. Tensions of mind and will are seen into with cool gravity during its course: "I should like to believe that it is some evidence of love when I can truthfully say: *Desire, even in its wildest tantrums, can neither persuade me it is love nor stop me wishing it were.*" But the seer doesn't hesitate to tell jokes on himself as he goes: "*I will love You whatever happens, even though You put on twenty pounds or become afflicted with a mustache:* dare I promise that?" And there is scarcely a single moment when this enterprise in precise definitions fails to entertain.

Even, indeed, when the costliest, most unjocular refining of meaning is in process, even when the reader is aware that a confrontation of one or another truism (Modern Man Is Rootless, The Age Is Corrupt, etc.) is becoming a painful self-encounter— even then pleasure isn't necessarily foregone. The central subject of rumination in James Merrill's "An Urban Convalescence" is Manhattan impermanence—streets torn up, buildings torn down, huge cranes "[fumbling] luxuriously in the filth of years." And an entirely serious contest is waged inside the feverish, inefficiently tranquilized East Sider who speaks in the poem—a contest between habitual lapses into cultural commentary on megalopolis and the impulse to speak an immediate and personal response to things seen.

Since habit is powerful (cultural commentary is the most honorable substitute nowadays for details of feeling), the contest isn't swiftly won. The stroller remarks that the new buildings do nothing for architecture. He remarks that the situation would be unchanged even if the new buildings did a lot for architecture, for they are no less impermanent than the old ones:

> The sickness of our time requires
> That these as well be blasted in their prime.

But always as he speaks in this too familiar tongue, categorizing, dismissing, the sense of an inner resistance is vivid, and at length the imprecision of such talk is directly confronted:

> There are certain phrases which to use in a poem
> Is like rubbing silver with quicksilver. Bright
> But facile, the glamour deadens overnight.
> For instance, how "the sickness of our time"
>
> Enhances, then debases, what I feel.

And this instant of clarity frees the man. Possessing himself newly, momentarily released from jargon, he perceives the immateriality of the quality or age of buildings, understands the difference between houses of brick and stone and true tenancies of life. The truth of his response to interiors weathering in public view can't be expressed in mutterings about cultural decline; battered houses, wallpapers flying, bring before him his own emptiness, not the culture's, show him the heart's deprivation, the heart's endless need:

> . . . to make some kind of house
> Out of the life lived, out of the love spent.

No jokes, no pleasant sallies, merely a steady movement away from cant toward the center of a genuine response. But the movement is highly affecting, and there isn't a hint of dry or airless inquiry in "An Urban Convalescence"—no surplus solemnity, no pretense.

Still, when all is said, it won't do to pretend that the chief point about poetic zeal for exactitude is simply that it isn't invariably boring, or that, in any event, accuracy pure and plain is a value. What matters much more is that people who insist on saying "exactly-what-they-mean" are insisting on their own human importance, claiming a uniqueness of being, asserting their pride. Implicit in Auden's comment that his poem must be written "in such a way that no reader could misread *I Love You* as I love you" is a belief in the supreme significance of individuality of feeling.

And Auden is scarcely alone in the faith. "Poetry is feeling," said e. e. cummings, "not knowing or believing or thinking." And this means that poetry is "expressing nobody-but-yourself in words," because "whenever you think or you believe or you know, you're a lot of other people: but the moment you feel, you're nobody but yourself." As for the value of expressing "nobody-but-yourself": well, said this poet, it's also "the most wonderful life on earth."

Perhaps. But it is just here that the negative voice wants another, possibly over-dour word. It wants, in particular, to remark the traces of self-indulgence and self-congratulation in the life in question. Is it not, after all, faintly fatuous, this swelling happily-approvingly in thoughts of being nobody-but-myself? What are the social consequences of faith in the almighty significance and perfect differentiation of separate egos? Is the sight of a man turned silent by depletion of ego so vastly more depressing then the sight of a man preening himself over his nonacculturated bits of being, the unsmoothed wart on his elbow, his odd turn of phrase?

True enough, the classic poetry of the immediate past—Yeats, Eliot, Whitman, Wordsworth, the others—is more than preening; in this body of work, self-certitude, pride, conviction of identity, separateness, personal meaning are struggled after, not assumed. And, true enough, poems still appear that are recognizable as human attempts to escape from the mass by knowing the full truth of massification—witness Denise Levertov's jagged, shocked, protesting verses on the superhighway:

> And the people—ourselves!
> the humans from inside the
> cars, apparent
> only at gasoline stops
> unsure

eyeing each other
drink coffee hastily at the
slot machines and hurry
back of the cars
   vanish
   into them forever, to
   keep moving—

Or witness those lines of Joel Oppenheimer's that, beginning with
gentle reflection on one woman, one pregnancy, one birth, run on
almost helplessly into the ugliness of *un*individuation, brooding
about:

   . . . all of us who turn heavily
   on our beds at night. of the
      heart
   which ponderously grasps its
   way back, great sea creature
      caught
   far up on the beach, a mon-
      strous polyp or
   jellyfish. of the lungs painfully
   beating in used air to bring us
      back
   sweating to face air. of the
      nameless
   faceless images we dealt with,
      giving
   our all. of the snorts and grunts
      and
   great cracks of wind exhaled
      fighting
   off the wild animals, keeping
      the beasts
   at bay, while we slept. of all the
      legs
   that might be slid between, all
      the
   buttocks held firm and resilient,

all the nipples erected and
    tweaked
between thumb and first finger.
of all the bodies male and
female to be made love to
beneath the grinding of light,
air, darkness, all the
constituents and elements.

Yet the small reservations return and return. Conceivably their source is mere envy of the personality-monger, the self-advertiser, the triumphant eccentric, the mindless Giant of the day. But whatever the source, the result is, in one (overworked) word, a state of ambivalence. —Singers, in your precision is my beginning. Singers, you alone nourish belief in the significance of private feeling; you alone strengthen faith in the possibility of unique response. Right you are, the world of pure outerness, of unrelieved G.N.P., m.p.h., SAT, Rep.-Dem., prep-high, Brooks-Barney's is unbearable. Only here, only on pipe nights with the beautiful, thin books that nobody sends for Review or for Prepub Comment, that nobody wants Returned to Library or even Paid For (bookshops bill embarrassedly for poetry, doubting they ever stocked the thing that the slip says was bought)—only here does the inner self bloom, stretch, breathe, look about. There must be room for the inner self.

But how much room? How much human pride is supportable? What feelings in the noble "nobody-but-myself" can sanely be detached from the general cultural conditioning and called "uniquely mine"?—*I, I, I,* you keep saying, you voices in the thin, beautiful books. You *are* your precision, and I am the sense of personal difference created in me by my responsiveness to you, my love of your tune. But do you truly believe that this voluptuous dream of differentiation, this fine slaking of my lust for Uniqueness, does much for the survival of humanness? The sense of aversion, antipathy, remoteness from others that grows stronger in me as I read you, the distaste for public anguish and public joy and public words: suppose we grant that it built the present civilization, will it not also wear it down?

—Common stuff, characteristic contemporary quandaries, problems that can't be made to come out. They are, like everything on earth, merely more matter for poetry: reasons or occasions, maybe, for one or another precisionist to repeat to himself, in private, that, like Miss Marianne Moore, "he too dislikes it," and thereafter go on to explain—"exactly-what-he-means."

Reading, Writing,
Reality, Unreality ...

Success and fame at last: I'm invited to speak at the annual meeting of "my" professional association—the Modern Language Association, membership ca. 28,000—on the subject of English Teaching, How to Improve. Do I know, without being told, what is wanted for this talk? I do indeed. Something about Relevance, assuredly. Something about Involving the Kids and Using the Media. A sample turned-on test question perhaps? (Joseph Andrew was the first Beatle. Discuss.) —My feeble mockery is of course insincere: I'm pleased and flattered to have been invited. I accept.

Still, there are some problems. To speak truthfully, I've been at English teaching for years and years without ever having been fully comfortable in the work as it's generally understood. Or, rather, I've never felt close to the profession. Or, rather—why trim?—I've felt downright remote from it. And not just from the mainstream, but from the improvers and reformers as well, when we've worked together at conferences. It's as though there were two languages, one that's natural to me in the classroom, another that comes forth when talking about teaching with fellow teachers. Suppose, Famous Successful Doctor of Phil, suppose this time you spoke from the center of your experience. Suppose you laid out your inner assumptions—the ones that really determine how you work in a classroom. Suppose you said, Well, now, just here and here is where we differ, just here is where I've had hard going in the past with colleagues no matter what their circumstances or mine, just here is where, despite my thousand assurances that I care about books, am no philistine, deeply believe in literary criticism as a significant act of mind, etc.—just here is where the tide of suspicion and hostility begins running too hard on the bow, and I slide off my point. Suppose, in short, on this occasion you were to take up spikiness, Stand Firm, say what you really believed? The earth would shake? They would censure the Program Committee?—And in any case (they can censure whom they will), in any case, what would it sound like? How would you begin? What exactly do you say when you speak the Whole Truth about yourself as an English teacher and lay about you, all boldness and megalomania, to abuse The Others? . . .

—Friends, you say, my first assumption is that it's by no means fatuous to attend to poems as real objects, autonomous, autotelic, free-standing. Everyone who reads decently knows the extraordinary experience of raptness, selfless joy, tranced involvement in the movement of a poem or story. Everyone who teaches decently knows that this experience—the entrance into the story as a world—in some sense "is" art, and that the moment we turn our backs on it and chatter about courtly love or the Elizabethan world view, there is no return to the spell, no fresh habitation of the work of art as "a world." And everyone also knows that there *are* ways of acknowledging the fact of a spell or an illusion. When we ask our questions about internal organization, point of view, rhetorical modes and the rest, we do show forth to our students our own fascination with the texture of the seizing hand on our wrist, our own interest and wonder at the ways in which we have at once been worked on and have ourselves worked in the encounter with the poem or story. And the uses of such acknowledgments aren't inconsiderable; students and teacher are elevated by them. They are momentarily privileged to care for something beyond themselves; they are seeking to actualize (I apologize for the cant word) the range of humanness which flows from the capacity of men to investigate their own delights and to arrive at the mode of consciousness that gives birth to standards.

The critical redskin who doubts the worth of such activity is, among other things, a man out of touch, someone unaware of the evidence about what repeatedly happens to human beings as a result of their effort to speak in acknowledgment of the spell or illusion of a work of literary art. Several times a year, each of us reads an essay about poem or book or *œuvre* proving in itself that a human being can be ennobled by such effort. Nor is it true that you invariably have to look hard for such work: Last year, for instance, two successive issues of one literary magazine provided just the sort of proof I have in mind. (I am thinking of the issues of the *Sewanee Review* that carried Mr. John Crowe Ransom on T. S. Eliot's "Gerontion," and Mr. Donald Pearce on Keats' Nightingale Ode.)

But to say this isn't to say that in most classes about structure and design (nature of the speaker, relations among images, linguistic continuities, interplay between dramatic units, etc.) that the aim of effecting a return to an experience, a reenactment, is sufficiently clear. Rather, these classes often resemble efforts to touch the bones of an object that never was alive, that never had laid a hand on anyone. The laws of anatomy are brought into the center of the classroom, and the humanness and livingness of lyric and narrative cease to count. And the English class becomes a place distinguished chiefly by total obliviousness to Whitman's great words:

> The process of reading is not a half-sleep, but, in highest sense, a gymnast's struggle . . . the reader is to do something for himself, must be on the alert, must himself or herself construct indeed the poem, argument, history, metaphysical essay—the text furnishing the hints, the clue, the start or framework. Not the book needs so much to be the complete thing, but the reader of the book does.

That such obliviousness can become a rule seems to me symptomatic of the English teacher's forced retreat to the periphery of his subject; his frequent inability to escape a community- and profession-imposed obligation to triviality—an obligation to names, not things; apparatus, not inquiry; the window rather than the view. When I speak of a "retreat," I am simply saying that I believe the English teacher isn't usually and primarily engaged in the activity of encouraging students to find the bearing of this book and that poem and this "composition" on their own lives; he is not using the authority of art, the actualities of the imagination, as they can be used. I believe the English teacher is inhibited about giving himself to the labor of drawing men into an effort to reflect upon and understand their own experience (a labor that art—and student composition—make much easier). I believe that while he declares allegiance to tradiional slogans about his subject, while he goes on announcing the supreme relevance of literature to the development of character, imagination, responsiveness to life, goes on declaring that books truly do "connect," he, nevertheless, concentrates in his day-to-day teaching on other matters. He busies himself introducing students to arcane literary hierarchies—the mystique of Great Books, etc. (Take a book, any book, *this* book.) The high school teacher and the college teacher function here in much the same ways. They assign on opening day a reading list—*Silas Lapham* or *Marner* or James Joyce or *Hard Times* ("You must have the trad, you see") or whatever. Everyone takes in, by implication, that this is the Subject: the first fact about literature is that there is high art and low, and Teacher knows the high. (The low is what other people read.) And Teacher will tell you which is which even if you don't ask. The key illumination he offers is that the low—often the student's own or "natural" choice—is beneath mention, does not organize life, does not lay an order over against experience, cannot be usefully attended to with an eye toward discovering *its* relevance to human life.

He, the teacher, introduces students to arcane literary hierarchies, and, in addition, introduces them to "objective" structures, designs, and effects. And he introduces them to the history of literature, the history of language, the lives of the great writers, their "philosophical outlook," and the development of literary form. (Shakespeare liberated the sonnet from Petrarch, John Donne liberated the sonnet from Shakespeare, then came the heroic couplet as released from Milton, and soon the Romantic poets protested against the heroic couplet on behalf of the sloppier quatrain, and then we have Ezra Pound.) And the teacher sees himself always as the enemy of a slovenly enterprise known throughout the trade as "identifying." He is bound by professional convention to oppose student involvement with the text, "identification with the hero," and the like. The student may "identify," God forgive him, on his own time, but please to keep the muck of your life out of my classroom. Yet, simultaneously, the teacher is telling himself that *of course* he's concerned with the relation between literature and life. But there is a "field" to be "covered," isn't there? We do have a discipline, a design to be held in view? And "they" do have to be shown what good books and spelling really are, do they not?

For an inkling of the meaning of the situation I describe, I believe you have only to consider for a minute what the teaching life of men in other fields would be, were they placed in a relation to their subject comparable to that of many present-day English teachers. The professor of chemistry would be a professor of test tubes, the professor of fine arts would be a commentator on paint and brushes, the physicist would be an authority on bouncing balls. Heat, light, electricity, organic compounds, energy in the one case, images of man and God and nature in the other—these would vanish as matters of inquiry, if an emasculation comparable to the emasculation of English were accomplished elsewhere. In place of a subject, an area of life, a portion of nature, or existence, the disciplines would be empty—contentless, dimensionless, insubstantial.

How much can be said about English before it was emptied of content? (I am still setting forth assumptions, and it will be over in a moment.) What is its lost dimension, its lost substance? The substance of English is dramatic and presentational, a fullness, an embodiment, a wholeness, not an isolate or a swiftly nameable concentrate: not energy, not heat. But, as already indicated, a way toward a true sense of this subject does exist—one that leads through negatives. "English" is not centrally about the difference between good books and bad. It is not centrally about poetics, metrics, mysteries of versification, or the study of balance and antithesis in the Ciceronian sentence. It is not centrally about the history of literature, not centrally about changes in moral and philosophical systems as these can be deduced from abstracts of selected Great Works. Still more negatives: the English classroom is not primarily the place where students learn of the majesty of Shakespeare and alas for Beaumont and Fletcher. It is not primarily the place where students learn to talk about the structure of a poem or about the logic of the octave and sestet, or about the relation between the narrator and author and speaker and mock-speaker and reader and mock-reader of the poem. It is not primarily the place where students learn to mind their proper manners at the spelling table or to expand their vocabulary or to write Correct like nice folks. It is not a finishing school, not a laff riot with a "swinging prof," not an archaeological site.

It is the place—there is no other in most schools—the place wherein the chief matters of concern are particulars of humanness—individual human feeling, human response, and human time, as these can be known through the written expression (at many literary levels) of men living and dead, and as they can be discovered by student writers seeking through words to name and compose and grasp their own experience. English in sum is about my distinctness and the distinctness of other human beings. Its function, like that of some books called "great," is to provide an arena in which the separate man, the single ego, can strive at once to know the world through art, to know what if anything he uniquely is, and what some brothers uniquely are. The instruments employed are the imagination, the intellect, and texts or events that rouse the former to life. And, to repeat, the goal is not to know dates and authors and how to spell *recommend;* it is to expand the areas of the human world—areas that would not exist but for art—with which individual man can feel solidarity and coextensiveness.

So much for rough assumptions and opinions about where we are. If they are obnoxious opinions, they aren't so because held by an art-baiter. Their root is the simple sense that the teaching of writing and reading can become an enclosed, sealed-off enterprise, locked into terms of discourse which, whether identified as those dominantly of historicism, aestheticism, professionalism, or technicism, are too unrelenting self-referring to be worth praise.

I come now to my examples, intending to show what I complain against is visible in public reality.

Late last summer at Hanover, New Hampshire, some forty or fifty English professors from England, America, and Canada sat together, under the auspices of the Carnegie Foundation, the National Council of English teachers, and MLA to attempt to arrive at some good and just assumptions about English teaching. After a week or so of attitudinizing and speechmaking, people came to realize that they were being self-indulgent. The way to establish what one felt about teaching was to do some teaching, expend energy each before the other. So a committee chose a poem; our group was divided into classes of six or seven, and we were asked to brood about the chosen poem and then to suggest an age level or grade for which the poem seemed particularly suitable. With this grade in mind, we were to speak to: "What objectives would you hope to move toward in your classroom handling of the poem, what methods and approaches would you use?"

The Hanover crowd was not undistinguished, by and large; some citizens were well known throughout the profession. But the episode in question was, in my view, a disaster. Talk about classroom objectives degenerated almost instantly into rancorous dispute about Taste. How good was the poem? "I hate it." "It's bad Hardy, ekshly." (I shall come in a moment to "the poem itself"; the paradigm is what matters here.) "Don't you think something a *little* better could have been found? I mean, can't he *tell* the difference?" etc. Next: a question about the relation between the poem and the genre, dramatic monologue: What other poems might be put into the equation? Next: Would the poem be read in class, when, by whom, how? So there were demonstration readings, and it was agreed by the group that two of our number read well. But the question of the uses of the poem, the question how to place it in the classroom, how to set up vital relations between the student and these lines: those matters seemed more or less without interest. Here was a bit of poetry which, like many another bit of poetry, would strike an inexperienced reader as "clipped out" from somewhere, torn from context, quite mystifying at first glance, a kind of uninvited guest, all unexpected. Yet, even the probable surprise of the poem to inexperienced students wasn't enough to shake the discussants out of the vacuum of taste and genre talk. Before I come back to the poem itself and make a commitment about proper classroom objectives, let me deal, in similar paradigmatic manner, with a classroom situation involving writing.

We are at the same conference. A successful high school English teacher from Cheyenne, Wyoming, presents a paper about grading compositions—in particular, about how to teach young people to revise. The teacher's exhibit is a paper written on the theme of "an important decision." The answer in the unrevised and revised theme that we are asked to consider draws on an uncommon experience from the world of sport. It is, at bottom, a world not only of sport but of cruelty—cruelty which the student, because of his closeness to a local culture, is unaware of. The instructor, calling for revision, directs his energies not to the task of awakening the student's consciousness to the cruelty of which he is oblivious; instead he deals with the problem as one of "technique," and calls for more colorful, precise "details"; as though the use of writing isn't to seek deeper comprehension of experience but to tart up "theme topics" with Timese.

But, of course, from this distance the rights and wrongs of both episodes aren't visible. Let me first quote the poem just mentioned, Hardy's "The Man He Killed":

> Had he and I but met
> By some old ancient inn,
> We should have sat us down to wet
> Right many a nipperkin!

But ranged as infantry,
And staring face to face,
I shot at him as he at me,
And killed him in his place.

I shot him dead because—
Because he was my foe,
Just so: my foe of course he was;
That's clear enough; although

He thought he'd 'list, perhaps
Offhand like—just as I—
Was out of work—had sold his traps—
No other reason why.

Yes; quaint and curious war is!
You shoot a fellow down
You'd treat if met where any bar is,
Or help to half-a-crown.

What should one *care* about when one is teaching this poem? I must change the question quickly in order to fit it to my classroom, for I think it is probably a mistake to begin flatly with any poem, to begin any class as though the prime aim were to "do justice to the poem." I would say that the teacher does well to remind himself that the poem is the third voice in the room, and that he himself is not merely the servant of the poem, but the defender, interpreter, even perhaps celebrator, of the life and world of feeling. Saying it again: Only in his classroom are details of immediate, living, individual thought and feeling and response legitimate areas of interest and speculation. Well and good if he wants to say to himself: How can I show the organization of this poem? But he should add other words in the line of self-exhortation. He should remind himself that most men don't know what they feel, hence sometimes feel nothing; and the literature teacher and the writing teacher are men whose gifts and sensitivities are means by which others can be awakened to contrarieties and puzzles of ordinary response. The map of human relations and feelings known to the young is all Sahara usually; few marks on it except what the culture (or the rebel-culture) scratches—love of parents or hatred, pride in nation, pride in self, ambition, dutifulness, loyalty, unfocused cynicism. Flat counters, simplicities, socializing abstractions. Again and again, the work of imaginative literature populates the desert spaces, fills the blank tracks with probabilities of feeling.

At an interesting, though not primary, level, "The Man He Killed" is a poem about meetings, about strangers encountering each other, establishing ways of acting toward each other, controlling the terms on which they will be known. But the poem is first of all a small rendering of a single man's experience of fathoming for himself the relation between bits of his own behavior and feelings, and the grand impassive concerns of the machine of is-ness beyond him—state, nation, army. Hardy is always brilliant at imagining and revealing the responses of relatively simple minds to enormous events or issues. John Wain once said that Hardy's eye looks straight enough into homely, normal, workaday reactions to permit his reader to see how little truth there is in the notion that homely, normal, workaday reactions truly exist. A teacher with ability to retain control of his class while moving freely from conversation to text and back to conversation might decently and honorably begin with a question about how we place ourselves in relation to the state or nation. Do you ever have a citizen-feeling? When? Can you say much about it? Describe it? The Lincoln Memorial at night? Leaving New York harbor, returning? Watching an Inauguration on TV? What is it like to be a loyal citizen, do you think? What are the elements of this experience? Have you ever been in a quandary about where you are in relation to an Official Policy, a Public Decision, the Country itself? "This is my country"—how much ownership do you feel in the "my"?

I would think a teacher beginning this way would want to turn away after five or ten minutes, proposing a poem as another voice in this conversation. There need not be endless agonizing about a perfect reading or about the goodness or badness of the poem. Neither item matters as much as our opportunity to move with young minds to consciousness of how people go about making a sense of themselves as related in significant ways to the public weal, public choices, issues, wars.

But we won't move at all, will we, if we fail to do justice to the third stanza, sounding it as it should be sounded? More questions here. Shall we read it as though the man were answering confidently? No? Why so? Why is he not confident? How does he answer? You might say, with a sort of faintly overacted concentration, frowning, bemused, overacted cudgeling of brains, "I am taking this problem very seriously, because I happen to be (within my limits—and do not think I'm without pride, I've got as much of that as the next man!) a serious, independent, thoughtful person." The questions here seem to point us not only at the man's way of working out a quandary but at the art of the poem as well. For a great part of the latter does, after all, lie in the strained turning of the lines to follow simple hesitation and pauses on to the release of a wry, hand-lifted shrug. The movement of the words does indeed register the movement of a mind, a simple man seeming to think it out, seeming to "work something out for himself."

But we must get to the central point. How does the man "solve" this problem? Does he solve it? Here is somebody trying to fathom a public mystery: Why do I shoot and kill another man, under the sponsorship of the state? What does this fathoming amount to? Well, it amounts to a gesture and a tag: Life is paradoxical, "quaint and curious." The man meets his need by acting in a certain way. By doing a kind of homely philosophical turn. By making a kind of profundum-sound. By lifting a shoulder in a manner that says, We're not so dumb, y'know. We at least know we don't know anything and when we say that, we at least know a lot more than your super-educated blokes—them what thinks they know bloody well everything.

How shall we "finish" our class? Perhaps not with homage to a poem. We may trail off asking whether, now that we are familiar with the way in which questions don't get answers, we ourselves will be less inclined to accept our own pseudo-answers, our own postures of reconciliation, etc. Are we not protected? Will we know enough to press on to "real" answers? Why? Why not? And then at the end, what will the teacher tell himself? All I did today "in English" was show forth a little of the manner in which human beings face their puzzles, bridge the gap between their slim certainties and the complicated rationale of events, bridge it by accepting their socially imposed obligation to behave as though everything does finally add up. I have asked some questions that might oblige somebody, at some future moment when he is saying: Well, we know life is a racket—or a paradox—or a joke—that might oblige such a man to stay a minute longer inside the mystery, instead of cutting it off with the word "paradox."

And, I say defensively, in these actions, I haven't much defaced the poem. The stillness in Hardy's stanzas, the part of the organization where for an instant the poem becomes quite good, is the moment at which the poem bodies forth in a speech rhythm a certain expressive curve of hesitation, followed by release toward "comprehension." The achievement of the poem is to give formed substance to a human effort to comprehend what is beyond comprehension. The triviality the mind offers in such efforts is carried in the silly-rote patness of the sounds—*foe, so, foe, though.* The small messy cluster of rhymes introduces words as words into the equation at just the instant when the man is discovering a word as a word—*foe* is "just a word," somebody's taught word. Just a foe, just so. Right. *Foe*'s the right word. It is "right" because there is no way to move out of the suspension of thought in cliché, empty sound, or half-smiling gestures of reconciliation.

But we are not teaching the poem in order to celebrate a snippet of craft. No, no more than we are teaching it in deference to "life" or to "experience." Our deference is to the formed substance that the poem has made—the reality of one single man's particular way at a particular time with a particular companion of masking incomprehension as "understanding of a sort," the sense of what it is like to inhabit the skin of someone at the moment when he behaves as though he believes he "understands" what in truth is beyond his power of understanding. Our class hasn't precisely been "taught a poem." It has been in a conversation about understanding and blindness; and while the best voice in the conversation is the poem's voice, it is that only because *we* took it in, we showed ourselves what it created and how that creation comments on gestures of our own. And (one last point here), the teacher's art, if the conversation comes to anything, doesn't lie in his mastery of the poem alone. It lies in his or her approach to the great vision of the humanistic investigator found in Kierkegaard's *Concept of Dread:*

> . . . just as the psychological investigator must possess a greater suppleness than a tightrope walker, so that he can install himself within men's minds and imitate their dispositions: just as his taciturnity during periods of intimacy must be to some degree seductive and passionate, so that reserve can enjoy stealing forth, in this artificially achieved atmosphere of being quietly unnoticed, in order to feel relief, as it were in monologue: so he must have poetic originality within his soul, so as to be able to construct totality and orderliness from what is presented by the individuum [student or poet, I want to add] only in a condition of dismemberment and irregularity.

Less needs to be said about the other instance I cited: the writing episode. I want only to say that it doesn't seem to me that the good teacher of writing can see himself as a tutor in the craft of adding details, color, vividness, etc. His obligation is to move the student closer to the thing, to find the talk that will create a subject for the student, create a need for utterance, an eagerness to name a truth beyond the truth begun with. Here is the original paragraph which the Cheyenne teacher read to us. It is about bullriding:

> I had been riding bulls for 2 summers and wasn't doing too bad at it, when I was chased up a fence by a bull in Thermopolis. This didn't seem to affect me and I went right on riding; however, in Douglas this summer I rode a bull, and bucked off; and the bull

came at me, hit me, then tried to bury me. After that I swore I wouldn't ride bulls again. In the same rodeo my buddy was riding a bareback horse and he fell under it getting kicked several times. Then I swore I would never ride horses or bulls again.

And here is the revision, produced after the teacher asked for more details:

The day was on the chilly side. The sky was overcast and the wind was strong. Most contestants wore jackets when not up. Bull riding was the first event, and I was second out on a good spinning bull named Corkscrew. He was a big blue-gray brahma with long horns protruding from his head like his big sagging ears.

I nodded my head and the chute gate sprang open, and I then knew that this was going to be no picnic. He jumped high and began spinning to the left as if he was going to screw himself into the ground. I was just getting with the spinning bucks when he ducked out from under me, throwing me hard on my left shoulder. As I was rolling over from the force of the fall my eyes caught the huge animal throwing up dirt with his front feet, preparing to charge. I jumped to my feet and didn't waste any time getting to the fence, but my ton and a half friend was right on my tail. His head was lowered and snot was streaming out of his reddened nostril.

The snot in the nostril does not, I think, change the bull. It is one more bit of objective timese, one more "balding" or "blue-eyed" or whatever, one more pretense that the viewer does not affect the object viewed. The right question to ask the bullrider was, perhaps: What about the canvas strips wrenched up under the animal, crushing his scrotum? How can you think of them? Have you thought about why the animal bucks? Why does the animal not shriek? Why do we do this to them? Have you imagined this pain? Why do you yourself and I myself not care very greatly about it? Here is a dreadful, needless affliction of torment—a creature backing, rocking, tearing itself apart in air—and we are oblivious to the shrieking in these motions. Why so?

Questions of this sort seem to me to be analogous to the questions I wish to ask about the poem. They seek to remake a situation for the reader and the writer; they seek to shift the relation between the writer and the subject, edging him closer to the thing, pressing for the human response.

Someone tolerant of looseness but, nevertheless, troubled by all this asks: What makes you believe every teacher doesn't do exactly what you've just been talking about? I would instance, in answer, the papers I have read in the bound volumes of the last few Yale conferences of English teachers; I see no point in quoting passages, and I do not mean to set up against literary criticism, but these papers are presented as aids to teachers, and they seem to me by and large to speak to English teaching in different terms from those just set forth. And then, too, there are the episodes I cited, two among scores, from a recent and reputable international conference of teachers of English.

Someone else may ask: How could teachers with a subject as exhilarating in its contemplation as English let it slip from their hands? Especially when so many great voices, not mere doctors of philosophy like you, Professor D., have said loud and bold: Study the *thing*. (Do not talk to me of artistry: Van Gogh. Tell me about the mudbank over there. Or Turgenev: If you want to know my stories, then know my *things:* "All the images rose up before me as things:" Coleridge.) Why should things—objects, feelings, situations—not stand in better with English teachers than they do? Nothing short of a book suffices to tell that story. There are enormously complicated community pressures toward innocuousness and toward a bootless "mastery of mechanics" (the citizen with no ideas, no vision of himself worth punctuating, but with a clear grasp of "punctuation mechanics" is the desiderated product). And there are a number of intellectual influences that are scarcely less important. One of these is the advent of special traditions of professionalism among literary men and teachers—first, the cult of historical research, later, the cult of design and structure. Another is the powerful thrust (coming partly through the Symbolist aesthetic) toward dismissal of the referential nature of works of literary art: The poem became a set of relations within itself, a fascinating clockworks that told no time. For different reasons, the student composition had already become something analogous—a lesson in the mastery of a particular progression of paragraphs, rather than a raid on the unexpressed. Still another distraction was the noisy, pointless dispute between historicists and new critics—an argument in which both parties were in agreement on a fundamental principle: Students should not be encouraged to study poems and novels as discoveries or clarifications or embodiments of life itself. (The teacher who chose up sides in this dispute had the illusion of opting for something "concrete"; in fact, he merely took on another abstraction.) There is, in addition, the tendency of some literary men of positivistic cast to aspire to the condition of scientist; in other words, clear out the human junk. Above everything, perhaps, there is the widespread and ignorant conviction that only the mindless can speak with interest about details of feeling. But what person who has ever sought intensely and responsibly to know his own feelings in a particular situation could accept an account of that enterprise as intellectually unchallenging? The surest proof of the excruciating difficulty of achieving consciousness of one's own or another's responses is the rarity of effort toward that end. It is much easier to settle for public cant and private self-deception than to reach for the innerness of a man.

But the present need, as I said at the start, isn't for etiological surveys. Neither is it for long ponderings on the possibility that teaching which recovers a decent interest in the life embodied and represented in works of literary art (and in student composition) will lead to loss of taste, critical inexactitude, ignorance of our literary heritage, dumbness before the wonder of language. (The love of a melody cannot be lessened by attention to what the melody expresses, the pieces of life set in order and related one to the next within the tune.) Nor is it useful to agonize about the possibility that to deal with substantive matters in the English classroom means decreasing the distance between teacher and student and accepting, as a normal classroom event, face-to-face, abrasive encounters of assumptions, doubts, and longings.

For the truth is that the gains that could come from releasing the English teacher and student into the living world of their subject hugely outweigh any possible losses. These gains can even be fairly expressed in terms of significant national interests. It is the free man's awareness of himself as possessing a distinct life of feeling, a singularity of response, an individual tendency in time, that alone gives meaning and relish to the idea of freedom. And in the contemporary state there are massive forces ranged against every small encouragement and stimulation of that awareness, forces blandly denying the dream of individuality and the dream of self-knowledge. The English classroom is, ideally, the place where the latter dream is set under scrutiny, understood, valued, and interpreted. To reduce the classroom to a lesser place, to evade the substance of English in the name of stylistics, correctness, acquaintance with the classics, taste tests, colorful composition, is therefore to deny youth a good defense against the fate of mass men.

What is being said here can be mocked, I must admit now at the end, as amounting to a merely therapeutic conception of the study of literature and composition. But there is nothing on earth, after all, that cannot be defaced with a *merely*. The argument that the right course for English studies or humanities courses is one that prizes the poem and the play as windows opening on a livingness that would otherwise be unseen and dead to the human eye need not run into extravagance. There is no implicit claim that any man can be "saved" simply by such views and visions, simply by talking about his own relation to the state before meeting a poem embodying perplexities in that relation, simply by being pressed to consider the torment of the bull as well as the "need for lively detail." The argument holds only that the teacher and student who speak together of the things that books make palpable, who tell each other what they see and why they believe or disbelieve their eyes, can awaken in each other a stronger consciousness of humanness than that issuing either from an absorption in metrics or design or the hierarchy of taste. Is it not a fact that whatever serves the interest of that consciousness—the interest of a man's awareness of the immediacy of himself—also serves the highest interests of the highest art as well?

Turning On and Off
with Student Rebels

They turn you on, the student strike-and-bust stories—*Red Flag/ Black Flag* (1969), the Paris tale as told by reporters for a London weekly, *Up Against the Ivy Wall* (1968), by Columbia undergraduate reporters, the narrative chapters of the Cox Commission Report. If you're a prof and your school hasn't been hit and you've got a grievance, you read them hand running, excited, believing, all hot-pugnacious-involved . . . Up against the wall, Prex! Suck eggs, Trustee!

—There are funny bits, to be sure. A drill leader (Mark Rudd or Cohn-Bendit or gorgeous Sauvageot) calls a command on the wrong foot and piles a column of rebels up on the ground; an emergency faculty meeting chokes on amended amendments. And there are horror passages as well. (Bad in New York and elsewhere, the "campus" bust was obviously worst at the Sorbonne—more fury in *flics* than in pigs.) But even in the most hideous reading moment, a sense of heightened life and promise hangs on. And when it burns off, as it does in the end, leaving the rebels strung out in the bare air of their fantasy, the sequel is nevertheless not depression. For there are lessons in these stories, as well as excitations, and, as it happens, brooding on them doesn't bring a man down.

About one excitation they offer—vicarious revenge—a critical word does need saying. Perfectly understandable why faculty types relish such revenge. You and three other chaps and some students hustled, say, for six months as an "environment committee," inventing a workable substitute for a rotten fraternity system—whereupon The Trustees, blithe, lordly, misinformed, killed your proposal over a drink. Or you were invited onto a minor Trustee subcommittee—pals at last—only the group never met thereafter, the Chairman merely sailing your thoughtful suggestions over the transom to the Board for friendly unexplained dismissal. . . . With these or other remembered frustrations or humiliations in the equation, teachers can be forgiven for taking pleasure in the sight of administrative snottiness (Columbia- or Sorbonne-style) getting its what-for—sweating in phone booths, being lashed by foul (student) tongues, pleading with faculty fixers, grasping too late that "something dangerous is happening." But blameworthy or not, such pleasures aren't improving. Arrogance is universal in academe, nobody's exempt—and insofar as the riot tales muffle that truth, insinuating that teachers and students somehow escape the great Establishment Sin, they're bad for the moral character.

On other fronts, though, to repeat, the books are impeccably moral—meaning they teach as well as excite. The chief lesson taught is about the uses of interruption to thinkers, and about the deadness of intellectuality as routine. Strike days at Columbia after the first bust saw much larking about—sunbathing in South Field, pot festivals, and the like. But *Up Against the Ivy Wall* shows that students and professors in impressive numbers were also talking straight and hard to each other in this period about how to restructure the school:

> Students had time to spend long hours engrossed in discussions with the professors they had met in front of buildings during their vigils, or with the other students who had been inside the buildings with them. Freed from the fetters of habit and routine, students were able to work on the Strike Committee's many projects. . . . Some attended the Strike Committee's "free university" liberation classes; more met with their teachers in dormitory lounges, apartments near campus and on South Field to talk about the strike as well as their course material.

More important, during the insurrections themselves students won extraordinary triumphs over their own lassitude, complicity in is-ness, conviction of powerlessness. Both in the "communes" of Morningside Heights (Hamilton, Fayerweather, Avery, Math Hall, Low) and in the Grand Amphi at the Sorbonne, youth itself took in, half astonished, that civilization does begin anew with every child, and that the terms of substantive human relations, obligations, aspirations, are ever open to change:

> For the thousands of young people taking part, it was a delirious and unforgettable experience, one of the most formative they might ever live through. If the May Revolution was anything at all, it was this roaring mass of spontaneous student committees and assemblies running its own affairs.   [*Red Flag/Black Flag*]

> Now, insulated from the norms and forms of American culture by several feet of office furniture and barricades, the students inside the "liberated" buildings were able to create social patterns of their own. The takeover of the buildings had begun as a political tactic designed to bring about the goal of social reconstruction. It quickly evolved into the realization, on a small scale, of that very goal. . . . Students could, within the strike context, *make the decisions that affected their lives.*   [*Up Against the Ivy Wall*]

There were puerilities, naturally—witness the candlelight marriage ceremony performed by a Reverend Starr for student rebels in Fayerweather. ("Do you, Richard, take Andrea for your girl?" "Yes." "Do you, Andrea," etc. "I now pronounce you children of the new age.") And everywhere there was vagueness—especially in the proposals for educational reform. *Red Flag/Black Flag* tantalizingly mentions a "marathon debate from mid-May far into June, drawing in students, teachers, and artists in all fields," held by a "Committee for the Preparation of a Reform of Artistic Teaching" in France. Complaints are registered against art-teaching that's overprofessionalized, remote from general education, "cut off from living art." *Voilà.* What are the counterproposals, new strategies, new teaching ideas? Not a word, not a single word.

And yet despite puerility and vagueness the sense of promise remains. A frozen world unblocked, the gates of faculty-student habitude swung wide, young and old speaking seriously to each other, perceiving freshly the shortness and preciousness of the life adventure, aiming anew to make something of it by acts of mind . . . Only a murderous stoniness could read of such hours unmoved.

Where then is the fantasy, the silliness at the core? According to Charles Frankel, a Columbia professor lately returned to campus from the culture wars of the State Department, the fantasy lies in the notion that if you're upset about Vietnam, racism, poverty, or the general quality of life, the bridge to blow is College. Only a dreamer or a fool would attack "those institutions in our society of which [these] ills are least characteristic," says Frankel in *Education and the Barricades* (1968).

According to the Cox Commission, on the other hand—these are the patient lawyers headed by Harvard's Archibald Cox whom Columbia retained to find out what really happened in spring 1968—the fantasy lay in the belief of reform-minded students that civility wasn't a cornerstone of academic enterprise at its best. (". . . the essential postulate" for young and old to remember, said the Commission, is "that the university is dedicated to the search for truth *by reason and civility*. . . . The survival—literally the survival—of the free university depends upon the entire community's active rejection of disruptive demonstrations.")

And according to still others, the fantasy was a matter of false optimism. For James Ridgeway, for instance—he is the author of *The Closed Corporation* (1968), an attack on the American university as a "center of industrial activity"—the rebels' error would be that of failing to understand that change is now quite out of the question. ("It is too late for the myth. The universities were bought by the Pentagon long ago.")

But for most readers the rebels' key delusion will probably not seem to be any of these. The center of the students' "thinking" appears to have been the notion that, after you've liberated a few buildings on a main campus, or paraded about town (Paris) with a union mob, your revolution is done and done. In *Obsolete Communism: The Left-Wing Alternative* (1969), Daniel Cohn-Bendit argues that the Sorbonne uprising of May 1968 proved that "revolution is possible even in a highly industrialized capitalist society." And certainly it's true that, in Paris, workers and students did march together, and several joint student-faculty-administration committees did come into being, and various reforms of admissions policy, curriculum, exam procedure, parietal rules did come under discussion. At Columbia, moreover, significant changes occurred. No gym. An end to footsie with the Institute for Defense Analyses. New committees at work. Fresh efforts at communication with the Harlem community.

Still the dream of Instant Transformation must remain a dream. The reform of a university, as of most institutions, requires excruciating effort, wearing struggle against dailiness, habit, the bondage of ready-to-wear ideas. "The longer I live," said Péguy, "the less I believe in the efficiency of an extraordinary sudden social revolution, improvised, marvelous, with or without guns and impersonal dictatorship, and the more I believe in the efficiency of modest, slow, molecular, definitive, social work." But how exhausting is that work! How long it takes! "A universal, one might say *untiring* laziness pervades the world." And, further problem, the delicious memories of the liberation interval fade fast for those engaged in this work. ("The spirit inside was beautiful," says the Hamilton Hall girl about the occupation, squinting to remember. "There was singing, talking, dancing to music from small phonographs, watching TV, participating . . .") Which of us who never heard that music can contemplate without whining the task of creating new, genuinely flexible-interesting-joyous learning situations? "Preventing people from sliding down their natural slopes—what is it but giant's work?"

And there are no giants, just us—and the work hasn't been done—and the rebels are, as Grayson Kirk, in his thin-lipped rage, insisted, "transitory birds"—and, dammit, like every gang of kids, they won't pick up their mess. And they're forever inventing newer, grander messes to make. And they really didn't try to imagine the future as particulars of feeling—seemed to want eternal hate as much as they wanted revolution.

—But bless them bless them bless them, they did interrupt. Bless them for that. Against the enormous weight of habit, their own included, they set a strong shoulder, and shoved. *They inserted themselves.* Not for long, not for nearly long enough, and always with too much larking to too many "small phonographs." But the light they saw out the tunnel, the little music they made, these frail new committees, surprising quivers of guilt—in the line of growing points, pray, what else exactly have we got?

The Man Who
Imagined Imaginations

The author hasn't changed my life, doesn't qualify as a Neglected Figure, wouldn't be thrilled (might be amused) at the idea of being rattled on about for a stretch in print. He bears an unexciting name—Charles Horton Cooley. He was long dead when I began reading him. (Cooley's dates are 1864–1929.) In his most attractive book—*Life and the Student* (1927)—he set down his thoughts on "our time," human nature, the university and literature in odd little not quite epigrammatic, often contradictory paragraphs, four or five to the page. (Far from fretting about the contradictions, Cooley relished them.)

And the circumstances under which I took up the book were of a kind that often makes for edginess and hypercriticism in a reader. (I was on a self-improvement bender, learning Sociology on my own, studying "seminal thinkers"; among Americans in the field Cooley ranks as a seminal thinker.)

Still, I warmed to the thing—Cooley's *Life and the Student*, that is—from the start, and it hasn't stopped growing on me yet. Partly of course this means simply that I'm easy with the author, or at least with his most visible side—the prof side, the kind voice, the alert head. Cooley was an attitudinizer who went around setting traps for himself, but the fatuities he catches himself in remind me of mine. He claimed that he hated faculty meetings because of the parliamentary fidgeting, the distraction from significant mental labor, etc. Since that's my supper-table line too, I felt it when suddenly he needled himself into admitting the real reason faculty meetings depressed him was that "I do not shine on these occasions."

He was in addition (so he implies in the book) the sort of teacher who's prone to exalted views of his own motives and work, seeing only the noble character-builder in his disciplinarian self, never the sly cynic or cop. Since again I'm that way myself, his excursions—in a chapter called "Academic"—on the meaner teacherly seedinesses also have, for me, an edge.

And, as might go without saying, I share many of his opinions about the wider academic scene. He seems solid (to me) on the question, Can a teacher be made into an administrator? (Certainly, is his answer, as easily as a car can be made into a truck: "Stiffen the frame and lower the gear.") I admire him for complaining, four decades ago, that "no teacher or official becomes aware of the student as a human whole; he is known only by detached and artificial functions." I also admire him for saying publicly—harder to do so then than now—that, since faculty and students have "somewhat different interests," the student is often wrong when he is docile, and right "when he does not behave as the faculty would like to have him." There's usually, furthermore, a blade in his irony, as when he praises the contemporary (1927) zeal to suppress radical ferment ("though stupid, [this zeal] should probably be encouraged as a possible incentive to rebellion"). Yet neither his feeling for the worth and separateness of the undergraduate interest nor his enthusiasm for social transformation sucked him into stereotypes (like ours) of The Student as surefire savior or hero:

> College students are not the homogeneous crowd that some imagine. As in other societies, there is a dominant type or form that more or less imposes itself upon the whole, but underneath there are variants, many of them maladjusted and more or less psychopathic. In the eye of each, if you look for it, you may see an individual spirit, a self, often only partly at home with its fellows.*

* No mystery about how Cooley came by his academic knowledge. Born in Ann Arbor, educated in Ann Arbor, married to an Ann Arbor girl, he climbed the faculty ladder in that place—the University of Michigan—and

But easy as it is for my prof side to cotton on to Cooley, the reason his book grows on me doesn't really have much to do with academic soul-brethren ties. The truth is I use *Life and the Student* as what's called inspirational reading; the book incites to optimism, and I'm vulnerable to the special style of its prodding. For one thing, there's little sentimentality in these pages, and no high marks for innocent or brainless virtue:

> Too long we were taught that good will was the same as goodness. We now see that most evil is done by those who mean well. What we urgently want is knowledge—true perception of the working of each part on every part of the common life of men.

For another, Cooley's vocabulary of uplift, while old-fashioned, is work-oriented and practical, nothing mysterious or godly to turn a person off. (Recurring phrases are "constructive imagination," "mental energy," "mental stability," "persistent cumulative labor," and the like.)

And, best of all, Cooley is longer on showing than telling. He does, true enough, have some general propositions to sell. Chief of them is that people should learn to push their minds to comprehend "personal" ideas held by others:

> Society is an interweaving and interworking of mental selves. I imagine your mind, and especially what your mind thinks about my mind, and what your mind thinks about what my mind thinks about your mind. I dress my mind before yours and expect that you will dress yours before mine. Whoever cannot or will not perform these feats is not properly in the game.

Or again:

> . . . the imaginations which people have of one another are the solid facts of society. . . . I do not mean merely that society must be studied by the imagination . . . but that the object of study is primarily an imaginative idea or group of ideas in the mind; that is, we have to imagine imaginations.

But that belief doesn't emerge as an abstract formula; it appears instead as a mode of behavior, a set of actions. The mind

---

died there, at sixty-five, having spent but a year or two of his life away from a campus town.

inside *Life and the Student* constantly puts itself under pressure to know and feel from some other position besides that which is habitual—to know how another point of view is held, what vectors of decency, viciousness, obliviousness, fear, or whatever hold even the maddest eye on its bearing. Cooley ventures into crazy jut-jawed anti-Semitism and speaks from within this obtuseness. He broods on an actor's minute-to-minute experience on the stage, speculating on its inner quality and texture. At one moment he spends himself imagining the anxieties of the thoughtful and sensitive man:

> His self-consciousness is awakened and intimidated by strange people. It is fear in the dark. Every new person is a fresh glass in which he is impelled to see himself. Hardly a child comes into the house but he finds himself imagining how he appears to it and wishing to appear well.

At the next he's smiling into the minds of two ladies who bump into each other on the street, each gotten up in a new outfit, each imagining the other's inner idea of her own splendor. And, far more commonly, he's working into paired self-images of the rich and the poor, blacks, whites, immigrants, natives, placing the innerness of the privileged at its precise distance from that of the others—for, as he says, "one sees into life only as he has the fullness of spirit to enter into it." Cooley isn't, in short, a stand-off theorizer about "how to know," how to sympathize, etc. His paragraphs are mainly acts.

And, as I say, these acts serve—whenever I think to remember them—as counters to pessimism. Pessimism about good works, for example—attempts to make yourself useful where the help that's needed is of a kind it's feasible to give. I have a small, paid job at the moment that takes me occasionally into ghetto grade schools in Washington, D.C., to teach. Coworkers in the project —two able young writers named Sam Cornish and Lucille Clifton—are black. Kids and teachers are black. None of us is wasting his time, and usually I take for granted that my "services" have value. But there are bad days. A middle-aged Ivy

WASP can easily miss the boat, act condescending, hurt some-body unintentionally, misunderstand a remark, make a tactless joke, read a face wrong, etc. etc. —Cleaver has clout at such times, a lot of it—Cleaver, Jones, Baldwin. You want to forget them and hear somebody encouraging, somebody saying, You can do better, can imagine more clearly, aren't locked in. Hang in there, Teach. Cooley, a calm coach, is the right medicine. Keeping him in mind meets a need and shakes off self-pity.

And the man is no less helpful in the other area wherein, for me, pessimism is hard to take—the work desk, the typewriter. Not to mince words, editors have been known to knock my stuff as hard to read. Too much brambly qualification, too much roundabout-again, fella, don't twist and turn so. Relax. I don't cave in instantly when this happens. I explain to myself that I'm out to represent "views of my views," hope to slip inside and tell how ideas or feelings fit together, within, for somebody else. But any writer, when knocked, is in the market for support, and Cooley is extremely supportive. He speaks up for a "persistent endeavor to see all around one's ideas, to assimilate them with fact from every standpoint, so that nothing of their meaning may escape." No "life made easy" character, a complicator not a simplifier, he's a fine corner man for writers whose "Let's try a rewrite" mail looks like mine.

Fair to ask: Why settle for so little? Is Cooley the only optimist, the only bearable recommender of imagination, complication, and the rest? Nowhere a more powerful voice? What about Péguy?

The most powerful living writer on Cooley's themes is, to my mind, Hannah Arendt; issues addressed in *Life and the Student* —and in Cooley's other works—appear in a clear and profound light in many books from her pen. No greater crier-up of hard, imaginative labor than this analyst of totalitarianism, no stronger advocate of effort that "does not tire of interminable dialogue and 'vicious circles,'" that alone "bridges abysses of remoteness until men can see and understand everything that is too far away from us as though it were our own affair." In a superb essay on "Understanding and Politics," Miss Arendt says straight out:

Without this kind of imagination, which actually is understanding, we would never be able to take our bearings in the world. It is the only inner compass we have. We are contemporaries only as far as our understanding reaches. If we want to be at home on this earth, even at the price of being at home in this century, we must try to take part in the interminable dialogue with its essence.

The note is well beyond Cooley's range—not much tragic grandeur in *Life and the Student.* But the lack is made up for by the supply of specific workaday notions in his pages about how to "try to take part in the interminable dialogue." Tricks, hints, dodges, ploys—much of what you learn does, to be sure, come down to that. Homely matter. Cooley says if I stand "at the classroom door and seek the eye of each student as they come in I [will] get a human sense of them that makes it easier to talk to them. A strange crowd facing you is oppressive." And I chuckle —what a gimmick!—and am sorry for my need for such guid-ance. Still, I'm glad to have it. Partly for the thing itself—this ploy and the hundred others in *Life and the Student,* partly for the glimpse of the frail counterpuncher who's nevertheless ready to mix it with oppression, disinclined to break the habit of hope.

And here's the essence of it, finally, the secret of the closeness I feel—the scale of the Cooleyan struggle. A gloom-fighter, a chin-up lad, Cooley is nevertheless human and unheroic, utterly unintimidating. No "towering mind," not even a faculty-meeting star, cheerful man, "just a prof"—yet he presses himself, thinks he can get out. Looking across the table he says, "Living on a little requires genuine freedom of mind—meaning you've got to imagine otherness from within and see yourself from without— and push and push and push. Tricky job. Still it's possible. You work piece by piece, elbows in, hands up. Stretch your head, don't waste time arguing and contradicting, look to learn, try to *find* the other fellow as he's known to himself. You'll be fasci-nated, wait and see. Life will seem absorbing, you may wind up thinking something can be done." I want to buy that, as it happens, so I wind up rereading this little book.

Existential:
Sixties' Cinderella Word

Pop question: Can *existential* make it big?

Prospects were poor until recently. A foreign entry, heavy, hard to pronounce, fast in the forties, faded in the fifties, the word looked a foot too long. Worse, it came from philosophy instead of from showbiz or sports. And as for the timing of its sixties' bid—crazy. Camp, charisma, nitty-gritty, dialogue, relevance, thrust—jargonville was jammed to the rails with winners: how could a "newcomer" break through? Despite the handicaps, though, *existential* is breaking through. Improving its place steadily, unfazed by cheapening, inflation, or technical correction, it's closing once again on high fashion. Given a boost from nonlinear media, its future could be immense.

As might be guessed, adaptability plays a key part in this success story. Useful in a variety of fields, *existential* has won strong support across a whole spectrum of nontechnical writing—magazines, newspapers, and books. (In the space of a week this season it was used in public prints to distinguish revolutionaries from gamblers, rioters from students, party candidates from write-ins, and the ovum from sperm.) But other elements besides adaptability figure in the tale—in particular, an Image Factor. Embarrassing to mention that, of course; it implies (falsely) that *existential* is just another contemporary blur-word, no core of meaning at its heart. (The standard pop core is as follows: Existential, adj.—*Not-knowing-what-will-happen-next.* Cf. Norman Mailer at the New York Theater for Ideas: "It was existential [the

Columbia strike], because these kids went out and did something that they had never done before, and they did not know how it was going to turn out." Or cf. Steve Cohn, in the Amherst College literary magazine: ". . . the trick is not to know what's going to happen next, that's existential, that's being."

But embarrassing or not, image-talk is necessary. You can't understand *existential* today without leaving the narrow denotative band and seeing the term in its largest dimensions, as an item closer to trade names than to ordinary parts of speech. Like Marlboro, Mustang, or Ma Griffe, the word sings, has mystery in its nimbus, casts a shadow, evokes the gut response. Charged atmospheres gather at its mention—the unexpected, the reckless, the unconstrained, the spontaneous, the indomitable, the solitary, the purified, the intense, the elemental. . . . The "meaning" of *existential* lies, in short, in the content of the Existential Image— beautifully controlled intimations of safe audacity swinging round the don't-know-what-happens-next core. And, as indicated, the goodwill roused by these intimations already ranks as a major popcultural capital reserve.

Writers who draw on the capital aren't hung up about how and where to spend it. Neither are they oblivious to its potential as a prestige-builder—a means of instant sanctification both of oneself and the cause one favors. For Nat Hentoff the cause one favors is the Concerned Parents movement, pro-community control of schools—therefore he describes the cause as that of "existential education" in his column in *The Village Voice.* For Charles Marowitz (another *Voice* column) the cause one favors is that of the Living Theater, the La Mama Company and Tom O'Horgan —therefore he cries up *Hair* as "existential thunder." For Mary Ellmann the cause one likes is female superiority; hence in her *Thinking About Women* (1968) she identifies sperm as humdrum and herdlike ("jostling masses, swarming out on signal like a crowd of commuters"), and finds the ovum to be adventurous-glamorous-existential ("the ovum travels singly . . . in [a] kind of existential loneliness . . . a daring and independence").

Connotations of daring and independence are by no means the

term's only plus values. *Portentousness*—a sense that something grave and grand, though incomprehensible, is nigh—also enfolds the word. One is aware of it, a misty penumbra, in a *Commentary* essay by Diana Trilling, wherein instead of the flatness of "special" or "peculiar," we savor the excitement of *existential:* "In the meanwhile one's friendly neighborhood suffered in its own existential fashion and went unnoticed. . . ." One feels it, too, in an article by Robert Somma in the *New York Free Press Critique,* wherein *existential* stands in deliciously for "usual" ("negation, despair, abulia [are] not the existential conditions of super spades or super stars"). And the Reverend William Jones, of Brooklyn's Bethany Baptist Church, achieves portentousness by dropping *existential* in to replace *real:*

> "[State Trustee] Johnson was just a puppet. He was not a free man. The existential question is: Is Firman free?"
>
> [*New York Post,* December 4, 1968]

There is, as should be acknowledged, a squarish pop usage, one that takes the term as synonymous with phrases like "existing, that which is," or "pertaining to real life." In *Cinema Now* (1968) the film maker Stan Brakhage reflects on the Beat Generation as a "form of life which is destructive of the self," and recalls that he used to say, when asked to comment on it, "We've got beyond the stage of existentialism, we've got to the stage of desistentialism."* And the word does have a few snipers, characters who concede its prestige grudgingly or ironically, if at all. The dustjacket of a first novel published this month—*Yes,* by Bibi Wein—is sniffish about the book's hero on the ground that he "accepts love incidentally," and "romanticizes the existential

---

* Surprisingly, something of the same flavor—*existential* as pertaining to that which is, concrete life—turns up in Mr. Nat Hentoff's recent remark, in *Evergreen Review,* about the congressional education of Allard Lowenstein:

> As for transforming the Democratic Party into the agent of our salvation, that too is not in the immediate future as Allard Lowenstein, for one, is going to find out existentially in encounters with his party leadership in the House.

freedom he thinks he wants." And a recent Sunday *Times* magaziner about the 20th Century-Fox production of *Che!* quotes an extra praising the star of the film for seeing Che Guevara as a businesslike "casino gambler" rather than as a wildboy "existential" type.

On the whole, however, disrespect is rare. When Michel Crozier, the sociologist, invokes "the existential anguish of the hippies" as an opposing force to the business-government faith in the "science of decision-making . . . the omnipotence of reason," he isn't knocking hippies. When Michael Rossman, the New Left leader, writes in the *American Scholar* that the student activist movement is beyond politics, and works in "unstructured temporary groups in which the dominant themes are existential involvement and effective (potent) freedom," he's not lamenting the Democratic decline. When Margot Hentoff declares in *The Village Voice* that her voting-booth decision to write her own name in on the presidential ballot was an "existential act," she isn't confessing she's a silly woman. When David Cohen, of Country Joe and the Fish, tells *The New Yorker's* "Talk" reporter that he had a breakdown—"the beginning of the existential dilemma—I just fell apart"—as a student at Los Angeles State College, he doesn't see himself as a cloddish, insensitive chap. And when Miss Renata Adler writes, in *The Times*, that Steve McQueen has "existential" features, she hardly means the man looks bad. The plain case is, to repeat, that *existential* has come through, bears no negative scars, has a uniformly positive valence: at the end of the sixties it means good, like pop knows it should.

For the student of popular culture, the questions arising from this evolution are these: How and why has the word arrived at its present state? What were the chief stages of its progress? And neither question is quickly answerable offhand. It seems likely that when the American *existential* record is thoroughly investigated, significant contributions to it will prove to have been made in two books by one author—*Advertisements for Myself* (1959) and *The Presidential Papers* (1963) by Norman Mailer. For while *existential* did have an early run in the forties, it dropped from pop sight thereafter—until Mr. Mailer set it on a comeback trail. *Advertisements* was the first publication in book form of the author's ruminations on the Hip and the Square—chat that freshened the association of *existential* and romantic. And *The Presidential Papers* was no less notable, partly because it laid down the first pop definition of the word ("an act . . . is existential precisely because its end is unknown"), and developed the themes of existential glamour adumbrated in *Advertisements,* and partly because it was dense with suggestive new coinages— "existential legislation," "existential orgasm," "existential politics," "existential vibrations," "existential fatigue," "existential heroine" (Jacqueline Kennedy), to cite just a few. —But these notes on the *existential* past are at best scratchy impressions: the subject demands at the minimum a solid AmStuds doctoral thesis or two.

Nor are AmStuds' doctors the only likely researchers. For students of the history of philosophy this evolution also presents interesting problems, namely, How could a term be so efficiently, swiftly, ruthlessly stripped of intellectual content? What distinctively American gifts figured in the transformation? —Irrepressible American humor clearly had something to do with the redefinition. (Jean-Paul Sartre himself acknowledged this, indirectly, upon learning in 1947 that the American producers of *No Exit* had brightened the piece, and were playing it strictly for laughs. M. Sartre's churlish comment at the time was that "Les Américains ne comprendront jamais rien à l'existentialisme.")

And American production genius was also involved. Changing the meaning of *existential* sharply reduced the amount of time needed to produce a philosopher, even a "first philosopher of hip," and eliminated the need for mental labor. In former days talking philosophy of any kind required extensive training— profitless, time-consuming—in the analysis of concepts, and some consciousness of intellectual tradition as well. Talking existential philosophy was especially burdensome, furthermore, because on its strong side (the phenomenological side, developing from Husserl through Merleau-Ponty) this school conceived the philosophical task to be that of laboriously, responsibly uncreating previous philosophies, descriptions, perceptions, standardized structurings of experience, in order to begin the infinitely difficult task of knowing a thing.* For the American market a substitute was vital—some means of enabling people to sound philosophical without suffering the pain of thought. And the drive to meet this need helped to create the automated, or Hentoff, philosophical style—that device by which a man can think existential by signing his name, pulling the lever, uttering the word.

And finally, some degree of influence on the redefinition may have been exerted by American theories of experience and self-realization, and by the national idealization of isolated, autonomous, closed-system selves. European existentialists tend to be, if a frank word may be spoken, a shade chicken in their concept of freedom, stressing that, while I can realize my being in conflict with others, I must understand that others are themselves engaged in realizing their being in conflict with me; the resulting tension *between* freedoms defines the general human struggle and is the root of our need for balance. Americans are less inhibited, as the theme of creative violence in Norman Mailer attests.† We know better than to be distracted by complications stemming from too much brooding on the truth that, although human beings can be treated as objects, none is less than a

* ". . . we bypass [the world of perception] in critical thought—almost to the point of forgetting the contributions of perception to our idea of truth. For critical thought encounters only bare propositions which it discusses, accepts or rejects. Critical thought has broken with the naïve evidence of things, and when it affirms, it is because it no longer finds any means of denial. However necessary this activity of verification may be, specifying criteria and demanding from our experience its credentials of validity, it is not unaware of our contact with the perceived world which is simply there before us, beneath the level of the verified true or false."—Merleau-Ponty, *The Primacy of Perception.*

† Writing from a European, hence narrowly critical, point of view in a coterie journal called *Minnesota Review,* Samuel Hux recently remarked that "Mailer tends to force 'conflict with' to an insane logic, to change it to 'destruction of.' No longer does he realize himself in the *tension* of inevitable conflict, but in the apocalypse of chosen violence . . . This is not existentialism, but popular surrealism."

subject to himself. We also know better than to be gulled into the idea that thinking is a kind of experience; we know, as did our lesser forefathers from the beginning, that reflection is at bottom an evasion of or even escape from experience—and Experience is All. And this knowledge has in turn nourished the determined American effort to simplify existentialist key-terms.

As goes without saying, though, these matters of genesis, influence, etc. are at bottom purely academic. What counts isn't the nature of the forces that are shooting this word into the center of popular consciousness, but rather the simple fact that the word will arrive there, will have a life in pop usage. There are, admittedly, many unknowns in the equation. (How will the word make itself at home in social discourse? My unusual weekday-night third martini, for instance, formerly known as an extra drink—will I come to call it my existential belt?)

And there will also be, in time, some sadness. Older types, witnessing the slow descent of the term into phone-book listings—Existential Bagel, Existential Body and Fender, Existential Casket—will keen to each other, asking how a word could have been so corrupted. How could such rot be taught? Learning without studying . . . Thinking without thought . . . Philosophizing without wisdom . . . But this elitist rant, this maundering about yesteryear, won't for an instant turn the trend. For way out on the what-comes-next precipice, free, giddy, gutsy, orgasmic, alone, there's no nostalgia, Pops, no looking back over the shoulder—so man like uh y'know what cat in that crib *could* give a good existential goddam?

In and Out of Universal City

Bad moment for bringing out a new novel. Especially bad for a little book, familiar pattern—love, renunciation . . . Current Critical Trend Unfavorable. New Involved Journalism is all the rage. Involved Journalism is a personification of a vision, says Nat Hentoff (following Norman Mailer) in the *Evergreen Review*. "Who needs fiction?" says Professor Kazin in the *Atlantic Monthly*. "Who needs fiction in order to learn what is constantly reported by . . . the magazines, newspapers, college textbooks, and television set?"

—The line is hard to dispute. You want to say: "Involvement is a cage. Freedom is precious. Stories liberate." But merely saying so—it sounds whiny. What's the point? And as for demonstrating, actually trying to show where and how storymaking (and reading) can straighten people out, keep a man in one piece: could you even begin to do that without soaring into hubris—or tailing off into another tale?

The time is early May, close to the end of term. A foundation aide up from New York talks awhile in my office and then offers a gig. Fly out to Hollywood, observe some TV film-making, write answers to a few questions about the production dynamic, supplies of unused talent and imagination, etc., and add any thoughts bearing on the immediate business (the immediate business is Educational Television, Methods of Improving). The trip can be scheduled in reading period, guidance on "the coast" assured (an independent producer attached to Universal City promises to cooperate). As for—oh, yes—money: we're staying in tight on this, but "a skinny hundred a day and expenses," will that do? . . .

The flight west (at the end of the month) is cozy, and I settle in on a Sunday night at a motel I've stayed at before—a block or two off Hollywood Boulevard, on the corner of Yucca and Something Else. (I'm not totally green. Behind me a year or two is a stretch as a writer-consultant in ETV, and a turn, before cameras, as an interviewer—in Hollywood, at that.) In the morning I go to work. I drive out to Universal City, meet my people, observe shooting on sound stages and the back lot, attend a script conference, a casting conference, a rap session and a gabfest, and begin "interviewing" producers, writers, coordinators, directors. Succeeding days are the same, and the notes pile up. ("Carol, darling, take your own time to sit down. Don't feel obligated to do it on the cue." . . . "Okay, it's *between* a rewrite and a polish." . . . "Are you going to eat that during the shot?" . . . "We need an inch under Ben." "Give Ben an inch and he'll take a mile." . . . "Roll 'em and go." . . .)

On toward dinnertime in the evening I walk over with the producer and his helpers to the projection room to watch the day's prints. (The footage is for *Run for Your Life,* a serial dramatic show about a young man with a year to live.) Afterward, sliding out of most invitations, I drive back to my motel, swim in the pool, mix a drink, eat alone, late, at this or that Pow Beefhouse along La Cienaga, and return home to work for an hour, pulling notes into paragraphs. Several days of this and I say my thankyous, pack up, and fly home. My "report" takes a weekend to finish (the foundation man likes it)—whereupon exams come in and the gig's up. . . . A trip, another carbon MS in a manila folder, a vanished check—day in the life of a culture reporter/professor . . . The story in theory ends here.

Suppose for a moment, though, that we wanted to go on with it—in the New Style, in Involvedese—with an eye to clarifying differences between new journalism and old novels. Could it be done? Is there a formula to follow? Guidelines for tyro In-

volveders? Hints? Rules? The answer is Yes of course, rules a-
plenty. In some particulars, indeed, the forms and conventions of
Involvedese are as tight as those of an aubade. (The conventions
include a set tone—conscientious embitterment; a set conflict—
Good Guy vs. Bad Guy within the reporter; a set pattern of
character development—the reporter is first a clown, then a heel,
then a seer, and a set climax or reversal or peripeteia—exposure
of the Involved Audience's vanity and hypocrisy.) —But why so
many words, as the wave said to the fisherman. Let's run the
junket through the involving machine and look at the scenario
that comes forth.

The first sight, naturally, is my public Universal City self,
angled to reveal a naïf, a Country Joe clownishly enjoying the
local magic, sloping about in a mist of stock responses. . . .

Item: a projection-room audition. After the dailies, the producer watches clips of starlets—casting is incomplete for a segment due to start filming in the morning. A face pleases him.
Backwind: he looks again. The girl speaks only a single line in
the clip. Striking wide eyes. "Get her," is the word to the casting
people. They set out on a telephone search. My heart races. I'm
hot for the sweepstakes: will A Star be born? They give up after
half an hour, and in a different but still charged mood, I think:
Sad, sad . . . Poor child. So near yet so far. Who'll ever know?

Item: A moment on the sound stage. Star and ingenue playing
to each other. (PAUL [almost a whisper]: "I'm sorry, Kate. I'm
sorry." KATE: "Oh, Paul . . . I've never blamed you—") Beautiful. I love it. I sigh with the ingenue, turn away with her, share
the inexplicability of things that keeps them from life together, a
future. . . . The director snaps his fingers, signaling the end of
the take, and delightedly I catch a glance—shy? approving?—
that passes between Star and girl. They like each other, then?
They're together, really together? I'm in rapture.

Item: Script conference. A new young director calls on the
producer to complain about the logic of the script he's to direct
the following week. A recent Harvard grad, producer of the

undergraduate version of Kopit's first play. Attractive, person-
able . . . I don't follow the talk closely enough—miss my chance
to find out how sharp the lad is, whether he's another slumming
Harvardian or someone earnestly trying to redeem his assignment. Plain enough why I wander off: "in my heart" I already
know the score. He's a Harvard, isn't he? That means he's okay.
Harvard in Hollywood sticks up for integrity, and rightly so.
People respect people who stand up for themselves. You're damn
straight. Up quality! Up taste! Reinhart!

—Well and good: we've got a tease and a theme—reporter as
nit. It needs underlining and development. More confession,
more personification of the vision. How about a backward glance,
like so—

I've always been a boob out in Hollywood. I gorged on stereotypes the last time too. In my educational telly days, I plumped
for a D. W. Griffith bio-special that presented the man as a noble
artist-voyager afloat on a sea of muck. (Camera tight on bronze
Hollywood Boulevard sidewalk star bearing Griffith's name, as
the voiceover laments—during pullback to twoshot—the chewing
gum that pedestrians grind into his memory.) Nor is that the half
of it. I'm forever sucking up to local values out there. It's true.
Was I not ecstatic—on this trip—when asked for my views at a
script conference? Did I not become embarrassed about my drab
professorial rented compact car? At home it's easy to be properly
sniffish about posh car conspicuousness, but out there— The
truth is, I'm *extremely vulnerable to corruption.* Going in and out
of the gate I avoided the guard's eyes; I was downright furtive.

And the night I accepted an invitation to dine with a Biggie—
more sin. We climb out of the chauffeured car in Bel Air; I follow
the cigar through the voluptuous house, single-file line of march,
children, maids, dogs, hanging on, hoping to delay our passage.
(Same bit every night, the man says, patting this one, shaking
that one off.) And we slip out a side Dutch door through a lush
garden to a pool house—domesticity left behind, sweet young
bird waiting on pool terrace to make drinks. "We" three eat by
ourselves, chuckling, happy, *yé-yé*, we here, they there. . . . Did

I speak up for the family? for good solid middle-class values? I did not. I read my way deep into this alien pattern: two worlds, eh? servants and children in one, yes, grown-ups separate, hmmmm. Mmmmmmmmm?

—Pause here, frowning—a moment of perplexed search for self-understanding. Or for self-justification or for a rationalization. Perhaps my finkery was actually good manners. (Would it not have been rude to confront hospitality with a solemn endorsement of family togetherness?) Perhaps the sucking up was determined in my youth—spells cast over me in the Fantasy Theater off Sunrise Highway in hometownville. Saturday afternoon, enfolded, glass bell over me, hurrying away from the flicks. Safe in the schoolyard, screened from sight, I fight the air and smash chins (if the flick's been Gable or Garfield), or, if it's Sophisticated Comedy, I light my Sensation with Bill Powell's insouciance and speak out in Cary Grant's voice. Having once adored the glamour, having once given up my whole self to it, having once become a mere echo, could I have expected to break out of myself in the real Hollywood? . . .

—Okay: we've made it to the middle. Our line thus far—for the Involvedese Scenario—is that in the daytime Uni-City was Fun City for me. A place where my mind cut off altogether and I shuttled about from one act of identification to another—fool, fraud, boozer, comic, happy sunshine sycophant.

But at night—here's a key moment: we're turning toward The Deeper Guilt—at night and the following weekend I stopped shuttling. Another character rose up in me and held the floor: the foundation fink, the "culture critic." I try to be fair to him at first. I say, In a way the culture critic was doing the best he could. We have to have people like that. It's a condition of The Culture. The Culture Critic had specific questions to answer about morale, taste-levels, and the like. He was just doing his job. Ah but *no*, dammit. (This is an emotional outburst.) I *loved* the job. I was shameless. My behavior as Culture Critic was downright treacherous. Did I so much as hesitate, for instance, before invoking alienation theory behind my hosts' backs? No, I did not, witness this paragraph of my report:

> . . . no community interest or shared sense of responsibility for the finished segment of a series show unifies production staff and performers, directors, men on the set. . . . The executive producer. . . and his immediate associates are usually visible to others chiefly in entrepreneurial roles: they are artificially drawn off into a separation—as "coordinators" of ungraspable multiplicities. . . . Stereotypes of art versus business harden. Tensions, frictions, suspicions deplete trust. Feelings of powerlessness burgeon. . . . The performer retreats into a reductive sense of himself, experiences no sense of control over the production as a whole, and at length dwindles into self-pity. . . .

Furthermore I savaged the product itself, never hinting how I dug The Stars:

> *Run for Your Life* is fairly described as a fantasy. The *shtick* is the imminent death of the hero, which places him beyond ordinary moral chastisement (whatever the behavior, decency would feel compelled to forgive it). The hero has a positive obligation to sin. He was created as a sophisticated, attractive, appetitive hero—and if such a figure were to form a permanent relation with a girl, he would be guilty of self-indulgence, or even of cruelty itself. The character of his situation therefore establishes or suggests a world in which promiscuity is probity—and that world is scarcely unwelcoming to mass fantasy and desire. If the imminence of death were constantly stressed, true enough, the fantasy would be contained or qualified. But here again the executive producer is alert—too alert—to the substance of the program's appeal. He remarks that he avoids scripts which make much of the death theme and turn the viewer's face too blankly toward reality.

Even at the moment of final survey, I held to my lying condescension, and spoke in pained distaste:

> There are elements of garish pseudo-sophistication in various segments of *Run for Your Life,* and the dialogue abounds in three-dot waffle. (Sample provided.) But the precedents for this warmed-over

Sagan—if not for promiscuity and bloody socking matches—in the radio soaps of the thirties and in sentimental ladies' fiction of the late nineteenth century are past counting. Neither show nor hero is an inexplicable phenomenon, a freak of culture. Both are continuous with America, part of a seamless cultural whole. What is unappetizing about them is also unappetizing about Ford Galaxies, Holiday Inns, Hollywood Boulevard between Highland and Vine, the teary-sincere orator in LBJ, the smile of the airline stewardess, *Valley of the Dolls*, many commencement speeches, and perhaps half the articles in this month's issues of the "quality" magazines. Style, discipline, clarity of thought, fullness of understanding are lacking—and the heart is nevertheless somehow vaguely felt to be in the right place.

Am I not a wretched soul to have set myself up so high! Am I not a hypocrite to have left my own clowning goof-off response so far behind!

—Time for the kicker, the close. We need a moment wherein "I" the Involved Reporter get it in the ear, am *caught out* in my fundamental insincerity and guilt. No problem: life supplies the *shtick*. Within months of my trip to "the coast" my two opposing selves—Detached Critic and Secret Showbiz Buff—clanked against each other noisily in public, did they not? Knowing only the part of my nature that I cheesily dressed out for them, the producers of *Run for Your Life* trustingly wrote me into one of their scripts. Ben Gazzara, Star, takes down a book "By Benjamin DeMott" from the shelf of a new girl friend's apartment, and comments in a way suggesting that anyone who reads my work must be highly educated and a person of Natural Taste. At the time I was asked to release my name for this use, I was touched. Showbiz, ah, Showbiz! But time passes. They catch up with you. At the end of a class last spring, a spiky straight-A student wheels up to incorruptible me and says, You were on TV last night, a real lousy show, how come? Feeling the tide of his disillusionment (Say it isn't so, Prof), I hang there suspended, as I hang here in the final paragraph of this swell piece of Involved

Reportage. I hang suspended and then pretend puzzlement, not having the courage to face him.

But though I acknowledge no complicity, turn away, I am—at least for an instant—nailed. And you know it, Reader, don't you? You wanted it. You want to whip me. Chew me. You're rejoicing because I got what I deserved, right? So you see? *You're another.* No compassion. We're all [obscenity] together and it was ever thus. Whereupon we

GO TO BLACK

As should be said at once, an essay that fleshed out the model above with appropriate details, intensities, and dirty words wouldn't by any means be useless. It could put a reader in touch with several bits of conventional wisdom about contemporary life—as for example that even on holiday people see their inner world as conflict-ridden; and that a man's fantasies rouse contradictory responses—joy, shame—inside him; and that the objectifying culture which seeks to neutralize "the personal" imposes strains and falsehoods; and that, responding to this pressure, people discipline themselves, separate their parts and arrange them in hierarchies, in order to create a viable professional self.

But despite these reminders, these occasional gestures at something beyond the Involved Reporter, the actual function of such writing isn't, as the small scenario should show, to bring a world into general view. On the contrary, the function is to explore a literary mode of self-suspicion. The explorations are often witty, sometimes intense. There is a certain play within the tone of embitterment. It's flexible enough to accommodate ruefulness and embarrassment (see Andrew Kopkind on serving *Time* in the *New York Review of Books*), as well as earnest, caring, self-chiding (see Murray Kempton defining, in *The Spectator*, his feelings of guilt after the murder of Bobby Kennedy). A disciplined reporter occasionally makes his guilt felt in a piece without explicitly focusing on it—see Tom Wolfe's piece on a father-son, adman-hippie confrontation in the Village (*The*

Kandy-Kolored Tangerine-Flake Streamline Baby), or Rex Reed's account of a family Sunday at the Paul Newmans', unaccredited sightseers and tourists milling outside while Reed is well treated within (*New York Sunday Times*, September 1, 1968).

But too often the impression, no matter what the precise tonal register or level of discipline, is that form has preceded substance. Selection of details both from outward events and inward response lights up discontinuity, opportunism, insincerity; personal rumination curves repeatedly, deterministically, toward the occasion when the reporter "finds himself out." Conscious from the start of an obligation ever to inch his way toward a more solidly cynical idea of a person, the writer speaks always with a self-deprecatory tic.

The tic has a history, naturally, and a sociology as well. Reductive versions of humankind have been standard items in Western thought for longer than a century. Psychiatry has enlarged the market, as Seymour Krim—his essay "Making It" (1968) is a landmark in the development of Involvedese—once pointed out:

> In the climate we all make it in, the age of suspicion, putdown, sneer, needle, it's almost inevitable that a swinging person is going to probe himself for the hidden motivations in the way he acts, makes his little scenes. Introspection is the private playground of every brain around, there's no escaping it, and especially in New York where psychiatry has gotten such an incredible play is there a used condom of doubt that drags down every full-hearted gesture into the subway mire of the psyche's triple-dealing [*sic*]. Face it, man—nothing is safe in our world from the meanest interpretation, nothing is pure or uncomplex, nothing but *nothing* escapes from the enlarged vocabulary of analysis that our quick and unhappy minds grind out for sheer dissonant sport.

And the appetite for cynical views of the person is now fed everywhere in the media. Think of the endless series of Feiffer cartoons (Instant John Osborne, Instant Underground Man) showing sad-faced middle-class types abusing their moral character, and then being congratulated by their audience:

Your Honor [says a Feiffer character in panel one] . . . Ladies and Gentlemen of the jury [panel 2] . . . I have great potential but no follow through [3]. . . . I have contempt for the values of success but I secretly hunger to be successful [4]. . . . I don't know what love is, which is why I avoid all serious relationships [5]. . . . I make a great show of interest in other people but I'm *really* only interested in myself [6]. . . . I've never deliberately hurt anyone in my life but I always feel guilty [7]. . . . I throw myself on the mercy of the court [8]. . . .

In the next-to-last panel the jury speaks:

The jury finds the defendant a fine, insightful person who is not afraid to be brutally honest with himself.

And in the last panel the man departs, slick, buoyant, smug in briefcase and cigarette holder. "Justice triumphs," is his conclusion. The message is: Self-love is a disease beyond remedy. You cannot confess without strengthening your sense of invulnerability. "He who despises himself esteems himself as a self-despiser." The evil in me is beyond my capacity to name and know. From the trap of guilt there's no possibility of escape.

Or think of the insistence with which the same ground theme sounds in the work of the literary masters of Involvedese—witness the central passages of Norman Mailer's *Armies of the Night*, wherein the writer details his guilt at not spending another night in jail:

. . . a failure of nerve always presented the same kind of moral nausea. Probably he [Mailer] was feeling now like people who had gone to the Pentagon, but had chosen not to get arrested, just as such people, at their moment of decision, must have felt as sickened as all people who should have marched from Lincoln Memorial to the Pentagon, but didn't. The same set of emotions could be anticipated for all people who had been afraid to leave New York. One ejected oneself from guilt by climbing the ladder—the first step back, no matter where, offered nothing but immersion into nausea. No wonder people hated to disturb their balance of guilt. To become less guilty, then weaken long enough to return to guilt was worse than to remain cemented in your guilt.

"That passage," says Mr. Hentoff, not only "draws you in," it "brings you the news about the rest of your life." And again the news is that "for the rest of our life" we must wear another man's dirty shirts.

News of this kind resembles dogma more than things as they are, and some who are in close touch with their own full human complication are likely to resist it. Sustaining an uncomplacent, non-beamish resistance is impossible, however, without protection from cynicism about the person—and what protection can be found? I can mumble commonplaces and truisms at guilt-mongers. I can talk to myself about the connectedness of human parts, about the interdependency of self-love and self-criticism, about the intimate relation between human fantasy and social hope. I can remind myself that the common (and absurd) day-dream of escape from conditioned existence into Absolute Integrity or Beauty or Guiltlessness is at the same time a force charging me to invent new models of life, and reinvigorating old standards of assessment. I can lay it down that men's dignifying severities of self-scrutiny have roots in indulgence, that responsibilities begin in irresponsibility, and that the compulsion to believe the worst of ourselves—the style of conscientious embitterment, dutiful self-hatred—is in fact a vanity, a fleece-lined hair shirt, bearing no relation to genuine humility or genuine pride, and invariably deflecting both understanding and the will to modify or re-create the conditions.

But, expressed thus, these truths are the merest chat, worthless until the meaning is known from inside. And the case is—coming at last to the point—that there are few surer ways into that meaning than through imaginative writing. To say this, to say that fiction alone draws us out from the cage of self into caring, knowledgeable concern for the life that is not our own, isn't to claim that novelists and storytellers are untouched by high-fashion self-hatred. Neither is it to say that journalism by literary men never draws a person out in the fashion described. (There are hints of conscience-nagging in George Plimpton's *Paper Lion;* the writer once or twice damns himself for an interloper, etc. But because his subject permits lightheartedness, and because he himself has virtually a lover's feeling for the charm of his own fantasy, he can bear to let his reader see beyond him.)

It is to say, though, that creating a story, whether as writer or reader, is an act capable of liberating people from the boring predictabilities of self-regard. That creation is a means of living into the interdependency of "best self" and "worst self," and of pushing beyond artificial borders, beyond official moral simplifications of human motivation, beyond this year's lit-establishment tone and style of self-assessment, into a clearer, denser, fresher world. Reading or writing, I indulge my desire or need to be someone else, to be a different person in a better world—and am reminded that this desire is at once an indulgence and a moral distinction—and am lifted (briefly, that is true, only briefly) by this "literary" experience to a kind of behavior both as judge and as fantasist that possesses unfaked dignity. I oscillate between permissible identifications with other human beings and an attainable detachment. I sense contrarieties pressing inside the next man. I'm elevated by the act of judging deeds that aren't mine, but that are yet known to me from within.

And it *is* the judgment—that act of judging—that's most exhilarating. Reading and writing fiction is far from a murky love-in or flower kiddies' ball. It is an act requiring sympathy, since "understanding" is the goal—but not an extravagant sympathy of the kind that chokes the sense of justice. Reading *Anna Karenina* I'm not simply bewildered or amused that Oblonsky can at the same time be wretched about his faithlessness to Dolly and tickled by some wisp of recollection of the "bewitching" governess. I don't simply take this response or conduct in a forgiving spirit, or regard it as a determined event, inescapable. I come at its inevitability from within. I feel the regrettable yet, for him, oddly pleasing limitlessness of what we cannot control. I understand that the conscience that pains Oblonsky also delights him by reminding him of his personal attractiveness. I am unremittingly aware of the reciprocities of what is called "virtue" and what is called "vice," conscious of the hollowness of appeals to Integrity as a separable entity in itself, alert to the complex process by which new vanities and new moral aspirations wake to life simultaneously within human beings. And *yet none of this knowledge paralyzes me.* I assess the relative significance of the character's conscience in my inward experience as I read; I understand that Oblonsky is a small man, less than a man can be, and in the act of understanding I rise for a while above the naïf or gull within me, above my smallness, and out of chichi self-contempt.

A voice says: It sounds mysterious. Reading and writing fiction equal judging yourself from outside, judging another from within. . . . Can you tell it simpler, please?

It's not, finally, a simple matter, I suppose. And for that reason people who talk about fiction in terms of volume of news, competition with Huntley-Brinkley, or with Mailer at a convention, or Capote at an execution, seem to me (I confess) dim. A story is an orchestration or score of sympathy and judgment, penetration and objectification: now the one predominates, now the other, but both are always at hand, stimulating each other, letting us out of ourselves, calling us back to judge our trip. I need such scores for several reasons. Partly because through them it's possible to touch a life of feeling or an idea of personhood superior to the one in current journalistic fashion, yet not so far beyond me as that still proposed by the religious establishments. Partly because the possession of a means of motion forth from the self spins me out of simplicities of self-laceration and doom-mongering. Partly because, through the novel—again: either by writing or reading it—I touch my borders, such as they are, become an expanded constructive sympathy, an expanded self. No more rewinding myself perpetually onto the spindle of a passive shame: I spring with the word toward its target and take the force of the impact from within.

—Fine, oh, fine, says a harsher voice: I get it. Writing fiction is an ego rub. It builds self-satisfaction. It lets you like yourself. —You think that's proper? In a time like this we should go about savoring our beauties and excellences?

Well, it hurts to say so, true. And no use pointing out, defensively, that there are complacencies in stylized guilt (the news of my whole life) as well as in shrugging self-acceptance. For, once that point is made, you're back again in abstract argument, speaking up solemnly for some famous elusive "balanced attitude toward life," etc. Who can know what balance is? The best I know is that I like truth of the sort implicit in Thoreau's lovely springy sentence: "When I am condemned and condemn myself utterly, I think straightway, 'But I rely on love for some things.'" I like, that is to say, a truth of resiliency, a truth about how we spring out, spring back, aren't by any means "indomitable," yet seldom are put down by sorrow or guilt, can cross over, can know from within. Such truth doesn't belong to the new journalism; the mode is too uniformly blackish and self-accusatory. But in the bright book of life, the novel, you can sometimes touch it—which is why, even in a bad moment, people will get on with the work.

—Well and good, says one last voice, kinder and more relaxed. But you've not said how it really went out there, have you? Out in Hollywood? You remember you started—

How it *really* went? In the end that's another subject, not at all close to the one in view here (is fiction finished?). It is the subject of values shaken, the challenge of fantasy—not fit stuff (to repeat) either for Involvedese or for the lingo of the Culture Critic. The subject does come up, though, in something of mine available for a price downtown—a book that has, for a stretch, a Hollywood setting. The work is called A Novel, and I can speak of it at any time without feeling pushy, guilty, or the like. For the idea of speaking of it is only to rouse a pleasant memory. Thinking back on "the work," talking about it, I remember writing it—the experience rushes into mind, the freedom, sense of perfectability. . . . How happy I was!—happiness being nothing more nor less than a road by which it does seem possible truly to get there from here.

Acknowledgments

The author thanks Theodore Baird, Fred Baron, Seelye Bixler, John Cameron, Muriel Crosson, Larry Dilg, Barbara Hardy, George Kateb, Leo Marx, Bea McKie, James Merrill, Floyd Merritt, Dave Michelmore, Lewis Mudge, Franklin Patterson, William Pritchard, Edwin Rozwenc, John Simon, James Steinman, and Rosa White for generous help of many kinds.

PRENTICE-HALL

Foundations of Cultural Geography Series
PHILIP L. WAGNER, Editor

RICHARD E. DAHLBERG, Series Cartographer

*In Prentice-Hall's Foundations of Economic Geography Series, also.

Foundations of Cultural Geography Series

RICHARD E. DAHLBERG, *Series Cartographer*

The
Cultural Geography
of the
United States

WILBUR ZELINSKY

Professor of Geography
Pennsylvania State University

PRENTICE-HALL, INC., Englewood Cliffs, N. J.

CARL A. RUDISILL LIBRARY
LENOIR RHYNE COLLEGE
HICKORY, N. C. 28601

Library of Congress Cataloging in Publication Data

Zelinsky, Wilbur.
    The cultural geography of the United States.

    (Foundations of cultural geography series)
    Bibliography: p.
    1. United States—Civilization.   2. Anthropo-geography—United States.
    3. National characteristics, American.   I. Title.
    E169.1.Z38   917.3'03   72-4503
    ISBN 0-13-195503-9
    ISBN 0-13-195495-4 (pbk.)

© *1973 by Prentice-Hall, Inc.*
Englewood Cliffs, N. J.

All rights reserved. No part of this book may be reproduced in
any form or by any means without permission in writing from
the publisher. Printed in the United States of America.

10   9   8   7   6   5   4   3   2   1

917.303
ze3c
92963
april 1975

PRENTICE-HALL INTERNATIONAL, INC., *London*
PRENTICE-HALL OF AUSTRALIA, PTY. LTD., *Sydney*
PRENTICE-HALL OF CANADA, LTD., *Toronto*
PRENTICE-HALL OF INDIA PRIVATE LIMITED, *New Delhi*
PRENTICE-HALL OF JAPAN, INC., *Tokyo*

to the land I have loved the most

Foundations of Cultural Geography Series

The title of this series, Foundations of Cultural Geography, represents its purpose well. Our huge and highly variegated store of knowledge about the ways that humans occupy and use their world becomes most meaningful when studied in the light of certain basic questions. Original studies of such basic questions make up this series of books by leading scholars in the field.

The authors of the series report and evaluate current thought centered on the questions: How do widely different systems of ideas and practice influence what people do to recreate and utilize their habitats? How do such systems of thought and habitat spread and evolve? How do human efforts actually change environments, and with what effects?

These questions are approached comparatively, respecting the great range of choice and experience available to mankind. They are treated historically as well, to trace and interpret and assess what man has done at various times and places. They are studied functionally, too, and whatever controlling processes and relationships they may reveal are sought.

Diverse tastes and talents govern the authors' attack on these problems. One deals with religion as a system of ideas both influencing and reflecting environmental conditions. Another evaluates the role of belief and custom in reshaping plant animal species to human purposes. Some consider the use and meaning of human creations, like houses or cities, in geographic context; others treat of the subtle and complex relationships with nature found in agricultural systems of many sorts. One author looks at an entire country as a culturally-shaped environment; another analyzes the mechanics of the spread of customs and beliefs in space. All work toward an understanding of the same key problems. We invite the reader to participate actively in the critical rethinking by which scholarship moves forward.

PHILIP L. WAGNER

"E pluribus unum" presents a worthy problem for cultural geography. How did the United States become indeed united, and just what *is* truly united about the country and its peoples? What are the many out of which the one is constituted, and how do they express their own distinctiveness?

A longtime keen and careful student of American cultural features, Professor Wilbur Zelinsky here attempts a broad interpretation of the United States as a cultural geographic phenomenon, relating its diversity of values and perceptions, cultural currents and diffusions, landscapes and regions, to the larger national unity.

Philip L. Wagner

Contents

PART *spatial expression*

PART 1 background

CHAPTER ONE

Origins

Why the United States?

"What, then, is the American, this new man?"[1] After nearly two centuries, de Crévecoeur's haunting question still cries out as piercingly and urgently as ever. Wherever his home and whatever his calling, the concerned citizen of the late twentieth century must persist in the endless job of interpreting and understanding the most powerful and innovative nation in the world. The literature on the United States—on its land, its people, and their ways and institutions—has grown to mountainous proportions; but new questions arise constantly, and more quickly than the old ones can be answered.

It is to one of these emergent themes that this volume—the first attempt to view the cultural geography of the United States synoptically—is addressed. In what ways has the particular configuration of the American cultural system shaped spatial processes and structures in this nation? How has it molded the visible, and invisible, features of the landscape, or the ways in which the American has evolved his behavior over space and his perceptions of, and interactions with, other people, his habitat, and with ideas both near and far?[2] And how, in turn, have these areal facts modified and channeled the development of the cultural system? In brief, what can a reading of the spatial dimensions of American culture contribute to the unfinished chore of explaining this mighty, dynamic outpost of mankind's future? Obviously, "America watching" is a mandatory activity for those who care about the welfare of the species *Homo*

1 J. Hector St. John de Crèvecoeur, *Letters from an American Farmer* (London: Thomas Davies, 1782), p. 51.
2 The concept of culture is defined and discussed in detail in A. L. Kroeber, *The Nature of Culture* (Chicago: University of Chicago Press, 1952). For general introductions to the field of cultural geography and its concepts and methods, consult Philip L. Wagner and Marvin W. Mikesell, eds., *Readings in Cultural Geography*

sapiens or for those who are simply smitten with affection for this lovely and fragile planet. It is also an effective strategy for the scholar intent upon tracking down abstract scientific truth.

Indeed for the student in quest of lawlike statements about cultural geography, the United States is almost too good to be true. He would be hard pressed to identify—or invent—a better country for accumulating facts, for asking basic questions, or for experimenting with new approaches. Given the recent origin of American culture, along with the relative simplicity of its areal expression, America is as nearly ideal a laboratory as could be desired. The cultural landscapes of much of the Old World might be characterized as intricate and ancient, of uncertain origin, revealing multiple time levels and the handiwork of many ethnic groups. In the United States, on the other hand, we deal with what we have come to regard, all too ethnocentrically, as a virtual *tabula rasa* at the outset of European settlement. Actors entering a nearly bare stage play out their roles rapidly, directly, and with few complications of plot. In addition, through pure happenstance, the texture of the "natural" landscape upon which American culture evolved and spread so rapidly tends to be coarser than in most parts of Europe, Asia, or Middle America. Its physiographic, climatic, and biotic provinces are broader and less often punctuated by minor irregularities that might catalyze and shelter local cultural peculiarity. Yet the American cultural scene is by no means a dull, uniform, featureless affair; there is sufficient variety from place to place and through time to entice the student of culture, but not so much as to frustrate or bewilder him. All in all, the accessibility of the American record and its relative transparency as to essential cultural structure and process is an open invitation to scholarly investigation.

A further attraction is the almost embarrassing abundance and variety of raw data, from the beginning to the present. The entire process of European exploration, occupation, and development was richly documented by many literate, alert, and fascinated participants and visitors from earliest days onward; and a great store of words, drawings, pictures, maps, digits, and other durable artifacts have been generated. Thanks to the infrequency of domestic disturbances and large-scale property destruction, most of this material endures. The major problem is selection and digestion.

If scientific expediency and an extraordinary availability of facts (neglected though many of them may be) were not adequate excuses for settling on the United States to demonstrate some basic concerns and devices of cultural geography, we can return to the ultimate argument. By definition, all places are unique; but the United States is unique in

(Chicago: University of Chicago Press, 1962); Philip L. Wagner, *The Human Use of the Earth* (New York: The Free Press, 1960); George F. Carter, *Man and the Land; a Cultural Geography,* 2d ed. (New York: Holt, Rinehart & Winston, Inc., 1968); Joseph E. Spencer and William L. Thomas, Jr., *Cultural Geography; an Evolutionary Introduction to Our Humanized Earth* (New York: John Wiley & Sons, Inc., 1969); and Samuel N. Dicken and Forrest R. Pitts, *Introduction to Cultural Geography* (Waltham, Mass.: Xerox College Publishing, 1971).

a manner that transcends the parochial pride or interest of its citizens. Quite clearly the United States is the most powerful nation of the contemporary world in both economic and military terms. This nation also retains much of its traditional strength as a moral force, and has had few recent rivals as a generator of science and technology, or as an exporter of tourists, religious and linguistic influences, and a varied cargo of the popular and fine arts. Thus the cultural personality and behavior of American man is literally of worldwide importance, and quite possibly crucial in deciding the survival or further progress of the human species.

Basic Processes of American Cultural Development

The origin and development of some of the distinguishing features of American culture must be sketched before treating its geography. Basic to this entire discussion is the premise that the United States belongs to the Greater European cultural realm, and that in all essentials our culture is derived from that of Northwest Europe and, most particularly, of Great Britain. This is not to claim that non-British or non-European sources have not contributed to the peculiar American cultural blend, for they obviously have, but simply to assert the powerful genealogical fact that British cultural parentage underlies all else. But if one glances at some of the more extreme forms of American cultural development and then compares them with developments in England past or present, any immediate kinship may be difficult to detect. How, then, did American culture come to be what it is today? The following five processes would seem to have been at work and, in combination, to account for that rapid, massive transformation of Old World elements into the singular American compound.

1. *The importation of selected individuals and, hence, selected cultural traits.* As crucial an item as any in the formation of American culture was the fact that the immigrants who shaped it were not random samples of the Old World population from which they were drawn. Instead, they were selected, consciously or otherwise, for specific attributes; and these attributes, in turn, were probably decisive in imparting to the new cultural system the specific shape and direction it was to follow.

2. *The simple fact of long-distance transfer of people and their cultural freight.* The very act of transporting settlers from Europe (or Africa) across the Atlantic to North America served to initiate social and cultural alterations of some consequence. We have here a "sea change" phenomenon: the forced shipboard association for some weeks or months of persons who had been strangers; the all-too-frequent traumatic impact of the voyage itself; the thrust into unfamiliar physical surroundings; the struggle to establish a viable community during the critical early months in America. Inevitably, the transferred group was noticeably modified by this experience. This is illustrated by solicitous attempts at transplanting certain European groups intact and arresting change in their new setting. In the case of New France and New Spain or some minor groups along the Atlantic Seaboard, the product was

still a colony distinct from the antecedent society.[3] One way of interpreting the founding of a New England is that it was in part an effort
to restore the pristine purity of a vanishing, perhaps imaginary ideal
England. The result, however, was again a community quite different
from the intended model.[4] In brief, then, the abrupt relocation of people
across great distances inevitably generates cultural change, however
zealously the immigrants may try to prevent such change.

3. *Cultural borrowings from the aboriginal populations.* The adoption of certain cultural items from the Amerindians—or, more precisely,
the process of cultural interchange between aborigine and newcomer—
was a minor factor, except perhaps locally and temporarily, in the creation of the Euro-American cultural system. Nonetheless, the immigrants
did not enter a total human vacuum; and there was some transfer of
items, despite the great cultural gap among the peoples involved and,
especially, the vast disparity in levels of socioeconomic achievement.

4. *The local evolution of American culture.* With the coming of
various groups of selected immigrants to North America, their survival
past the first critical episodes of contact with a strange land, and perhaps
some dealings with the aboriginal folk, there began in earnest the evolution *in situ* of a recognizably American set of cultures, later to form a
single national system, through the operation of at least five processes,
as follows:

   a. There was selection of cultural traits from among those transmitted
   from overseas. Obsolete or irrelevant items (for example, most of the
   feudalistic social and landholding practices) withered and died, but
   others, previously latent or minor but now of major survival value
   (for example, woodcraft, hunting and fishing techniques, and systems
   of slave or contract labor), flourished and developed new variants.

   b. In a fashion analagous to the genetic drift observed by biologists,
   small random cultural mutations occurring at all times to all groups
   may emerge as events of lasting effect amidst minute groups living
   under isolated conditions. Thus it is quite possible that in the earlier
   days of colonization, when settlements were small and scattered,
   miles were longer, governmental control was quite inefficient, and
   communications were slow and uncertain, pure chance may have
   nudged cultural evolution in specific directions in different regions.

   c. The interaction between new settler and various phases of the
   physical habitat almost certainly engendered cultural change. This

---

[3] The processes of cultural transfer and transformation are treated in illuminating fashion in George M. Foster, *Culture and Conquest; America's Spanish Heritage,*
Viking Fund Publications in Anthropology No. 27 (New York: Wenner-Gren Foundation for Anthropological Research, 1960).
[4] The phenomenon is well documented in an exemplary case study: Sumner
Chilton Powell, *Puritan Village; the Formation of a New England Town* (Middletown, Conn.: Wesleyan University Press, 1963). A similar story of the difficulties
of transplanting the traditional social order and mode of landholding is detailed in
Richard Colebrook Harris, *The Seigneurial System in Early Canada; A Geographical
Study* (Madison and Quebec: University of Wisconsin Press and Les Presses de
l'Université Laval, 1966).

came about either more or less directly through the settler's physiological or psychological responses to novel environmental stimuli or, indirectly, as a byproduct of an economy that, in turn, reflects physical circumstances. This description is not intended to revive the hoary controversy over environmental determinism. Indeed any single-factor, unidirectional determinism must be rejected in the quest for geographic explanation. What must be considered instead are complex *interacting* entities, in this instance the human ecosystem, in which man is assumed to be part of an intricate biophysical system. Within such a set of relationships, cause and effect are inextricably enmeshed so that a given phenomenon is seldom unequivocally one or the other. It would be just as unrealistic to expect the land surface, soils, biota, waters, or microclimates of the country to be unaffected by modern American man as to declare that his pattern of bodily and mental activity and, thus ultimately, his cultural configuration were untouched by the nature of the land.[5]

5 But, after all these disclaimers, there still remains the stubborn likelihood that the specific size, location, and physical characteristics of the American territory were relevant factors in the shaping of American culture; or, to be more realistic, the ways particular people at particular times and places perceived and interacted with these factors did somehow influence the course of cultural development. Unfortunately for scientific purposes, the United States was formed only once; and we can never know with any assurance what might have happened if all other variables were held constant and the same batch of settlers had elected Brazil, Kamchatka, or South Africa. But suppose that instead of a roughly rectangular tract of 3,000,000 square miles some 3,000 miles from the homeland with a very large package of known and available physical resources, those very same British colonizers had picked a small, bleak, roundish, sub-Arctic island only some 800 miles from their ports of embarkation, as did the Norse who tried their luck in Iceland, or a long, narrow, humid tropical island like Cuba, one with little immediate potential beyond the agricultural and pastoral. Would the resultant culture have been the same? The question answers itself. Or does it? The entity whose origin we seek to explain is a set of basic national characteristics common to all members of a large population inhabiting a land of considerable physical diversity. If there is no one single American physical environment, or even a dominant one, or any sensible possibility of arriving at a meaningful *average* environment, then it is indeed hard to say with what universal physical entities the people in question were interacting to produce a unified national culture, or even that such interaction was truly meaningful. Some escape from this dilemma can be sought in certain pervasive, general qualities of the land that transcend local variability in climate, land forms, soil, and biota. These qualities include sheer vastness, wildness, and plenitude of exploitable natural wealth, and a genuine remoteness from ancestral sources and centers of imperial control. There is also the persuasive, but hardly conclusive, positive correlation between the degree of difference from Britain of the general physical habitat and the regional personality of American culture. Thus, for example, the Southern California cultural pattern seems to deviate from that of Great Britain to a greater degree than does New Hampshire's, roughly to the extent that the Southern California habitat is more unlike the British than is New Hampshire's. Put as simply as possible, it can be asserted, but scarcely proved as yet, that some quite broad physical attributes of the American land—matters of location, bulk, level of resource endowment, but not any specific local habitat—*may* have played a role in the genesis of the *general* structure of American culture. At the same time, regional variants from the national pattern *may* be explainable, in part, in terms of particular local sets of environmental conditions.

d. The appearance of new social and economic patterns, in part in symbiotic response to the local habitat, but more meaningfully perhaps in recognition of deeper forces, promoted cultural change. Although the rules of socioeconomic process and change are embedded in the larger cultural system, when such change does finally occur, it can have some reciprocal impact upon basic cultural structure. That the profound and rapid development of American society and economy did indeed modify many aspects of culture, including some not directly social or economic, and even perhaps some of the basic postulates of the cultural system would seem to be an incontrovertible proposition.

e. Finally, the spatial juxtaposition in America of social and ethnic groups that had been widely separated in the Old World led spontaneously to cultural interchange and the diffusion of old and new ideas and thus must have contributed materially to the forging of the special American identity. In particular, as population grew and internal communications improved, the circulation of messages, goods, and travelers could not help but rise sharply and with a pronounced effect upon cultural patterns. The spatial reshuffling of Old World elements yielded interesting cultural consequences.

5. *A continuing interchange with other parts of the world.* Despite chronic problems in transportation, at least up to the present century, the United States has never been isolated from, or uninfluenced by, the cultural evolution of the remainder of the world.[6] The umbilical cord between immigrant and homeland was seldom totally severed and, in fact, much return migration took place. But beyond such personal ties, the country as a whole has been sensitive to cultural currents elsewhere. This was notably the case during the earlier phases of settlement when the Europeans were restricted to small beachheads, each of which was dependent upon a European metropolis. Later on, with national independence and the shift inland, international cross-pollination was less obvious, though still important. More recently, with a sharp acceleration in the tempo of communications, in the commerce of power, goods, and ideas, and in the circulation of visitors, the impact of the outer world on Americans has grown markedly. At the same time, the effects of American culture on other groups has been magnified even more remarkably.

By dismembering in so clinical—and perhaps pedantic—a fashion, by essentially deductive logic, the confused, untidy narrative of American cultural evolution, we may seem to know more than can be truthfully claimed. In essence, we would like to ask who and what came from where, when, and how, and how they behaved after they got here, in dealing with the land, the people they found on it, and their neighbors

---

6 This subject has not yet received the attention it merits, outside the realm of high culture (that is, the fine arts, architecture, letters, and music); but an interesting exploratory attempt is available in Robert O. Mead, *Atlantic Legacy; Essays in American-European Cultural History* (New York: New York University Press, 1969).

near and far. In effect, the preceding paragraphs have outlined an ideal treatment of the historical geography of American culture. Such a monograph is indeed badly needed, and perhaps some day will be feasible; but it is not attempted now, chiefly because our theoretical grasp of the processes of cultural and social change, and of human ecology in general, is still far too primitive to support such an effort. Only fragmentary answers are at hand for any of the queries stated above: it is unlikely that we shall learn very quickly how to analyze fully the ongoing culture changes enveloping us at the moment, much less ever recover enough of the past record to reconstruct unequivocally how Americans came to be the kind of people they are. Furthermore, it is not yet feasible to assign relative weights to the various processes and subprocesses enumerated above. Thus, out of sheer necessity, the basic strategy followed here is descriptive, with only occasional allusions to fundamental process or to larger theory. Nonetheless, although the bulk of this essay is given over to defining sources and end results and to plotting the spatial and temporal contours of our cultural landscapes, with only an occasional boring to the rock-bottom of cultural process, it is in that dark, uncharted realm that we must begin to grope for the larger scientific answers in the not-too-distant future.

Parallels with Other Parts of the World

It cannot be said too often that the means whereby American culture acquired its present form are not peculiar to this part of the world, or that this national pattern is by no means unique. On the contrary, it is useful to classify the United States as a member of a rather large set of countries: the neo-European lands whose culture, population, or both were derived from European sources and implanted successfully at some distance from the homeland, beginning in about 1500 A.D. More specifically, the United States can be viewed as belonging to either of two intersecting subsets of this larger group: a Western Hemisphere area, taking in all of the Americas; or that scattered collection of countries that might be labeled neo-British, namely Canada, Australia, New Zealand, South Africa, Rhodesia, and perhaps Eire, the British West Indies, Bermuda, and the Falklands, in addition to the United States.

The identification of a Pan-American cultural realm is hazardous. Aside from whatever fusion of ideas and behavior might result from a none-too-great spatial propinquity and a certain parallelism in political and settlement history, it is hard to put one's finger on cultural features shared by Anglo-America and Latin America.[7] That there may be an underlying pervasive mood, some exclusive set of shared values, is as yet an open question. Are we the victims of wishful geopolitical thinking? At the very least, however, productive analogies, leaving matters of

---

[7] The strong diversity to be found in Latin America is dealt with in John P. Augelli, "The Controversial Image of Latin America: a Geographer's View," *Journal of Geography*, 62, No. 3 (1963), 105–12.

genuine kinship in abeyance, can be worked out with at least two nations: Brazil and Argentina.

The existence of the neo-British cultural community is too obvious to be argued. Despite great spatial intervals, locations in frequently dissimilar habitats, and envelopment within strikingly alien indigenous and immigrant groups, the family ties and continuities of these sibling countries persist. If ever there were a ready-made laboratory situation for the cultural geographer, here it is. Given two groups of settlers of British background living in two different areas that may, or may not, be physically analogous, how does this or that cultural process develop? Some interesting comparative work has been carried out in the fields of settlement and economic geography,[8] but, rather surprisingly, virtually none aimed directly at cultural issues. Such analyses might be especially worthwhile along the United States-Canadian border, where the only obvious differentials are political and cultural.

The Cultural Legacy of the Old World

We are faced with the problem of describing how much of what was imported into the United States, and to what effect. The matter is immensely complicated by the fact that for the past few centuries Europe has been in a state of swift, even convulsive, change. Adopting a crude metaphor, American immigrants have leaped onto North American soil from a rapidly moving train. Anglo-American culture originated in the very same region that also served as the cradle of modernization. For more than four centuries it has witnessed revolutionary change of a scope, variety, and ultimate planetary impact unmatched in man's million-year existence upon this earth. And if there were profound shifts in the social, political, demographic, scientific, and technological realms, it follows that European cultural patterns were not immune to change.

If we wish, then, to learn what sort of culture the formulators of the American system brought along with them, the current European scene will not be too enlightening. The investigator must resort instead to a rich documentary and archaeological record. Thus, for example, any concern with European antecedents of American folk architecture takes one to old verbal and graphic descriptions and to carefully selected survivals from the past, then to an assessment of basic processes, forms, and meaning—a job, by the way, still waiting to be done properly. A survey of recent construction would be only partially relevant.

A curious byproduct of European cultural dynamism is the fact that

---

8 For example, John E. Brush and Howard E. Bracey, "Rural Service Centers in Southwestern Wisconsin and Southern England," *Geographical Review*, 45, No. 4 (1955), 559–69; Walker D. Wyman and Clifton B. Kroeber, *The Frontier in Perspective* (Madison: University of Wisconsin Press, 1957); Marvin W. Mikesell, "Comparative Studies in Frontier History," *Annals of the Association of American Geographers*, 50, No. 1 (1960), 62–73, and D. W. Meinig, "A Comparative Historical Geography of Two Railnets: Columbia Basin and South Australia," *Ibid.*, 52, No. 4 (1962), 394–413.

some isolated relics of late medieval or early modern European cultural communities have survived in odd corners of the New World, though suffering extinction in the homeland. Thus a reasonable facsimile of the life of seventeenth-century France or the Rhineland can be glimpsed in veritable living museums in the less accessible tracts of Quebec or amidst the Old-Order Amish of Pennsylvania and other states—and found to be utterly different from present-day France or Germany. Much the same story might be told about survivals of early English and Scotch-Irish traits in the remoter tracts of the Appalachians[9] or about the Volga Germans and Doukhobors. Similarly, the student intent upon learning the pre-Socialist culture of the Polish peasant or the eastern European Jewish *shtetl* would be well advised to try Hamtramck, Chicago, or some isolated North American rural colony for the former and Brooklyn for the latter. Within a wider context, the cultural anthropologist seeking a relatively undisturbed pre-contact West African culture would fare better among the Bush Negroes of the Guyana or Surinam hinterland than among the partially modernized tribes of Ghana or Nigeria.

Even though we cannot decipher too many specific items on that crucial early bill of lading of cultural exports from Europe to America, one outstanding conclusion emerges from fragmentary, indirect evidence: the bearers of this culture were not in any sense a representative sample of the people back home. Instead, we find migrants selected, through external circumstance or by themselves, for specific qualities. The movement of Old World natives to the United States—by all odds the largest migrational shift in human history—was largely spontaneous and uncontrolled. Only in the last few decades, and too late to be of decisive effect, has there been any official screening and rejection of entrants. Although a great mass of public and private documents could be mined to ascertain the kinds of people who decided to hazard their fortunes in America, their motivations, and the processes of selection, to date historians and others have barely begun this monumental chore. However, even the present-day demographer, working with voluminous current data and with living informants who can be tested in great depth, confronts severe problems in measuring motivations or in interpreting differentials in skills, intelligence, and personality traits as between migrants and stay-at-homes or among various categories of migrants. Although selectivity is, and has been, of major import, it need not be simply slanted in one direction, nor is it invariant through time and space.

What, then, was unusual, or nonrandom, about those immigrants who came to be the makers of American culture? First of all, as with almost any modern, long-distance migrational stream, the immigrants were largely young adults, sometimes accompanied by children, and a disproportionate number were male. And, as is also characteristic of most

---

9 The persistence of Scotch-Irish cultural practices within North America in general is explored in E. Estyn Evans, "The Scotch-Irish in the New World: an Atlantic Heritage," *Journal of the Royal Society of Antiquaries of Ireland,* 95 (1965), 39–49, and "Cultural Relics of the Ulster-Scots in the Old West of North America," *Ulster Folklife,* 12 (1966), 33–38.

contemporary voluntary movements, they came in the main as single families or individuals rather than in larger groups, although clusters of kinfolk or former neighbors would frequently arrive sequentially in a "chain migration." More to the point, certain countries were overrepresented in the passenger lists—Great Britain initially, others later; from within each of the countries in question, regional representation seems to have been quite uneven. This has been well established for seventeenth-century British migration to Massachusetts and Virginia,[10] and is unquestionably just as true for France, Germany, Italy, West Africa, or any other major generator of migrants. Since the degree of cultural diversity among subnational regions was undoubtedly greater during the crucial early colonial period than is the case today, such localization is of more than passing interest. There was probably also some bias in the recruitment of migrants as between urban and rural areas; the city folk may have been overrepresented, but perhaps not consistently.

Too little genuine research has been done on prior education, occupation, or social class of early (or later) American immigrants for any summary statement. Dismiss, if you will, such silly stereotypes as the Virginia Cavalier or the Georgia convict—the former canonized in local myth as the noblest of human material and the latter seen in a quite different light. One plausible generalization is that, contrary to popular belief, poverty was not the chief spur driving the hopeful across the ocean (except, of course, for such panic migrations as followed the Great Potato Famine in Ireland). More probably, a certain critical threshold of incipient affluence, and the appetite for even more, had to be breached before passage was booked. The regional patterns in the historical geography of American immigration seem to support the assumption that simple wretchedness could not do the trick alone. The African immigrant was subject to selective forces beyond his control. The imbalance between sexes among Africans taken as slaves was unusually great, and there was ruthless weeding out for physical stamina. In addition, particularly accessible areas and tribes furnished the bulk of the slave cargo.

We reach much more solid ground in treating the religious composition of the transplanted Europeans. Quite clearly, the immigrants tended to favor the aberrant creeds, whether of the theological left or right. Thus we find gross overrepresentation in colonial America of such nonestablishment groups as the Congregationalist, Presbyterian, Quaker, Mennonite, or Moravian, and perhaps British and German Baptists; and virtually all the French minority in the American colonies were Huguenot. (See Table 1.1.) There is much more to such a strong incidence of churchly dissent than may meet the eye. Adherence to such "fringe" groups no doubt reflected, and reinforced, certain nonmodal personality types and, it is not too bold to assume, deviant political proclivities.

---

10 Charles O. Paullin and John K. Wright, *Atlas of the Historical Geography of the United States* (Washington, D.C. and New York: Carnegie Institution and American Geographical Society, 1932), 46–47, Plates 70–C, 70–D.

Table 1.1.   Religious Congregations: United States, 1775-1776

Congregational	668	Moravian	31
Presbyterian	588	Congregational-Separatist	24
Episcopalian	495	Mennonite	16
Baptist	494	French Protestant	7
Friends	310	Sandemanian	6
German Reformed	159	Jewish	5
Lutheran	150	Rogerene	3
Dutch Reformed	120	Others	31
Methodist	65	Total	3,228
Catholic	56		

Adapted from Charles O. Paullin and John K. Wright, *Atlas of the Historical Geography of the United States* (Washington, D.C. and New York: Carnegie Institution and American Geographic Society, 1932), p. 50.

Would the American Revolution have succeeded, or even have begun, had the voyagers to the New World been a good stratified sample of the originating population?

The most baffling question for the student of migration is that of the intrinsic quality of those involved. How do they rank in terms of native intelligence or various inherent talents? And what about such vague, but important, psychological traits as aggressiveness, achievement drive, gregariousness, docility or its converse, inner-directedness, other-directedness, and a long list of others? All of these are extremely difficult to define and even harder to observe and measure, and are not readily scored on a simple linear scale. Quite possibly the American settlers may have deviated in personality structure to a significant degree, but in complex ways, not always in the same direction, from those they left behind. The existence of a distinctive American national character would indicate either that such an entity reflects the cumulated propensities of just such individuals, who gave American culture its decisive early twist, or that the peculiar conditions of early American life would have led to the same end in any event, or, more plausibly, that some convergence of both these factors took place. That is, a rather special cohort of immigrants interacted with one another and a novel physical and socioeconomic setting to form a strikingly new culture.

The identity of the earlier American immigrants is a question reaching well beyond normal antiquarian curiosity. This is because the colonial record so ideally exemplifies the Doctrine of First Effective Settlement, roughly analogous to the psychological principle of imprinting in very young animals. Whenever an empty territory undergoes settlement, or an earlier population is dislodged by invaders, the specific characteristics of the first group able to effect a viable, self-perpetuating society are of crucial significance for the later social and cultural geography of the area, no matter how tiny the initial band of settlers may have been. As an obvious corollary to this statement, we can ignore the nonviable

experiments, for example, the Raleigh group in North Carolina or some
ephemeral shore parties in pre-Puritan New England and elsewhere.[11]
Thus, in terms of lasting impact, the activities of a few hundred, or even
a few score, initial colonizers can mean much more for the cultural
geography of a place than the contributions of tens of thousands of
new immigrants a few generations later. The history of the northeastern
United States clearly illustrates how indelibly the early colonial patterns
have marked its cultural landscape.

It is assumed that the culture of the colonial Atlantic Seaboard and,
hence, of the later continent-spanning Republic was basically, decisively
British. But at least three other distinctively non-British groups were
notably active in the colonial arena, and may have contributed to the
evolving American culture: the aboriginal, the African Negro, and various continental European ethnic groups. Let us look at each of these
in turn.

The Aboriginal Contribution

The aboriginal presence was important for the first wave of pioneers,
not only for the early scattered groups along the coast but for most of
the later vanguard pressing into inland frontiers as well. Friendly Indians
could well tip the balance for physical survival during the very first

11 This is as good an occasion as any to note the fascinating riddle of pre-
Columbian contacts between the Old and New Worlds. Their relevance to the
cultural history and geography of Anglo-America seems much more dubious than
may be the case for the Meso-American and South American civilizations. Yet it is
increasingly obvious that some voyagers did cross the ocean, perhaps more often
by chance than design and not always returning to tell the tale. Indeed it would be
extraordinary if such adventures had not occurred. A number of Chinese, Japanese,
and other Asian vessels must have drifted to the northwest coast of North America;
many undocumented trips between western Europe and eastern North America must
have taken place during the fifteenth century or even earlier; the documentary and
archaeological evidence for at least intermittent Scandinavian exploration, settlement,
and commerce in northeastern North America is irrefutable; the probability of even
earlier Celtic voyages is strong; and the possibility of an occasional transatlantic
excursion during ancient times cannot be dismissed. But, for our purposes, the net
result of all such events is virtually nil. It is barely credible that a few new words
were introduced into aboriginal vocabularies and the odd artifact or custom transferred to the Amerindian; but thus far no convincing argument has been advanced
for a significant modification of either the pre-Columbian North American or any
Old World culture through such casual, shallow contacts. The materials on early
transatlantic contacts are summarized and discussed in Gwyn Jones, *The Norse
Atlantic Saga* (London: Oxford University Press, 1964); Carl O. Sauer, *Northern
Mists* (Berkeley: University of California Press, 1968) and *Sixteenth-Century North
America; the Land and People as Seen by Europeans* (Berkeley: University of California Press, 1971); and Douglas R. McManis, "The Traditions of Vinland," *Annals
of the Association of American Geographers*, 59, No. 4 (1969), 797–814. The
broader range of substantive and theoretical questions concerning early inter-
hemispheric cultural contacts is ably explored in a major symposial volume, Carroll J.
Reilly, J. Charles Kelley, Campbell W. Pennington, and Robert L. Rands, *Man
across the Sea: Problems of Pre-Columbian Contact* (Austin: University of Texas
Press, 1971).

years; less amiable tribes might pose major strategic problems if they chose to maneuver against the white settlers on their own or in league with hostile European powers. Nevertheless the sum of the lasting aboriginal contribution to the North American extension of British culture was distinctly meager, and certainly a great deal less than the European impact upon the aborigines.

First of all, a small absolute number of Indians were available to offer their cultural wares, a number that generally dropped sharply during the initial encounters.[12] In many instances, in fact, the tribe simply vanished through abnormally high mortality or flight, leaving the frontiersman with scarcely any aboriginal contacts. This attrition of Indian populations may have been well advanced in many areas before any face-to-face confrontations took place between the two groups. Casual early meetings along the coast probably introduced European infectious diseases that moved rapidly into the interior with highly lethal effect. Equally devastating were European firearms and metal weapons that were carried quickly along well-established trade routes. Thus, for example, when Penn initiated his colony in 1682, it was in a territory already virtually deserted, with the few survivors badly demoralized after nearly a century of indirect onslaught by European maladies and artifacts (and where, incidentally, it was thus prudent to experiment with a humane Indian policy).

A second reason was the unbridgeable cultural chasm between aborigine and European. They differed so profoundly, not only in level of material achievement but in the essential style or shape of cultural pattern that genuine communication was nearly impossible. This basic incompatibility was exacerbated by the spatial accident that British culture was first implanted, and the embryonic American culture gestated, in what chanced to be a backwater region of aboriginal America, the stretch of littoral from the Carolinas to southern Maine. It was late in the colonial era, much too late to redirect the design of a rapidly crystallizing pattern, that American settlers in interior Georgia and the Carolinas first encountered Indian groups whose social organization and level of agricultural technique approached their own. This is quite contrary to the course of events in Spanish America, where the conquerors pushed singlemindedly into the climactic regions of Indian power and culture, expropriated them, then worked outward toward the peripheral zones, and during the process affected a hybridization of both race and culture.

The sharp cultural disconformity between newcomer and aborigine in eastern North America, and later further west, meant a chronic incapacity to formulate a workable social apparatus for accommodating the two disparate groups. To this day, official policy, which once in effect

---

[12] The statistical evidence is meager and grossly defective, especially for eastern North America. The most comprehensive survey of the material—although probably much too conservative in its numerical estimates—is Alfred L. Kroeber, *Cultural and Natural Areas of Native North America* (Berkeley: University of California Press, 1939).

condoned outright extermination, has dithered between the ghetto approach—coralling the survivors into open-air museums called reservations,
there to preserve whatever scraps of the ancestral way of life they could—
and forced assimilation, that is, transformation into good, copper-skinned
WASPs. Both policies have had generally dismal results. No serious
attempt has been made, except perhaps in the Hispanic Southwest, to
forge either a spatially intermixed, but socially stratified, plural society or
a fully, freely fused amalgam of bloodlines and cultural heritages, as
has occurred in portions of Latin America, New Zealand, or Hawaii.
The point might be one of purely academic interest if the Amerindians
would generously agree to vanish, as was thought to be happening around
the turn of the century; but now their number is growing at a rate far
ahead of that for the general population and one that shows no sign
of abating.

What, then, was the Indian contribution?[13] Perhaps the most meaningful gift was a partially humanized land and much valuable information
about its contents. The territory entered by explorer and homesteader
was not covered by the forest primaeval but had already been grossly
modified by aboriginal hunting, burning, forestry, and planting. Therefore much open woodland, or even parkland, was interspersed with
fairly large clearings or "Indian old-fields."[14] Indeed in the subhumid
regions of the continent, the creation of prairies and grasslands may
have been the work of the aborigines. The fact that much practical
geographical knowledge was passed on to the new settlers is reflected
in the survival of many thousands of place names of Indian origin on
the contemporary map. These occur despite the infrequency of Indian
words fully integrated into American English, except for those referring
to specifically American plants, animals, and land forms. Geographical
briefing of the invaders also included data on trails and settlement sites,
so that the toil of roadmaker and town founder was somewhat eased.
In the case of certain obvious highway routes and town locations, Indian
pretesting may simply have hastened the selection.

Considerable knowledge regarding the local biota was handed on
to the Europeans. The American pharmacopoeia was immeasurably
enriched by Indian lore; and some useful sources of industrial raw
materials, such as dyes, fibers, and poisons, were identified by our
predecessors. Only a few fully domesticated species seem to have been
taken directly by the European settler: maize, various species of beans
and squash, the sunflower, and the Jerusalem artichoke. In addition, of
course, many other items, some of the utmost importance, were derived

13 For a useful summary, see A. Irving Hallowell, "The Backlash of the
Frontier: The Impact of the Indian on American Culture," in *Smithsonian Report
for 1958* (Washington, D.C.: Smithsonian Institution, 1959), pp. 447–72.

14 The general prevalence of savannas and other forms of partially open land
at the time of the first European incursions into the South, thanks to the activities
of the Amerindians, is discussed in Erhard Rostlund, "The Myth of a Natural Prairie
Belt in Alabama: an Interpretation of Historical Records," *Annals of the Association
of American Geographers*, 47, No. 4 (1957), 392–411.

from tropical America, often by quite roundabout routes, but not from local sources. Among these are: cotton, tobacco, the white potato, the peanut, the tomato, the sweet potato, the turkey, the avocado, and the guinea pig. The local indigenes also shared their knowledge of some semidomesticated and wild food plants, among them the sugar maple, the sassafras, wild rice, the pecan, the persimmon, and a goodly number of fruit, nut, and berry items; and the adoption of various ornamental flowers and shrubs may have been aided by information acquired from the Indians.[15] There are also several minor, but striking, aboriginal items in modern American material culture, notably the canoe, certain forms of basketry, the mocassin, and some types of palisading and crude temporary shelters. No spontaneous transfer at all seems to have occurred in the realms of music, dance, the plastic arts, literature, or religion. Finally, there is the image of the Indian, his mythic role in American literature and folklore.

It might be hypothesized that, had the European colonists found an utterly unpopulated continent, contemporary American life would not have differed in any major respect from its actual pattern. Although some interesting minor nuances can be attributed to interaction with Indians, no basic assumption, attitude, institution, or process seems to have been altered materially thereby. There is the immediate objection: What about the decisive influence of maize in the American farm economy? The fortuitous local presence of this wondrous plant was indeed convenient; but had it been missing, *Zea mais* would surely have been imported from tropical America, probably via Europe, just as soon as a genuine demand for it materialized, precisely as happened with Virginia tobacco shortly after initial settlement, upland cotton from Mexico, soybeans from the Far East, grain sorghum from Africa, or brahmin cattle from India. In any event, Indian corn was totally transformed into a European crop. European, not aboriginal, modes of cultivation were adopted; and it was to play the role first of a bread grain, analogous to wheat /or oats, then that of a livestock feed in a manner completely alien to Indian practice, and as a source of completely un-Indian industrial raw materials, for example, mash for bourbon. But if the Indian impact upon Europeans was ultimately negligible, the reverse is certainly not true. When it has endured, the aboriginal culture has been profoundly affected, even fundamentally revised. The now extinct equestrian buffalo-hunting culture of the Great Plains, the Iroquois men who have become so adept at assembling structural steel, and the quite lively Navaho tribe, so strongly focused on sheep (and so adroit in silversmithing) derived from Europe, are only three of the more dramatic examples. Since such battered, but viable, cultures will account for a mounting percentage of the national population, their acculturative practices merit the attention of social scientists and humanists.

15 U. P. Hedrick, *A History of Horticulture in America to 1860* (New York: Oxford University Press, 1960).

The African Contribution

African Negroes and their descendants, nearly all of them slaves, were present in significant number from 1619 onward and accounted for one-fifth the total population of British North America by the late eighteenth century; and in some parts of the South they greatly outnumbered Caucasians. Under these circumstances, it would be quite extraordinary if some transfer of African culture traits did not occur; but the question of precisely what or how much has not yet been settled at all adequately. A basic reason is that until recently—specifically the publication of Herskovits' deliberately provocative, but scholarly, manifesto[16]—no one had bothered to ask, and that since then much of the work has been partisan in nature. During most of American history, the Negro was invisible to most historians and social scientists, or considered only as the passive occasion for the Civil War. When viewed at all in a social or cultural context, the "obviously inferior" Black was looked down upon as an *Untermensch,* poorly mimicking the master culture. "The myth of the Negro past" is that the slave reached these shores in a condition of utter cultural nakedness or amnesia, quickly jettisoning all of his African heritage or being quite incapable of practising any of it even if he had wished to do so.

The peculiar nature of the slave trade and the process of "breaking in" new slaves did indeed guarantee the obliteration of all but a small residue of the African cultural pattern. Slaves were collected by purchase or capture from much of Black Africa; but the traffic was especially vigorous within West Africa, culturally the most advanced portion of the continent south of the Sahara, except for the Ethiopian Highlands, and clearly the source for most North American slaves. Much mingling of persons from different tribes must have gone on in the ports of embarkation; and if there was an intermediate stopover in the slave markets of the West Indies, further intertribal scrambling took place. This clearly protective tactic of dividing and demoralizing persons who could seldom understand one another's language was carried another step by plantation foremen in the American South. Thus they had at their disposal gangs of slaves who had no choice but to learn a form of English and other facets of the dominant culture when they were thrown together with other detribalized strangers.

It is a marvel that anything at all was retained, but it is plain that a certain, not yet fully specified, residuum of Africanisms has survived. The fact that Africa and Europe, as segments of an Old World in intermittent contact, did share some cultural elements, makes it hard to decide, for example, the source of a particular proverb or folk tale found in America but long current in both Africa and Europe. As in comparable areas in the Antilles and South America, the retention rate for Africanisms is highest in isolated localities where Negroes have been strongly dominant

---

[16] Melville Herskovits, *The Myth of the Negro Past* (New York: Harper & Row, Publishers, 1941).

numerically. A prime instance is found in the Sea Islands of South Carolina and Georgia where the Gullah, or Geechee, dialect seems as much West African in syntax and vocabulary as it is English.[17] Something of the same situation may be seen in the Creole speech used by some Louisiana Negroes and introduced from the French West Indies. As in the Caribbean, a vigorous "pidgin" or "Creole" English prevails among American Negroes with little formal schooling. Although formerly denigrated as a degraded or substandard form of English, many linguists now accept the thesis that this form of speech is a legitimate, full-fledged dialect with its own phonetics, vocabulary, and a distinctive grammar, and that African influences were critical in its formation.[18]

It is seldom feasible to relate Africanisms in the American South, unlike those in Cuba or northeastern Brazil, to specific African tribes. But there are some items whose viability in the United States was enhanced by the fact that they transcended tribal lines in Africa. This argument has been made for certain forms of worship and burial practice (including the burial society and methods of grave decoration), and for some types of dance, coiffure, and costume. A very few plants, notably okra, the watermelon, and the peanut (originally, of course, from South America), can be attributed to the Negro slave. There is still much controversy over whether American Negro family structure reflects African tradition or has a later origin. Few African words have been admitted to the standard American English vocabulary, though the score may be better for slang; but there is some possibility that African phonetics may have had their effect upon the general speech pattern of the American South. Musicologists may quarrel endlessly as to just how the blues were born; but it is hard to imagine jazz as having originated without some African inspiration, just as it would equally be far-fetched to think of it springing full-blown out of Africa. It is also the one significant cultural complex of presumable African ancestry, except possibly certain dance forms, to have diffused throughout the entire country.

In other respects, the African cultural contribution, whatever its total extent, was initially limited almost wholly to the Southern culture area. Later, during the post-independence fusion of colonial cultural strains into a national pattern in the trans-Appalachian West, some traces of African culture would automatically have been included in the Southern parcel of traits, and thus might appear in quite dilute form in the national culture. The recent self-conscious revival of African practices by the more determined Black Militants—notably in costume, coiffure, and personal names, with some discussion of adopting African languages—is extremely interesting in its own right as another example of the deliberate

17 Lorenzo Dow Turner, *Africanisms in the Gullah Dialect* (Chicago: University of Chicago Press, 1949).
18 William A. Stewart, "Continuity and Change in American Negro Dialects," *The Florida FL Reporter* (Spring 1968). Bibliographic citations for much of the useful literature on this intensely controversial topic are to be found in this provocative essay.

manipulation of symbols in synthesizing ethnic self-awareness; but these ultra-visible gimmicks are items from the library or the travelogue, not treasures dug up from the cellar of folk memory. Those few Negro Americans who have lived or visited in Africa for any extended period are quickly, acutely made aware of the profound cultural gulf between themselves and their racial brethren. Similarly, there is a sharp separation in both physical and cultural space between the repatriated Americanized Negroes of the Liberian coast and the indigenous communities of the interior.

The Continental European Contribution

As they solidified their hold upon the Atlantic Seaboard from Maine to Georgia, the British (that is, the English, plus the Anglicized Welsh, Cornish, and Scotch-Irish) willy-nilly acquired title to an appreciable number of non-British settlers, namely some antecedent Dutch, Flemings, Swedes, and Finns in the Hudson and Delaware valleys and vicinity. In addition, large numbers of Germans and Swiss began entering Pennsylvania and Maryland from about 1700 onward. Further ethnic spice was added elsewhere by smaller contingents of Highland Scots, Irish Catholics, Sephardic Jews, and French Huguenots. With the great territorial expansion of the American Republic, a major community of French-speaking folk was annexed in southern Louisiana and smaller clusters elsewhere in the Mississippi Basin and the Great Lakes country. Similarly, a goodly number of persons of Spanish and Mexican stock suddenly found themselves within the borders of the United States in 1848. Finally, the Russian presence had made itself felt, however fleetingly, in northern California as well as in Alaska. How great a contribution did these varied non-British European groups make toward the formation of the American culture, regionally or nationally?

In the case of the colonial hearth areas, that is, the nodal zones along the Atlantic Seaboard that proved to be the incubators for the national cultural pattern, the Doctrine of First Effective Settlement does not apply at all to the few Swedes, Finns, and Dutch along the Delaware Valley. These settlers and their way of life were promptly swamped by subsequent British and Teutonic colonization. The Dutch were more successful in clinging to some shreds of identity for more than two hundred years in Manhattan, Long Island, New Jersey, and the Hudson Valley; but eventually they too were smothered by the greater weight of British, or general American, population and culture. Some lingering traces of their cultural presence may be noted locally, but any contribution to national culture is problematic. Similarly, such small, exotic enclaves as the Salzburgers in Georgia, colonies of Swiss and Huguenots in South Carolina, or Highland Scots in North Carolina were quite local and ephemeral as regards the genesis of national patterns.

The case of the so-called Pennsylvania Germans is more complex. This appellation fits a rather heterogeneous set of German-speaking

Protestants from Switzerland and the Palatinate and other sections of Western Germany. They began arriving in force in Pennsylvania and Maryland quite soon after English-speaking settlers had firmly occupied these tracts, and were thus just barely among the first effective settlers. Soon thereafter, the Pennsylvania Germans formed a significant part of the frontier contingent in the Appalachian Piedmont and valleys from Virginia through Tennessee, and were among the first groups to penetrate the eastern Middle West. This ethnic group may account for a major share in culture formation within an influential area centering on the Delaware and Susquehanna valleys, and, by means of migration and diffusion, may have contributed consequentially to the national mix. The question is muddied by the fact that, within the Old World, the British, Germans, and neighboring folk were co-members of a cultural subrealm with rather efficient internal communications.[19] Thus it is usually difficult to assign a particular trait or innovation to a specific source. Take the introduction of log-building techniques in house and barn construction. This may have been the work of the Pennsylvania Germans, but an equally strong case could be pleaded for the seventeenth-century Swedes and Finns.[20] In any case, the Pennsylvania Germans—and, with major reservations, the African Negroes—would appear to be the only credible nominees as non-British participants in the critical early phases of creating a national American culture.

The fate of the annexed non-British ethnic groups is of some interest, at least locally. The Florida Spaniards and California Russians can be written off immediately, for they quickly sank out of sight. The tiny nodes of French settlement in the Mississippi-Great Lakes territories (for example, Detroit, Michilimackinac, Prairie du Chien, Vincennes, Kaskaskia, Ste. Genevieve, and the eastern Ozarks) succumbed only a little less rapidly, leaving as their lasting legacy only a few place names and an esoteric land survey geometry. Despite much romantic (or commercial) self-deception, the same story must be told for the Colonial Spanish and Mexican cultures in California. Their contribution, especially in the agricultural sector, might have persisted more strongly had the transition to a new regime been smoother; but the antecedent cultures were simply pulverized under the massive Anglo-American avalanche, leaving little more than a few ruins, place names, and archaic grant boundaries, and some items of agriculture and animal husbandry.[21]

Genuine survival and durability are found in French Louisiana and particularly in the Hispanic Southwest. The Cajuns, speaking a French patois, have managed, in part because of relative isolation, to cling to

[19] The point is argued strongly in James T. Lemon, *The Best Poor Man's Country; a Geographical Study of Early Southeastern Pennsylvania* (Baltimore: The Johns Hopkins Press, 1971).

[20] The problem is handled definitively in Harold R. Shurtleff, *The Log Cabin Myth* (Cambridge, Mass.: Harvard University Press, 1939).

[21] H. F. Raup, "Transformation of Southern California to a Cultivated Land," *Annals of the Association of American Geographers*, 49, No. 3, Part 2 (1959), 58–78.

their linguistic, religious, and, to a degree, political identity, so that despite a powerful dose of Americanization and a certain culturally schizoid tendency in consequence, they retain their ethnicity, and may do so indefinitely. In New Mexico and southern and southwest Texas, and some segments of Arizona and Colorado, the political and economic supremacy of the Anglos and a strong recent in-movement from the East have not yet fully overcome the cultural stubbornness and demographic vigor of an Hispanic or "Chicano" (and in New Mexico a partially Hispanicized aboriginal) population.[22] Their staying power is abetted by the continuing immigration and circulation of Mexicans and a constant flow of cultural currents from the neighboring motherland. The Hispanic Southwest remains a battleground of cultures, the major example of cultural pluralism in the United States, and, in some respects, an accidental political (and ecological?) protrusion of the Anglo-American realm beyond its logical limits into the periphery of Latin America. In any case, the strong non-British heritage of the Hispanic Southwest, like the Gallic tradition of southern Louisiana, is a local affair. With the possible exception of the range livestock system and the attendant "cowboy complex,"[23] little has been exported past regional boundaries; the mainstream of national culture is unaffected.

Significance of Sequent Waves of Immigration

The chronicling of American immigration and a discussion of the major processes at work are most pertinent to any analysis of American cultural geography.[24] The sequential ordering of unequal parcels of ethnic groups was a material factor in the development of the national culture. Their initially irregular spatial assignment promoted regional distinctiveness among culture areas; and the persistence of ethnic areal segregation is, of course, a topic of consuming interest in and of itself.

A survey of the more than 360 years of foreign immigration into

22 Richard L. Nostrand, "The Hispanic-American Borderland: Delimitation of an American Culture Region," *Annals of the Association of American Geographers*, 60, No. 4 (1970), 638–61; and Donald W. Meinig, *Southwest: Three Peoples in Geographical Change* (New York: Oxford University Press, 1971).

23 Walter Prescott Webb, *The Great Plains* (New York: Grosset & Dunlap, 1957), 205–15. For a dissenting viewpoint, see Terry G. Jordan, "The Origin of Anglo-American Cattle Ranching in Texas: a Documentation of Diffusion from the Lower South," *Economic Geography*, 45 (1969), 63–87.

24 The voluminous literature on American immigration is listed in Stanley J. Tracy, ed., *A Report on World Population Migration as Related to the United States* (Washington, D.C.: George Washington University Press, 1956). Among the more outstanding treatments of the subject are: Oscar Handlin, *The Uprooted: the Epic Story of the Great Migrations that Made the American People* (New York: Grosset & Dunlap, 1951); Marcus Lee Hansen, *The Atlantic Migration, 1607–1790: A History of the Continuing Settlement of the United States* (New York: Harper & Row, Publishers, 1961); Conrad Taeuber and Irene B. Taeuber, "The Immigrants," in *The Changing Population of the United States* (New York: John Wiley & Sons, Inc., 1958), pp. 48–70; and Maldwyn Allen Jones, *American Immigration* (Chicago: University of Chicago Press, 1960).

the territory of the United States suggests a division into five distinct periods, as follows:

 I. 1607–1700: The initial, strongly English and Welsh wave, along with a major complement of Africans;
 II. 1700–1775: A still predominantly English, Welsh, and African movement, but with strong Teutonic and Scotch-Irish components as well;
III. 1820–1870: The Northwest European wave—heavily British, Irish, Teutonic, and Dutch, but including the vanguard of other European groups and some Asians, Canadians, and Latin Americans;
 IV. 1870–1920: The Great Deluge—large numbers of eastern and southern Europeans and Scandinavians joining those from Northwest Europe; Asians, Canadians, and Latin Americans in significant quantity;
 V. 1920 to present: A highly miscellaneous influx—less than in the preceding period but still of major absolute magnitude—from western and southern Europe, Latin America, Canada, and some Asian lands, with Latin America registering especially steady and major gains.

Firm quantitative values cannot be assigned to these periods. Official statistics are lacking prior to 1821; and, since then, many illicit entries have eluded detection. Furthermore, the official figures indicate gross rather than net immigration, for a considerable percentage of the foreign-born do eventually leave the country, and there is an outward trickle of native Americans as well. If a rough guess must be hazarded for immigration before 1820, then a net total of far less than one million seems plausible.

The cultural impact of these five periods is inversely related to their recency, in keeping with the Doctrine of First Effective Settlement. Thus the few tens of thousands who arrived before 1700 were much more consequential for our cultural heredity than the 26,240,000 tabulated for the 1870–1920 period. To adopt a somewhat fanciful biological analogy, Period I could be likened to cultural infancy, Period II to childhood, and the last three periods to adolescent and mature development. Behaviorally, the earlier formative years are the important ones. Carrying the metaphor even further, it must be admitted that the act of conception in western Europe was probably the most critical event of all; but its exegesis lies beyond the limits of this essay.

These five periods can be grouped into two larger eras that are quite distinct in terms of the acculturation process: a colonial period up through 1775, and a national period following 1820. During the first, the migrant gave no thought to cultural adjustment, whatever other problems may have beset him. He left Great Britain with the realistic expectation of remaining very much the same sort of Englishman he had always been, for acculturation was subtle and painless. Even the former residents of the Rhineland planned to preserve their identity; and after settling in fairly cohesive territorial blocks, most did succeed, as have many of their desendants after some two and a half centuries. Those who came after the resumption of large-scale immigration in the 1820's were faced with a new situation: a dynamic, evolving national culture already sharply divergent from its European forebears. Active member-ship in it meant paying heavy dues: education in a new language or dialect and indeed learning a whole new way of life, even for the British newcomer. In brief, immigrants experienced "culture shock" followed by total acculturation, if not in the first generation, then certainly in the second or third. It could not have been very long before the immigrant began to anticipate the ordeal. The fact that so many millions of the foreign-born and their children agonized their way through a prolonged personality crisis deeply compounded the chronic American dilemma. For after they had paid the stiff psychological entrance fees, the "new Americans" had joined a club whose older members were and are forever searching out their elusive identity, consciously trying to decide what the new land and the new man are to be.

Exemption has been granted only to those immigrants who were not forced to snap the ties with the homeland abruptly: the French-Canadians, Mexicans, and Puerto Ricans. Those French-Canadians filter-ing into New York and New England from Quebec and New Brunswick, but still commuting socially and psychologically, if not physically, be-tween domicile and homeland, have not yet all been Americanized past the point of no return. Exactly the same situation prevails for those Mexi-cans crossing northward into Texas and the Southwest in general. The tether binding Puerto Ricans and Virgin Islanders to their home islands is a short one, in hours and dollars, if not in miles; and their comings and goings are frequent enough to subvert acculturative tendencies.

That the first effective wave of immigrants (1607–1700) was so largely British (or, in the case of Canada, French) is one of the pivotal facts of North American human geography. The exploitation and settle-ment of eastern North America by Northwest Europeans—primarily the British, of course, but, in descending order, the French, Dutch, and Swedes as well, were not quite as inevitable as may now appear. For more than a century, the Spanish failed to exercise seriously their military and legalistic option on North American real estate, confining themselves to a few flimsy coastal missions in Georgia, the Carolinas, and Chesapeake Bay, and their pathetic outposts in Florida. Several excuses can be cited: lack of sufficient manpower and naval strength; a general preoccupation with the administration of New Spain; the poor missionary prospects offered by the North American aborigines. The basic reasons, however, were probably that the Spanish found the region physically and econom-ically uninviting and, in any case, had not yet attained that stage in their internal development when large numbers of emigrants with capital could be ejected from the homeland. The British found eastern North America a much more attractive place than the Spanish did and by 1600 were economically, demographically, and otherwise primed for for-eign adventure and the spawning of a series of new Englands. After a century and a half of combat with like-minded continental northwestern Europeans, the British swept eastern North America clear of competition by virtue of superior military, institutional, and economic strength.

The Seventeenth-Century British immigrants were drawn from most sections of the island of Great Britain (and in much smaller number from the British West Indies). A great deal of interregional scrambling took place in the assembling, trans-Atlantic passage, and subsequent inter-actions of the travelers, so that original distinctions were blurred or totally erased. Only the most deviant group, the Welsh, managed to hang on to much of their parochial identity, and then only temporarily, as in parts of southeastern Pennsylvania. In effect, a sort of basic Pan-British kit of culture traits survived and was implanted, in precisely parallel fashion to what has been noted for New Spain, where a basic Pan-Hispanic pattern was transmitted, in part through formalized edicts and codes, to all corners of a vast empire. The result was unmistakably British, but regional contributions could no longer be sorted out.

The eighteenth-century wave of immigrants witnessed greater ethnic diversification with the arrival of shiploads of the quasi-British Scotch-Irish, the quite un-British Teutons, and a trickle of others. Even earlier, in Philadelphia and Nieuw Amsterdam-New York and their respective hinterlands, the ethnic and religious mix was more varied than elsewhere. Small Dutch, Flemish, Jewish, French, Spanish, and Italian groups were to be encountered, in addition to the substantial communities of Germans and both slave and free Negroes. Up until the suspension of major move-ments in 1775, the emigrant ships disgorged their cargoes mainly within a limited number of harbors from Portsmouth, New Hampshire to Hampton Roads (movement inland from the Carolina and Georgia coast was feeble). The newcomers fanned out northward, inland, and south-westward in a great, irregularly pulsating arc.

After more than four decades of military disturbances in both America and Europe, significant immigration resumed around 1820 and, with momentary quiet periods caused by war or economic depression, increased until an all-time peak was reached in the opening years of the twentieth century. The veritable flood that had poured across the ocean for nearly a century was finally reduced to a modest trickle by World War I. It is convenient to divide this great mass movement into two fifty-year periods, before and after 1870. During the first, natives of Great Britain were joined by an extraordinary outpouring of famine-stricken Irish, swarms of Germans, and lesser, but significant, groups of Swiss, Netherlanders, and Belgians (but surprisingly few French). Since the importation of Africans had been outlawed in 1808 and the contra-band slave trade was minor, this phase can be fairly characterized as Northwest European.

From about 1870 onward, the flow from Northwest Europe continued but was augmented dramatically by immigration from Scandinavia and from eastern and southern Europe. Poles, Hungarians, Lithuanians, Jews, Russians, Ukrainians, Czechs, Slovaks, Croats, Serbs, Italians, Mace-donians, Portuguese, and Greeks were all abundantly represented. In addition, the influxes from Canada, Latin America, China, and Japan, already in progress before 1870, gained in volume.

Viewed at the macroscopic scale, Europe's development moved steadily outward in wavelike fashion through time and space from a hearth area around the North Sea toward the north, east, and south; and it is clear that the capacity and impetus for intercontinental migration was a major symptom of the achievement of a certain significant level of advancement. (See Table 1.2.) In fact, one can rather accurately date the inception of significant modernization for individual nations by close study of emigration data.[25] A mirror image of the migratory impulse in the European subcontinent was the spatial zonation of ethnic groups in the United States and Canada, especially within the rural population. (As time went on, immigrants gravitated toward the cities at a greater rate even than native Americans.) The late arrivals were more likely to seek opportunity in the open spaces of the central and western United States than in the eastern third of the country, where the more inviting rural niches had been preempted. And there is indeed a special concentration of Germans in the upper Middle West, of Scandinavians in the north central states, Italians in California, or of various Slavic groups from Kansas northward and northwestward.

As the settlement frontier rolled westward, there seems to have been a gradual change in the size of ethnic blocs. Within the original colonies, large blocks of land were dominated by single groups—whole counties or even provinces. Thus we find that, formerly at least, almost all of New England had much the same ethnic composition, as did much of the South. Even in heterogenous Pennsylvania, specific groups would tend to dominate specific counties. At a later stage, during the settlement of the Middle West, rural immigrant blocs seldom prevailed beyond the township scale, giving rise to intricately meshed mosaics in such states as Wisconsin or Kansas;[26] and each major city might have several distinct ethnic neighborhoods. In the final stage, in the Far West, large uniform areas of any single European group have been rare; within the city, group dominance seldom goes beyond the single residential block, and one block may hold several nationalities. A similar pattern is found in the western countryside. Evidently, there has been a growth through time, and thus with distance westward, in the spatial porosity of American society, possibly because of a lessening need for territorial clannishness, but more probably because of the nature of land law and private land speculation in recent decades.

In the final, current phase of immigration, both the volume and national composition of the movement are controlled by federal statute. But even without such official restriction, the flow would have ebbed. The American "pull," especially for the relatively unskilled laborer, had become weak by the 1920's, and so had the economic (if not sociopolitical) "push" to abandon Europe. In any case, immigration from Latin America, largely uncontrolled, has grown rapidly and is now clearly the largest regional category. Although present-day immigration has had

25 The phenomenon is mapped in *Atlas of the Historical Geography of the United States,* Plates 70–E through 70–O, and discussed in Donald J. Bogue, *Principles of Demography* (New York: John Wiley & Sons, Inc., 1969), 804–10.

26 J. Neale Carman, *Foreign-Language Units of Kansas. Historical Atlas and Statistics* (Lawrence: University of Kansas Press, 1962).

Table 1.2. *Immigrants to the United States, 1820-1969, by Region or Nation of Origin and Percent of Decadal Total*

| | Northwest Europe | | | | Germany | Italy | Spain, Portugal and Greece | Eastern[b] Europe | U.S.S.R. and Baltic States | Asia | Canada | Latin America[c] | All Other Countries | Total No. (in thousands) |
	Great Britain	Ireland	Scandi-navia	Other NW[a] Europe										
1820–1829	20.5%	40.2%	0.2%	9.3%	4.5%	0.3%	2.1%	–	0.1%	–	1.8%	5.8%	15.2%	129
1830–1839	13.8	31.7	0.4	8.4	23.2	0.4	0.5	0.1	–	–	2.2	3.7	15.6	538
1840–1849	15.3	46.0	0.9	6.4	27.0	0.1	0.1	–	–	–	2.4	1.1	0.5	1,427
1850–1859	15.8	36.6	0.9	4.4	34.7	0.3	0.4	0.1	–	1.3	2.3	0.7	2.7	2,815
1860–1869	25.6	20.5	4.6	3.4	34.7	0.5	0.4	0.2	0.1	2.6	5.7	0.6	0.9	2,081
1870–1879	21.1	15.4	7.6	4.3	27.4	1.7	0.7	2.6	1.3	4.9	11.8	0.8	0.4	2,742
1880–1889	15.4	12.8	12.8	3.8	27.6	5.1	0.4	6.9	3.5	1.3	9.4	0.6	0.3	5,249
1890–1899	8.9	11.0	10.6	3.3	15.7	16.3	1.3	17.7	12.2	1.6	0.1	0.9	0.4	3,694
1900–1909	5.7	4.3	5.9	2.2	4.0	23.5	2.9	26.3	18.3	2.9	1.5	1.9	0.6	8,202
1910–1919	5.8	2.6	3.8	2.5	2.8	19.4	5.7	19.9	17.4	3.1	11.2	5.7	0.3	6,347
1920–1929	7.9	4.8	4.7	3.2	9.0	12.3	3.8	12.1	2.1	2.6	22.1	14.9	0.4	4,296
1930–1939	7.7	5.1	2.4	4.6	17.1	12.2	3.3	10.0	1.3	2.6	23.3	9.5	0.8	699
1940–1949	14.6	2.6	2.6	8.7	13.9	5.9	2.4	3.9	0.5	3.5	18.8	19.5	2.9	857
1950–1959	12.4	2.4	2.1	6.3	24.6	8.0	2.8	5.6	0.1	5.7	15.3	12.6	1.8	2,300
1960–1969	7.1	1.3	1.4	3.7	6.5	6.2	6.0	3.6	0.1	11.0	13.5	38.9	1.1	3,212
Total No. (in thousands)	4889	4714	2,473	1,635	6,896	5,149	1,155	5,384	3,387	1,431	3,942	3,087	463	44,588
	10.9%	10.6%	5.6%	3.7%	15.2%	11.5%	2.6%	12.1%	7.6%	3.2%	8.9%	6.9%	1.0%	100.0%

a Belgium, Netherlands, Luxembourg, France, and Switzerland.
b Albania, Austria, Bulgaria, Czechoslovakia, Hungary, Poland, Rumania, Turkey in Europe, and Yugoslavia.
c Not including persons born in Puerto Rico, Virgin Islands, or Canal Zone.

Adapted from Donald J. Bogue, *Principles of Demography* (New York: John Wiley & Sons, Inc., 1969), p. 807 and *Statistical Abstract of the United States,* 1969 and 1970.

far less impact, qualitatively or quantitatively, than that of the past, the admission each year of 300,000 to 400,000 persons is greatly in excess of the number reported by any other nation.

In no case, with the possible exception of the French-Canadian invasion of Aroostook County, Maine and the northern segment of Vermont or the sudden Cuban surge into Miami, has foreign immigration displaced or fundamentally reordered the American culture. Nevertheless, it may have brought about major modification. Thus large parts of Minnesota and the Dakotas are unmistakably Scandinavian and American; the Germanic character of portions of south central Texas[27] and the Dutch imprint upon southwestern Michigan is plain to see,[28] as is the recent Jewish-American characer of the Catskills; and much of Pennsylvania's and West Virginia's coal belt has been markedly slavicized. The personalities of several major metropolises have been deeply affected by large ethnic settlements. The Germans of Milwaukee and Cincinnati, the Poles of Detroit and Buffalo, the Irish of Boston, the Puerto Ricans in New York City, and the Cubans and Jews of Miami come immediately to mind.

Territorial Patterns Among Ethnic Groups

The whole grand theme of the ethnic diversity of the nation, considered in its full spatial range, from the major region down to the fine, intraurban details, merits much more attention than it can be given here.[29] We limit ourselves here to suggesting a few major processes that

27 Terry G. Jordan, *German Seed in Texas Soil; Immigrant Farmers in Nineteenth-Century Texas* (Austin: University of Texas Press, 1966).

28 Elaine M. Bjorklund, "Ideology and Culture Exemplified in Southwestern Michigan," *Annals of the Association of American Geographers*, 54, No. 2 (1964), 277–41, and John A. Jakle and James O. Wheeler, "The Changing Residential Structure of the Dutch Population in Kalamazoo, Michigan," *Ibid.*, 59, No. 3 (1969), 441–60.

29 It is rather surprising how little attention has been devoted, at the national scale, to the ethnic-racial composition of the American composition, as viewed in spatial perspective. The most recent cartographic treatments are: S. I. Bruk and V. S. Apenchenko, eds., *Atlas Narodov Mira* (Moscow: Main Administration of Geodesy and Cartography, 1964), 94–95, (a map depicting no less than 54 different groups); and *Atlas of the Historical Geography of the United States*, Plates 67B–70B, 71–76A. The textual notes for the latter (pp. 46–48) provide references to earlier census atlas coverage of immigrant stock. There is a brief but useful overview of the broader geographic patterns in Richard Hartshorne, "Racial Maps of the United States," *Geographical Review*, 28 (1938), 276–88, and a more extensive, but only intermittently geographic treatment in Donald Keith Fellows, *A Mosaic of America's Ethnic Minorities* (New York: John Wiley & Sons, Inc., 1972). A number of studies dealing with individual groups, mostly at the state or local level, are listed in Wilbur Zelinsky, *A Bibliographic Guide to Population Geography*, Department of Geography, Research Paper No. 80 (Chicago: University of Chicago, 1962). The recent literature on Afro-Americans is listed in Donald R. Deskins, Jr., "Geographical Literature on the American Negro, 1949–1968: a Bibliography," *Professional Geographer*, 21, No. 3 (1969), 145–49. Among the more interesting post-1961 items analyzing ethnic geography at the micro scale are Daniel F. Doeppers, "The Globeville Neighborhood in Denver," *Geographical Review*, 57, No. 4 (1967), 506–22; and Gerald D. Suttles,

may have helped create the territorial zonation of ethnic groups. In the first instance, there is the distance-decay effect, or the importance of relative proximity. This has already been shown to operate for the French-Canadians of the Northeast and the Spanish-Americans of the Southwest. It is also the principal factor accounting for the Pacific Coast concentration of the Chinese and (especially before World War II) the Japanese (Figure 1.1) as well as the lesser number of Filipinos, Koreans, and East Indians, and for Cubans in Florida and along the Gulf Coast. Less obviously, this consideration governed the locational choices of the colonial British, Germans, and Scotch-Irish, so that often nothing more mysterious than the question of the nearest available real estate was involved. Spatial friction also explains, in part, the great piling up of nineteenth- and twentieth-century immigrant groups in the major ports of entry.

With much trepidation, it can be hinted that the factor of environmental affinity—the selection of familiar and preferred kinds of habitat—might bear looking into. Certainly other causes played their part in the heavy Scandinavian concentrations in the North Central states; but the availability of terrain, plant cover, soil, and, less convincingly, climate reminiscent of the homeland or responsive to known skills is to be considered. This is particularly true for certain marginal tracts claimed by Icelanders and Finns, which were ignored by members of a less hardy breed. Similarly, the success of Dutch farmers in polderizing marshlands in Michigan and Ontario supports the hypothesis, as may the flocking together of Italians and Armenians in sections of California's Central Valley that are crudely analogous to their motherlands.[30] Environment may be involved only obliquely, as when specific groups are introduced because of occupational specialization. Thus Basque shepherds are concentrated in various parts of the Intermontane West, Japanese horticulturists in Southern California, Portuguese fishermen around Cape Cod, Greek sponge-divers in the Tampa area, and Cornish miners in southwestern Wisconsin. And there is the overwhelming geographic fact of a large Negro population corresponding to the plantation system. Other ethnically linked occupations, however, are only weakly place-specific: Jewish peddlers and merchants, Greek restauranteurs, and Chinese laundrymen.

Once a viable ethnic nucleus takes hold at a given location, chain migration may be triggered. If communication lines are kept open between the new settlements and relatives and neighbors back home, positive information may induce the latter to pack up and follow. In this way, a great many urban and rural ethnic neighborhoods have expanded. This mechanism has also reinforced the ranks of at least one major religious

---

The Social Order of the Slum; Ethnicity and Territory in the Inner City (Chicago: University of Chicago Press, 1968).

30 The location of the Italian-American population is presented and discussed in Joseph Velikonja, "Distribuzione Geografica degli Italiani negli Stati Uniti," *Atti del XVIII Congresso Geografico Italiano, Trieste, 4–9 Aprile 1961* (Trieste, 1961), 1–20.

1-a
AFRO-AMERICAN

○ Primary metropolitan concentration
• Secondary metropolitan concentration

1-b
JAPANESE & CHINESE; SCANDINAVIAN

Scandinavian rural concentrations
Japanese & Chinese rural concentrations

JAPANESE & CHINESE
□ Primary metropolitan concentration
○ Secondary metropolitan concentration

SCANDINAVIAN
✕ Primary metropolitan concentration
• Secondary metropolitan concentration

1-c
AMERINDIAN

• Secondary metropolitan concentration

1-d
GERMAN

○ Primary metropolitan concentration
• Secondary metropolitan concentration

Primary rural concentration

Secondary rural concentration

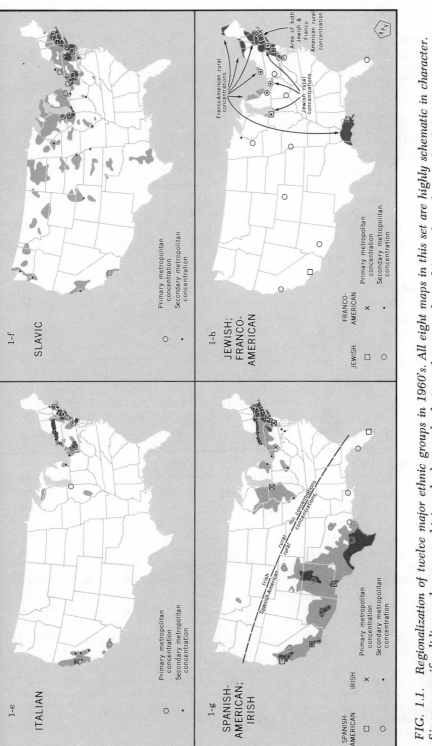

1-e

ITALIAN

○ Primary metropolitan concentration
• Secondary metropolitan concentration

1-f

SLAVIC

○ Primary metropolitan concentration
• Secondary metropolitan concentration

1-g

SPANISH-AMERICAN; IRISH

SPANISH-AMERICAN
□ Primary metropolitan concentration
○ Secondary metropolitan concentration

IRISH
✕ Primary metropolitan concentration
• Secondary metropolitan concentration

Irish rural concentrations
Spanish-American rural concentrations

1-h

JEWISH; FRANCO-AMERICAN

Franco-American rural concentrations
Jewish rural concentrations
Area of both Jewish & Franco-American rural concentration

JEWISH
□ Primary metropolitan concentration
○ Secondary metropolitan concentration

FRANCO-AMERICAN
✕
•

FIG. 1.1. Regionalization of twelve major ethnic groups in 1960's. All eight maps in this set are highly schematic in character. Since a specific sliding scale, one combining absolute and relative values, was devised for each, and since the definition of ethnicity and the quality of data vary sharply from one group to another, it is not advisable to make quantitative comparisons between any pair of maps, or portions there of.

group transcending etʜɴic lines: the labors of nineteenth-century Mormon missionaries abroad inspired many British, German, Scandinavian, and other converts to make their way to Utah.

There is one large section of the country that has failed conspicuously to attract the foreign-born Caucasian in significant numbers: the American South. Even before the Revolution, the South had been peopled largely by pioneers trekking overland from Pennsylvania, Maryland, and the Upper South rather than by direct penetration of its coastal plain. Subsequently, all but a minute fraction of the vast immigrant horde avoided Southern destinations. The only notable regional exceptions are a portion of Texas and (if it is indeed southern) southern Florida. The apparent explanations are: an inferior array of economic opportunities, even after Emancipation; a social climate that few immigrants found enticing; and a xenophobia that may have been both cause and effect of the low incidence of aliens. In any event, the absence of any immigrant leavening of the solid WASP-cum-Afro-American regional culture of the South affords some negative insight into the nature of the immigrant impact upon the North and West.

The validity of that perennial cliché, "the American Melting Pot," merits at least passing notice here, for, in fact, the problem has already spawned a whole bookshelf of publications.[31] The question of whether felt ethnic differences will gradually vanish from the American scene is obviously one of great theoretical and practical import for the student of culture or society. The confident forecast of a few decades ago that the powerful forces of assimilation would grind down ethnic distinctions and mold a standardized American has not been borne out. Some foreign groups do assimilate rather rapidly, notably the English, British Canadians, and many Scandinavians; in fact, the propensity to assimilate seems to be a function of the specific culture—and of generation, with the second the most susceptible. The phenomenal territorial mobility of Americans and a high rate of intergroup marriages also help to tear down ethnic and religious barriers. Yet, despite the obvious forces pointing toward ethnic entropy, the sense of difference and affinity for particular places shows no signs of disappearing in either rural neighborhoods or urban centers. Indeed, in the latter case, some ethnic strongholds have been staked out in suburban and exurban tracts as well as kept within the inner cities. The Melting Pot, it turns out, contains a lumpy stew; and though ethnic groups may have thickened and enriched the All-American broth—except in the southeastern quadrant of the pot—the lumps will not cook away, at least not for a good many more years. We can now expect diversity to persevere for many years. It might be added that we lack any serious geographic analysis at the local scale of

31 Two of the more interesting recent approaches to the problem are Milton M. Gordon, *Assimilation in American Life: the Role of Race, Religion and National Origins* (New York: Oxford University Press, 1964); and Nathan Glazer and Daniel Patrick Moynihan, *Beyond the Melting Pot: The Negroes, Puerto Ricans, Jews, Italians, and Irish of New York City*, 2d ed. (Cambridge, Mass.: M.I.T. Press, 1970).

the processes of ethnic assimilation or the lack of it in the United States and that such efforts might be exceedingly useful.

How great was the effect of the post-1820 immigration upon the character of the American cultural system or its geography? The general answer must be: quite considerable in outward detail, rather little in inner substance. By the year 1820, the essential business of modeling a new national culture and consciousness with its special set of assumptions, drives, and rules had been completed. On a superficial level, it is easy to comment on how our lexicon has been enlivened by additions from the German, Irish, Mexican, or Yiddish vocabularies or how our menus have been similarly enriched by immigrant cuisine. On a national scale, the exotic addenda of the past century and a half have diluted certain characteristics and strengthened others; but none of the central defining attributes, as set forth in the next chapter, has been revised. Perhaps the major effect has been to reinforce something already in progress, the move from an English to a native American ethos, despite our continuing "special relationship" with Britain. An ecumenical ingathering of nations has given substance to the dream of a brotherhood of common ideals and virtues open to all (but most cordially to Caucasians) rather than a shared ancestry—of a voluntary utopia in place of the doctrine of blood and soil.

The Turner Thesis

No discussion of how American culture originated could be complete without treating the most popular, and certainly the most vigorously debated, of the general hypotheses set forth to date, that of Frederick Jackson Turner, first enunciated in 1893, and further elaborated in later writings by Turner and his disciples.[32] Ignoring the many interesting tangential questions that spring from it, the essential argument is quite simple: The central fact of American existence has been the experience of the advancing settlement frontier and its effects upon the rest of the country and later generations. Turner maintained that the American national character was forged on the frontier and that the meaning of American history and institutions can be read only in the light of the peculiar social, economic, and psychological conditions of that transient zone. The lively controversy that has raged between the strongly polarized proponents and opponents shows little sign of abating even now, with only a few scholars working toward a compromise; but it is only in such an intermediate position, I believe, that the merits of both sides of the argument can be realized.

[32] The essential utterances can be found in Frederick Jackson Turner, *Frontier and Section: Selected Essays* (Englewood Cliffs, N.J.: Prentice-Hall, Inc., 1961). The various viewpoints in the Turnerian controversy are competently handled in George Rogers Taylor, ed., *The Turner Thesis*, Problems of American Civilization, Vol. 3 (Lexington, Mass.: D. C. Heath & Co., 1956); and Richard Hofstadter and Seymour Martin Lipset, eds., *Turner and the Sociology of the Frontier* (New York: Basic Books, Inc., 1968).

The contention that the general attributes of nation and citizen originated in the frontier or in its availability as a "safety valve" for an overcrowded East cannot be supported by factual analysis or general cultural theory. Given its very thinly occupied territory, with minimal social or political coherence, a precarious economy, and quite defective communications both internally and with the well-settled portions of the nation, it is hard to visualize any mechanism whereby the frontier could have wielded a commanding influence on the evolving life of the United States. Since the percentage of national territory or population accounted for by the frontier was slight at any given time (except during the earliest years of European settlement), this would have been a case of the tail wagging the dog. Furthermore, all that we know of cultural process indicates that innovations tend to diffuse outward from nodes of relatively intense social and cultural interaction, usually from those core areas where there is a concentration of power, wealth, and talent. Only in rare instances do new ideas or inventions seep back from periphery to nucleus.

This argument may seem to run counter to our earlier espousal of the Doctrine of First Effective Settlement, but on closer examination it does not. The identity and behavior of the first effective settlers were indeed of critical importance for the later development of their own areas, in both the colonial Atlantic Seaboard *and* derivative frontier zones. The Turnerian thesis, on the other hand, implies that despite the variety of peoples, economies, and other aspects of frontier life, there was some transcendent set of general conditions—an overall "frontierness"—uniting all segments and epochs of the American frontier. This overriding quality, in turn, ultimately shaped the personalities and behavior of all our citizens and helped mold the nation's fundamental institutions. That is a proposition that has not been established through solid historical research and probably cannot be.

If the Turner thesis lacks a firm basis in historical data, we are still left with the phenomenon of its remarkable vitality in academic circles and also, in less articulate fashion, in popular thought. Responding to this fact, one can suggest that if the various settlement frontiers failed to act upon the larger society and culture in ways we can measure, nonetheless the *idea* of a potent frontier spirit has been very much alive in the general consciousness. Mythological fact may be as triumphant as historical fact. Seen in this light, Turner's writings emerge as the first conscious evocation of a great quasi-religious folk legend, a codification and celebration of a fundamental article of the national ethos. It remains to be seen why Americans, most of whose ancestors had no direct encounter whatsoever with frontier life, should reach out almost instinctively toward the rather mystical notion that the unique strengths and virtues of the country are the legacy of a heroic frontier era. But the fact of such a groping is incontestable; and since nothing is stronger or more durable than an idea, it is almost irrelevant whether it is connected with actual events and conditions or not. To the degree that the Turner thesis is a formal declaration of an important state of mind, putting aside as secondary the question of strict historical veracity, it is valid and useful. But if we wish to discover how American culture really developed, we must turn elsewhere.

Why Did A National Culture Come to Be?

Thus far we have managed to evade perhaps the most fundamental question that could be asked about American culture: Why does it exist as a distinct national entity, with a certain coherence and personality of its own and with a recognizable continuity over so broad a territory and within so great a population? For there is no doubt that such a basic cultural and psychological unity does prevail, beneath the much more visible monolithic economic and political entity. The processes whereby the transplanted cultures of modern North America came to diverge from those of the ancestral strains of the Old World have been sketched. The relative contributions of various areas and of numerous national groups arriving in varied number at different periods have been described. But still it is not clear why a sense of budding nationhood should have surfaced among the people of thirteen British North American colonies (but not those in Canada or the West Indies) in the latter half of the eighteenth century, or even less whether it was inevitable, given the centrifugal forces of great distance, disparate habitats and ethnic and religious characteristics, and varied social, political, and economic interests.[33] A balkanized North America would appear to have been the more likely alternative. (Consider the fragmentation of New Spain after 1820.) Then there is the further difficulty of accounting for the survival, growth, and spread of the new nation and its freshly minted cultural pattern, despite formidable odds. Obviously, there was a complicated set of factors—geopolitical and commercial prominent among them—interacting in very complicated ways to bring about the birth of the United States. It is equally clear that once the viability of the political state has been explained, its cultural cohesion readily follows, or that this sequence of steps could just as easily be reversed.

Fortunately, such an explanation, although highly desirable, is not truly central to our purpose. Furthermore, it is simply unavailable as yet, except as a series of unproved speculations. Let us, then, accept as a primitive postulate the improbable fact of the existence of this large, populous, apparently durable nation-state with its special cultural geography. We turn next to an examination of what manner of special identity was wrought from the eclectic cargo of people and ideas carried to these shores from the Old World.

---

[33] For some stimulating approaches to this question, consult Karl W. Deutsch, "The Growth of Nations: Some Recurrent Patterns of Political and Social Integration," *World Politics*, 5 (1952), 168–95; Hans Kohn, *American Nationalism; an Interpretative Essay* (New York: Crowell Collier and Macmillan, 1957), and Richard L. Merritt, *Symbols of American Community, 1735–1775* (New Haven: Yale University Press, 1966).

CHAPTER TWO

Identity

On Capturing the American National Character

Anyone seeking to explore the special qualities of American culture finds a Comstock Lode of source material. The young Republic and its denizens were objects of intense curiosity on the part of visitors from the Old World, many of whom were not at all reticent about putting their observations into print; and the popularity of "America-watching" has slackened only slightly in recent years.[1] In addition, Americans themselves have been deeply concerned, almost obsessed, with their image and with their public and private identity, so that national self-analysis has been a thriving indoor sport among a number of native writers. In fact, this narcissistic attitude is itself one of the more extraordinary facets of the national character. Thus the literature dwelling on the peculiar nature of the American scene would fill many yards of shelf space; and much of the better material is of direct value to the cultural geographer. Some of the more precious insights into the basic design of American culture are to be derived not only from the better travel accounts and scholarly probes but from the revelations of creative artists. Such authors as Emerson, Thoreau, Whitman, the quintessential Mark Twain of

[1] Comprehensive guides to the early travel literature for the United States are to be found in E. G. Cox, *A Reference Guide to the Literature of Travel*, Vol. 2, *The New World*, University of Washington Publications in Language and Literature, Vol. 10 (Seattle: University of Washington Press; 1938) and W. G. Vail, *The Voice of the Old Frontier* (Philadelphia: University of Pennsylvania Press, 1949). The most important group of foreign commentators are listed and analyzed in Jane Louise Mesick, *The English Traveller in America, 1785–1835*, Columbia University Studies in English and Comparative Literature (New York: Columbia University Press, 1922) and Max Berger, *The British Traveller in America, 1836–1860*, Columbia University Studies in History, Economics, and Public Law, No. 502 (New York: Columbia University Press, 1943).

"Huckleberry Finn," Henry James, Hart Crane, Robinson Jeffers, Eugene O'Neill, and F. Scott Fitzgerald speak to the central issues, and so too the music of Charles Ives, George Gershwin, or Aaron Copland, the choreography of Martha Graham, and the architecture of Frank Lloyd Wright. More oblique and gnomic, since they purport to deal with extra-American realms of experience, but perhaps ultimately even more illuminating, are the works of Herman Melville or Austin Tappan Wright.[2]

In formal scholarly analysis, two fields of research have actively worked to delineate the core of American culture: American Studies and community studies.[3] Outside these two academic groups, several outstanding individuals, mainly in the fields of history or higher journalism—F. J. Turner, Alexis de Toqueville, Walter Prescott Webb, T. J. Wertenbaker, Perry Miller, Oscar Handlin, and Daniel Boorstin, for example—have delved into the mysteries of the cultural identity of the United States with noteworthy results. Among geographers, there has been a modest amount of work on specific cultural phenomena (see chapter 3), but surprisingly little aimed at questions of essential theme or process. Indeed the only explicit thrust in that direction would seem to be the work of J. K. Wright and David Lowenthal and of French geographers André Siegfried and Jean Gottmann.

2 The reference is to Austin Tappan Wright, *Islandia* (New York: Farrar and Rinehart, 1942), an extraordinary novel about an early twentieth-century American's encounter with a vividly imagined continent, a volume whose great literary and extra-literary merits are, like those of *Moby Dick*, only slowly and posthumously coming to be recognized. For a brief, but warm, appreciation, see Lawrence Clark Powell, *A Passion for Books* (Cleveland: The World Publishing Company, 1959), pp. 97–111.

3 The interdisciplinary entity known as American Studies, which is scarcely three decades old, has displayed much vigor, despite uncertainty over methodology and larger objectives. It represents the efforts of a cluster of scholars in the humanities, chiefly American literature but also history, music, architecture, folklore, and art, and some sociologists and anthropologists as well, to combine the techniques of cultural anthropology and humanistic analysis in interpreting American civilization holistically, and possibly contributing something toward a general theory of cultural process and change. American Studies is analogous to a number of other regionally oriented interdisciplinary consortia, for example, Sinology, Indian Studies, or Islamic Studies; but one may detect the implicit assumption that American civilization may differ in kind from others, that the central questions are unusual in nature and urgency. This movement has produced a number of works of interest to the geographer, and its practitioners merit close attention on the part of anyone seeking to define the essence of America. The topic is comprehensively and critically reviewed in Robert Meredith, ed., *American Studies: Essays on Theory and Method* (Columbus, Ohio: Charles E. Merrill Books, Inc., 1968).

An impressive series of community studies has been executed by a number of sociologists and anthropologists. In analyzing the social structure and behavior of small groups, usually within a single city or other small locality, these studies have confronted cultural issues, but generally as items of secondary concern. Their contribution toward the charting of national cultural patterns has been implicit rather than overt, but still of substantial value. The accomplishments of the community studies movement are summed up in Maurice R. Stein, *The Eclipse of Community; an Interpretation of American Studies* (Princeton, N.J.: Princeton University Press, 1960) and Conrad M. Arensberg and Solon T. Kimball, *Culture and Community* (New York: Harcourt Brace Jovanovich, Inc., 1965).

Much time and energy has been squandered by social scientists in debating the validity of the concept of "national character."[4] There has been much confusion over the meaning and implications of the term, and even more over the wisdom of applying generalizations about a nation to the behavioral patterns of its individual citizens. There is also legitimate fear lest studies in national character perpetuate—or create— false national stereotypes. Fortunately, for our purposes, this Gordian knot can be severed neatly with three observations:

1. Useful nonstereotypic statements can be made about the cultural idiosyncracies (that is, national character) of an ethnic group taken as a whole;
2. the population of the United States does indeed form a single large, discrete ethnic group;
3. statements about the character of the larger community cannot be, indeed should not be, transferred to individuals because of sharp discontinuities of scale.

These points deserve some elaboration.

The validity of national character analysis is dubious when a political state is an arbitrary slice of a larger national entity or is inhabited by a heterogenous collection of unassimilated peoples. What useful general statements could one make about the national character of Cyprus, Malaysia, Togo, or Surinam? It is an utterly different story when nation-state and ethnic group coincide. By definition, ethnic groups form one of the principal categories of cultural communities. Along the cultural continuum from the individual or family to such vast, diffuse entities as the Sino-Japanese or the Greater European Cultural Realm, the ethnic group stands at a critical juncture. It is the largest group to arouse a sense of gripping emotional commitment, one that in moments of crisis may be more precious than life itself; its members share a common symbol pool and are co-owners of the same basic value system and historical or mythic memories. The true ethnic group is also a true nation, in the most primitive, meaningful sense of that term. The ethnic nation may find political consummation in a nation-state, or, if it is less fortunate, it will be a submerged fraction of a larger political entity or distributed over the territory of two or more such states. The origin of ethnicity is immaterial. The group may date back to prehistoric times, with traditions so deeply rooted in a specific tract of land that the emergence of a modern nation-state is a spontaneous, almost unconscious act. In some instances, such as Yugoslavia, Czechoslovakia, Israel, or India,

---

4 The anthropological literature on the topic, which is large and inconclusive, has been reviewed in P. J. Pelto, "Psychological Anthropology," in B. J. Siegel and A. R. Beals, eds., *Biennial Review of Anthropology 1967* (Stanford, Calif.: Stanford University Press, 1967), pp. 140–208; and J. J. Honigman, *Personality in Culture* (New York: Harper & Row, Publishers, 1967). An excellent general bibliography is available in Michael McGiffert, ed., *The Character of Americans; A Book of Readings* (Homewood, Ill.: Dorsey Press, 1967), pp. 364–68. The most recent explicitly geographic treatment of the question is Robert D. Campbell, "Personality as an Element of Regional Geography," *Annals of the Association of American Geographers,* 58, No. 4 (1968), 748–59.

there may be some real or legendary basis for affiliation; or the new ethnic group may be a totally modern assemblage from immigrant or conquered groups, as has been the case with Canada, Brazil, Argentina, or the Soviet Union.

It is suggested that the population of the United States is a genuine ethnic group recently fused from quite miscellaneous materials through a combination of spontaneous fermentation and deliberate engineering by a powerful socioeconomic state apparatus. This group very nearly coincides with the political territory governed by Washington; but one must exclude the more culturally recalcitrant aboriginal Indians, the small Gypsy group, and a few other tiny, aberrant, or transient groups, and the people of Puerto Rico, the Virgin Islands, Samoa, the Trust Territories of the Pacific, and other alien areas currently under American rule. Similarly, there are minor, mostly temporary, exclaves on foreign soil of persons who are totally American in identity.

Once again, by definition, every ethnic group, including the American, possesses a distinctive cultural pattern. We have already agreed that American culture is a member of the Greater European Cultural Realm and no other, even though it may have been affected to some slight degree by non-European cultures. Our immediate problem is to identify those attributes of American culture that are particularly distinctive and important from the viewpoint of the cultural geographer. A complete catalog of American culture would amount to an almost endless list; and even given perfect knowledge, compiling it would prove to be a Herculean chore.[5]

What we are after is the most critical set of cultural attributes, the small package that will most parsimoniously signal the complex totality. The term "culture core" perhaps states most succinctly what is desired. As originally used by its author Julian Steward,[6] it refers to the basic livelihood arrangements of a community, those aspects of the human ecosystem or man-land relationships whereby a group obtains those goods deemed necessary for an adequate existence. Although understanding this system is, of course, critical to the study of any culture, the American livelihood pattern is not basically different from that of several other advanced nations.

As an alternative definition of the culture core, consider instead the central assumptions, the basic values and axioms that define aspiration and direction, even if they seldom describe actual performance.[7] The

---

[5] Some of the more useful items are listed in this volume under *Selected References*, pp. 141–54.

[6] Julian Steward, *Theory of Culture Change* (Urbana: University of Illinois Press, 1955), p. 37.

[7] This point is adumbrated in a remarkable chapter, "The Influence of Manners and Religion on Democratic Institutions in the United States," in a remarkable book, Alexis de Toqueville, *Democracy in America* (New York: Oxford University Press, 1947), pp. 195–220. This was initially published in Paris, 1835–1840. The term "manners" is never adequately defined, but in context appears equivalent to "ethos" or "basic values." De Toqueville states his argument vigorously: "The importance of manners is a common truth to which study and experience incessantly direct our attention. It may be regarded as a central point in the range of human

ethos—that elusive but powerful mood of this and all other distinctive cultures—is the product of many forces. Probably all facets of human experience enter into it, and it, in turn, molds the universe of its participants and the ways they comport themselves within it. Ethos changes through time, but slowly, so that there is a recognizable continuity between the mental world and shared values of colonial Americans and those of our contemporaries. There are also notable variations from place to place, but well within the limits of a sharply bounded national cultural system.

Unfortunately, there is as yet no rigorous, objective method for arriving at the nonmaterial culture core of an ethnic group. The analyst is obliged to feel out a hazardous subjective route. If the following scheme—admittedly an experimental one—is only one of a number of possible ways of defining the central attributes of the national character, it does have the advantage of being congruent with the judgments of many perceptive observers of the American scene, and of being supported rather well by those aspects of the land and people that can be mapped or measured.

Given all the foregoing conditions, it seems possible to chart the geographically relevant, locally distinctive character—the ethos—of American culture in terms of four pervasive themes or motifs, as follows:

1. an intense, almost anarchistic individualism;
2. a high valuation placed upon mobility and change;
3. a mechanistic vision of the world;
4. a messianic perfectionism.

The importance of these motifs, in both absolute and relative terms, varies markedly within the country and as between historical periods, but not so much as to vitiate their validity. This strategy of characterizing so vast and populous a nation in so very curt and cavalier a fashion would not be workable were there not a surprising degree of relative uniformity among the various regions and social segments of the country. As R. M. Huber describes it, "American culture, by its astonishing standardization of thought and uniformity of values in relation to size and population, permits us to make generalizations which would be far more difficult—perhaps impossible—to formulate for many other countries in Western Civilization."[8]

Keep in mind again that we are describing a culture, not the individuals who participate in it. Obviously, a culture cannot exist without bodies and minds to flesh it out; but culture is also something both of *and beyond* the participating members. Its totality is palpably greater

---

observation, and the common termination of all inquiry. So seriously do I insist upon this head, that if I have hitherto failed in making the reader feel the important influence which I attribute to the practical experience, the habits, the opinion, in short, to the manners of the Americans, upon the maintenance of their institutions, I have failed in the principal object of my work." (p. 213)

8 R. M. Huber in Meredith, *American Studies.*

than the sum of its parts, for it is superorganic and supraindividual in nature, an entity with a structure, set of processes, and momentum of its own, though clearly not untouched by historical events and socioeconomic conditions. The example of language is relevant, for it is both a major component of, and paradigm for, the totality of culture. Languages have a life of their own, and the forces that change their content and structure are beyond the conscious control of any set of individuals. Furthermore, the basic syntax of language, its axiomatic implications concerning the meaning of meaning, are a decisive factor in the ways we think about and look at the world. It is just as correct to say that a language speaks us as to declare that we speak a language. In the same way, a culture practices us even more than we practice it. Thus the fact that most American citizens are not stereotypical embodiments (but how many are!) of the four postulates briefly noted above does not destroy their usefulness as illustrations of the essence of American culture. (It is a moot point, and one falling outside the orbit of this essay, whether it is possible for participants in a culture to alter its basic structure, even if they become fully, unhappily aware of it.)

None of the critical themes treated here is uniquely American. In fact, at least three may be found in similar form in other places or periods. But the particular strength and conformation of each and, most especially, their specific combinations are emphatically unique. Moreover, these traits are all borrowed from European sources in which they were latent, and they reflect a continuing interaction with Europe. If the special American tangent is to some degree idiosyncratic, we also have here a behavioral pattern that fits beautifully the needs of the modernization process, unquestionably the major event of recent world history. In fact, it would be difficult to imagine a culture more efficiently programmed for expediting progress toward the most advanced technologies and socioeconomic organization; and for at least the past 70 years the United States has indeed held a commanding lead in most phases of modernization. Are we witnessing a cultural pattern responding to the inner logic of the modernization process? Or has this process been initiated (by cognate cultures elsewhere earlier) and then been catapulted upward by the extraordinary favorable. thrust of American culture? It is probable that both situations have prevailed. In any event, if there is no necessary association between the specific American cultural pattern and the phenomenon of modernization, in all the countries where it has occurred there are some interesting resemblances.

The Theme of Individualism in American Culture

The heroic self-image of the lone, self-reliant, upward-striving individual, sharing equal rights and opportunities with all and liberated from the shackles of tradition and authority, is possibly the single most dominant value in the cultural cosmos of the American. This fanatical worship of extreme individualism, indeed an almost anarchistic privatism, affects so many phases of our existence so deeply that no one can interpret either the geography or the history of the nation sensibly without coming to grips with it. To a much greater degree than the other three themes treated below, this idea is something of which most citizens are actively, even fiercely, aware; it flourishes at the personal as well as the collective level. This creed reflects an ideal goal rather than an everyday reality. Few persons have the resources to carry individualism to such methodically logical extremes as did, say, Henry Thoreau or William Randolph Hearst. But, nonetheless, the reverence for individualism has been a critical force in so many decisions, both private and collective, that it has had an incalculably strong effect in shaping the cultural landscape.

Americans are so conditioned to accepting individualism as the only proper or natural mode of behavior that it is difficult for them to realize that it is actually a quite late, deviant development in social arrangements. Until a few centuries ago, everyone's behavior was tradition-bound. The rules for personal, social, economic, political, and all other forms of activity were a matter of inherited or ascribed status in a family, sex, caste, village, occupation, or church, which, in turn, was determined by the accidents of place of birth and ancestry. It was only with the dawn of the modern age in Northwest Europe, and later elsewhere, that individualism became either possible or widely accepted. In fact, one can now neatly distinguish the modernized, relatively advanced and prosperous countries of the world from the traditional, less advanced societies by the presence or absence of the individualistic philosophy. And any recent success in achieving modernization can be measured by noting how firmly individualism has taken root in the evolving country. What is truly remarkable in American culture is not the existence of a trait shared with the people of Sweden, Switzerland, Rhodesia, Hong Kong, and Siberia, but rather the extremes to which it has been carried both ideologically and materially.

The doctrine of individualism has expressed itself in many ways, but there are three particularly interesting forms: the Frontier Myth; the Protestant Ethic; and the Success Ethic. The apotheosis of the frontiersman as the resourceful, isolated fighter against the wilderness, triumphantly carving out his own autonomous barony, the virile libertarian, jack-of-all-trades, and rough-and-ready paragon of all democratic virtues, has captured the popular imagination, and has survived lustily in folklore, drama, and fiction. To a surprising degree, this is still the role in which many Americans cast themselves in their private daydreams. The result has been a search for the physical or moral equivalent—in technology, the arts and sciences, overseas, in outer space, and elsewhere—for the vanished settlement frontier. There is also an atavistic acting out of the Frontier Myth in many phases of the settlement landscape, recreation, and political behavior.

The familiar, if controversial, Protestant Ethic has, it is claimed, been a potent force in American economics and theology,[9] though quite

---

[9] The thesis of the Protestant Ethic was initially presented in Max Weber, *The Protestant Ethic and the Spirit of Capitalism* (London: G. Allen & Unwin,

unevenly as between different epochs and regions. The emphasis laid upon individual spiritual salvation seems to have been translated into material terms as the parallel doctrine of worldly salvation through constant industry and frugality. Predictably, its self-denying practitioners took a rather dim view of aesthetic experience. This and their hostility toward idleness and pleasure for its own sake have lingered on in the American mind, and have not been completely erased even today.

The Success Ethic, one which is dominant in the United States today, though hardly unique to this country, seems to be a rather simplified product of the Protestant Ethic. Instead of spiritual salvation, however, it holds the greatest good to be the greatest possible individual success. Unfortunately, the definition of success and the scales for measuring it are not clearly understood. Some look upon it as a form of inner satisfaction or ego gratification, but most see it competitively, as the attainment of maximum social approbation, envy, or status, or power. However, under the fluid social conditions prevailing in America, status and power are elusive, and absolute personal success is seldom certain. Contrary to popular myth, simple monetary greed is not the governing passion in American personal behavior, as an expression of individualism or anything else. The bona fide miser is a newsworthy rarity in the United States. Money is a neat numerical device for keeping the score in the scramble for success, not the goal itself. Conspicuous generosity is a mark of success; and the American who has arrived may work as hard at giving away or spending his wealth as he did in piling it up.

Beyond any question, the unusual freedom and mobility given the individual to capitalize upon his innate capacities and to create or grasp new opportunities has been as potent a factor as any in the unequalled material accomplishments of the Americans. But the other side of the coin is the heavy psychological price they pay for freedom and prosperity. It is found in a constant sense of insecurity, of having no final anchorage in things, men, or the supernatural. The American is born into an uncertain place in an unstable society, never quite sure of his identity, and spends his life in a quest for an elusive ego satisfaction. The powerful solvent of individualism has begun to weaken even the most intimate and cohesive of social groups, the nuclear family.[10] The

---

1930) and is critically discussed in Robert W. Green, ed., *Protestantism and Capitalism; the Weber Thesis and its Critics* (Boston: D.C. Heath and Company, 1959). The complex interplay among theology, business practice, and science in early New England, an area of peculiar significance for the later evolution of the nation, is treated in Dirk J. Struik, *The Origins of American Science (New England)*, rev. ed. (New York: Cameron Associates, 1957).

10 The point has been made by a Chinese-American anthropologist with the unusual advantage of being able to view American culture from both inside and outside. "We have seen that mutual dependence is the outstanding Chinese characteristic, and that this deep-seated tendency to rely upon other persons, especially those within the primary group, produces in the Chinese a sense of social and psychological security. . . . The self-reliant American, however, strives to eliminate from his life both the fact and the sense of reliance upon others. This unending struggle to be fully independent raises the threat of perpetual social and psychological insecurity. A close parental bond is severed early in life; the marriage which replaces

consequences may be unpleasant for both individual and society. Furthermore, the practice of individualism has sometimes gone past the point of optimum return and has become dysfunctional, even in a narrow material sense.

The enthusiastic pursuit of individualism has yielded some paradoxes. Americans are at the same time the most acquisitive and the most generous of folk; they are intensely private people, yet at the same time unusually gregarious; and individualism goes hand in hand with sheeplike conformity. These seeming contradictions do make sense, however. The accumulation and the giving away of property are equally proud badges of success, the one following the other. The rootlessness of the private person, lacking any secure base in family, clan, neighborhood, or any other system of mutual dependence, impels him to turn to a series of churches, political causes, lodges, clubs, jobs, and other shallow, transient associations. Masses of insecure individuals find refuge and solace in mob camaraderie, in mass conformity within narrowly prescribed ranges of individualistic behavior.[11] (The genuine certified eccentric abounds in Great Britain, where the individualist can indulge his whims as a kind of obligato above a relatively steady social base; he is almost unknown in the United States.) In the final analysis, individualism, as it is enshrined in national tradition, is hardly a viable way of life in a complex, advanced society of 205 million persons. The illusion of its supremacy and potency may fade in some sectors, notably the economic, but the idea survives. Faith in the absolute goodness of letting every individual do almost anything he wishes is writ large across the American landscape. It will be a long time before the student of American cultural geography can ignore its pervasive effects.

Individualism Manifested in the Cultural Landscape

POLITICAL PATTERNS. If the individualistic strain in the American cultural fabric reveals itself in many geographic phenomena, it does so as strikingly and basically in political behavior as in any other form.

---

it is unstable; heroes come and go; class affiliation is subject to a constant struggle to climb from one level to another; and the alliance with God, though less ephemeral than the preceding relationships, is nevertheless affected by the same divisive forces. For, given the ideal of total self-reliance and its concomitant version of a God who helps those who help themselves, Americans seek their final anchorage in harbors other than men or the supernatural." Francis L. K. Hsu, *Americans and Chinese: Two Ways of Life* (New York: Abelard Schuman, Ltd., 1953), pp. 279–80.

11 And such mass conformity can hardly produce any genuine sense of community. It is not putting things too strongly to state: "There is very little true local community or government in the United States. We are a collection of shallow and spurious and artificial communities, and it is one and the same thing to say about us that we need more national government and that we have hardly any real local government at all. . . . What we do have—mostly the corporations and similar 'private' organizations—is barely recognized for what it is." David T. Bazelon, *Power in America: the Politics of the New Class* (New York: New American Library of World Literature, Inc., 1967), p. 44.

Imbued with the notion of the sovereignty of the individual, the American generally regards government as a necessary nuisance at best and thinks that government best which governs least. The overtones of the epithet "politician" have always been unflattering. Fear and suspicion of authority run deep, and the more remote the seat of power, the sharper the antagonism toward it. The fiction that each of the 50 states is indeed a sovereign kingdom is one that many in public life actually seem to believe, and to which many more pay lip service. Many a function that could be performed more efficiently at less cost at the federal or regional level is jealously hoarded by the state, county, or even municipality.[12] It is truly remarkable—and contrary to much expert early opinion—that the United States achieved federal union in the 1770's and has maintained it continuously ever since. This fact argues the existence of other forces, and, most basically, that mysterious sense of nationhood combined with the free migrations of many persons within the national space, powerful enough to counteract the intrinsic anarchism of the American. But if Americans by the millions were prepared to lay down their lives for the abstract idea of Union, few would lift a finger to strengthen the national government. Indeed many pious platitudes are still being uttered about the urgency of decentralizing administrative functions now based in Washington when, in fact, the national government is still woefully impotent in many vital areas. Among the larger advanced nations of today, one would have to turn to other neo-European lands of similar bent, for example, Australia or Canada, to find local affairs so feebly managed or even ignored by the central authorities. There is something deeply symptomatic in the absence of a national police system[13]—the very thought of it causes most Americans to recoil in horror—or the parcellation of the National Guard into 50 quasi-sovereign entities. Even in so simple a matter as a national system of highway signs, Americans find it impossible to reach consensus.

The chronic antiauthoritarianism of the people has made it virtually impossible for governmental agencies to chart or carry out any form of long-range social and economic planning, except fitfully during such cataclysms as World Wars I and II or the Great Depression. Indeed it was not too long ago that the term "planning" was considered a dirty word by many Americans. Effective planning is practiced, for quite valid, selfish reasons of profit and efficiency, only by the larger privately

[12] As of 1967, there were no less than 3,049 counties, 18,048 municipalities, and 17,105 townships in official existence in the United States; and these local governments, in turn, called upon the services of 508,720 *elected* officials, plus many more appointed employees on wages or salary. U.S. Bureau of the Census, *Statistical Abstract of the United States: 1969*, 90th ed. (Washington, D.C.: Government Printing Office, 1969), 405. The amount of administrative inefficiency implicit in these figures staggers the imagination.

[13] Yet, in keeping with the ambivalence of the national character in matters of privacy, there is little general indignation over the elaborate surveillance systems being developed, often quite covertly, by various governmental bureaus and credit organizations, for the collection and filing of the most intimate kinds of information about individual citizens.

owned corporations and the military and technological branches of the government. The dynamics and larger design of American life, and thus of our human geography in general, are the products of autonomous, essentially uncontrolled social and economic forces and the interplay of numerous competitive special interests.[14]

In spatial terms, the fragmentation of political authority is extraordinary, and it is not just a product of historical happenstance. This is most painfully obvious in the urban centers where some three quarters of the population now lives or works. Except for some smaller places, cities, which operate as unified socioeconomic areas, are balkanized into a number of politically sovereign entities. The larger the metropolis the more numerous and irksome these divisions, and the greater the problems of effecting treaties and alliances whereby the urban area can somehow transact its business. In extreme cases, a single metropolitan area may contain several hundred distinct governments. There are not simply the nominal territorial units (city, village, township, and so forth) but also a multiplicity of special jurisdictions for administering water supply, sewage disposal, pollution control, highways, harbors, schools, hospitals, airports, police, planning, zoning, parks, charities, and many other things. Each of these has some degree of independence. Clearly the costs in time, money, and mismanagement are burdensome. Attempts to rationalize the situation through annexation of outlying places or by creating consolidated metropolitan governments have met with very modest success. Of the 230 Standard Metropolitan Statistical Areas now in existence, only one, Miami (Dade County), Florida, has anything approaching a unified government; and even that experiment is not yet beyond jeopardy. Superficially, the explanation for the slow progress of the "metro" idea lies in the technicalities of state law. More fundamentally, however, the crazy quilt of local authority reflects a deep-seated American individualism; laws and institutions ultimately express the inner temper of the collective mind, in this case a centrifugal, anarchistic mood, the displaced frontiersman's deep, dark dread of "city hall." Psychically, the stockade around the suburban fort seems to be worth the heavy penalty.

In rural areas, the persistence of some two thousand county governments and tens of thousands of minor civil divisions into the late twentieth century cannot be explained in rational terms. These miniature principalities did make sense in the days of horse-drawn vehicles or even the railroad, but are completely anachronistic in an automotive era. In

14 One of the more remarkable facts about a society that is normally so engrossed with facts and figures is that so very little is known about who owns the physical and productive resources of the nation and how basic decisions are reached concerning their allocation, or other matters of national life or death. It is also remarkable that so few academics have bestirred themselves to find out. Apparently this is the most indelicate of subjects, much more so than sex or any of the standard vices. For a massive, irascible, fact-laden, and ultimately persuasive attempt to explore the unmentionable, see Ferdinand Lundberg, *The Rich and the Super-Rich: a Study in the Power of Money Today* (New York: Lyle Stuart, 1968).

any case, the majority of these areas have suffered absolute loss of population. Only a single state, Connecticut (the location may be significant), has stripped its counties of obsolete functions. Once again, the symbolic value of these vestiges of a bygone democratic rurality may operate, if only at the subconscious level, to prolong their life.

SETTLEMENT PATTERN.   Nowhere is the individualism that suffuses the American cultural pattern so legibly inscribed as in our rural settlement patterns or in that general ruralism that is inescapable in American thought and action. Except for New England, the isolated rural farmstead readily became the dominant form of settlement throughout British North America, just as the single-family dwelling is now standard in all but the oldest cities. Even in New England, the general nature of the land and economy *and* a seemingly irrepressible urge toward spatial dispersion and private land speculation brought an end to group colonization and agglomerated villages during the closing phases of frontier advance in the eighteenth century.[15] Other colonial projects for farm villages, for example, the plans framed by William Penn for the immediate Philadelphia hinterland, quickly came to naught, if they were actually implemented at all. Except for the firmly disciplined Mormons and a few other pietistic groups, all subsequent attempts to cluster farm families met with failure.

The explanation for the prevalence of the isolated farmer lies neither in European precedent nor in economic logic. Many of the early immigrants who were destined for American farms had probably been city-dwellers. Although the European source areas were among the most highly urbanized anywhere in the seventeenth and eighteenth centuries, by conservative estimate more than 90 percent of colonial Americans were rural residents.[16] Most of the colonists drawn from rural portions of Europe must have been living in clustered farm villages, since that mode of settlement was general there. Where it was not, the distance to a central place and the rural dispersion of traditionally urban or village functions tended to be less than in the New World.

After 1787, with remorseless rectangularity and with the greatest possible disregard for the sphericity of the earth and the variable qualities of its surface, more than two million square miles of public domain were blocked off into 36-square-mile townships and these, in turn, subdivided into 36 sections, each one mile square. This simplest of possible geometries represents a distillation of earlier Colonial experience and thought, especially that of Virginia and New England—an indefinite projection westward of the Jeffersonian model of an agrarian republic

15 Glenn T. Trewartha, "Types of Rural Settlement in Colonial America," *Geographical Review,* 36, No. 4 (1946), 568–96.

16 For a detailed account of the most rural of the American colonies, see Harry Roy Merrens, *Colonial North Carolina in the Eighteenth Century: A Study in Historical Geography* (Chapel Hill: University of North Carolina Press, 1966), esp. pp. 142–72.

peopled by sturdy independent yeomen. Note the lack of provision for town sites; any urban development was to be an excrescence upon a thoroughly rural design.[17]

The layout of roads and, more particularly, the shape of individual properties and the placement of farmsteads within them, reveal a strong bias toward solitude. It would have been feasible to combine rural residence on sizeable farms with a degree of sociability, as has been done in rural Quebec, by letting the farms run back a full mile or more from relatively narrow road frontages, so that homes could be set in close proximity.[18] Instead, individual properties tend to be compact or square; only exceptionally do three or four farmsteads occupy the common corners; and quite often the farmhouse is located so far back from the highway as to be completely hidden from its nearest neighbors. Although there are obvious functional advantages in living on one's farm instead of commuting daily from a central place, there are also social and economic drawbacks. A far more efficient road system could easily have been devised to serve at less cost an equal number of farmers holding the same amount of land, but with a great reduction in mean distance between homes.

As many ordinary central place functions as possible were ruralized, and some remain so to this day. Only in rare instances could the town be dispensed with totally, as happened in much of Tidewater Virginia or among the larger southern plantations.[19] Itinerant merchants were numerous until recently, the mobile library flourishes, and many completely rural county courthouses still exist.[20] In accordance with the Northwest Ordinance, rural schools prevailed, most of them no more than a single room in size. Rural churches seem greatly to have outnumbered urban congregations; and that thoroughly American phenomenon, the outdoor camp meeting, abounded in various times and

17 Excellent presentations of the historical geography of American systems of land division are available in Francis J. Marschner, *Land Use and Its Patterns in the U.S.*, U.S.D.A. Agriculture Handbook No. 153 (Washington, D.C.: Government Printing Office, 1959) and Norman J. W. Thrower, *Original Survey and Land Subdivision: A Comparative Study of the Form and Effect of Contrasting Cadastral Surveys*, Monograph Series of the Association of American Geographers, Vol. 4 (Chicago: Rand McNally & Company, 1966).

18 As described in Richard Colebrook Harris, *The Seigneurial System in Early Canada: A Geographical Study* (Madison and Quebec: University of Wisconsin Press and Les Presses de l'Université Laval, 1966); or R. Louis Gentilcore, "Vincennes and French Settlement in the Old Northwest," *Annals of the Association of American Geographers*, 47, No. 3 (1957), 285–97.

19 The impulse toward the spatial segregation of homes as an expression of individualism may well have been in the air in Europe at the time the United States was settled; but there were the practical difficulties of a landscape thoroughly encumbered with relict patterns and structures. When reform of the settlement pattern was effected, mainly for economic motives, as happened during the British Enclosure Movement or the parallel breakup of the agglomerated village in eighteenth-century Sweden, the practical problems were staggering.

20 Edward T. Price, "The Central Courthouse Square in the American County Seat," *Geographical Review*, Vol. 57, No. 1 (1968), 38.

places. These isolated religious establishments and the later grange halls and annual county fairs offered the physical basis for much of the organized social life of the nation. At the same time, there was a corresponding atrophy of the social side of the small towns, which, like the larger cities, have always been overwhelmingly economic in function. The recent dwindling away of rural schools and churches is more the result of declining farm population and improved transport facilities than of any slackening in the psychological impulses that led to their generation. Possibly the one visible landscape item that most poignantly discloses the intense individualism and rurality of the American is the isolated country graveyard. In sharp contrast to most European and early colonial custom, whereby burial was restricted to municipal cemeteries or to village or city churchyard, the American custom has been the family plot and bucolic community graveyard.

The contention here is that economic necessity was buttressed by cultural predisposition to make rurality more than a temporary measure: it became the pure, natural fruition of a powerful individualism. The evidence for this is the tenacious grip of rural values upon the mass mind long after the nation has ceased to be essentially agrarian, as can be shown in analyses of modern literature and political behavior. The somewhat fictitious self-sufficient family farm remains one of the durable central symbols around which American mythology is organized, for city folk as for others. Conversely, there lurks in the American mind a clear repugnance toward and distrust of the large city.[21] It is only against the background of such an antiurban bias that one can rationally explain the inordinately long delay in electoral redistricting of state legislatures so as to give urban voters equal representation. Likewise this bias explains that haunting suspicion in the city-dweller himself that he is a moral pariah and hence the political inferior of his uncorrupted country cousin. Similarly, the extremely rapid territorial explosion of the American city, faster and more patternless perhaps than that of any other nation, is undoubtedly abetted by the same sentiments. The diffuse urbanoid periphery represents an uneasy compromise between a rural tropism and the functional imperative of the city. The case for the significance of individualism in the American culture complex need not be made exclusively from rural evidence. The haphazard morphology of the American city and the nearly universal lack of any aesthetic or functional association between adjacent structures also speak volumes.

21 This rural tropism and antiurban bias is rather overstated in Morton and Lucia White, *The Intellectual Versus the City* (Cambridge, Mass.: Harvard University Press and M.I.T. Press, 1962). The question is perceptively treated within a broader context in such works as Leo Marx, *The Machine in the Garden: Technology and the Pastoral Ideal in America* (New York: Oxford University Press, 1964); and Frank R. Kramer, *Voices in the Valley: Mythmaking and Folk Belief in the Shaping of the Middle West* (Madison: University of Wisconsin Press, 1964); while the theme of an ambiguous attitude toward cities is explored at length in Anselm Leonard Strauss, *Images of the American City* (New York: The Free Press, 1961). An adequate full-scale study of how Americans think and feel about cities, concretely or in the abstract, still remains to be done.

ECONOMIC PATTERNS.   The theme of individualism in American economic activity is so thoroughly shopworn it scarcely calls for elaborate argument or documentation. Such catch phrases as "rugged individualism" or "the free enterprise system" eloquently testify to the American businessman's image of himself and the system to which he belongs. If there is a good deal of substance to the myth of the completely unfettered entrepreneur—and trustbusting would not have been socially acceptable were it not in basic accord with the theme of individualism—there is still a wide gap between the ideal and the real. American businessmen have indeed been a remarkably free-wheeling lot in comparison with their confrères in almost any other society, so that the speculator in land and commodities is not only tolerated but is an honored member of the community; but even the most rapacious "robber baron" was subject to a few restraints. The failure rate among smaller entrepreneurs has been dismal; and the majority of American farmers, now as in the past, have been either tenants or deeply indebted to mortgage lenders. The compelling logic of maximizing profit and minimizing risk has nurtured the giant, impersonal corporation; and entire industries find it most lucrative to eliminate serious competition and to regulate prices and other practices by mutual agreement. But reverence for the myth and an incurable antagonism toward truly effective government that is so integral a strain in the general cultural pattern make it impossible thus far to achieve a totally rational economy. Nowhere is this more evident, and nowhere are the geographic implications more direct, than in the transportation and communication industries.

To a degree unmatched in other lands, these industries have been controlled by (ostensibly) competitive enterprises owned by individuals or private corporations. This was true for earlier eras when some postal services, most improved roads, ferries, canals, and toll bridges—many of them needlessly duplicating the services of others—were in private hands. The history of the American railroad industry, understandable only against the backdrop of individualism, is one of chaotic growth, wholesale duplication of lines, and a frustrating proliferation of terminals in major cities. Only slowly, against a rear guard action by public opinion and federal bureaucracy, have the necessary, inevitable mergers taken place. Even now there is no truly nationwide line; and unlike almost every other modern nation, the coterminous United States has virtually no federally owned or operated trackage except a recently introduced, severely truncated passenger system. The recent history of air transportation is essentially a replay of the railroad saga, with the significant exception that technical factors have compelled the local consolidation of terminal facilities: the same duplication of lines and services; the same uneasy combination of competition and cooperation and grudging reliance upon governmental semi-control and subsidy. And what other self-respecting nation lacks that glittering status symbol, the national airline? The ghost of individualism still stalks the land.

At an even broader level, the universal mood of economic privatism has made it impossible to draw up, much less execute, the sort of comprehensive transport system that is urgently needed, one that would integrate railroads, trucking, airlines, bargelines, pipelines, busses, and mass transit in a manner that could save enormously in terms of costs, time, annoyance, and space. At the other extreme, the unrivaled supremacy of the private car in the ground transportation of passengers, and the correspondingly dismal results of efforts to maintain or revive mass transit systems, argues a deeply ingrained bias toward personal autonomy, symbolized by the metal-and-glass bubble around each American.

In communications, the picture is much the same. Only postal services are a federal near-monopoly; but perenially some business spokesman has uttered the primordial tribal cry of "Turn the Post Office over to sound private businessmen!" until the recent restructuring of the system within an autonomous quasi corporation. Again, in contrast to like facilities in every other civilized country, our telegraph, radio, and television facilities are, with minor exceptions, operated for private profit, and with wretched results. In the case of telephone services, elsewhere a government monopoly, the free enterprise system has acquitted itself more nobly, in part because a single corporation bestrides the field. But a glance at a map of franchise territories reveals a surprising number of local companies, and indicates that here again the theme of individualism has achieved spatial expression.

RELIGION AND EDUCATION. The stubborn insistence upon individual autonomy and the most absolute freedom of choice possible has yielded unique results in American religious life. Not only is the number of denominations and subdivisions thereof far in excess of anything recorded anywhere else at any time, but many groups united in name or theory are, in fact, almost totally disunited at the regional or congregational level (and dissension within the single congregation is a popular indoor sport). Diversity is not only doctrinal but also spatial and behavioral. The number and range of local churches is unequalled elsewhere, so that a rather small village may boast a half dozen denominations, and only rarely does a single creed dominate even a single locality. The American lacks any fixed locus in spiritual as well as in social or physical space. Members of a single family may belong to two or more churches simultaneously; a given individual may join several different churches in the course of a lifetime. He may even patronize two or more churches on successive sabbaths, in a thoroughly egalitarian spirit. In contrast to the economic and political realms, where it can be demonstrated objectively that individualism yields dysfunctional results in contemporary America, strong arguments can be adduced for either side of the issue of external freedom of choice in matters religious: it is a mixed blessing.

The structure of the American educational system also confirms the individualist streak in the national character. The prevailing pattern seems so natural to Americans that it is startling to realize how truly aberrant it is when set against worldwide norms. Public education at the primary and secondary levels—and often at the collegiate level—is under strict local control by municipality or county, with only a mild

CARL A. RUDISILL LIBRARY
LENOIR RHYNE COLLEGE
HICKORY, N. C. 28601

degree of supervision by the state government and none at all at the federal level. Although technical or financial assistance may be forthcoming from Washington, strenuous efforts are made to prevent overt interference with local school policy. Thus there is no federally operated system of schools, except on Indian reservations and in the military services, and any advocacy of such would be political suicide.

In addition to the proliferation of public, parochial, and private elementary and high schools found in many American communities, there is an abundance of privately endowed and operated colleges. Many are, or were, denominational, but most appear to have been founded for purposes of gain, philanthropy, the propagation of particular points of view, or the perpetuation of the donor's name. Private colleges are genuine rarities in other parts of the English-speaking world or elsewhere. Their profusion in the United States attests not only to the nation's material wealth but also to the free range given individual initiative. Little work has been done on the geography of education in the United States and none apparently on the historical geography of higher education. An analysis of colleges, especially the private liberal arts college, might yield important insights into the cultural geography of the nation.

MISCELLANEOUS SYMPTOMS. The extremely high valuation placed on individual effort and freedom in American culture surfaces in many other aspects of the national scene. The following items would seem to have considerable potential for the geographic analyst, but remain almost totally unexplored. The American hospital system offers a close parallel to our schools in its mixture of public, religious, and private endeavor and the occasional proliferation—and probable duplication— of facilities in certain fortunate localities. The emphasis on profit-making proprietary hospitals and homes for the convalescent and elderly is probably stronger than in other societies. Their spatial configuration awaits the explorer. The vast number of privately endowed philanthropies (about 18,000 at present), not only for schools and hospitals but for many other forms of activity as well, is the result, in part, of phenomenal affluence and the peculiar structure of the tax laws, but is also a ringing assertion, usually posthumous, of the personal triumph of the lavish individualist. The United States would also be far in the lead in any international competition in voluntary associations, whether in absolute quantity (more than 15,000 are listed in the standard source)[22] or number per capita. These groups, which may be fraternal, athletic, recreational, charitable, occupational, business or professional, scientific, artistic, political, criminal, neighborhood, or related to any of a limitless variety of other special interests, reflect both a footloose individuality and the somewhat shallow gregariousness that develops among people adrift without a secure social

[22] Margaret Fisk et al., eds., *Encyclopedia of Associations*, 2 vols., 6th ed. (Detroit: Gale Research Co., 1970).

base. Again, it would be most profitable to look into their geographic manifestations.

A final suggestion that could plunge one deeply into the American cultural psyche concerns the significance of attitudes toward firearms. There seems to be something peculiarly symptomatic of an extreme individualism in a rate of private rifle and revolver ownership far exceeding that of other urban-industrial lands. Clearly this is a socially dysfunctional phenomenon. Even more symptomatic is the sheer volume of the recent uproar over the real or imagined threat to what many consider an inalienable individual privilege. Once more, the seductive image of the frontier hovers over the land.

The Theme of Mobility and Change

All societies change. This truism has held since time immemorial, but it is only in the past few centuries that it has had any real meaning for individuals. Only recently have things moved so rapidly that one is unable to overlook major change within a single lifetime or shorter intervals.[23] For members of most cultures, change is profoundly disturbing and unwelcome, something to be resisted and shut out. The American attitude is remarkably different. Here necessity has become a virtue; the external imperative has been internalized. Once again we have a cultural trait pandemic throughout the modernized world, but with the United States blazing the way, riding the cab of the locomotive of history, happily stoking the fires. The love of change and of all forms of mobility, an innate restlessness, is one of the prime determinants of the structure of American national character. Living in a world of swift and sudden transitions and constant acceleration in the pace of innovation, Americans revel in the new and the rapid; they are sulky or bored with the old and the static. Choice, change, movement, and progress are the new gods. Nowhere else does the cult of youth have so many devotees; and nowhere else is it so uncomfortable or even disgraceful to reach an advanced age. It is no accident that the United States has spawned and developed jazz music to such sophisticated levels. Indigenous art forms reflect the core of a culture; and jazz ideally embodies the feeling of hurtling momentum, imbalance, fluid relations, and inner uncertainty.

Perhaps the briefest acceptable definition of the uniqueness of its culture is this: America is process. This understandably exaggerates a universal principle, for the comprehension of process is fundamental in studying any society; and process and structure are everywhere lashed together in a never-ending embrace. In the case of the United States, however, the processual side of reality is the more obvious. The rate and complexity of change are so overpowering and process so rapidly evolutionary that the resultant structural arrangements tend to be fleeting and

---

[23] The first book length discussion of this new phenomenon is Alvin Toffler, *Future Shock* (New York: Random House, Inc., 1970).

unobtrusive.[24] A more basic statement about the quintessential nature of its culture is that the United States is a country of constant decision. The existentialist point is well stated by Perry Miller:

> He who endeavors to fix the personality of the American in one eternal, unchangeable pattern not only understands nothing of how a personality is created, but comprehends little of how this nation has come along thus far... he fools himself if he supposes that the explanation for America is to be found in the conditions of America's existence rather than in the existence itself. A man is his decisions, and the great uniqueness of this nation is simply that here the record of conscious decision is more precise, more open and explicit than in most countries...being an American is not something inherited but something to be achieved.[25]

The ways in which time, space, and other apparently absolute elements of experience are actually perceived can vary widely from one cultural group to another.[26] One of the basic postulates of the American cultural system—and one to which nearly all its members subscribe—is that time is a peculiarly precious thing; literally, time is money, as we are told a dozen times a day. Another is the axiomatic belief in the directional, linear flow of time. In many, perhaps most, cultures, time is felt to be either patternless, with no discernible rhythm beyond that of the year or generation, and is seldom thought about consciously, or it is vaguely circular, with grand recurrent cycles and subcycles. In either case, events are enacted within an ultimately immutable universe. In the American cosmos, on the other hand, events flow purposefully and rapidly from a dim, unregarded past along a straight, narrow groove toward an indistinct but brighter future. This notion can be neatly symbolized as an arrow in upward trajectory. Such a linear patterning of space and spatial behavior, is, of course, closely paralleled by an equally linear patterning of space and spatial behavior.

As a group, Americans are profoundly insensitive to, or uninterested in, any segment of time except the present and the immediate future. Unlike more static cultures, whose members dwell companionably with memories or relics of past generations, the American is often nearly oblivious to his history, or even takes positive pleasure in demolishing older artifacts and replacing them with newer (= better) ones. What visible evidence is there, for example, that New York City has existed continuously for more than 340 years? Insofar as there is any enthusiasm for the past, it is for a neatly segregated, sanitized, romanticized package in museum form, vide Williamsburg, Greenfield Village, Sturbridge Vil-

---

24 The theme of incompleteness and rapid change in a future-oriented visible landscape is dwelled upon in David Lowenthal, "The American Scene," *Geographical Review*, 58, No. 1 (1968), 61–88.

25 Perry Miller, *Nature's Nation* (Cambridge, Mass.: Harvard University Press, 1967), p. 13.

26 Edward T. Hall, *The Hidden Dimension* (Garden City, N.Y.: Doubleday & Co., Inc., 1966).

lage, or the never-never land of the Western film—a synthetic past uncannily mirrored by the equally shallow, museum-display futures exhibited in our world fairs and the science fiction movie.[27] Although Americans are powerfully propelled toward a future in which present expectations will be consummated and current incongruities in our visible landscape are to be patched up, it is a very short-range future—the lifetime of living individuals. The remote future is almost never thought about.

The high esteem accorded time by Americans, who have a correspondingly weak awareness of space, is apparent in many ways. Geography courses are rare in secondary schools and lacking in many a college, but the teaching of history is well-nigh universal. (We may not have much true feeling for the past, but at least we feel we ought to.)[28] The number of clocks in public and private places is noteworthy. Most individuals feel almost naked without their wristwatches, but how many carry compasses, maps, or field glasses, or can identify cardinal directions or the local river basin? Here again the United States carries to an extreme a motif that first appears in early medieval Europe with the elaboration and first widespread, communal use of mechanical timepieces. Promptness is celebrated, and time is chopped into tiny slices to be doled out grudgingly. Particularly revealing is the relative status of time, space, and substance. Americans will go to great lengths to conserve time, including the abolition of distance for all practical purposes, and a spendthrift wastage of physical resources. In fact, almost anything is permitted if a few moments can be saved. Linear distances are automatically translated into temporal terms: it is so many hours between cities, or so many minutes between home and job. This interchangeable spatial-temporal linearity is strongly developed at the sacrifice of territorial acuity, so that the perception of two-, three-, or four-dimensional space is quite feeble in a land of ephemeral human landscapes.

The overwhelming emphasis on haste, speed, and change in the American cultural pattern has had endless repercussions upon the social and economic behavior of our citizens. An innate receptivity to innovation, a hunger for novelty, and a tolerance of, even an eagerness for, the built-in obsolescence of many products from paper tissues to skyscrapers have affected our social and economic geography in ways too numerous and obvious to be recounted here. Suffice it to say that even in the short run the immense, rapid turnover of things and people, through space and processual channels, cannot be fully justified on

[27] David Lowenthal, "The American Way of History," *Columbia University Forum* (Summer 1966), pp. 27–32.

[28] Books and periodicals dealing with American history in a popular style have proved quite lucrative in a number of instances; but, unlike Great Britain, Germany, and other countries, where such publications flourish, we have no successful mass-audience journal concerned with matters geographical. The financial success of some essentially touristic ventures or those dealing with natural history does not vitiate the argument.

strictly rational economic grounds or otherwise. Taking a deeper, longer view, it is clear that the vigor of the various American circulation systems —of migrant, artifact, information, and so forth—is less a response to narrow monetary impulse than to the essential mold of the cultural matrix. By hustling, wandering, experimenting, "developing" themselves and their land, and consuming space and treasure at a prodigious rate, Americans are scratching a very basic itch indeed.

In geographic terms, this inner restlessness is expressed most purely and simply as spatial mobility. The phenomenon can be classified into two major categories: *migration*, that is, change in permanent residence; and *circulation*, that is, temporary or pendular movements. Although the available data and measures for migration in the United States are far from ideal, they do clearly indicate that the great majority of Americans shift residence at one time or another and that a significant minority do so with great frequency and over considerable distances.[29] Unfortunately, the information at hand does not permit useful comparisons with other nations.[30] A survey taken in 1958 indicated that only 26 percent of Americans 18 years and older had not changed residence since birth. According to the Bureau of the Census' Current Population Survey, between 18.6 percent and 21.0 percent of the total population had moved to a different house within any given year since 1948; between 5.6 percent and 7.1 percent migrate to a different county annually, and about half that number to a different state. As far as can be inferred from the rather unsatisfactory figures, there has been little rise or fall in internal migration rates in the United States over the past 100 years, but a sharp increase in average distance of move. In any case, the persistent pattern of high mobility reinforces the belief that the footloose behavior of Americans is not a transient frontier phenomenon.

In recent years the outlines of a rather complex lifetime cycle of migration for the typical American citizen appears to be emerging. After a childhood during which his family may or may not move, and upon graduation from high school, the American may change residence one or more times as a result of marriage, military service, or college education. Then, with or without such an intervening phase in early adulthood, the adult participates for forty years or so in the labor force, during which time change in employment may prompt change in residence. In addition, continuing affiliation with a large corporation may mean shifts from one of its plants or office locations to another. Marriage and divorce

---

29 For useful discussions of the historic and geographic migrational patterns within the United States, consult Conrad Taeuber and Irene B. Taeuber, *The Changing Population of the United States* (New York: John Wiley & Sons, Inc., 1958), pp. 92–111, and Donald J. Bogue, *Principles of Demography* (New York: John Wiley & Sons, Inc., 1969), pp. 776–800.

30 One of the first serious attempts to confront this question is Larry H. Long, "On Measuring Geographic Mobility," *Journal of the American Statistical Association*, 65, No. 331 (1970), 1195–1203. This article tends to support the assertion that Americans are more mobile than citizens of other lands.

often bring about migration, especially for women. After retirement, the individual may elect to move his household to an area he considers attractive or comfortable. Each of these forms of migration produces important geographic effects.

The more casual and ephemeral movements in which Americans engage are poorly documented; but their aggregate volume, if it could be quantified as mileage or hours in transit, is enormous and probably well exceeds the level that could be recorded for any other advanced, nominally sedentary country.[31] Included here are several kinds of patterned, cyclical trips and a miscellany of one-time or irregular travel experiences. Among the former, the daily journey to work bulks largest. Only a tiny minority of American workers live within walking range of place of employment; and among the commuters, the 1963 Census of Transportation reports, 24 percent travel 11 miles or more to their destination and an appreciable number 30, 40, or more miles, generally by private auto. In addition, there are millions of weekend trips to vacation cottages or resorts or trips by college students from home to campus, innumerable delivery routes in retail and wholesale enterprises, and the complex odysseys of salesmen and business executives. Less repetitive in pattern are long-distance journeys by tourists and members of the military at home and abroad and a great volume of local (up to 50-mile) excursions to see friends, relatives and seek cultural or athletic diversions. In fact, the state of physical rest seems to be the exception.

Even though statistical details on various forms of American mobility can be elusive, the theme of dynamism is emphatically inscribed upon our settlement morphology. The highway has become *the* controlling element, the most vital social organ in contemporary life. No longer is it simply a bumpy, dusty nuisance linking densely settled places; it has been transformed into a spinal column, with cities and almost all else more and more dependent upon it for sustenance and growth.[32] The manner in which mountains and rivers are moved and great swaths slashed through cities with little heed to financial, social, or historic cost to make room for new highways testifies to the priority of values. (A century ago the same story could have been told about the imperious railroad.) The basic drives and motifs of a culture can be most clearly read along its growing spatial edges, where it is essentially uninhibited by the physical and social detritus of the past. This is perhaps the fundamental appeal of the settlement frontier of pioneer days to the social historian and cultural geographer. Today it is the suburb and ribbon settlements along our highways that speak most eloquently about

[31] On the significance of territorial mobility in general and the American situation in particular, see Wilbur Zelinsky, "The Hypothesis of the Mobility Transition," *Geographical Review*, 61, No. 2 (1971), 219–49.

[32] Some of the most thoughtful observations on the modern American highway and its attendant features are scattered through the issues of *Landscape*, in the form of brief essays by its former editor, John B. Jackson. See, for example, "The Abstract World of the Hot-Rodder," *Landscape*, 7, No. 2 (Winter 1957–1958), 22–27.

our essential selves; and even stronger clues are visible in the largely twentieth century cities that have sprouted in the relative emptiness of Texas, California, and the Southwest with their extraordinary dispersion and diffuseness and nearly total reliance upon the internal combustion engine—and the near extinction of the pedestrian.[33] There we find the logical physical embodiment of a society in which almost everyone, even the pauper, owns an automobile and the most significant rite of passage is the acquisition of a car or motorcycle after a childhood of roller skates, scooters, and bicycles. It is also a society where many aspire to motor-boats, skis, snowmobiles, and the private airplane: in short, speed is supreme.

Perhaps the most interesting physical expression of our theme of mobility is found in the large new suburban shopping center, with its sprawling parking lot or the developments that have mushroomed around important highway interchanges and airports, veritable autonomous cities, reminiscent of the almost totally self-contained large hotels of major metropolises—which, in turn, were spawned by railroad terminals. But there is also abundant evidence in the details of roadside enterprise within and between cities. The fact that the wheel has become an almost organic extension of the American's anatomy is illustrated by those indigenous inventions, the motel and the drive-in restaurant, cinema, and bank. Recently, drive-in post offices have begun to appear; and there are well-founded reports of drive-in churches and funeral parlors. In addition to the more conventional shops and services that stretch along the road for mile after mile, each with its parking lot, there are the many enterprises that would not exist without the auto, truck, or bus: filling stations, garages, accessory shops, new- and used-car dealers, drag strips, car laundries, and auto junkyards. Quite literally, travel has become an end in itself: the American never arrives; he is always on his way.

We have looked at only a small fraction of the evidence that could be amassed to prove that most Americans ardently subscribe to a value system granting lofty status to mobility in all its forms—travel, speed, haste, change—most obviously in physical space but in other dimensions as well. This is a proposition that will recur again and again in our further examination of spatial process and structure in the American cultural system.

---

33 To a marked degree, the American city has been the creature of transport technology from the very beginning. See, for example, John R. Borchert, "American Metropolitan Evolution," *Geographical Review*, 57, No. 3 (1967), 301–32. One can define a sequence of urban morphologies identifiable with each major mode: first the city shaped by the needs of ocean or river transport, pedestrians, and horse-drawn vehicles; then the patterns engendered by railroads and, somewhat later, by streetcars; and currently the morphological response to auto, truck, and airplane. The basic point remains the same, however: the overwhelming importance in urban design of moving people and things. Cities tend to be marts and transfer points; all else is subsidiary.

The Theme of a Mechanistic World Vision

Another basic postulate upon which American culture is constructed is that the universe is a fundamentally simple, mechanical system subject to human control: this is the vision of the world as machine, one that can be improved and accelerated.[34] (Note the peculiar prominence of the term "fix" in the American vocabulary.) This belief applies not only to the cosmos in general, but to the various subsystems and territorial units within it, as well as to individual human beings. Although this theme is ultimately as meaningful for the human geography of the United States as the notions of individualism or dynamism, its spatial expression is rather less direct, so that it can be expounded here briefly.

A mechanistic model of reality leads quite readily to a series of related ideas: the desirability of keeping the machine and its components nicely adjusted and working at optimum efficiency; a cleanliness fixation; a highly elaborated pragmatism; hence a utilitarian attitude, with a corresponding denigration of abstract thinking and aesthetic considerations; a passion for the precise measurement of things; a love of bigness and growth; a strongly extroverted personality pattern; and a firm belief that brute nature can be subjugated and made to behave rationally for the benefit of its human masters. Only some of these beliefs call for further comment.

Within the adjustable world-machine envisioned by Americans, the human actor is a detachable, freely mobile, perfectible cog; and we achieve the convergence of our previous two themes with that under discussion. Eli Whitney's invention of the system of interchangeable parts, perhaps the first truly major American contribution to world technology, provides a neat paradigm for the larger pattern of reality as sensed by his compatriots: the interchangeable Yankee, highly versatile and movable, and eager to insert himself into the locus of maximum advantage to himself and thus, of course, to the system.[35] The phenomenal social, economic, and spatial mobility of the individual thus becomes a rational way for lubricating and putting into a state of frantic productivity all those gears, wheels, levers, springs, and pulleys that comprise the physical and social world. The pressures within the cultural milieu tend to mold people into flexible, adjustable, cheerful, conformable units for operation in the social as well as the economic sphere. If a machine is to work well, its parts must be washed, dusted, and carefully cleaned and polished; and for this reason, among others, we find an obsessional interest in personal cleanliness, which carries over

---

[34] This notion is developed with great power and depth in two volumes by Lewis Mumford, *The Myth of the Machine: I. Technics and Human Development* (New York: Harcourt Brace Jovanovich, Inc., 1967) and *The Myth of the Machine: II. The Pentagon of Power* (New York: Harcourt Brace Jovanovich, Inc., 1970).

[35] Daniel J. Boorstin, *The Americans: The National Experience* (New York: Random House, Inc., 1965), esp. pp. 3–48.

into the internal design of the American house. But it must also be noted that while the American is so concerned with the neatness of his person, clothes, and home, this interest fades past personal property lines, so that he feels almost complete indifference to the appearance of public spaces.

A mechanistic world is a quantifiable one, so that it is hardly surprising to find everything numbered and counted, or to note the ardent accumulation of statistics by a people who dote on digits. The observable universe is converted into dollars, hours, miles, acres, tons, decibels, input-output tables, foot-candles, wavelengths, millibars, TV ratings, grade-point averages, and a long list of other indices. It scarcely needs saying that the dominant themes and methods in American social science are set by the general cultural conditioning of its practitioners. In territorial terms, the rectangular land survey, already mentioned for its effectiveness in dealing with the craving for personal isolation, has the additional virtue of numerically coding even the smallest tract with its unique combination of letters and numbers, so that both size and location can be identified almost instantly. The great majority of American cities are wholly or partially laid out on a rectangular grid; and many of them have their major thoroughfares named in numerical or alphabetical order. The practice of methodically numbering all buildings within a city (and all rooms within buildings) by distance and direction from a baseline or point of origin seems to be an American innovation, probably one initiated in Philadelphia. It is now almost universal within the United States, but has been adopted and executed with equal rigor in relatively few places outside North America.

A reverence for number and quantity combines with the pervasively dynamic quality of the American cultural system to produce a fervent worship of both growth and bigness. The theme of giantism—paralleled in modern times only by the Russian passion—is constantly obtruding in American behavioral patterns and the visible landscape. In many American cities, the skyscraper makes more sense as symbol than as rational investment.[36] Humorous braggadocio and the tall story seem indigenous, and Texan expansiveness in myth and jest is a quintessential expression of this impulse. There is an irresistible urge to achieve—and proclaim—the quantifiably superlative—the biggest, highest, costliest, loudest, or fastest—frequently without any dollar-and-cents justification. This compulsion cannot be ignored in analyzing the economic or population geography of the nation; indeed it merits book-length treatment in its own right.

The American value system casts its members in the roles of Promethean heroes bringing light and imposing order upon a somewhat unruly, but ultimately domesticable, wilderness. As subjugators and transformers of nature, Americans tinker with or rebuild its machinery and make it run faster and more smoothly. In the short run, this strategy

[36] Jean Gottmann, "Why the Skyscraper?" *Geographical Review*, 56, No. 2 (1966), 190–212, and Larry Ford, *The Skyscraper: City Structure and Urban Symbolism*, doctoral dissertation, University of Oregon, 1970.

has generally succeeded, at least in bookkeeping terms, even though the long-term resolution of the ecological problems of man in North America is cloudy at best. The march of settlers westward across the continent can be viewed as a series of environmental traumas or conflicts, in each of which the modern American has won the immediate decision through a technical knockout. The principle in every case has been that the land must be made economically profitable, to respond quickly and effectively to human endeavor; it is a simple commodity to be sliced, cubed, sold, processed, and squeezed of its intrinsic wealth.

Through a fluke of environmental fate, the culture hearth within which these ideas were first fully hatched and tested was the northeastern United States, an area reasonably analogous in physical characteristics with the Northwest European source area. Few concessions were necessary. Within the humid subtropics of the American South, on the other hand, the traditional modes of rural economy did not work very well. But instead of coming to ecological terms with an unfamiliar land, the Southerner persisted in his Promethean ways and inflicted upon the region a totally inappropriate mode of cultivation. In the case of cotton and tobacco, the early profits were reassuring, even though growing conditions, especially for the former, were marginal; but the ultimate cost in environmental and social havoc was incalculably great. It is only in the twentieth century that ways have been found to make Southern land productive for long periods at fairly high levels; but, again, through a synthetic technology willfully imposed by men who are still not psychologically at home in the region.

In less dramatic form, the minor crisis of the encounter with thick-sodded humid grasslands in the Middle West was overcome with the aid of technology; and the land was "broken in" promptly and efficiently. The chronic environmental tensions in the Great Plains and further west within more arid regions have never been fully resolved. Instead there has been a series of technological adventures, some of them failures, others temporarily successful, whereby the American conquistador has tried to tame the land. On an even larger scale, there is growing concern over the long-term biological and psychological results for the American population as a whole, and not just the physical impact upon land, water, and air, of the runaway explosion of a technology that ignores the habitat, or else treats it in a highly simplistic fashion.

The Theme of Messianic Perfectionism

Perhaps the most extraordinary facet of the American national character is the power and durability of an idea only weakly, fitfully developed in other cultures: the notion that the United States is not just another nation, but one with a special mission—to realize the dream of human self-perfection and, in messianic fashion, to share its gospel and achievement with the remainder of the world). This moral expansiveness (some would call it "moral imperialism") exists over and beyond the usual flexing of economic or military muscle that all modern nation-states of any size seem to indulge in quite automatically in response to some general law. If it transcends standard nationalism, neither is it just the normal afterglow of revolutionary fervor. Indeed the American Revolution was much tamer in its initial ideological content than other modern revolutions have been. But if there is a predictable time-decay function for the Islamic, French, Russian, and presumably the Mexican, Ghandian, Maoist, Castroite, and lesser political and religious convulsions of recent centuries, as the curve representing zeal for converting the heathen droops steadily lower each year, quite the opposite seems to have happened with the American sense of mission.

From the very beginning of serious settlement along the Atlantic Seaboard, potent strains of a visionary perfectionism were mingled with more mundane economic and political considerations, and not only in the New England colonies. In this errand into the wilderness, there was a quite conscious attempt to seek out or build a New Zion—later the New Athens or New Rome—the City upon the Hill, or quite literally, an earthly Eden with a Manifest Destiny.[37] It is not too extravagant to claim that collectively, the country thinks of the land as a literal, real-world utopia. Thus it is that many a citizen can quite solemnly speak of "God's Country" or the "American Way of Life." Even the term "Americanism" carries with it a sense of uplift, special earnestness, and quasi-religious connotations; no other language has a parallel term.

Insofar as cultural geography is concerned, this is a major, but generalized, theme more important as basic premise or mood than as specific, mappable expression. But the American penchant for messianic perfectionism does attain tangible form in at least two ways, neither of which has received the geographic analysis it deserves. If one might debate the propriety of treating the entire nation as a utopian experiment, the case is clear for early New England and other colonial settlements, notably Penn's Holy Experiment. Some scores of churchly and secular utopian colonies have been founded in the United States from the

---

[37] This idea is implicit in many writings on the character of life and thought in the United States but is seldom advanced explicitly. Among the more noteworthy statements are Hugo Münsterberg, "The Spirit of Self-Perfection," *The Americans* (New York: McClure, Phillips & Co., 1905), pp. 347–64; Jean Gottmann, "Prometheus Unbound," *Megalopolis: the Urbanized Northeastern Seaboard of the United States* (New York: Twentieth Century Fund, 1961), pp. 23–79; Charles L. Sanford, *The Quest for Paradise: Europe and the American Moral Imagination* (Urbana: University of Illinois Press, 1961); and J. Wreford Watson, "Image Geography: the Myth of America in the American Scene," *Advancement of Science*, 27 (1970–1971), 1–9. The argument is especially fully and eloquently developed by Sanford, and one of his central statements is well worth quoting:

Liberals and conservatives alike have been moralists, forever pitting themselves...against the fancied evils of life, forever demanding changes, improvements, cure-alls. Since Colonial days, in fact, there has been a marked tendency to regard America as having greater moral obligations than other nations and therefore to consider her sins more heinous than those of other nations.

An unfortunate result has been much exaggeration of America's deficiencies by patriotic citizens and an equally unfortunate exaggeration of her innocence and uniqueness in terms of moral (material, political, economic) superiority. By their great prestige as culture heroes, Franklin and Jefferson contributed significantly to a national superiority complex which alternated between an isolationism which would retreat behind a *cordon sanitaire* of protecting oceans to a hermetically sealed paradise in the Mississippi Valley, and a messianic internationalism which would make the world over in the American image. (p. 134)

eighteenth century onward.[38] The movement may have peaked during the last century, but new, ever more inventive utopias are still being formed. Usually quite short-lived and practicing some form of primitive communism, such visionary schemes were not unknown in Europe and in other neo-European areas; but their incidence and their impact upon national thought has been far greater here than elsewhere. In one instance, the Great Basin Kingdom of the Mormons, the enterprise has flourished, endured, and had a decisive effect upon the human geography of a truly extensive tract of land.[39] Although these utopian adventures account, in sum, for only a small fraction of the population, they are deeply symptomatic—a kind of psychodrama, acting out the daydream haunting the American cultural soul.

In their choice of place names, Americans have also revealed various facets of their world outlook, including a vigorous strain of self-improvement and upward aspiration. Almost any corner of the country will do, but a casual scanning of the Pennsylvania map yields the following more or less inspirational town names:

Acme	Frugality	Philadelphia
Arcadia	Harmony	(City of Brotherly Love)
Concord	Independence	Pleasant Unity
East Freedom	Industry	Progress
Edenville	Liberty	Prosperity
Effort	New Hope	Salem (Peace)
Enterprise	New Jerusalem	Unityville
Freedom	Paradise	Zion

But it is in larger, less concrete manifestations that the force of this faith in America's unique burden has been greatest. The pervasive feeling of optimism and enthusiasm, one that does appear in the normal behavior of most individuals, reflects this inner faith; and it has supplied much of the drive toward extraordinary exertions in the economic arena or in the physical manipulation of the habitat. The remarkable, unabating vigor of American religious missionary activity abroad, usually dispensing Americanism, covertly or otherwise, along with a particular brand of Christianity, bubbles up from the same cultural wellspring.[40] American philanthropies—educational, technical, medical, and charitable, including the Peace Corps—exert strenuous efforts in almost every corner

[38] Among the more useful accounts are Charles Nordhoff, *The Communistic Societies of the United States from Personal Visit and Observation* (New York: Harper & Row, Publishers, 1875) and Mark Holloway, *Heavens on Earth; Utopian Communities in America, 1680–1880* (New York: Dover Publications, Inc., 1966).

[39] Donald W. Meinig, "The Mormon Culture Region: Strategies and Patterns in the Geography of the American West: 1847–1964," *Annals of the Association of American Geographers,* 55, No. 2 (1965), 191–220, and Richard V. Francaviglia, "The Mormon Landscape: Definition of an Image in the American West," *Proceedings of the Association of American Geographers,* 2 (1970), 59–61.

[40] "A geography of missionary operations, both Catholic and Protestant, is needed for a proper evaluation of Christianity's role as a carrier of Western culture to the non-Western world, especially since 1800. Unfortunately, a comprehensive

of the globe. In a quite fundamental, but often unrealistic way, the basic postulates and decisions in American foreign policy have been affected by the enduring conviction of an ordained vocation.

On the domestic scene, the intensity of various ameliorative movements—for temperance or prohibition, for the abolition of slavery, for civil rights, for women's suffrage—and of the counter-movements has reached a pitch beyond that justified by the immediate practicalities and may attest to a streak of fanaticism. In the geography of each of these, their regional evolution through space and time, and the interaction with other social and cultural items, much could be learned about the larger issues of American cultural geography, but little serious work has been attempted to date.

Finally, the American quest for a secular paradise has had specific implications for the physical scene of much interest to the geographer. Recent studies have richly supported the suggestion of a pastoral vision as a major component of the American Dream.[41] The United States has been regarded, subconsciously by most, but with a dawning awareness by writers and artists, as a bucolic Middle Landscape, a humanized, parklike blending of the best of wild nature with civilization's blessings, neither wilderness nor city, but a blissful balance between the primitive and the urbane. The self-sufficient single-family farm tilled by virtuous Jeffersonian yeomen has been the physical embodiment of this ideal. And a persistent reverence for this rural Eden and the only slightly less idyllic small town still lingers in the folk memory. The strangely ambivalent attitude toward wilderness derives from this vision, as does the chronic allergy toward the completely urban life. One might also conjecture that the almost intuitive westering urge of the American migrant, a momentum that has not spent itself more than seven decades after the official closing of the frontier, or the peculiar obsession with East Asian affairs cannot be fully explained as the search for economic advantage or for physical delights, neither of which is necessarily fully realized by these pursuits. We may be witnessing the pursuit of an ever-receding mythic landscape, a pastoral perfection that has always lain to the westward, first for the European, and later for the American.

---

mapping of the extent and intensity of Christian missionary activity does not exist." David E. Sopher, *Geography of Religions* (Englewood Cliffs, N.J.: Prentice-Hall, Inc., 1967), p. 70. And there is indeed a striking paucity of serious geographic work on this promising geographic topic. Most of the important cartographic and other endeavors in this sector are noted in Hildegard Binder Johnson, "The Location of Christian Missions in Africa," *Geographical Review*, 57, No. 2 (1967), 168–202. This essay is one of the most substantial contributions to date on missionary geography.

41 Among the better presentations of this theme are Henry Nash Smith, *Virgin Land: the American West as Symbol and Myth* (Cambridge, Mass.: Harvard University Press, 1950); Sanford, *The Quest for Paradise;* Marx, *The Machine in the Garden;* Peter J. Schmitt, *Back to Nature: the Arcadian Myth in Urban America* (New York: Oxford University Press, 1969); and Watson, "Image Geography."

P**A**RT 2 *spatial expression*

In the two chapters that comprise Part Two, our approach becomes more conventionally geographic as we explore some explicitly spatial attributes of American culture. A general statement concerning the basic spatial processes operating within the cultural system of this country will be attempted in chapter 3. First, we must begin by backing off and examining some fundamental issues in the study of culture and of cultural geography in particular. Then, after tying these general items into the specific conditions of the American scene, we will treat briefly two sharply contrasting sets of phenomena—the American house and the geography of American religion. The purpose of this exercise is to show how basic cultural processes achieve specific geographical expression, and also to document the relevance of the critical traits of national character discussed in the preceding chapter. The final chapter takes up one of the more important and interesting, mappable manifestations of the processes in question—the culture area—and examines the identity, origin, structure, and significance of American cultural regions and subregions, past and present.

There is some precedent for the initial chapters of this volume, although it must be sought largely in the nongeographical literature. There appears to be none for chapters 3 and 4, which represent, however haltingly, an effort to treat the spatial behavior of American culture systematically and with some rigor. Therefore some general definitions of concepts are in order, as is a confession of the inadequacy of our knowledge and methods.

CHAPTER THREE

Process

Explaining the Spatial Aspects of Cultural Change

What processes have been most influential, within the total cultural system, in shaping the geography of the country? And how have they operated? The question may also be rephrased to read: How and why has American culture changed through time and space? The problem has already been approached in chapter 1 in which we described, or speculated about, the ways in which a distinctive American culture came into being during the colonial and early republican periods. A major part of the answer was seen to be the spatial transfer and subsequent interaction of selected people and traits from foreign sources. The simplest way to attack the questions just posed might appear to be to pursue this strategy further—to discuss the spatial transfer of objects (people, things, and ideas) within the United States and a continuing interchange with other parts of the world.

In actuality, however, several distinct processes have been at work. These are:

1. The selective transfer of immigrants and cultural traits from the Old World;
2. The interaction of the newcomers among themselves and with new habitats in several early cultural hearths;
3. Differential participation by various groups in the advance of the settlement frontier from these cultural hearths;
4. Differential mobility of different groups of people during the post-pioneering period;
5. The spatial diffusion of a great range of specific innovations;
6. Deep structural change in society and culture that is expressed at different times and rates in different tracts.

All these mechanisms of change have been, or will be, noted (though in rather different order); but special attention should be accorded the one that may be the most important, yet the least amenable to direct observation: the deep structural changes experienced by a society and culture as a community evolves upward from a relatively primitive set of conditions toward an ever more complex civilized existence. The vast question of the degree to which the evolutionary paths of developing societies are followed in blind obedience to fundamental historical laws or, on the contrary, are coincidental in nature or the result of contacts among different societies, is one of the most difficult and controversial facing the cultural anthropologist.[1] Thus a final decision may never be reached as to whether the suggestive similarities between the social and ecological structures of early Middle Eastern and Middle American civilizations constitute two special cases of the same universal and inevitable progression or are simply coincidental.

In any case, if one were to amass all possible data on local inventions, the diffusion of innovations, interaction with the local habitat, the spatial movement of people and influences, and all the other discrete events that contribute to culture formation, there would still be a large, unexplained residuum. Much of what has happened in the slow character-building process in the culture history of a locality would seem to be transacted at the unlit subterranean levels of consciousness, as a series of extremely gradual, subtle shifts in modes of thinking, feeling, and impulse in response to basic alterations in socioeconomic structure and ecological patterns. There is no reason to believe that such has not also been the case with the United States and its various subregions, even within the relatively brief time this society has existed.

Some Basic Cultural Propositions

Before we can begin exploring the how and why of spatial and temporal shifts in American culture we must take a hard definitional look at what is being studied: the concept of culture. Only within the past few decades have students of mankind begun to recognize the existence of an entity called "culture," something within, yet beyond the minds of individual human beings.[2] It is a very large, complex assemblage of items, which, taken together, may be as important a variable as any in explaining the behavior of individuals or societies or the mappable patterns of activities and man-made objects upon the face of the earth. The late emergence of any semblance of a "science of culture" can be

[1] Carroll Quigley, *The Evolution of Civilizations: An Introduction to Historical Analysis* (New York: The MacMillan Company, 1961); and William T. Sanders and Barbara J. Price, *Mesoamerica: The Evolution of a Civilization* (New York: Random House, Inc., 1968).

[2] For extended discussions of the concept of culture and its significance, see Leslie A. White, *The Science of Culture* (New York: Farrar, Straus, & Giroux, Inc., 1949); and Alfred L. Kroeber, *The Nature of Culture* (Chicago: University of Chicago Press, 1952).

attributed in part to the extraordinary difficulty of observing and objectively measuring the characteristics of so complex and elusive a phenomenon. The idea that the traditional ways of thinking and acting of one's group are not absolute and that there is some coherence in the seemingly chaotic kaleidoscope of beliefs and customs of alien societies required a bold leap of the anthropological imagination.

The history of scientific thought also helps account for our inability to offer a fully rigorous definition of culture or to suggest many firm ideas about the structure of cultural systems or the laws governing their behavior through space and time.[3] The physical and chemical properties of inorganic matter are the most obvious, measurable items for the curious mind searching after some underlying order in the universe; and their study initiated formal modern science, as we know it. The methodical observation of plants and animals appeared soon after as another scientifically respectable endeavor, despite the greater difficulties involved. Very much later, the human mind began to be inquisitive about itself and the properties of our nervous system and personality, and the science of psychology was born. It is when the scientist approached groups of things in complex interaction that both observation and analysis posed the most formidable challenges. Sociology and political science are new, and their achievements relatively modest. So are the "scientific" approach to history[4] and the study of ecology, that is, the "societal" aspects of plants and animals coexisting within specific habitats.[5] The systematic understanding of the culture of human groups calls for sophisticated techniques of an even higher order. Not the least of the problems is achieving adequate objectivity, a relatively minor matter in the physical and biological disciplines. The student of culture must somehow strip himself of his native preconceptions. It is difficult enough to do so when looking at alien folk; it entails a near miracle when investigating one's own culture, as in the present work.

Much ink has been spilled in the effort to reach a satisfactory definition of culture. Perhaps the most successful to date is that offered by Kroeber and Kluckhohn in 1952 after an exhaustive critique of the literature:

Culture consists of patterns, explicit and implicit, of and for behavior acquired and transmitted by symbols, constituting the distinctive achievement of human groups, including their embodiment in artifacts; the essential core of culture consists of traditional (i.e., historically derived and selected) ideas and especially their attached values; culture systems may, on the one hand, be con-

3 Of the many recent works on the history of science, the most useful would appear to be J. D. Bernal, *Science in History*, 4 vols. (Cambridge, Mass.: M.I.T. Press, 1971).

4 David S. Landes and Charles Tilly, eds., *History as Social Science* (Englewood Cliffs, N.J.: Prentice-Hall, Inc., 1971).

5 The emergence of the fields of biological and social ecology is thoughtfully reviewed in Otis Dudley Duncan, "Social Organization and the Ecosystem," in R. E. L. Faris, ed., *Handbook of Modern Sociology* (Chicago: Rand McNally & Company, 1964), pp. 37–82.

sidered as products of action, on the other as conditioning elements of further action.[6]

The full exegesis of this statement could, and did, require a full volume; and some cultural anthropologists would take exception to all or part of the definition. But all would agree that culture is an assemblage of learned behavior of a complexity and durability well beyond the capacities of nonhuman animals. Following the Kroeber-Kluckhohn formulation, culture can be regarded as the structured, traditional set of patterns for behavior, a code or template for ideas and acts. It is highly specific to each cultural and subcultural group, and survives by transfer *not* through biological means but rather through symbolic means, substantially but not wholly through language. In its ultimate, most essential sense, culture is an image of the world, of oneself and one's community.

It will be helpful to spell out several general attributes of culture implied in the definition above that are of importance to geographers and other students. First of all, culture is indeed an exclusively human achievement. In fact, it is *the* critical human attribute, the one exclusive possession that sets mankind far apart from all other organisms. With the appearance of cultural behavior at least one million years ago during the organic evolution of man-like creatures, true human beings can be identified. The capacity for abstract thinking, for the mental juggling of symbols and inventing of ideas, is something no other species has attained, as far as we can tell.[7] Given this ability, enormous stores of information and ideas can be accumulated, sorted out, retained and bequeathed to later generations, and added to; an unlimited variety of recipes for thinking and behaving can be assembled from this vast larder of knowledge, then adopted, revised, or abandoned. Thus the pace of cultural evolution far outruns that of the slowly mutating germ plasm. Such plasticity and inventiveness, certainly not any inherent physical prowess, accounts for *Homo sapiens* having become the dominant species on this planet. Implicit in all this is a very great variability in modes of behavior as between groups, places, or periods, much more than might normally be expected of members of the same species. At the same time, there is also a strong intrinsic conservatism in many phases of a culture, so that only a small fraction of all combinations have ever been realized.

The power wielded over the minds of its participants by a cultural system is difficult to exaggerate. No denial of free will is implied, nor is the scope for individual achievement or resourcefulness belittled. It is simply that we are all players in a great profusion of games and that in each cultural arena the entire team, knowingly or not, follows the local set of rules, at most bending them only slightly. Only a half-wit

[6] A. L. Kroeber and Clyde Kluckhohn, "Culture, a Critical Review of Concepts and Definitions," *Papers of the Peabody Museum of American Archaeology and Ethnology,* 47, No. 1 (1952), 181.

[7] Try teaching even the brightest chimpanzee or dolphin the meanings of the words "mother," "yesterday," "kilometer," or "flag."

or a fool would openly flout them. But as in chess, the possibilities for creativity and modulation are virtually infinite. It is enough to have experienced "cultural shock," the sudden immersion in another culture without special briefing, or the almost equally painful reentry into one's own community after such an episode, to realize that many of the habits one regards as natural or logical are so only for one's own group. Most of the norms, limits, or possibilities of human action thus are set as much or more by the configuration of the culture as by biological endowment or the nature of the physical habitat. It is futile to evaluate or give relative weights to the various determinants that shape the affairs of men, since none can operate without the others. The survival of a cultural pattern is dependent upon inherited human capabilities and upon a certain range of habitats, and its functioning is subject to whatever constraints are intrinsic to these; but, on the other hand, cultural expression also makes a deep impact upon the outer world. Thus culture is a powerful agent, but always in complex interaction with other powerful systems.

A cultural system is not simply a miscellaneous stockpile of traits. Quite to the contrary, its many components are ordered. Moreover, the totality of culture is much greater than the simple sum of the parts, so much so that it appears to be a superorganic entity living and changing according to a still obscure set of internal laws. Although individual minds are needed to sustain it, by some remarkable process culture also lives on its own, quite apart from the single person or his volition, as a sort of "macro-idea," a shared abstraction with a special mode of existence and set of rules. This point becomes clearer if one examines some specific cultural complexes that share this attribute of superorganic existence with the total culture. Thus an economic system—*vide* the famous "Invisible Hand" of Adam Smith—has been perceived to evolve and act according to its own private code, at least in pre-Keynesian times, without the effective intervention of its participants. Languages constantly change, though at variable speeds, in accordance with complex rules we are only slowly beginning to grasp, but utterly without calculation or effort by their speakers. Any sensitive linguistic observer who has watched the dizzy pace at which American English has altered during the past generation can testify to a sense of lying helpless in the path of large anonymous forces. Similarly, there is a distinctive personality to be recognized in almost any viable organization—church, college, army, corporation, or government bureau—that almost literally lives and breathes, persists and develops, quite independently of the personal sentiments of its members.

The nation-state idea is perhaps the neatest illustration of the transpersonal character of cultural systems; and the origin, growth, and perpetuation of the idea of a United States of America is a superb example. Whatever the genesis of the idea, it was certainly not the conscious fabrication of any identifiable cabal of nation-builders, but rather a spontaneous surge of feeling that quickly acquired a force and momentum of its own. This idea was so powerful that millions of men were ready to sacrifice their lives for it. Individuals who entertain the nation-state idea are born and die, and some may even have doubts or reservations; but the idea marches on, quite clearly beyond the control of anyone. Even if it were a matter of dire necessity, it seems impossible to devise any program, excluding mass annihilation, whereby the idea of a United States or a Russia, France, or Germany could be disinvented.

The structure of cultural systems is rather loose and open. If we regard culture as a system in the technical sense of the term, it is rather special by reason of both complexity and sheer size. Probably the only other system of greater magnitude is that including all interacting subsystems on and near the face of the earth that comprise total terrestrial reality and the subject matter of geography. There may be certain quintessential ideas and practices that cannot be tampered with without profoundly revising the larger cultural pattern; but, in the main, the total structure can absorb much change or contamination, including addition or subtraction of elements in specific departments of culture without great impact upon the whole. Thus two centuries of radical technological and economic change have not basically revised the structure of the American family—at least not yet. And the near-disappearance of men's straw hats, electric trolleys, or Spencerian handwriting seems to have had minimal effect upon basic American life patterns. But if one could imagine anything as unimaginable as a mass conversion to ascetic Buddhism, the substitution of the Arabic language for English, the abolition of the achievement motive, or the adoption of a joint family system, the reverberations all through the cultural matrix would be fast and shattering.

Even among so-called "primitive folk," a single cultural system encompasses an enormous range of information. Each cultural group has a certain common fund of traits—a full count of the individual bits of information would probably run well into the millions—that is acquired, usually quite unconsciously, during the early months and years of childhood. But, in addition, there are any number of special groups or activities, ranging from a half-dozen or so in the simplest of societies to literally hundreds of thousands in the most complex, each with its own distinctive subculture. Even in a Micronesian village or a band of Bushmen, no single person commands the full complement of traditional practice and lore. In the United States, even the most diligent and brilliant of scholars could not begin to master more than a minute fraction of the aggregate cultural package.

The problem of how to take an inventory of all traits or complexes that make up the total system, or how to classify the full range of subcultures and other major dimensions present within a given community, has not been solved. But the situation can be indicated roughly in diagrammatic form (Figure 3.1). Consider the full rectangular solid as representing the total culture, with one dimension equivalent to the range of traits and complexes that make up the totality of any culture or subculture. A second dimension (here the vertical one) represents an additive (and overlapping) set of subcultures: for example, males and females, farmers, ditchdiggers, Presbyterians, mountain climbers, convicts, Freemasons, bowlers, and drug addicts. (The number of strata

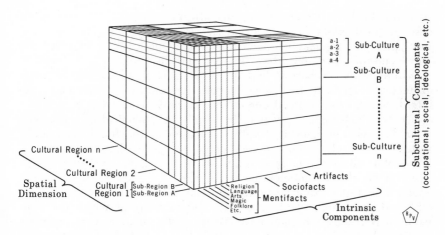

FIG. 3.1.   A schematic, three-dimensional representation of cultural systems.

shown in the diagram is, of course, highly schematic.) The third dimension indicates variability through space, that is, the set of cultural regions and subregions that one can identify within the territorial range of the cultural system in question. Further dimensions—especially time—might be added to this scheme, but not without transcending the possibilities of graphic representation. Note that if the cube is sliced either horizontally or vertically (at an angle normal to the spatial face), the result is a regional or subcultural parcel of cultural phenomena that run the gamut of human ideas and practices: for example, courtship, facial expression, superstition, pronunciation pattern, motor skills, social etiquette, and burial customs.

For our purposes, it will suffice to adopt one of the simplest ways of categorizing the components of a culture, among the almost limitless array of possible schemes. This is a tripartite classification into artifacts, sociofacts, and mentifacts.[8] Artifacts are those elements of culture that are directly concerned with matters of livelihood or, somewhat more broadly, the entire technology of supplying wanted goods and services. The variety of artifacts can barely be suggested: all tools, weapons, and other man-made objects; manufacturing in all its many aspects; the shelter system; the production of food and drink; the transportation system; medicine; property-holding and land-use systems; clothing; and many other phenomena. Sociofacts are those phases of the culture most directly concerned with interpersonal relations: kinship and family systems; political behavior; education; social etiquette; voluntary organizations; reproductive behavior; child rearing; and a host of others. Mentifacts are basically cerebral, psychological, or attitudinal in character, and include religion, along with other ideological baggage, magic and superstition, language, music, dance, and other arts, funerary customs,

    [8] Julian S. Huxley, "Evolution, Cultural and Biological," *Current Anthropology,* 7 (1966), 16–20.

folklore, the basic value system, and abstract concepts of all sorts. In a sense, the mentifactual is the innermost, least mutable, "holiest," and most precious segment of the culture—the glue holding together the entire cultural mass and setting its tone and direction.

In practice, it is hard to find any single facet of culture that is purely artifactual, sociofactual, or mentifactual. These arbitrary categories are interdependent to a marked degree. For example, house design and construction, which might appear to be wholly technological or artifactual, is, in fact, closely associated with the nature of the family and social system and so also with religious or cosmological ideas. In any case, if the total culture can be seen as a loose, yet somehow structured, assemblage of an almost innumerable set of elements, viewed from another angle, it is also a package with many subcultural compartments, each with a decided amount of autonomy, and to many of which the individual may belong simultaneously. To make this thought more concrete, consider the single man, the microcosmic building block of a larger cultural universe, who carries his own unique collection of cultural attributes, and may also be a participant in many subcultural groups. Imagine someone who is, among other things, a Czech-American Lutheran plumber, a member of the VFW, an ardent Cleveland Indian fan, a radio ham, a regular patron of a particular bar, and a member of a car pool, the local draft board, the Book-of-the-Month Club, and the Republican party, and a parent whose son attends a particular college. Each of these subcultures will tend to have its own array of gear and physical arrangements, spectrum of economic and social beliefs and practices, cluster of abstract concepts, and, not least important for our purpose, distributional spread in physical space. The one man and his friends and associates move through many worlds. It is only by taking into account the relevant multiplicity of components and dimensions at the particular scale chosen for observation, and also the fact that they are changing through time, that a realistic understanding of a given culture can be reached.

It has been implied that virtually the entire range of human activities might be regarded as the acting out of various cultural systems. Consequently, one might make the technical claim that cultural geography is equivalent to the entirety of human geography. But this sort of academic imperialism is impractical. For most purposes, it is more efficient and profitable, at least in the short run, to extract major subsystems from the total culture, then treat them independently of other aspects of the larger system, holding other things constant. This has been done with conspicuous success in the case of the economic, demographic, and political subsystems, especially when the analyst restricts himself to a single reasonably homogeneous cultural realm. It is even convenient, when working at the international scale, to assume universal economic, demographic, political, and perhaps other principles that override and suppress local cultural peculiarities. One result is that the normal domain of the cultural geographer includes only those items that are overtly ideological or traditional, such things, for example, as language, religion, ethnicity, the settlement landscape, or diet, or whatever is least susceptible to rigorous systematic analysis and the prompt distillation of general propositions.

As it happens, we confront here a profound, but as yet poorly under-stood, methodological dilemma. Each body of human geographic phe-nomena stands at the intersection of two large systems: that of its local culture and that system of ideas or relationships governing the branch of knowledge in question. Thus the geography of land use in the United States can be approached either as one of the outward ways in which the indigenous culture is manifested, or simply as the local expression of a group of universal economic principles that we have had some success in capturing. At the moment, the latter strategy is rather more immedi-ately productive, although an ideal plan would find some way of merging both perspectives. On the other hand, if we seek to understand the phys-ical morphology of rural settlement in this country, it is more expedient to work within the context of the national cultural pattern rather than to appeal to universal postulates, since we still have only rather fuzzy notions of what those might be.

As is true for any geographical phenomenon, the question of scale is critical in dealing with cultural systems. As used here, "scale" is not simply the problem of the fineness of the detail under scrutiny or, as with map scale, the ratio between the real object and the abstraction. There is the even thornier matter of bounding the cultural facts to be studied. How large a group or territory is to be observed? Cultural sys-tems are loose, open affairs with hierarchical tendencies and with few sharp natural boundaries. (We ignore such trivial exceptions as the island or oasis community isolated over long periods.) There is an un-broken continuum of cultural units—of boxes within boxes, so to speak—extending downward from the whole of humanity, living, dead, or yet to be born, to the single contemporary individual, and each of them is unique. Obviously, neither extreme is too useful in an operational sense. (There is also the related question of temporal duration. When is a culture born, when does it die, and how do we segment its lifespan into meaningful periods?)

Fortunately, we do have some fairly distinct, significant levels within the nested hierarchy. In the contemporary world, the nation-state—especially, the robust, strongly integrated, long-established nation-state—is a prominent, if not airtight, cultural compartment. The tactic of analyz-ing the cultural geography of the United States, which this volume attempts to do, is quite defensible; but the porosity and multidimen-sionality of culture is such that we must not fall into the trap of thinking that the official boundaries of the United States rigorously define the American culture area. There are ambiguous zones both within and outside the international frontiers. It is extremely difficult to say precisely who is or is not an American in many cases (the expatriate? the recent immigrant? the aborigine?); and many Americans are members of sub-cultures with foreign linkages. Rotarians, spelunkers, stamp collectors, gourmets, Baptists, movie buffs, student radicals, and xylophonists all have soulmates abroad.

There are other cultural aggregations cohesive enough to commend themselves to our attention. On the broadest territorial scale, we find the large cultural realm, for example, the Islamic realm or the European.

At the subnational level, one may look at ethnic groups and certain distinct subnational "culture areas," which have many of the traits of ethnic groups but do not quite aspire to nationhood, the critical feature of the full-fledged ethnic group. The student can even descend to the small tribe or the single village or band. In this work, we are concerned only with the culture of the American nation-state and of some of its more distinct culture areas, units ranging in size from a few thousand to some hundreds of thousands of square kilometers.

The one attribute of cultural systems that most particularly interests us is the fact that they almost always have spatial dimensions, that is, they exist within certain localities. Moreover, the general nature of the locality seems somehow to shape the culture and, in turn, to be influenced by it. In the strictest sense, the spatial component of culture is incidental. As a cerebral entity, a culture may flourish, move about, and propagate itself solely within the heads of a number of footloose individuals. Such extreme cases do occur, of course, but normally the facts of location and the processes of interaction with other localized or spatially structured phenomena do matter greatly. In fact, the territorial dimension is strong enough that it seems fitting to accord the regional aspect of culture an importance rivaling the technological, social, or ideological. This statement is especially valid when representatives of a culture have become deeply rooted in a specific place.[9]

A particular culture, or combination of subcultures, helps impart to an area much of its special character and behavioral design—which, fundamentally, is what geography is all about. Conversely, the character of a given place may be a strong formative influence in the genesis of a particular culture, which is the ultimate concern of the cultural anthropologist. This is especially so, it must be stressed again, after a cultural group has become established in a certain tract, or when such a group is transferred en masse to another tract. We do not yet understand the nature of the process. The facts of proximity or remoteness with respect to other cultures and the ease of travel or communication certainly enter into the equation. Many of the elements of the inanimate and the biotic environment are emphatically relevant. The perception of local opportunity with respect to all manner of economic and social activity—a special place as glimpsed through the special lenses of the culture—would also appear to figure importantly. The regrettable fact that we cannot analyze all these many, still quite mysterious place-oriented interactions does not exorcize them. It is this zone of intersection between cultural process and the total character of places that is the special domain of the cultural geographer. In this volume, we seek to begin illuminating

9 We are much less interested here in mappable but adventitious spatial patterns. Thus one could plot the distribution in western and central Europe as of May 1945 of some millions of highly diversified displaced persons and prisoners of war or of the hundreds of thousands of American servicemen, tourists, students, and businessmen currently sojourning on foreign soil and be suffused with feelings of geographic virtue. Indeed the analysis of such maps could be scientifically interesting for a variety of purposes, but the contribution toward understanding the cultures of the migrant persons involved or of the areas in which they happened to be would be quite minor.

this zone as it exists in modern America, and to chart some of its bolder landmarks. But we cannot pretend that this is more than a timid beginning.

Population Mobility as a Factor in Cultural Change

The American population has been characterized by unusually great mobility from the very beginning of its history. As already noted, immigration brought different combinations of ethnic groups to different sections of the country, a process that helps account for the specific structure of early American culture. But spatial movements, on the part of regular migrants or the transient traveler, have continued vigorously past the initial step of immigration or pioneer settlement, and almost certainly have been accelerating or changing in kind, or both.[10] The individual migrant carries with him an appreciable portion, though never all, of the culture in which he has been nurtured. If he arrives as an ordinary single stranger in a community, the chances of his having any impact upon the total culture are infinitesimal. On the contrary, the likelihood is for his eventual assimilation into the host society, while contributing at best only a trivial trait or two: a single word, for example, or a card trick or anecdote. There is, of course, always the outside chance that, given just the right circumstances, major innovations can be implanted by a single newcomer or a very small group. Thus the almost mythical transfer of silk from China to Rome by a pair of monks or the introduction of textile machinery into New England by Samuel Slater, or the propagation of the Christian gospel into heathen territory by the solitary band of missionaries. But, generally, any appreciable modification of a regional culture calls for the arrival of a goodly number of strangers.

This process has obviously been going on quite actively among post-immigration American populations. Most conspicuous are the spatial transfers of ethnic and racial groups. The mass migration of the rural southern Negro into some Southern cities, but in much greater volume to the metropolises of the North, has appreciably changed the cultural character not only of the cities in question but of the migrant communities as well.[11] With their large, new, culturally vigorous Negro minorities or majorities, Washington, Detroit, Chicago, and Cleveland can never

[10] Wilbur Zelinsky, "The Hypothesis of the Mobility Transition," *Geographical Review*, 61, No. 2 (1971), 219–49.

[11] The literature on the urban sociology and demography of our Afro-American population has reached such staggering proportions that one must hesitate before unlatching the bibliographic floodgates. Perhaps the single most useful recent volume is Karl E. Taeuber and Alma F. Taeuber, *Negroes in Cities: Residential Segregation and Neighborhood Change* (Chicago: Aldine-Atherton, Inc., 1965); but Gunnar Myrdal, *An American Dilemma* (New York: Harper & Row, Publishers, 1944) will always remain indispensable. Within the geographic canon, the most useful statement is John Fraser Hart, "The Changing Distribution of the American Negro," *Annals of the Association of American Geographers*, 50, No. 3 (1960), 242–66. For a micro-geographic analysis of change in community and migrant, see the same author's "A Rural Retreat for Northern Negroes," *Geographical Review*, 50, No. 2 (1960), 147–68.

recapture their pre-World War II cultural personalities. In such places as Harlem and Atlanta, an Afro-American culture has come into being unlike any that existed earlier in the nation. There has been a rather less visible spatial re-sorting of other representatives of regional cultures: the heavy flow of Appalachian whites to Cincinnati, Detroit, and other midwestern communities has appreciably transformed them, for example. The eastward diaspora of the West Coast Japanese in the 1940's has made itself felt in the microgeography of culture in various Eastern metropolises. The recent migrations and recreational circulation of American Jews initially domiciled in the cities of the Northeast has resulted in marked Jewish influences on a number of rural tracts in the Northeast and cities in the West and South. Although it has never been methodically analyzed, there seems to be selective summertime migration of Czechs, Poles, Ukrainians, and probably other groups to certain rural retreats, always with some lasting effect. The spatial reshuffling of distinctive ethnic and regional groups, on either the interregional or intra-metropolitan scale, may be more important than these few examples might suggest, for only the redistribution of the Negro population has attracted much scholarly attention.

Even less notice has been accorded the cultural repercussions of migrants selected in terms of characteristics other than ethnicity. As is the case with immigration from abroad, it is clear that patterns of internal migration do vary with age, sex, urban-rural residence, educational status, and class.[12] The evidence is much less accessible for migrational differentials among religious groups or occupations; but there is little doubt that they exist, are significant, and tend to produce new subcultural regional configurations. We may also speculate about correlations between propensity to migrate on the one hand and different types of temperament, levels of intelligence, political inclinations, and mental or physical health.[13] The possibilities for cultural evolution implicit in such movements are not limited to the simple concentration of similar individuals in certain areas or their weeding out from others. There is always the chance for some unanticipated reaction among newly juxtaposed cultural elements.

The primary motivation for migration into and within the United States has always been unquestionably economic. But from the beginning, the hope for monetary gain was supplemented strongly by other considerations. To take only the most obvious cultural facts, the decision by the potential European emigrant as to whether to try his fortune in

12 After more than three decades, the best general statement on the topic is still Dorothy Swaine Thomas, *Research Memorandum on Migration Differentials,* Bulletin 43 (New York: Social Science Research Council, 1938).

13 Some tentative findings are, in fact, available for the impact of mental disease upon the propensity to migrate. See Judith Lazarus, Ben Z. Locke, and Dorothy Swaine Thomas, "Migration Differentials in Mental Disease: State Patterns in First Admissions to Mental Hospitals for All Disorders and for Schizophrenia, New York, Ohio, and California As of 1950," *Milbank Memorial Fund Quarterly,* 51 (January 1963), 25–42.

America was closely related to ethnic, religious, and political identity. In the contemporary United States, with an exceptionally high spatial mobility and a general affluence that may be undercutting the primacy of the economic motive, it is logical to expect many persons to seek or shun specific places because of their personal cultural predilections. The implications of such a trend are examined in chapter 4.

The Diffusion of Innovations

The inducement of social, economic, and cultural change through the spatial diffusion of innovations has recently and justifiably received much attention from students of geography and other fields.[14] If this interest was initially centered on the outward propagation of various forms of technology on a macro scale by anthropogeographers and anthropologists,[15] the more recent focus has been upon the finer locational detail. A series of rigorous studies of the mechanics of contagious diffusion among neighboring individuals, the "telling" of unfamiliar information among pairs of persons, has led to clarification of what appears to be a stochastic process. Indeed, real-life situations can be simulated through Monte Carlo methods.[16] Insofar as such analysis is applicable to cultural geography, it carries with it the assumption that the total culture consists of a bundle of traits, a collection of particulate objects. This is at best a half-truth, but, up to a point, a quite useful one. Although the Hägerstrandian diffusion of innovations through personal contact among essentially stationary actors commends itself to the geographic analyst because it can be handled with relative methodological elegance and rigor, it is only one of three mechanisms whereby novel ideas can be spread from place to place: these are contagious diffusion; migration; and telecommunications. Under typical American conditions, the first of these may be the least important.

The movement of individuals from one cultural milieu into another also automatically means the transfer of their culture, at least within their minds. Whether there is effective transposition to the host population of any of the imported traits depends upon many variables. How

14 The seminal work in this area is Torsten Hägerstrand, *Innovation Diffusion as a Spatial Process* (Chicago: University of Chicago Press, 1967); and for developments since 1953 (the date of original publication), the "Postscript" (pp. 299–324) by Allan Pred, the translator and editor of the volume, is quite useful, as is Ronald Abler, John S. Adams, and Peter Gould, *Spatial Organization: The Geographer's View of the World* (Englewood Cliffs, N.J., Prentice-Hall, Inc., 1971), pp. 389–451.

15 Notable examples of the treatment of this theme by anthropogeographers at the macro scale include Carl O. Sauer, *Agricultural Origins and Dispersals* (New York: American Geographical Society, 1952) and a number of case studies scattered through Joseph E. Spencer and William L. Thomas, Jr., *Cultural Geography; an Evolutionary Introduction to Our Humanized Earth* (New York: John Wiley & Sons, Inc., 1969). See also George F. Carter, *Man and the Land: A Cultural Geography*, 2d ed. (New York: Holt, Rinehart & Winston, Inc., 1968).

16 As elegantly exemplified in Richard Morrill, "The Negro Ghetto: Problems and Alternatives," *Geographical Review*, 55, No. 3 (1965), 339–61.

many migrant carriers are involved? How permanent is the migration, or how prolonged the period of contact? What sorts of transactions occur between newcomers and older residents? What is their relative status? In addition to regular migrants, there are transients, for example, tourists, businessmen, students, servicemen, itinerant workers, conventioneers, and others. Such movement is particularly vigorous in the United States and further lubricates the cultural change already stimulated by large-scale migration.

The existence of several media for rapid, even instantaneous long-distance transmission of information adds a third major dimension to the phenomenon of diffusion. The early establishment of an effective American postal system meant the circulation of personal correspondence and printed newspapers, periodicals, and books to all corners of the land within a few days or weeks. The post was followed by telegraph and cable by the mid-nineteenth century; and later by telephone, teletype, mass-produced phonograph records and tapes, radio, and television. During the Paleolithic period, it might take millenia for a welcome innovation to reach all prospective clients, if indeed it ever did realize its outermost territorial range. By early modern times, the pace had quickened noticeably. It was then a matter of only decades or years, so that the acceptance of tobacco throughout the Old World was consummated in less than a century.[17] Today the appetite for novel artifacts can be excited literally overnight; and only problems of manufacture or delivery inhibit instant national or worldwide adoption.[18]

The veritable revolution in communications has been so profound and so sudden that its geographic implications have not been appreciated or seriously studied. Thus contagious diffusion, the dominant premodern mode of effecting cultural change spatially, may be giving way to migration and telecommunication, as new ideas and people vault rapidly over great distances and the spatial patterning of acceptors may be governed more by their ranking within one or more hierarchical systems than by propinquity alone. Thus the size or status of a city, college, or firm, or the standing of an individual in terms of social class, occupation, educational attainment, or ethnic or racial group may be decisive as to when an innovation is adopted.

If we turn to the earlier history of the United States, it would appear that the dissemination of innovations by mobile individuals was at least as effective as contagious diffusion in modifying the cultural map. Such studies as we have lead to two conclusions: (1) the most critical form of cultural diffusion was carried on by those pioneer settlers who estab-

17 Louis Seig, "The Spread of Tobacco: A Study in Cultural Diffusion," *Professional Geographer*, 15, No. 1 (1963), 17–21.

18 I can attest to this phenomenon from personal experience. In August, 1958, I drove from Santa Monica, California to Detroit at an average rate of about 400 miles per day; and display windows in almost every drugstore and variety store along the way were being hastily stocked with hula hoops just off the delivery trucks from Southern California. A national television program the week before had roused instant cravings. It was an eerie sensation, surfing along a pseudo-innovation wave.

lished the first effective settlements in various parts of the country; and (2) there were only a very few centers of especially active cultural ferment, of invention and elaboration, which acted as culture hearths, or in some cases funnels, from which local or exotic innovations spread over extensive areas during or after the period of frontier settlement (Figure 3.2).[19]

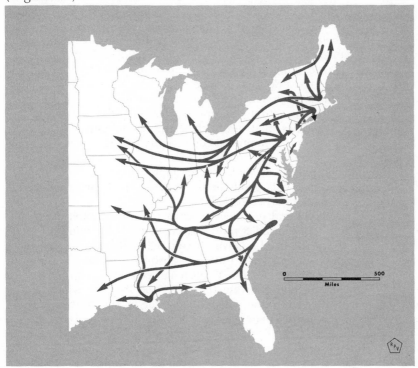

FIG. 3.2   *The movement of ideas in the Eastern United States (after H. Glassie).*

Care must be taken to avoid misleading analogies with other modes of spatial movement in discussing the diffusion of specifically cultural items. Although useful parallels can be drawn, and certain common mathematical formulations may apply to them all, the physical dispersion of gaseous or liquid substances, the spread of an epidemic, and the conquest of territory by a new plant or animal species do differ in fundamental ways from the spatial propagation of new practices among human societies. Furthermore, the diffusion of technological or economic inno-

[19] A marked localization of inventions and innovations in late nineteenth century America is indicated in an analysis of the location of patent applications in Allan R. Pred, *The Spatial Dynamics of U.S. Urban-Industrial Growth, 1800–1914: Interpretive and Theoretical Essays* (Cambridge, Mass.: M.I.T. Press, 1966), pp. 86–134.

vations is not quite equivalent to the processes involved in implanting novel cultural traits in alien soil. With the former, there are objective standards of performance, even though, of course, the ultimate definition of value is subjective. Competitive items can usually be readily ranked, so that if the freshly invented doodad can do the job better, it will be accepted as quickly as money and opportunity permit, whereas its predecessor is unceremoniously junked. Thus the stone axe never had a chance once metal tools appeared on the scene; the modern water closet has swept all before it; if you wish to see a leather tankard being made, you will have to visit Williamsburg, Virginia; and such things as the bicycle and plastic raingear have penetrated almost every part of the world, including some primitive societies otherwise adamantly set against any sort of change. Their virtues of low cost, compactness, or efficiency are just too compelling. Strong cultural barriers may slow down, but not stop, new technologies that are demonstrably superior. Thus many societies can fiercely resist improved contraceptive devices or better forms of nutrition, but usually such resistance is a rear guard action. Witness the growing acceptance of milk among Japanese youngsters who are being convinced that it is good for them, whatever their grandparents may mutter about the barbarous habit.

When purely cultural preferences are at issue, it is much more difficult to scale utility or to predict rates of acceptance. Is the miniskirt really better than the ankle-length gown? (And will either linger for more than a few months or years at a time?) Is abstract expressionism inferior to op or pop art? Why does the Englishman continue to prefer tea to coffee? Why should one cultivate the twist, the frug, or whatever the current craze might be rather than the foxtrot or the waltz? Is pizza really that much better than whatever edibles it has replaced in the American cuisine? Is the contemporary ranch house truly preferable to a turn-of-the-century Queen Anne house? All these questions and countless others are matters of taste and "fashion" controlled by unknown cultural-historical principles;[20] and there is no "rational" set of scales to measure whether choices among cultural options result in improvements.

We need not narrate in detail here the filling in of the American territory by pioneer settlers, with their cultural baggage. The general story has been well told, in word and map, in a number of publications,[21]

[20] The study of fashion is evidently still regarded as too frivolous by social scientists. Virtually the only serious general essay on its sociology is Herbert Blumer, "Fashion: From Class Differentiation to Collective Selection," *Sociological Quarterly* (Summer 1969), pp. 279–91. That it can prove to be a productive line of inquiry is amply demonstrated in J. Richardson and A. L. Kroeber, "Three Centuries of Women's Dress Fashions: A Quantitative Analysis," *Anthropological Records*, 5 (1947), 111–53.

[21] For example, Ralph H. Brown, *Historical Geography of the United States,* (New York: Harcourt Brace Jovanovich, Inc., 1948); Ray A. Billington, *Westward Expansion: A History of the American Frontier,* 3d ed. (New York: The Macmillan Company, 1967); and Randall D. Sale and Edwin D. Karn, *American Expansion: A Book of Maps* (Homewood, Ill.: Dorsey Press, 1962).

and the specifically cultural dimension of frontier advance is noted in the following chapter. The essential geometry of the taking of the American land is that of a frontier zone irregularly accelerating westward. This zone spread out from three nuclear nodes along the Atlantic Seaboard: southern New England; the Midland, based in the Delaware and Susquehanna valleys; and Chesapeake Bay. A fourth source, the French-American establishment along the lower St. Lawrence, proved to be of only ephemeral importance. Similarly, the various Hispanic-American and aboriginal groups swallowed by the dynamic Anglo-American frontier were minor sources of influence for the national culture. There has been some (two-way) traffic in cultural effects across the Mexican and Canadian borders; but most of the significant innovations have moved internally within and among American regions, or been transferred by specific regions through which overseas items are imported and spread inland.

Despite the stubborn romantic inclination to believe otherwise, the settlement frontier cannot be credited with the origination of any important inventions, material or otherwise. Even the new gear most closely associated with frontier life (for example, the Conestoga wagon,[22] the Colt pistol, the Springfield rifle) came from the "effete" East. But one cultural phenomenon, the unconscious rediscovery of a primitive or pan-European cultural substratum common to the varied ethnic strains that streamed across the Atlantic, is of more than passing interest. A groping backward into a half-forgotten past was resorted to by rusticated groups suffering temporary physical and social deprivation. We find evidence for it, for example, in the improvising of folk housing of a Ur-European character[23] and the resuscitation of some very early motifs in gravestone carving.[24] Such resurrection of the past is meaningful insofar as the frontier still persists physically in many a backwater tract, or ethereally as a strong mythic force in American thought. In general, however, the frontier played a passive role in the American cultural drama, as the remote destination for things, not as their source.

During the seventeenth century and much of the eighteenth century, Tidewater Virginia was preeminent in receiving fresh European ideas and disseminating them, if not in inventing new ones. This position is well indicated by such physical evidence as architecture and furniture;[25] and it is not unexpected in the light of the area's economic and political strength. Other early Southern coastal zones, such as those centered around Charleston, Savannah, and New Orleans, were much less influential at the national scale, largely because of weaker populations and

[22] Gary S. Dunbar, "Wagons West—and East!" *Geographical Review*, 55, No. 2 (1965), 282–83.
[23] Alan Gowans, *Images of American Living: Four Centuries of Architecture and Furniture as Cultural Expression* (Philadelphia and New York: J. B. Lippincott Co., 1964), p. 60.
[24] This notion is developed in some detail in Allan I. Ludwig, *Graven Images: New England Stonecarving and its Symbols, 1650–1815* (Middletown, Conn.: Wesleyan University Press, 1966).
[25] Gowans, *Images of American Living*, pp. 173–222.

economies and poorly developed connections with the continental interior.

By the end of the eighteenth century, cultural leadership had passed on to the more developed portions of New England, then rapidly ascendant in commercial and manufacturing activity. Throughout the nineteenth century, this region was clearly the most fecund and powerful, setting an example for the whole country in many departments of higher human endeavor. By virtue of the vigorous out-migration of New Englanders and the diffusion of ideas and objects through other means, the national patterns in industrial technology and mechanical devices of all sorts, higher education, science, literature and the other fine arts, theology, political ideas, manners, and domestic and public architecture were largely controlled by this single small region.[26] In fact, the cultural geography of nineteenth century America can be described, without serious exaggeration, as the continual pumping and spraying outward to west and south of a great array of novelties, locally invented or imported from abroad, from the New England reservoir. As New England folk and ways of life moved westward into upper New York State, there to intermingle fruitfully with other streams of settlement and ideas, a subsidiary culture hearth germinated within "New England Extended," especially within the "Burned-Over District" of west central New York.[27] What little work we do have on the cultural geography of the tract strongly suggests its potency in inventing and disseminating a variety of religious and social items.

How great a role the Midland culture area, centered in eastern Pennsylvania, may have played as a source of nationally significant items is much less clear. There was certainly some transmission of agricultural practices, religious denominations, and architectural forms (for example, barns and log construction) among other things;[28] but it is possible that the Midland's total contribution to the national cultural pattern may be less than would be suggested by its strategic location and early prosperity.

With the achievement of major national strength and an enormous settled territory by the mid-nineteenth century, the simple geometry of colonial cultural change and diffusion became decreasingly relevant. In place of a small set of Atlantic Seaboard metropolises and their immediate hinterlands, which conducted European cultural commodities

26 Lois (Kimball) Mathews Rosenberry, *The Expansion of New England: The Spread of New England Settlement and Institutions to the Mississippi River, 1620–1865* (Boston: The Houghton Mifflin Company, 1909); and Stewart H. Holbrook, *The Yankee Exodus: An Account of Migration from New England* (New York: The Macmillan Company, 1950).

27 Whitney R. Cross, *The Burned-Over District: The Social and Intellectual History of Enthusiastic Religion in Western New York, 1800–1850* (Ithaca, N.Y.: Cornell University Press, 1950).

28 Carl O. Sauer, "The Settlement of the Humid East," *Climate and Man: Yearbook of Agriculture 1941* (Washington: U.S. Department of Agriculture, 1941), pp. 164–66; Dunbar, "Wagons West—and East!"; Harold R. Shurtleff, *The Log Cabin Myth* (Cambridge, Mass.: Harvard University Press, 1939); and Edward T. Price, "The Central Courthouse Square in the American County Seat," *Geographical Review*, 58, No. 1 (1968), 29–60.

into North America or devised new ones, two other processes began to take over: the scattering of inventiveness, and an obvious cultural convergence. Welcome mechanical and social inventions could appear almost anywhere, except perhaps the remoter settlement frontiers, within a rapidly maturing, ever more self-assured society. Thus bourbon whiskey first appeared in Kentucky; an assortment of agricultural devices emanated from California and the Middle West; women's suffrage won its first major victory in Wyoming; the more daring experiments in educational practice were hatched on Middle Western campuses; and by 1900 Chicago may have become the most exciting place in the country for the writer or architect. If there has been a discernible reordering of peaks and valleys on the American map of relative cultural vigor over the past two centuries, the altitudes would now seem to be greatest in the Far West and Southwest. The Megalopolitan zone of the Northeast, most particularly Greater New York City and southern New England, may still originate and broadcast many ideas of note, but increasingly the newer modes of behavior and thought, as well as inventions of all sorts, seem to germinate most often in the metropolitan zones of California and neighboring states. However, the cultural map of late twentieth century America is not just the mirror image of the early nineteenth century. No longer is the simple physical flow of ideas and people through two-dimensional space the dominant process. The rules of the game have undergone profound, but poorly understood, revisions, so that the current mechanisms of change, thanks largely to radically different modes of communication and social structure, may bear scant resemblance to those of the past. One of the more obvious symptoms of the changing forms of change is the apparent homogenization of the nation, and indeed much of the world, through cultural convergence on a grand scale.

CONVERGENCE VS. DIVERGENCE. For the first 200 years of the European presence in North America, the forces of cultural diversification seem to have prevailed. By virtue of the differential migration over time and space of varied peoples and traits from overseas, the interaction of the newcomers with novel habitats and neighbors, and the spontaneous evolution of relatively isolated communities, the regions of Anglo-America diverged ever further from the parental European cultures, and each locality tended to become less similar to all others. Then, roughly during the period 1830–1850, a reversal of trend seems to have begun, as a set of powerful processes fostering national uniformity made themselves felt. A continental network of highways, canals, railroads, postal routes, and telegraph lines began to materialize, along with truly national business corporations. Mass production and mass consumption of anonymously made commodities began to edge out local artisans making individualized things for small markets.[29] Tastes and ideals were standardized with the proliferation of nationally distributed magazines, newspapers, books, popular songs and advertising, the itinerant dramatic troupe,

---

[29] John A. Kouwenhoven, *Made in America: The Arts in Modern Civilization* (Garden City, N.Y.: Doubleday & Co., Inc., 1948).

circus, and lecturer, and the great popularity of school textbooks (in vast editions), carpenter's and other trade manuals, manufacturers' catalogs, fashion books for ladies, and eventually mail-order catalogs. All these trends have, of course, accelerated in recent decades.

And they have gone well beyond our national boundaries. Better and faster methods for dispatching information and people hastened the acceptance of new trends in European technology, thought, and arts.[30] They also made possible a rapid, reverse flow of native American products, not only to Europe but to much of the non-American world. The cargo list of exports includes not only American variants of standard agricultural or industrial items (for example, motor vehicles, fabrics, and electrical goods), but many things that are undeniably American: chewing gum, basketball, comic strips, cornflakes, cola beverages, the major pesticides, jazz and its recent derivatives, casual clothing, the dominant forms of cinema and television entertainment, the supermarket, the drivein, the motel, Mormons and Jehovah's Witnesses, the Western genre in print and film, facial tissues, ballpoint pens, and hundreds of words, American in origin but now universal in currency.

To allay somewhat the accusation of foreigners that Americans seek to coca-colonize the world, we have taken as avidly as we have given. Few nations have become as cosmopolitan in consumer tastes in recent years as has the United States, for reasons going beyond our large, polyglot immigrant population. The menus of our restaurants and the shelves of our groceries are stuffed with delicacies from scores of exotic lands. Popular music has been deeply tinged by the styles indigenous to Brazil, Polynesia, Mexico, India, Israel, and a dozen other alien nations. Many forms of literature, music, painting, sculpture, architecture, theatre, and dance have been thoroughly internationalized. The American cognoscenti covet Eskimo carvings, African masks, Chinese ceramics, and performances on the koto, sitar, and bazouki. The ever-volatile styles of women's (and more recently men's) dress, jewelry, and coiffure appear to reflect every possible variation upon ethnic themes.

Evidence for the impact of modern technology and marketing procedures in smoothing out cultural irregularities is too abundant and blatant to be ignored. Within the United States, one suburban subdivision or shopping center may be almost indistinguishable from another. Motels, filling stations, magazine racks, drug stores, high schools, radio program formats, chain restaurants, and the seemingly unlimited array of franchise retail enterprises are all very much peas in a pod, whatever the city or state. Every place has become Anyplace. At the international scale, the casual visitor cannot tell one country from another by style of airport, hotel, airline, or apartment building.

But appearances can be deceiving. In trying to measure degrees of similarity among different places in a rigorous fashion, one must answer two basic questions: the precise specification of what it is that is being measured; and the application of suitable scales of measurement. For certain aspects of human activity, for example, demographic and eco-

30 Spencer and Thomas, *Cultural Geography,* 277–326.

nomic characteristics, generally acceptable definitions and modes of measurement are available. It has also been demonstrated rather convincingly that convergence has occurred in recent decades in both sets of characteristics within and among highly advanced nations (at least when populations are aggregated within sizeable reporting units).[31] In the cultural realm, and especially with sociofacts and mentifacts, the technical problems are much more severe. As noted earlier, cultural systems are exceedingly complex, many-dimensional entities. It is difficult to decide which dimensions particularly merit notice, what relative weights should be assigned to them, and how they might be measured; and the optimal mathematical procedures for comparing the resulting values as between places through space and time have yet to be specified.

Apparently only two serious attempts have been made to test the degree of cultural convergence among different sections of the United States. The first of these, using the results of various public opinion polls over a recent 30-year period, arranged by region and other variables, failed to disclose any convergence, and indeed suggested the opposite trend.[32] But some basic, intractable problems in interpreting the data suggest caution in accepting these results. In the other study, involving an analysis of choice of given names for males in selected counties in the eastern United States in 1790 and 1968,[33] a substantial amount of convergence, and an apparent erosion of earlier culture areas, was demonstrated, but again with some equivocation. The array of names in the later year was immensely greater and richer than in eighteenth century America; and it is entirely possible that aggregating data at the county level may have masked much within-county—or rather within-society—diversity in naming complexes. Paradoxically, the answer to the question of whether the United States (or the entire modernized world) has been becoming more homogeneous may be: "yes and no."

Within the familiar two-dimensional space used by geographers in their cartographic analyses, cultural distances among ever more complicated entities would seem to be shrinking; but modern man, torn loose from conventional bounds of place or social and biological descent, may well be feeling his way into a number of newly discovered dimensions. The opportunities for personal choice, more complete individuation, and the formation of new social and cultural entities may have been greatly enhanced. Thus although most places may have begun to look alike, in important ways not usually susceptible to casual visual observation they may have started down fundamentally different routes. In sharp contrast,

[31] Hope T. Eldridge and Dorothy S. Thomas, *Population Redistribution and Economic Growth, United States, 1870–1950, III. Demographic Analyses and Interrelations* (Philadelphia: American Philosophical Society, 1964); and S. Labovitz, "Territorial Differentiation and Societal Change," *Pacific Sociological Review*, 8 (1965), 70–75.

[32] Norval D. Glenn and J. L. Simmons, "Are Regional Cultural Differences Diminishing?" *Public Opinion Quarterly*, 31 (1967), 176–93.

[33] Wilbur Zelinsky, "Cultural Variation in Personal Name Patterns in the Eastern United States," *Annals of the Association of American Geographers*, 60, No. 4 (1970), 743–69.

the communities of the premodern past may have displayed the greatest imaginable superficial differences, but the most striking isomorphisms are revealed to the persistent analyst. The essential rules for society and culture were repeated in place after place, varied superficially but possessing the same components connected in similar ways.

This rather esoteric argument can be condensed into the following summary: the most advanced nations of the world, notably the United States, have entered an era of truly revolutionary social and cultural transformation such that the inward structure of society and culture may be skipping past a phase boundary into a totally new set of conditions. The results, insofar as they can be analyzed geographically, on maps or otherwise, are so nonconformable with the products of earlier situations that comparisons are awkward or impossible to make. To offer an analogy, the problem is rather like comparing the territorial range and activity patterns of birds with those of their earthbound reptilian ancestors.

The American House

Many of the generalizations on spatial processes in the preceding pages, along with those on the origins and special identity of American culture, can be fleshed out by considering two very different sets of phenomena: the American house and patterns of church membership.

We are concerned here with the dwellings of the great majority of the American population—what might be fairly characterized as "folk housing"—and buildings that never enjoyed the professional attention of architects.[34] Although basically an artifact and one serving some urgent physical functions, the house is also the product of a complex set of societal and psychological factors, all filtered through the sediments of history. It is really as much sociofact or mentifact as artifact. When fully interpreted, the form and uses of the house tell us much, not only about the physical locale and the technology of the place and era, but also about the source and dates of the builder or renovator, the contacts and influences he experienced, his ethnic affiliation, and possibly also class, occupation, and religion.[35] In a very real sense, the house is the family's universe in microcosm, the distillation of past experience and a miniature model of how it perceives the outer world, as it is or perhaps even more as it should be.

In essence, the American house is a European import. Or, rather,

[34] Geographers who are guilt-ridden in the knowledge that no set of phenomena is their exclusive disciplinary property may draw some solace from folk housing. It is an orphan topic in the United States, one neglected by architects and anthropologists, and given serious attention only by a few eccentric geographers.

[35] The tangible meanings conveyed by house morphology are probed in Amos Rapoport, *House Form and Culture* (Englewood Cliffs, N.J.: Prentice-Hall, Inc., 1969); and Peirce F. Lewis, "The Geography of Old Houses," *Earth and Mineral Sciences* (Pennsylvania State University), 39 (February 1970), 33–37. Deeper layers of significance are charted in James Agee, *Let Us Now Praise Famous Men* (Boston: The Houghton Mifflin Company, 1941); and Gaston Bachelard, *The Poetics of Space* (New York: Orion Press, 1964).

it is a uniquely new object reconstituted from a number of earlier European fragments, which then evolved in a special way in accordance with the peculiarities of American life. Ideas, usually subconscious, as to the proper way to construct a dwelling varied from place to place along the colonial Atlantic Seaboard, depending upon time, sources, and conditions of colonization. Quite early, distinct regionalisms in house styles began to develop. But equally early, the designs, and often some of the materials, of the homes for the wealthy were imported intact from northwest Europe. It was only about the time of American Independence that an indigenous professionalism in architecture for homes and public structures began to develop. Yet, if the homes of the common people of Massachusetts, the Hudson Valley, and North Carolina were all distinct from the beginning, they shared nevertheless some unmistakably American traits. These, in turn, reflect the primordial notions about house morphology underlying folk architecture throughout a good part of Europe. These could surface only under the relatively primitive conditions of new North American society. There was little borrowing of aboriginal building techniques, and then only locally and temporarily. And no African heritage can be discerned among the structures built by or for the slaves, except perhaps in the still unstudied rural Negro churches.

Each of the three principal colonial culture hearths—southern New England, the Midland, and the Chesapeake Bay area—developed its own set of house types and other sorts of buildings at an early date, and so also did a number of minor subregions. We can trace the westward thrust of settlers and ideas into the continental interior from these seedbeds of American style quite precisely in the field, at least up until the mid-nineteenth century, by plotting the location of surviving examples of these regional types.[36] And we can also observe the ways in which various strands of culture flowed together and sometimes produced new regional blends. In fact, the quasi-archaeological technique of studying older dwellings is one of the better, if more laborious, ways of charting the past or present extent of culture areas (or the microgeography of older cities) and of gaining insight into the historical geography of American ideas.

As in other departments of cultural practice, there is a striking depletion of individuality and inventiveness in building styles and ornamentation as one moves away from the early communities in the East to the relatively accessible regions of the West. In part this was presumably the result of relative isolation during formative years. In place of the truly riotous exuberance of form within a single long-lived New England village or even a single block in an eastern Pennsylvania

36 Fred Kniffen, "Folk Housing: Key to Diffusion," *Annals of the Association of American Geographers,* 55, No. 4 (1965), 549–77; Wilbur Zelinsky, "Where the South Begins: The Northern Limit of the Cis-Appalachian South in Terms of Settlement Landscape," *Social Forces,* 30 (1951), 172–78; Henry Glassie, *Pattern in the Material Folk Culture of the Eastern United States* (Philadelphia: University of Pennsylvania Press, 1968); and Lewis, "The Geography of Old Houses."

borough—a variety, by the way, still somehow harmonious—there is the monotony and stunted imagination of the Middle Western or far Western residential neighborhood. This tendency is even more marked within business districts. An attenuation of style is observable even within so simple a category as techniques of log-house construction; and in a study of Georgia examples, a striking contrast was seen between the earlier, richer repertory of log-house forms in the (older) North and the later, stripped-down set found toward the (younger) South.[37]

The structures built after about 1850 tell quite a different story from their predecessors. By that date there had been sufficient mingling and hybridization of the original colonial styles within the great central expanses of the country to produce a recognizably national group of building types; and the pervasive new modes of communication and manufacturing had started to iron out regional departures from mass norms. For the past century or so, domestic building styles are closely correlated with date, and are much more sensitive to rate of diffusion down a social or cultural hierarchy than to territorial location. Yet, however standardized American building practices may be becoming, the house, old or new, is still packed densely with information about the national ethos, the dealings between man and habitat, and the changing configurations of our cultural geography. Surely the geographer must concern himself with the form and meaning of the objects he studies if any real sense is to be made of their spatial array or of their processual linkages with other phenomena in space and time.

Several attributes of the American house, past and present, bespeak important peculiarities of the national character. Perhaps the most obvious is the lavish use of space, both in the sheer size of the house proper and in the largeness of the residential lot. Furthermore, a disproportionately small fraction of the population live in apartment buildings or other multiunit structures; many of those who do are college students, convicts, the indigent or ailing elderly, and other institutionalized populations.[38] Except in the most congested of urban settings, as in New York City, Boston, or San Francisco, the one-family dwelling is a free-standing unit, with at least a token patch of space between it and its neighbors. Row housing is a phenomenon restricted to urban neighborhoods in the Northeast that were built about two centuries ago, apparently in imitation of Northwest European models.

Although much of this expansiveness might be explained away, the residual cultural factor bulks large. Land was cheap and abundant, and still is relative to land in most parts of the world; but the urge toward very large, isolated, individual properties seems to go beyond any rational economic reckoning. This is most obvious in the isolated farmstead,

[37] Wilbur Zelinsky, "The Log House in Georgia," *Geographical Review*, 43, No. 2 (1953), 173–93.

[38] This aversion to apartment life may derive, in part, from British attitudes. Although statistics on housing characteristics are designed by various national governments so as to make valid international comparisons almost impossible, simple observation leads one to believe that the urban English are much fonder of the single-family dwelling than are any of their European neighbors.

for which no convincing argument can be made in terms of transportation systems or social utility. If the propensity of Americans toward larger lots is being more fully realized now with growing affluence and the lateral spread of cities, the cubic volume of the structure has been decreasing. This is largely because of rising costs of materials and labor, the scarcity of servants, and the shrinkage in average size of household. But American homes are still bulky by any universal criteria; and those of the nineteenth century middle class were often of incredible proportions, even after making all allowances for number of hired hands, children, and other kinfolk, or the provision of closets and storerooms for the accumulations of a super-productive economy. One cannot help but speculate that these dimensions reflect an optimistic, aggressively extroverted view of the world and the American's place in it.

The fact that Americans may be profligate with space but niggardly with time also appears in their building technology. Great store is set upon quickness of construction, and it is not by chance that the United States has originated or perfected most leading methods of building prefabrication, or that the technique of balloon frame construction, one that reduced costs and workdays for wooden edifices so markedly, won such instant, universal acceptance.[39] The commercial hotel as we now know it and its up-to-date offspring, the motel, both of which were nurtured in, and are ubiquitous throughout, North America, also embody the themes of haste and transience.[40] Note also the emphasis on the garage, often an integral, conspicuous part of the house, sometimes even threatening to dominate the nonautomotive segment of the structure. The stress on transience, clearly evident in the early shelters of pioneer settlers, has waxed rather than waned in recent decades. Few Americans build a house with the intention of occupying it for a lifetime or passing it on to their children;[41] indeed our population is so mobile that every other family changes its abode every decade. These urges toward transience and mobility receive their ideal embodiment in that superlatively American invention, the house trailer, which is virtually nonexistent outside North America. Nomadism as a way of life, though not yet well documented by the social scientist, may have made marked progress during the 1960's among some members of the so-called "counterculture," for whom the VW microbus or some other such vehicle in nearly constant motion may be the only true home. But even among the most respectable strata of American society, transience is revered. Witness the recent popularity of high-rise office and apartment buildings designed to obsolesce and be razed after a few years, but only after the maximum tax advantage has been squeezed out of them.

Partly because the ordinary American house is so transitory a phe-

39 Daniel J. Boorstin, *The Americans: The National Experience* (New York: Random House, Inc., 1965), 148–52.

40 Boorstin, *The Americans*, 134–47.

41 Such heirlooms are certifiable curiosities. In Michigan, farmhouses that have been continuously occupied by members of the same family for 100 years or more are designated "Centennial Homes" by a state agency, and are so identified for the passerby by means of a metal plaque.

nomenon, but basically because of a fundamental restlessness of character, we have witnessed a dizzying procession of building styles and fads, one following hard upon the heels of another. As already noted, the modern American house (or commercial or public building) is a much better indicator of date than of locality. So avid is the appetite for novelty that the architect has ransacked virtually every historic era and most regions of the world in search of inspiration.

A cheerful extroversion of personality is writ large in the American house and its surroundings, which do double service as status symbols as well as shelters. The penchant for large glass windows, a trend that shows no sign of abating, goes beyond a normal craving for natural illumination and creates some serious problems in heating and upkeep. With the advent of the picture window craze, it becomes especially clear that the house is designed to serve as a display case, to advertise to the world at large the opulence and amiability of the household. The same outward-going personality is visible in the extravagant development of the porch. Although the ultimate origins of the porch (or portico or piazza) are obscure—the British may have hit upon the idea in the West Indies or India—no other national group has seized upon the device with such enthusiasm. During its apogee around 1900, few self-respecting American houses were without one, and many houses were encased with a porch on two or three sides and possibly on the second as well as the ground level. These open-air extensions of the house—literally a perpetual "open house"—were the stages upon which much of the social life of the family was enacted during the warmer seasons. This obliteration of the distinction between inside and outside, totally at variance with Northwest European antecedents, is carried even further in much avant-garde architecture, especially in the Pacific Coast states.

The same impulses that favored the efflorescence of window and porch seem to lie behind the almost pathological fervor with which grass lawns are tended—and front fences or hedges are frowned upon. (Do we have here the democratization of the British baronial estate?) There is still much to be learned about the culture of a group, including the American, through the microgeographic analysis of their house gardens.[42] However, one peculiarity of American landscaping leaps to the eye: contrary to general usage, gardens are not invariably private spaces behind walls or hedges, but are often aggressively public, placed on the street side of the house. And since the lawn itself is basically ornamental or symbolic, intended much more for show than for any sort of play or foot traffic, it must be considered along with shrubs and flowers as a badge of membership in a cheerful, outgoing democratic society, but one in which the privileges of a powerful individualism must also be made manifest. The lawn is also significant as a shorthand symbol for the edenic ideal that is so strong an undercurrent in American thought. It is also appropriate to indicate here a rather cavalier disregard of

[42] Writings on Oriental gardens provide models that might well be emulated by American scholars. Some recent items are noted in Yi-Fu Tuan, "Man and Nature," *Landscape*, 15, No. 3 (1966), 32.

environmental conditions on the part of designer and homeowner, an attitude stemming from an overriding self-confidence and material abundance as much as from ignorance. Except for a tiny minority of interesting exceptions, ideas are *imposed* upon the land, however inappropriately (for example, lawns on the sands of Florida or picture windows in the subarctic). Climate, slope, drainage, geology, soil, and natural vegetation seem to matter little.

Paradoxically, despite its openness, the American house also attests to the supremacy of the private individual. We have already noted the aversion to inhabiting multifamily structures and the impulse to create token open spaces between neighbors. But it is in its internal arrangements, with the great stress upon isolation, the multiplicity of doors and closed spaces, and the segregation of specific functions, that the pervasive American privatism comes fully to the fore.[43] In addition, taking the house and grounds as a single entity, there is the starkest kind of contrast between the American's attitude toward his private bubble of space and that toward all public spaces. All self-respecting householders spend an inordinate amount of time caring for yard and garden and on keeping the interior as antiseptic and spotless as human ingenuity can manage. But public spaces, including sidewalks, thoroughfares, roadsides, public vehicles, parks, and many public buildings reveal a studied neglect and frequently such downright squalor that it is difficult to believe one is encountering a civilized community.

Finally, the American house quite neatly illustrates an all-powerful mechanistic vision of the world, for it is a carefully manipulated machine, a working model of what Americans feel the cosmos fundamentally is— or could be induced to be. The internal physiology of the American house represents a truly awe-inspiring triumph of the mechanical arts. The list of inventions promoting domestic comfort and convenience attributable to American ingenuity is long and fascinating. Elaborate and ultimately effortless central heating (and cooling) systems have been devised; then, like the other wonders noted below, made available to the world at large.[44] The water supply has been brought indoors, and thoroughly rationalized. American plumbing is the eighth wonder of the world, and the Great American Bathroom a veritable glittering cathedral of cleanliness. The kitchen is also a marvel of efficiency and clever design, incorporating a multitude of American "firsts." Similarly advanced are lighting, electrical wiring, laundry systems, and rubbish disposal. As already intimated, the layout of the house is thoroughly programmed, with a specific function, and usually no other, designated for each space. Thus we have carried to its logical extreme that spatial separation of place of work and place of residence that is so distinctive and important a feature of the larger landscape. This statement also applies to the farmer who

[43] The contrast between the internal plans of American and Chinese houses in this respect is almost total. See Francis L. K. Hsu, *Americans and Chinese: Two Ways of Life* (New York: Abelard Schuman, Inc., 1953), 68–70.
[44] We can forgive the British many things, but never their barbaric indifference to the virtues of central heating.

resides at his work place but works in different buildings on or near the farmstead from that in which he eats and sleeps. In almost every respect, then, the American house is a completely appropriate capsule world, fleshing out the main principles, myths, and values of the larger cultural system.

Geography of Denominational Membership

If the form, substance, and spatial patterns of American houses convey much vital information about the totality of the national culture, a great deal can also be decoded from the data on religious affiliation, but from a rather different perspective.[45] The trend in house morphology seems to be decidedly toward place-to-place uniformity; but, in terms of religion, the United States has been a land of phenomenal diversity from the very beginning, and this heterogeneity fails to show the slightest sign of slackening. In fact, no other nation begins to approach the United States in this respect. The best account available lists some 251 religious bodies able and willing to offer statistics on membership, but some scores of additional groups undoubtedly exist. Much of this variety was imported from Europe. From the Reformation onward, Great Britain has accommodated many different Christian groups; and the massive immigration from the European continent contributed many others to the American population. In addition, several groups of Old World provenance underwent further evolution and splintering in the New World; and the United States in turn has produced, and continues to produce, a prodigious number of its own native Christian denominations, some of them, like the Mormons, Adventists, and Disciples of Christ, claiming large memberships. This multiplicity of religious bodies is visible not only at the national or regional scale but even within a single small city, village, or neighborhood. At the most obvious level of explanation, this may be a matter of the doctrine of separation of church and state or of an economy rich enough to support a superfluity of congregations and church buildings; but it is much more meaningful as a ringing affirmation of the dogged individualism of the American. The freedom to choose one's church, to float freely from one group to another, or even to invent an original sect of one's own is deeply cherished, and is closely akin to other forms of personal mobility and self-assertion.

45 Church membership data are relied upon in this discussion not because they are ideal, or even satisfactory, indicators of the extent or intensity of religious practice but because no other measures are generally at hand. The strength of religious feeling on the part of individuals or groups is a phenomenon eluding easy quantification except for church attendance records, which are poor when they are available at all. Problems of American church membership and their interpretation are discussed in Wilbur Zelinsky, "An Approach to the Religious Geography of the United States: Patterns of Church Membership in 1952," *Annals of the Association of American Geographers,* 51, No. 2 (1961), 141–47. The discussion of denominational membership offered here is basically a brief paraphrase of this article. In addition, an indispensable fund of fact and interpretation is available in Edwin S. Gaustad, *Historical Atlas of Religion in America* (New York: Harper & Row, Publishers, 1962).

Yet, despite the luxuriation of creeds, it is also clear that religious feeling, at least in the conventional otherworldly sense, tends to run shallow in the United States. The incidence of church membership may be high and the financial investment in church property enormous, but traditional theological concerns scarcely ever enter the average citizen's head. At least, that has been the situation in recent decades, and the current is running strongly toward the further desanctification of thought and behavior. Such sacred occasions as Christmas, Easter, Passover, and the Sabbath have become largely secular and commercial, and church buildings have come to function more as community social centers than as houses of worship. Perhaps the most persuasive evidence for the casual role of the spiritual life in the American scheme of things is its relative invisibility in the physical landscape. In sharp contrast to the Christian, Moslem, or Hindu houses of worship of the Old World, or even those of neighboring Quebec and Mexico, the church building and associated activities are almost never located at the functional center of an American city, where land values are at their peak, but are relegated to peripheral sites.[46] Nor is tangible evidence of religion conspicuous in the country-side. And unlike most pre-modern communities of the Old World where daily existence and religion are mixed inseparably, the religious factor does not enter into the layout of town, field, or house, or the shaping of economic activities.[47]

On the other hand, in a new, emergent, perhaps unprecedented way, religion has become a potent force in the life of the country. There are hints of a novel mode of religion in the way in which imported creeds, including Roman Catholicism and Judaism along with the various brands of Protestantism, have become increasingly "Americanized," so that they now resemble one another much more than they do the same religions in the eastern Hemisphere. Furthermore, many of the more fundamentalist of the native churches, in what is not lightly called "God's Country," most vehemently identify themselves with extreme versions of patriotism.

Thus it can be said, without serious exaggeration, that Americanism has, in a most fundamental sense, become the true religion of Americans. The cult, which goes far beyond normal patriotism, is equipped with a full panoply of sacred writings, saints, rituals, and holy places. (The rise of Marxism-Leninism in the Soviet Union or Maoism in China offers some instructive parallels.) It would be difficult to find another object in human history so fiercely venerated as the American flag; and the heart-felt hysteria evident in flag-worship is a most convincing sort of religious testimony.

If Americanism does not fit neatly into the familiar mold of religion,

---

[46] The fact that Salt Lake City and Boston seem to be the only exceptions among larger American cities fortifies this contention, for these have been the metro-politan foci for the only two culture regions that begin to simulate theocracies.

[47] A theme pursued in detail in Pierre Deffontaines, *Géographie et Religions* (Paris: Gallimard, 1948) and David E. Sopher, *Geography of Religions* (Englewood Cliffs, N.J.: Prentice-Hall, Inc., 1967).

it may be that religion, like many other categories of human existence, is passing through a revolutionary set of changes as advanced societies enter a post-industrial age. The powerful strain of messianic perfectionism in the national character already alluded to is a major characteristic of this new faith (and of Marxism as well?). It is worth noting that the unabating vigor of North American missionaries, both Catholic and Protestant, in carrying the cross to Latin America, Africa,[48] Asia, and elsewhere is matched by their determination to spread the blessings of "the American way of life."

If virtually all the inhabitants of the United States are, consciously or not, adherents of a single religion in thought and deed, are the ordinary denominational classifications of any value to the cultural geographer? Most emphatically. When Americans categorize groups of people, the most important sets, beyond sex and age, are those taking into account race, religion, and ethnic group. If the racial boundaries are the most nearly impervious, the major religious faiths (Protestant, Catholic, Eastern Orthodox, and Jewish), are the next most stable, for it is more awkward to move or marry across interfaith lines than across almost any inter-ethnic line. Of central importance is the fact that religious associations seek out, accentuate, and preserve differences among persons. Not only can one's church affiliation denote national, ethnic, or racial origin, it also reflects rather strong urban-rural differentials, and in many parts of the nation the pervasive effects of regional culture. Thus there are significant correlations with larger spatial and temporal patterns. For that large minority of persons who elect to shift allegiance, the denomination may be a sensitive gauge of social, economic standing or aspiration, and psychological tendency.

There is some difficulty in providing usable maps of the major American religious denominations or derivative maps of religious regions (Figure 3.3) because of severe problems in defining membership and in procuring and evaluating statistics. But the results, imperfect though they be, are nonetheless instructive. It appears that, even though most denominational groups do tend, to a striking degree, to be national in distribution, no two groups display strongly congruent patterns, and each does have one or more major regional concentrations. These in turn can be attributed to specific events in cultural and demographic history.

More specifically, the spatial distribution of denominational members is the outcome of the following processes: births, deaths, migration, conversion (through casual contact or active missions), and apostasy. Although information is scanty, it seems that differential fertility and mortality are of relatively minor consequence in accounting for the size or distribution of religious groups. It is their spatial movements and success in attracting new members and holding old ones that are most critical. The contemporary map of American religion indicates four major sets of migrational events:

48 Hildegard Binder Johnson, "The Location of Christian Missions in Africa," *Geographical Review*, 57, No. 2 (1967), 168–202.

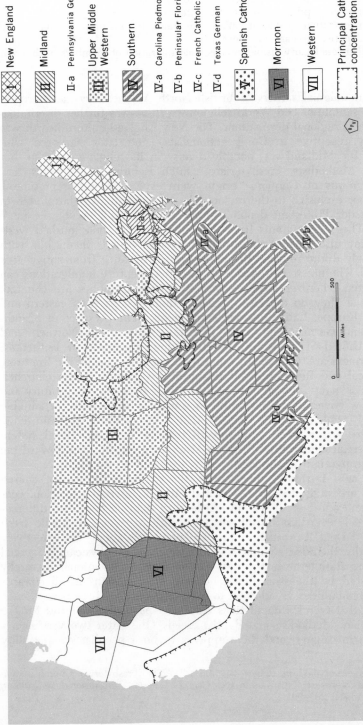

New England

I

Midland

II

II-a Pennsylvania German

Upper Middle
Western

III

Southern

IV

IV-a Carolina Piedmont

IV-b Peninsular Florida

IV-c French Catholic

IV-d Texas German

Spanish Catholic

V

Mormon

VI

Western

VII

Principal Catholic
concentrations

FIG. 3.3. *Major religious regions. (Adapted from: Wilbur Zelinsky, "An Approach to the Religious Geography of the
United States," Annals of the Association of American Geographers, 51, No. 2 [June 1961], 193.)*

1. the colonization of the Atlantic Seaboard by regionally distinctive groups;
2. their westward progression into the interior;[49]
3. the concentration of post-colonial immigrants from Europe, Canada, and Latin America in particular localities;
4. the rather less clearly visible interregional migration of members of different groups.

If the colonial settlers of British North America were an unrepresentative sample of Old World religionists, there was further discrimination in their regional destinations. The New England culture hearth was eminently receptive to Congregationalists (and later harbored Unitarians); the Midland was notably diverse in its religious makeup, but Quakers, Methodists, Presbyterians, Dutch Reformed, Lutherans, and various groups of Germanic origin were especially well represented, though not exclusive to the region. The early South was hospitable to all the major Protestant denominations of the period, except the more radical. Then, as migrants from these three nodal zones pushed westward, they also carried their religious identity with them, but with increasingly dilute regional distinctiveness as distance from native area increased. The nineteenth- and early twentieth-century immigrations can be detected wherever large clusters of Roman Catholics are counted, denoting as they do the Irish, various ethnic groups from eastern and southern Europe, Latin America, and Quebec. The presence of Scandinavians and German immigrants in many tracts of the Northern and Central United States is revealed by a high incidence of Lutherans; other Germans are traceable by the mapping of adherents of the Brethren, Evangelical and Reformed, and Evangelical United Brethren churches. Location of many immigrant church members over the past century and a half was governed by proximity to source or availability of suitable parcels of farmland. In one instance, that of the Jewish immigrant, however, there was a filtering downward through the hierarchical system of commercial metropolises, with the strongest representation toward the top of the pyramid in the larger cities.

The most intriguing questions in the spatial patterning of church members are suggested by differential rates of internal migration, conversion, and apostasy. If we have little hard data on migration differentials there is even less on differential ability to recruit and hold fresh converts. To put it in other terms, we know little about how effectively and rapidly the ideas in question diffuse through physical and social space. Gravitation toward certain points in the educational hierarchy is suggested by the strong concentration of Unitarians in all sizeable college communities, in addition to most large cities. There is also much evidence that frontier populations displayed particular affinities for the Presbyterian, Methodist, and Baptist creeds (the latter two very nearly American in origin); and there appears to be a peculiar compatibility

[49] As exemplified in Robert D. Mitchell, "The Presbyterian Church As an Indicator of Westward Expansion in 18th Century America," *Professional Geographer,* 18 (Sept. 1966), 293–99.

between Southerners and Baptism, especially after 1860. But what are we to make of the irregular map patterns displayed by Adventists, Disciples of Christ, or members of the Assembly of God and the Church of the Nazarene? The probability is that quite apart from accidents of ecclesiastical history, cultural forces we cannot yet identify have been at work in sorting out potential church members in terms of social and economic characteristics and preferences for particular areas and environments. Unfortunately, very little work has been done on the spatial array of religions at the micro scale in the United States, either within cities or in rural districts.[50] It is likely that even more puzzling questions of explanation and interpretation of the interrelations among location, religion, and other social factors would emerge from such documentation.

Further problems of theoretical interest are raised when regional boundaries are attempted on the basis of religious affiliation (Figure 3.3, p. 97). A total of seven primary regions are proposed, plus an additional five subregions, in an essay by this writer.[51] How closely do these regions resemble the more general culture areas delimited in the next chapter? Rather well in at least four instances. The Mormon realm is an admirable example of a region in which religion is the chief genetic factor as well as the strongest reason for a persistent distinctiveness. The special regional character of New England might also be attributed in part to its quasi-theocratic past and the unique blend of denominations housed within its boundaries. And religion is certainly a significant element in the maintenance of cultural identity within the Hispanic Southwest. In religion, as in many other respects, the Southern culture area tends to stand apart from the rest of the nation, although this distinctiveness seems to have materialized rather recently. This is because of the relatively high incidence of certain Protestant denominations, especially the Baptist, and the scarcity of Catholics and Jews, rather than because of any uniquely Southern group. On a lesser scale, an argument can be advanced for the Pennsylvania German area having acquired its unique geographic personality mainly because of its large quota of "peculiar people" and other staunch church members for whom religion has been a dominant force. On the other hand, the Middle West fails completely to assert itself in terms of a distinctive constellation of religions, and so too the West and its subregional components, excepting, of course, the Mormon area.

Thus, although we can do no more than lightly sketch the possibilities here, the spatial array of denominational members in the United States would seem to hold considerable potential in illustrating one major set of processes at work in shaping the more general cultural map: differ-

---

50 One of the rare specimens of this genre is Elaine M. Bjorklund, "Ideology and Culture Exemplified in Southwestern Michigan," *Annals of the Association of American Geographers,* 54, No. 2 (1964), 227–41.
51 Zelinsky, "An Approach to the Religious Geography of the United States," Fig. 26, p. 193. This initial attempt at regionalization should be used in conjunction with a more sophisticated drawing, Fig. 8, "Religious Affiliation in the United States, ca. 1950," Sopher, *Geography of Religions,* pp. 84–85. This contains additional information and a quite different mode of symbolization.

ential migration, or diffusion, of individuals and ideas at different periods. At a somewhat deeper level, it may offer raw material for the understanding of the still mysterious processes of region formation. And, finally, if we dare venture far beneath the arithmetical surface of denominations, members, and church buildings into the inner workings of religion in the larger sense, we may be witnessing one facet of a major structural transformation as a new mode of religious sensibility seizes the subconscious of a folk.

Other Aspects of American Culture

If the analysis of American house types and religious patterns can yield major insights into the nature and spatial behavior of the national culture, there are many other cultural items that might be eminently serviceable for the same purposes. Each reveals a special perspective, and none can be ignored without dimming our view of the vast, convoluted landscape that is the American cultural system. The following paragraphs include a listing of the more immediately profitable topics, with brief indications of what has already been done and, rather more pointedly, what can or should be done. Lack of space, however, precludes full-scale critiques or programmatic statements. In some sectors, practically no serious work has been executed by geographers or anyone else; but even where a significant body of work is at hand, as in the study of folk housing or religion, the amount of unfinished business still bulks immensely larger.

SETTLEMENT FEATURES. The settlement landscape offers a peculiarly attractive array of phenomena for geographic analysis, for it combines the effects of culture and tradition with those of habitat, economy, and technology in highly mappable ways. In addition to farmhouses, which until the turn of this century accommodated the great majority of the American population, there are the many varieties of barns, sheds, wells, and other farmstead structures meriting close attention. Enough work has been done on barns to indicate that they are perhaps the most conservative of structures in general use and may serve quite as effectively as house types to indicate sources, routes, and dates of settlers and the spatial outlines of culture areas.[52] Distinctive barn types are common to the South, others to the Midland and French Canada. Much of older New England is characterized by the readily recognizable connecting barn.[53] Enough work has been done on the fencing (wooden,

[52] The topic of barns as indices to early cultural identity is treated in Henry Glassie, *Pattern in the Material Folk Culture of the Eastern United States* (Philadelphia: University of Pennsylvania Press, 1968), pp. 60–64, 88–92, 133–41, 145–49; Eric Sloane, *American Barns and Covered Bridges* (New York: Wilfred Funk, Inc., 1964), and Joseph W. Glass, *The Pennsylvania Culture Region: A Geographic Interpretation of Barns and Farmhouses,* doctoral dissertation, Pennsylvania State University, 1971.
[53] A comprehensive bibliography for American barns is scattered through Glassie, *Pattern in Material Folk Culture.* For French Canada, see Robert-Lionel Séguin, *Les Granges du Québec du XVIIe au XIXe Siècle,* Bulletin No. 192 (Ottawa:

stone, stump, sod, hedging) used to bound fields and pastures to reveal some sharp regional differences and the probability that further research would be profitable, but not enough to suggest the nature of the ultimate findings.[54] A single study of the historical geography of the covered bridge is an admirable example of the leadership role of New England in devising new technologies, and of the mechanics of diffusion as well.[55] It also suggests the value of analyses of other bridge types or of the grist mills and country stores that punctuate the rural scene at frequent intervals. Another universal element in the American settlement land-scape, rural and urban, the church building, has been scandalously neglected by geographers. The architectural historians have confined themselves to the grander, professionally designed specimens, leaving vernacular church design in limbo. As an item responsive to ethnic, racial, temporal, socioeconomic, and urban-rural, as well as denomina-tional, differentials, the church building would seem to represent too rich an ore to be overlooked by cultural geographers or historians. There has been an equally puzzling avoidance of cemeteries by students of Americana, despite the abundance of field and cartographic material and the anthropological axiom that burial customs are among the more revealing departments of human behavior. The entire literature has been noted in a very brief statement that is also a forceful manifesto for the research that is so badly needed.[56]

In settlement studies, as elsewhere in American cultural geography, there has been a strong bias toward the rural and agricultural, so that scant attention has been paid to the urban scene and its artifacts. Thus we have virtually nothing on the historical geography or cultural impli-cations of factory buildings, warehouses, or shops, or of the public build-ings and spaces usually situated in towns (for example, schools, jails, depots, post offices, hospitals, hotels, zoos, theaters, parks, and other amusement places), or of the statues or other monumental constructions of such rich symbolic import. And such work as has been done on house types has largely ignored the specifically urban forms.[57]

The spatial configuration of settlement features has received at least modest attention from geographers, enough at least to indicate the promise of ampler rewards. The historical geography of land survey has

---

Musée National du Canada, 1963); for New England, Wilbur Zelinsky, "The New England Connecting Barn," *Geographical Review*, 48, No. 4 (1958), 540–53; and for the Midland, Alfred L. Shoemaker, ed., *The Pennsylvania Barn*, 2d ed. (Kutz-town, Pa.; Pennsylvania Folklife Society, 1959); and Glass, *The Pennsylvania Culture Region.*

54 J. Fraser Hart and E. C. Mather, "The American Fence," *Landscape*, 6, No. 3 (Spring 1957), 4–9; Wilbur Zelinsky, "Walls and Fences," *Landscape*, 8, No. 3 (Spring 1958), 14–20; and Glassie, *Pattern in Material Folk Culture, passim.*

55 Fred Kniffen, "The American Covered Bridge," *Geographical Review*, 41, No. 1 (1951), 114–23.

56 Fred Kniffen, "Necrogeography in the United States," *Geographical Review*, 57, No. 3 (1967), 426–27.

57 The situation is thoroughly reviewed in Kenneth E. Corey, *A Spatial Analy-sis of Urban Houses*, doctoral dissertation, University of Cincinnati, 1969.

CARL A. RUDISILL LIBRARY
LENOIR RHYNE COLLEGE

been usefully sketched by Marschner,[58] and the establishment of rectangular survey and a related road system in Ohio has been probed in some depth.[59] Only a single serious effort seems to have been made to examine the geography of field boundaries,[60] in contrast to the popularity of the topic among European scholars; but additional work on field, road, and survey patterns would probably repay the investigator many times over. Similarly, with the analysis of farmstead patterns, on which topic the pioneering essay still 'stands in splendid isolation.[61] Price's innovative study of the pattern of American county courthouse squares and their distribution through time and space has documented a most interesting series of diffusional processes and their impact upon urban morphology.[62] But, again in odd contrast to the European record, there are few other attempts to scrutinize urban street patterns. Such studies as we have indicate that the geometry of street layout (and the patterning of street names) may serve as effective tracers of cultural flows and one of the more reliable means for delimiting major culture areas.[63]

Casting a rather broader observational net are those geographers and other scholars who have looked at the composite visible landscape in the United States and tried to interpret it. In some local studies, such as those of Nelson on Southern California[64] or Swain and Mather on the "St. Croix Border Country,"[65] the cultural element is largely implicit. A number of recent critiques of the appearance of contemporary America, often sad or scornful in tone, have summoned up visual evidence in indicting some of the central values of the culture.[66] But other observers,

[58] Francis J. Marschner, *Land Use and Its Patterns in the United States,* Agriculture Handbook No. 153 (Washington, D.C.: United States Department of Agriculture, 1959).

[59] Norman J. W. Thrower, *Original Survey and Land Subdivision: A Comparative Study of the Form and Effect of Contrasting Cadastral Surveys* (Chicago: Rand McNally & Company, 1966); and William D. Pattison, *Beginnings of the American Rectangular Land Survey System 1784–1800,* Research Paper No. 50 (Chicago: University of Chicago, Department of Geography, 1957).

[60] J. Fraser Hart, "Field Patterns in Indiana," *Geographical Review,* 58, No. 3 (1968), 450–71.

[61] Glenn T. Trewartha, "Some Regional Characteristics of American Farmsteads," *Annals of the Association of American Geographers,* 38, No. 3 (1948), 169–225.

[62] Price, "The Central Courthouse Square in the American County Seat."

[63] John W. Reps, *The Making of Urban America: A History of City Planning in the United States* (Princeton, N.J.: Princeton University Press, 1965); and Richard Pillsbury, "The Urban Street Pattern As a Culture Indicator: Pennsylvania, 1682–1815," *Annals of the Association of American Geographers,* 60, No. 3 (1970), 428–46.

[64] Howard J. Nelson, "The Spread of an Artificial Landscape over Southern California," *Annals of the Association of American Geographers,* 49, No. 3, Part 2 (1959), 80–99.

[65] Harry Swain and Cotton Mather, *St. Croix Border Country* (Prescott, Wisc.: Trimbelle Press and Pierce County Geographical Society, 1968).

[66] Peter Blake, *God's Own Junkyard: The Planned Deterioration of America's Landscape* (New York: Holt, Rinehart & Winston, Inc., 1963); Ian Nairn, *The American Landscape: A Critical View* (New York: Random House, Inc., 1965); and Ian L. McHarg, *Design with Nature* (Garden City, N.Y.: Natural History Press, 1969).

such as Jackson, Kouwenhoven, and Tunnard and Pushkarev,[67] have been more temperate in their judgments; and Lowenthal and Prince's dictum that "Landscapes are formed by landscape tastes"[68] would seem a useful point of departure for the culturally attuned landscape-watcher, and for those concerned with the newly crystallized subfield of perceptual geography.

CULTURAL DEMOGRAPHY AND CULTURAL ECONOMICS. Demographers and geographers dealing with population matters have tended to restrict their explanations almost totally to traditional social and economic factors. But it would appear that in the United States, where fertility, mortality, and migrational differentials are not so largely shaped by economic considerations as in less affluent societies, more attention could be given to other modes of explanation. These could include not just the search for pleasure and the amenities, but also the role of cultural differences, regional and ethnic. Although such an approach might be especially pertinent in coping with migration, there are also interesting possibilities in terms of morbidity and causes of death.

To illustrate the point, consider a simple map showing homicide rates among the white population during a recent period. (See Figure 3.4.) The marked interstate differentials displayed in this drawing are not randomly distributed, but reveal instead a distinct variance by region. The risk of homicide is least in New England and the Northeast in general, and in those states that received major inputs of migrants and ideas from New England. The much higher rates in most of the South and West (with the interesting exception of Utah) may indicate a generally lower level of socioeconomic attainment but even more strongly the dilution of a New England cultural predisposition against personal violence. Unfortunately, earlier data to test this notion are not readily available.

Within the well-trodden field of economic geography, emphasis has consistently fallen on questions of production and distribution. Neither the statistical systems nor the curiosity of students has been directed toward the equally interesting problems of consumption. If, as we may legitimately speculate, cultural factors affect consumption in many ways, there has been a disturbing dearth of interest in patterns of food or beverage consumption, or in any aspect of dietary geography.[69] The few probes into this field are most provocative;[70] and again it seems

---

67 Christopher Tunnard and Boris Pushkarev, *Man-Made America: Chaos or Control? An Inquiry into Selected Problems of Design in the Urbanized Landscape* (New Haven: Yale University Press, 1963); and John A. Kouwenhoven, *The Beer Can by the Highway: Essays on What's American about America* (Garden City; N.Y.: Doubleday & Co., Inc., 1961). John B. Jackson's observations are scattered through many numbers of *Landscape,* usually in the form of unsigned editorials.

68 David Lowenthal and Hugh C. Prince, "English Landscape Tastes," *Geographical Review,* 55, No. 2 (1965), 186.

69 Herbert G. Kariel, "A Proposed Classification of Diet," *Annals of the Association of American Geographers,* 56, No. 1 (1966), 68–79; and Max Sorre, "La Géographie de l'Alimentation," *Annales de Géographie,* 51 (1952), 184–99.

70 Rupert B. Vance, *Human Geography of the South* (Chapel Hill: University

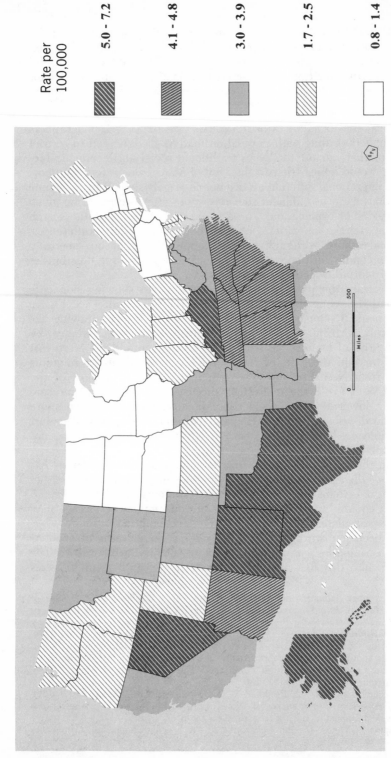

Rate per 100,000	
	5.0 - 7.2
	4.1 - 4.8
	3.0 - 3.9
	1.7 - 2.5
	0.8 - 1.4

FIG. 3.4. Age-adjusted homicide rate, white population, three-year average, 1959–1961. (Adapted from: National Center for Health Statistics, Homicide in the United States, 1950–1964, Public Health Service Publication No. 1000, Series 20, No. 6 [Washington, D.C., 1967], Table 2, pp. 16–17.)

clear that the intellectual payoff would be considerable for the geographic pioneer with the courage and persistence (and intestinal forti-
tude?) to assemble and analyze the disparate, often refractory data.
The same statement could be repeated for other consumer items, such
as clothing, cosmetics, furniture, jewelry, color preferences, and the like,
where choices are dictated by emotion, tradition, apparent whim, or
other "irrational" factors. The data presented in Table 3.1, subject though
they are to large sampling errors and despite the grossness of the areas,
suggest some rich possibilities. As in the field of electoral geography,
it is almost certain that valuable data have been compiled and analyzed
by advertising, manufacturing, wholesale, and retail corporations; but,
if so, most of it remains inaccessible to the public.

LANGUAGE. The one aspect of American culture that has been approached diligently in organized fashion—and with due regard to the
spatial dimension—is the vocabulary, pronunciation, and syntax of American English. This has been the accomplishment largely of a group of
linguists, with only fitful help from geographers.[71] The resultant maps
quite clearly indicate a close areal correspondence between the various
American dialects and subdialects and other phases of culture, material
and nonmaterial. Linguistic areas thus have proved to be excellent sur-
rogates for general culture areas in the United States, as in so many
other parts of the world. One can only hope that these linguistic endeavors will continue and reach the degree of sophistication and detail
achieved in European research.

As might be expected, the chief contribution by geographers to this
study area has been on the topic of place names.[72] The study of the

of North Carolina Press, 1935), 411–41; George R. Stewart, *American Ways of Life*
(Garden City, N.Y.: Doubleday & Co., Inc., 1954), 75–132; and Sam Hilliard, "Hog
Meat and Cornpone: Food Habits in the Ante-Bellum South," *Proceedings of the
American Philosophical Society*, 113 (January 1969), 1–13. The potential contribu-
tion of dietary studies to our understanding of the regional cultures of the United
States is illustrated in Don Yoder, "Historical Sources for American Traditional
Cookery: Examples from the Pennsylvania German Culture," *Pennsylvania Folklife*,
20, No. 3 (Spring 1971), 16–29.

[71] Most of the research effort by linguists on region aspects of American speech
has been devoted to an ongoing, massive project, *The Linguistic Atlas of the United
States*. The status of this work and the publications issued thus far are described in
Carroll E. Reed, *Dialects of American English* (Cleveland: The World Publishing
Company, 1967). The more noteworthy studies already published include Hans
Kurath, ed., *Linguistic Atlas of New England*, 3 vols. (Providence, R.I.: Brown
University, 1939–1943); and Hans Kurath, *A Word Geography of the Eastern
United States* (Ann Arbor: University of Michigan Press, 1949) and *The Pronuncia-
tion of English in the Atlantic States* (Ann Arbor: University of Michigan Press,
1962).

[72] For example, Robert C. West, "The Term 'Bayou' in the United States: A
Study in the Geography of Place Names," *Annals of the Association of American
Geographers*, 44, No. 1 (1954), 63–74; Wilbur Zelinsky, "Some Problems in the
Distribution of Generic Terms in the Place-Names of the Northeastern United
States," *Ibid.*, 45, No. 4 (1955), 319–49; and Meredith F. Burrill, "Toponymic
Generics," *Names*, 4, No. 3 (September 1956), 129–45 and 4, No. 4 (December
1956), 226–40.

Table 3.1. Regionally Distinctive Patterns of Consumer Expenditures for Selected Goods and Services, 1960-1961

Based upon Sample of 12,000 Nonfarm Households
National mean household dollar expenditure per item = 100

	Northeast	North Central	South	West
Flour	60.4	75.4	166.1	85.7
Macaroni, spaghetti, noodles	160.4	89.4	61.0	97.2
Rice	100.9	54.7	108.9	151.5
Cornmeal	22.7	45.3	259.3	30.1
Bread other than white	155.9	85.0	44.1	165.7
Beefsteaks, fresh and frozen	132.1	84.9	80.1	105.9
Bacon	79.2	94.3	120.3	105.9
Cold cuts	133.8	111.0	67.7	82.8
Smoked sausage	96.2	118.8	103.3	76.4
Fresh, frozen, smoked fish and seafood	162.2	66.0	76.3	97.1
Canned tuna	141.5	73.4	66.1	131.4
Fresh whole milk, retail	145.2	103.7	59.2	94.2
Pineapple juice	150.9	62.2	77.9	117.1
Fresh snap beans	107.5	58.4	164.4	42.8
Frozen green beans	183.0	60.3	50.8	117.1
Frozen lima beans	107.5	60.3	142.5	77.1
Frozen spinach	162.2	69.8	79.6	85.7
Butter	149.0	126.4	37.2	91.4
Margarine	92.4	90.5	106.7	114.2
Lard	43.3	66.0	210.1	51.4
Sugar	92.5	94.1	120.0	85.9
Syrup, molasses, honey	92.5	85.0	115.0	104.1
Tea	143.6	67.9	105.0	74.0
Cola drinks	75.4	92.4	145.9	71.1
Gingerale	220.8	73.8	35.4	65.6
Olives	136.0	105.9	50.8	120.0
Salt, other seasonings	94.2	83.0	105.0	116.9
Beer and ale	141.8	105.9	55.9	102.2
Blended whisky	173.7	100.0	50.8	71.1
Bourbon, scotch, straight rye	105.1	75.8	76.0	145.9
Cigarettes	114.8	96.2	91.5	97.0
Cigars	145.8	87.6	79.7	82.8
Other tobacco	77.5	73.8	174.2	48.6
Moving, freight, and storage	79.5	85.1	93.0	167.8
Writing supplies, stationery	114.7	98.0	75.9	120.0
Insect sprays, powders	92.0	53.8	133.1	125.9
Air fresheners, deodorizers	105.3	72.4	94.9	104.1
Electric blankets	60.1	61.1	114.0	197.0
Hats and caps, (men 18 years and over)	111.9	102.0	105.1	71.4
Slacks, shorts, dungarees (girls 16 and 17)	140.0	100.0	81.1	71.4
Hats (girls 16 and 17)	162.0	100.0	83.0	34.2
Gloves (girls 16 and 17)	128.2	114.8	94.6	60.0
Motorcycles and scooters	47.1	92.6	101.8	182.8
Indoor movies	130.1	87.0	74.1	108.5
Drive-in movies	83.0	89.0	101.8	140.1
Sports events	86.9	103.9	91.4	123.1
Concerts, plays, other admissions	170.1	85.2	47.2	108.5
Crafts, other hobbies	115.2	98.4	53.2	157.2
Pet food	117.1	78.0	87.9	128.7
Newspapers	132.1	103.9	74.1	102.9
Pocket edition books	109.4	81.6	79.1	134.1
Comic books	103.9	81.6	101.8	117.8
Hardbound books	89.0	89.0	96.3	130.1

Adapted from Fabian Linden, ed., *Market Profiles of Consumer Products* (New York: National Industrial Conference Board, 1967).

usage of generic terms singly or in groups over considerable tracts has proved especially fruitful in revealing the interaction of man and habitat and the spatial flow of ideas. There has been less interest in the geography of specific names; but an analysis of one particular type, classical town names, has documented nationwide, but irregular, dispersal from a west central New York hearth of a trait that is particularly diagnostic of the national culture.[73] Clearly there is much more to be learned by exploring our place name cover, whether through intensive local study[74] or through study of single terms, or classes thereof, over wider areas.

INSTITUTIONS, SOCIAL BEHAVIOR, AND FOLKLORE. The geography of social institutions is, potentially at least, a subject of considerable interest to the student of American culture. Unfortunately, there has been virtually no work done to date on the origin, spread, and geographical significance of such items as kinship groups; fraternal organizations; colleges; scientific, trade, and professional associations; and any of a vast array of other voluntary associations. A single attempt in this direction, an essay on the spatial career of county agricultural fairs, serves to whet the appetite.[75]

The record is equally blank as to social behavior, a field in which the interests of geographer, folklorist, sociologist, and psychologist intersect. Political geography, and more specifically electoral geography, might be included here, since the cultural overtones are loud; but it has begun to develop so vigorously of late that a brief note could not do it justice.[76] Among many other items, it can be suggested that the cultural geographer would be well rewarded by attending to all the many forms of recreation—field sports, children's games, card games, and holiday celebrations, among others. And, beyond that, there is the vast, enticing, and motley field known as folklore. It will suffice for the moment simply to list some of the many fertile topics that bear looking into: folk tales and legends; proverbs; riddles; superstitions; folk music; folk dance; handicrafts; gestures; social customs; and the many varieties of farm, household, and craft utensils.[77]

[73] Wilbur Zelinsky, "Classical Town Names in the United States: The Historical Geography of an American Idea," *Geographical Review*, 57, No. 4 (1967), 463–95.

[74] For a model study of this type, see Frederic G. Cassidy, *The Place-Names of Dane County, Wisconsin*, Publications of the American Dialect Society, No. 7 (Greensboro, N.C.: American Dialect Society, 1947).

[75] Fred Kniffen, "The American Agricultural Fair: Time and Place," *Annals of the Association of American Geographers*, 41, No. 1 (1951), 42–57.

[76] A good overview of the situation is afforded in the recent exchange of views between Cox and Kasperson: Kevin R. Cox, "Suburbia and Voting Behavior in the London Metropolitan Area," *Annals of the Association of American Geographers*, 58, No. 1 (1968), 111–27; Roger E. Kasperson, "On Suburbia and Voting Behavior," *Ibid.*, 59, No. 2 (1969), 405–11, and Kevin R. Cox, "Comments in Reply to Kasperson and Taylor," *Ibid.*, 59, No. 2 (1969), 411–15. For an ambitious survey—of sorts—of the political landscape of the nation, with heavy emphasis on ethnic and regional factors, see Kevin P. Phillips, *The Emerging Republican Majority* (Garden City: Doubleday & Co., Inc., 1969).

[77] Excellent introductions to the field are available in Richard M. Dorson, *American Folklore* (Chicago: University of Chicago Press, 1959) and Jan Harold Brunvand, *The Study of American Folklore: An Introduction* (New York: W. W.

The preceding pages may leave the reader with the impression that cultural geographers are enamored with quaint and arcane phenomena, and more excited over what is old, local, or special than in the pursuit of grander scientific quarry. This is at most a half-truth. In sampling specific topics that offer major potential for illuminating basic processes of cultural change through space and time, we have been obliged, for the sake of convenience, to divide what is really a whole. When the deeper layers of reality are probed, we can see that place names, barns, fences, diet, phonetics, voting patterns, burial customs, churchgoing, and much else are all related, interlocking phenomena, deeply imbedded within the immense matrix of culture. These seemingly disparate things can be the means to an end rather than the end of cultural research. In lieu of any options for experimenting in the laboratory or for applying strict deductive logic to the still obscure, but plainly very complex, processes at work in cultural change, the inductive route seems the most efficient strategy for identifying general cultural laws. And even though the job of systematically gathering, sifting, and collating information on a variety of spatio-temporal phases of American culture has barely begun, some hints of general process and larger structure are beginning to appear. For the geographer intent upon linkages among outwardly different items, and the larger designs of human thought and action through space and time, there is something particularly intriguing about the tendency for cultural patterns to fall into reasonably uniform territorial packages. In the final chapter, we examine such culture areas as they exist in the United States, and begin to explore some of the potentialities for expanding our theoretical frontiers in following such an inductive approach.

Norton & Co., Inc., 1968). One of the rare explicitly geographic ventures into American folklore is E. Joan Wilson Miller, "The Ozark Culture Region As Revealed by Traditional Materials," *Annals of the Association of American Geographers,* 58, No. 1 (1968), 51–77.

CHAPTER FOUR

Structure

Why Study American Culture Areas?

The cultural processes that have operated so vigorously in the Europeanized portions of North America over the past three and a half centuries have given us a set of reasonably homogeneous, contiguous tracts of territory whose inhabitants are at least dimly aware of a common cultural heritage and of differences from other territorial groups. Such tracts we can properly label "culture areas," even though they differ in some notable ways from the standard, classical culture areas of long-settled, slowly evolving communities elsewhere in the world. This chapter is based on the premise that the existence of these regions is a large, truly significant fact in the human geography of this nation, and that their analysis is a rewarding activity for the scholar in both a theoretical and a practical sense. At the most naïve level, Americans are spontaneously curious about the local peculiarities of their compatriots. Thus a favorite theme for social small talk is the distinguishing characteristics of the Yankee, Southerner, Hoosier, New Yorker, Texan, Pennsylvania German, or Southern Californian. At a more sophisticated level, it is plausible that the character of these more or less coherent spatial groupings of people has had a palpable effect upon social, economic, and political behavior at both the local and national levels, and that we need to know more about these relationships. An ultimate objective is to gain insight into some basic problems of culture theory.

In general, the differences among American culture areas tend to be slight and shallow as compared to most older, more stable countries, even though in one instance, that of the South, they helped precipitate the gravest political crisis and bloodiest military conflict in the nation's history. The often subtle nature of interregional cultural differences can be ascribed to the recency of American settlement, a perpetually high mobility rate, an elaborate communications system, and centralization of economy and government. Indeed a case might be built against the study of American culture areas on the grounds that they are quaint vestiges of a vanishing past, soon to be expunged from the living landscape and of interest only to antiquarians. But even if one concedes the likelihood that powerful forces are pushing many—but far from all!—departments of American thought and behavior toward standardization, the lingering effects of the older culture areas are still very much with us; and there is strong evidence that newer, quite potent ones are arising. Thus, for example, more than a century after the Civil War, the South remains a powerful political and social entity, and its peculiar status is formally recognized in religious, educational, athletic, and literary circles. In some instances indeed, the gap between South and non-South may be widening. But even more intriguing is the appearance of a series of essentially twentieth-century regions. The Southern Californian is the largest and most distinctive, and its quite special regional culture has yet to reach full bloom. Similar trends are visible in southern Florida and in the burgeoning Texas identity, and probably in the more flourishing segments of New Mexico and Arizona as well. At the metropolitan level, it is difficult to believe that such aggressively narcissistic places as San Francisco, Las Vegas, Dallas, Tucson, or Seattle are becoming that much like all other American cities. At the micro scale, some less obtrusively embryonic areas will be cited later. If there is any specific message in this chapter, it is that the subdued, yet meaningful, internal cultural heterogeneity of an older America is being supplanted by a novel mosaic, equally variegated but pieced together from newer materials and with new forces.

The Classification and Anatomy of Culture Areas

The culture areas of the world, past, present, and future, can be usefully divided into two classes on the basis of mode of origin. The first, and by far the more numerous, since it accounted for virtually all culture areas until the onset of the modern period and the emergence of some truly advanced, radically transformed populations, is perhaps best termed the *traditional region*. These regions are relatively self-contained, endogamous, stable, and of long duration. The individual is born into the region and remains with it, physically and mentally, since there is little in- or out-migration by isolated persons or families; and the accidents of birth would automatically assign a person to a specific caste, class, occupation, and social role. An intimate symbiotic relationship between man and land develops over many centuries, one that creates indigenous modes of thought and action, a distinctive visible landscape, and a form of human ecology specific to the locality. Although the usual processes of random cultural mutation, the vagaries of history, some slight intermixture of peoples, and the diffusion of innovations of all sorts prevents the achievement of total stasis or equilibrium, or complete internal uniformity, it would not be unfair to characterize such a traditional region as one based upon blood and soil. In the extreme, it becomes synonymous with a particular tribe or ethnic group.

The second class of culture area, the *voluntary region,* is still emergent, hence not yet clearly recognized. It is coeval with the process of modernization in Northwest Europe and the appearance of individuals who are essentially free agents, in spatial and other dimensions. It is in North America that the earliest, largest, and, to date, most advanced experimentation in devising voluntary regions has gone on. Our thesis is that the traditional spatial and social allocation of individuals through the lottery of birth is being replaced gradually by a process of relative self-selection of life style, goals, social niche, and place of residence.

This new, indeed revolutionary, mechanism can be detected from the earliest days of serious North American settlement onward. The colonists were motivated by a variety of considerations—religious, social, political, economic, and idiosyncratic. With some notable exceptions, however, they traveled as individuals or single families, gravitating toward those places perceived as best fulfilling their aspirations, and where they could hobnob with many strangers, of widely scattered origin but with similar tastes and proclivities. The entire process is beautifully exemplified in the founding of the Great Basin Kingdom by the Mormons. There we see a thoroughly self-conscious (and amply documented) routing into a remote, empty tract of like-minded persons of highly diverse background bent upon building a tightly structured, homogenous society. The same trends were at work in the occupation of the initial colonial nodes along the Atlantic Seaboard and later in the advancement of the frontier, but rather less visibly and distinctly, in part because of a large amount of random migrational jostling.

Once an American area had been effectively settled and had achieved some semblance of economic and social stability, there began a series of processes analogous to, but less intense than, those typical of the traditional region. Emotional and social roots were sunk into the land; man and habitat interacted in endlessly complex fashion; diverse people met and merged their ideas and ways of life; influences were given to and received from the outside. In short, a new culture area had crystallized. The older American case simulates, but cannot match, the premodern culture area in purity and longevity. With adequate isolation or richness of development, the regional culture might develop a persistent vitality of its own. But frequently the same forces of individualistic choice that led to its birth also promote its erosion and obliteration. The more enterprising elements in the population drift away to greener pastures; and the relict culture area may become the stage upon which new forces operate and newer voluntary regions take shape. It is altogether possible today to be a solid citizen of metropolitan New England or Philadelphia and yet be utterly oblivious to the historic cultural role of those places.

In late twentieth century America, the currents of voluntary migration are many and varied; they remain preeminently economic in character, but increasingly the quest for pleasure and the amenities plays a role in the decision to migrate. One might argue forcefully that the spatial

sum of millions of such decisions in a mass society is toward an unrelieved sameness from coast to coast, the progressive blotting out of
local deviation, especially in urban areas.[1] But a growing mass of evidence points in just the opposite direction: the spawning of new families
of voluntary regions, quite distinct in shape and structure from the older
traditional regions. Some of these regions are ephemeral in the extreme,
others have the promise of durability, but, in the aggregate, they amount
to a new geometry of culture, as mobile individuals seek ideal havens
on their journey of self-discovery.

The argument underlying this chapter, then, is that the system of
culture areas observable in contemporary America is dual in character.
There is the older set of places, originating during and just after the
period of First Effective Settlement. Some of these are relict in character,
others still prospering, but they are all hybrid creatures in the way they
combine elements of the traditional areas with those of the voluntary.
Partially superimposed over the older set are the many new voluntary
regions, some still quite indistinct, usually with scarcely any functional
connection with their predecessors.

A third, and trivial, type of region might be noted, then summarily
dismissed: the spurious or synthetic region. With two or three marginal
exceptions, we can so classify all 48 of the conterminous United States,
despite the strong popular inclination to think of each as somehow a
distinctive package of people. Falling into the same company are the
concoctions of the advertising agency and other vested interests—
"Chicagoland," Delmarva, TVA Country, "Pittsburgh Pirate Land," and
the like. Rather more interesting are the attempts of commercial promoters to breathe new life into genuine, but fading, cultural entities:
the Potemkin Village-like re-creations along superhighways of what the
passing tourist might expect Pennsylvania German country to look like,
or the largely fictitious simulations of frontier cowboy culture in towns
that mock reality by imitating the never-never land of movies and
television.

Let us define a culture area as a naïvely perceived segment of the
time-space continuum distinguished from others on the basis of genuine
differences in cultural systems.[2] The two characteristics that set it aside
from other varieties of geographic region are: (1) the extraordinary
number of ways in which it is manifested physically and behaviorally;
and (2) the condition of self-awareness on the part of participants. The
former trait has already been discussed, and the point made that no
other discrete category of geographic region, short of that elusive entity,
the holistic region, contains such a great variety of phenomena. The latter
characteristic is unique. One must insist that if self-consciousness is

---

[1] An idea advanced vigorously in Melvin M. Webber, "Culture, Territoriality,
and the Elastic Mile," *Regional Science Association, Papers,* 13 (1964), 59–69, and
in Alvin Toffler, *Future Shock* (New York: Random House, Inc., 1970), pp. 91–94.

[2] Joseph E. Schwartzberg, "Prolegomena to the Study of South Asian Regions
and Regionalism," in Robert I. Crane, ed., *Regions and Regionalism in South Asian
Studies: An Exploratory Study,* Comparative Studies on Southern Asia, Monograph
No. 5 (Durham, N.C.: Duke University Press, 1967), p. 93.

lacking (and it will suffice if it is present only at the subliminal level), then we are examining something other than a genuine culture area. The recognition of the area and one's affiliation with it can run the gamut from a raging sense of nationhood to fleeting, unemotional perceptions of small gradations of differences between one's local way of life and another.

A multi-tiered, nested hierarchy of culture areas might be postulated for the United States; but the most interesting levels, and those for which we can adduce the greatest number of general geographic principles, are the two topmost ones: the nation as a whole, and the five to ten (I prefer the former) of subnational regions, each comprising parts or all of several states. Given the fact that Americans have been vigorously expansionist all during their history, it is not surprising to find that the citizenry has filled up virtually the whole of the national space and spilled out far beyond into many military, diplomatic, missionary, scientific, and touristic exclaves. But, excluding such interesting outliers, which are scattered over much of the globe, and also various enclaves of unassimilated aboriginal or immigrant groups, there is a remarkably close coincidence between the conterminous United States and the cultural United States. In fact, our international boundaries present the neatest cultural cleavages to be found within North America. As the traveler crosses from this country into Mexico, he is negotiating a visible passage across a veritable cultural chasm, despite the intense Americanization of northern Mexico and the quite apparent Hispanicization of our Southwest border zones. If the contrasts are less dramatic between the two sides of the United States-Canadian boundary, they are nonetheless real, especially to the Canadian. Our northern border separates not only two distinct, if interrelated, political and economic systems, but also two different, yet closely fraternal, modes of cultural behavior. There is the abrupt, immediate change, for example, from one system of English pronunciation to another, and from one style of folk architecture to something noticeably alien. Undoubtedly other discontinuities could be recorded in other departments of culture. There is a major erosion of the cultural barrier along only a single major segment of our international frontier: that reaching from northern New York to Aroostook County, Maine. There a vigorous demographic and cultural invasion by French Canadians from Quebec and New Brunswick has gone far toward eradicating previous international differences.

But if the international boundaries are potent and precise as a cultural container, the interstate boundaries, on the other hand, are curiously irrelevant. In large part, this results from the fact that most were the relatively arbitrary creations of the federal Congress. But even when the state enjoyed a strong autonomous early existence, as did Massachusetts, Virginia, or Pennsylvania, subsequent economic and political forces have been powerful solvents, softening and washing away initial identities. In fact, our present set of 48 conterminous states is so anachronistic in the context of contemporary socioeconomic realities, not to mention cultural forces, that they could be readily scrapped and replaced by another, much better set were it not for the deterrent effect of inertia and various vested interests. And having served so long as spatial pegs (like professional baseball or football teams) on which we can hang signs stating our identity, however speciously, or as ersatz outlets for whatever vestigial "territorial instinct" lingers on in us, the wiping out of our state boundaries would set off a mighty uproar. Halfway convincing cases might be built for equating the states of Utah and Texas with their respective culture areas because of exceptional historical and physical circumstances—or perhaps Oklahoma, given a tardy European occupation and unique status as dumping ground for all the relict Indian groups of the East. But in the great majority of instances, the state either contains two or more distinctly different culture areas, or fragments thereof, or is a part of a much larger single culture area (for example, Iowa, North Dakota, Vermont). Thus there are sharp north-south dichotomies in Missouri, Illinois, Indiana, Ohio, and Florida; and Tennessee proudly advertises the fact that there are really three Tennessees. In one case, that of antebellum Virginia, the centrifugal cultural forces were so strong that actual fission took place in 1863 (into Virginia and West Virginia) along one of those rare interstate boundaries that approximates a genuine cultural divide.

Although geographers have devoted much attention to the structure of economic regions and the forces operating within them, we know very little about the anatomy or physiology of culture areas. The most interesting attempt to formulate general principles has been by Donald W. Meinig. He contends that, under ideal conditions (that is, given relative isolation over a long period, freedom from interference by others, and the opportunity for unhindered territorial expansion for a cultural group), three concentric zones will materialize. These he denotes, in order of decreasing degree of concentration or typicality, as the *core, domain,* and *sphere.* He defines them as follows:

> A *core* area...is taken to mean a centralized zone of concentration, displaying the greatest density of occupance, intensity or organization, strength, and homogeneity of the particular features characteristic of the culture under study. It is the most vital center, the seat of power, the focus of circulation.
>
> The *domain* refers to those areas in which the particular culture under study is *dominant,* but with markedly less intensity and complexity of development than in the core, where the bonds of connection are fewer and more tenuous and where regional peculiarities are clearly evident.
>
> The *sphere* of a culture may be defined as the zone of outer influence and, often, peripheral acculturation, wherein that culture is represented only by certain of its elements or where its peoples reside as minorities among those of a different culture.[3]

The necessary conditions are almost ideally met in the Mormon culture region of the western United States (Figure 4.1) and in that instance, theory comfortably coexists with fact. More recently, Meinig has applied it successfully, though with modifications, to the case of

---

3 Donald W. Meinig, "The Mormon Culture Region: Strategies and Patterns in the Geography of the American West, 1847–1964," *Annals of the Association of American Geographers,* 55, No. 2 (1965), 213–17.

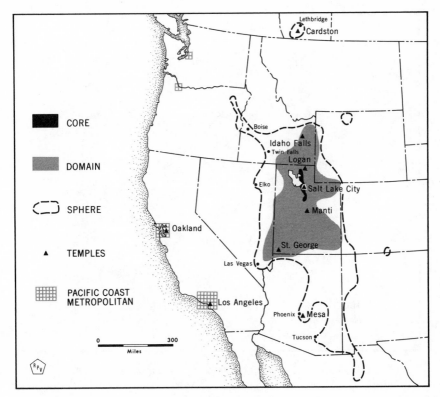

FIG. 4.1. The Mormon culture region. (Adapted from: D. W. Meinig, "The Mormon Culture Region," Annals of the Association of American Geographers, 55, No. 2 [June 1965], p. 116.)

Texas[4] (Figure 4.2). There the domain has been subdivided into a *primary domain* (which includes most of the state's territory) and a *secondary domain* (the northern section of the Panhandle); and he has also added a new fourth zone beyond the sphere—a "zone of penetration," evidently one of localized, "imperial" implantation of elements of Texan culture, lying within portions of New Mexico, Arizona, Colorado, Utah, and perhaps northern Mexico. What is most aberrant about the Texas culture area is the geometry of its core, a bulbous, hollow triangle whose three apices—the metropolises of Houston, Dallas-Fort Worth, and San Antonio—have interacted complexly and have shared the functions usually confined to a single compact zone.

This simple scheme, it must be stressed, works readily only under rather exceptional conditions and better at the national than the subnational scale. The growth and development of the great majority of traditional culture areas, not only in the Old World but in North America as well, has been inhibited by adjacent areas. The usual result is a

4 Donald W. Meinig, *Imperial Texas: An Interpretive Essay in Cultural Geography* (Austin: University of Texas Press, 1969), pp. 110–24.

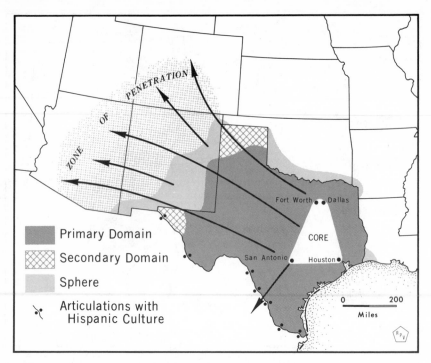

Primary Domain

Secondary Domain

Sphere

Articulations with
Hispanic Culture

FIG. 4.2. The geographic morphology of the Texas empire. (Adapted from: D. W. Meinig, Imperial Texas [Austin: University of Texas Press, 1969], p. 93.)

stunted, squashed, or misshappen area. The biological analogy is tempting: if you wish to see what an oak tree ought to look like ideally, find a mature specimen that has had a large meadow all to itself. Its brethren, struggling to survive in a dense grove, will have achieved very different sizes and shapes. Although the Meinig model accommodates the facts for the Mormon and Texas areas without much compromise, it can be made to work only with much stretching and bending in the New England, Midland, or French Canadian cases, and it is almost useless in describing or explaining other North American culture areas. It may be applicable at the national scale, with the Northeast (and especially Megalopolis) as the core; but the identification of domain, sphere or zone of penetration is a task still to be performed.

The cause and effect relationships between economic and culture areas in the United States and similar areas constitute another, largely unexplored subject. There is reason to believe that the two kinds of region were intimately associated during the colonial phase of our history, each taking form from and giving form to the other; but as time has gone on, the connections have become less clear. If one could, for example, formerly correlate New England (or at least its earlier, nodal segment) with a specific economic system, to do so is no longer feasible. It would appear that cultural systems are slower to respond to agents of change, whether endogenous or exogenous, than are economic or urban systems. Thus we have the spectacle of the American Manufacturing Belt—which happens to be a core region for many other social and economic activities than just manufacturing—now spanning major fractions of three traditional culture areas—New England, the Midland, and the Middle West—and the northern fringes of a fourth, the South. And its eastern facade and persistent nucleus, the great urbanoid sprawl known as Megalopolis, reaches from southern Maine to northern (or central?) Virginia, blithely ignoring the steep relict cultural slopes that are still visible in its more bucolic tracts.

The Major Traditional Culture Areas

AN HISTORICAL NOTE. The culture areas of the modern United States are European in origin, the result of importing European colonists and ways of life and the subsequent interactions among and within social groups and with a novel set of habitats. As suggested earlier, we can dismiss the aboriginal cultures as territorially insignificant, at least at the macro level.[5] Only in two subregions, the Southwest focused on the Upper Rio Grande and a portion of the Colorado Plateau (Figure 4.3) or the still indistinct Oklahoman subregion, does an Indian element merit consideration, and then only as one of several. Thus, except for the Southwestern Indian groups, pre-contact aboriginal areas can be safely ignored, but not without noting the curious coincidence or convergence of genetic factors in the case of western New York State. There the core area for the Iroquois Confederacy and its special near-civilization, which bloomed late in the pre-conquest period, matches perfectly a significant nineteenth-century culture hearth, which we are obliged to call, rather misleadingly for lack of a better alternative, the "Burned-Over District." In so far as North American aboriginal life attained a cultural climax outside the Mexican border zones, it was in the Southeast and Ohio Valley generally, and the lower Mississippi Valley most particularly. That area has no valid, latter-day Anglo-American descendant or counterpart. At the micro level, there are still many groups, some of mixed ancestry,[6] of local significance; but in almost every instance the culture in question has been greatly modified by European influences.

With some minor exceptions, the contemporary map of American culture areas (Figure 4.3) can be explained in terms of the genesis, development, and expansion of the three principal colonial culture hearths located along the Atlantic Seaboard.[7] Before taking up each in

---

5 Delimited in Alfred L. Kroeber, *Cultural and Natural Areas of Native North America*, University of California Publications in American Archaeology and Ethnology, Vol. 38 (Berkeley: University of California Press, 1939).

6 The geography of various triracial groups is presented in Edward T. Price, "A Geographic Analysis of White-Negro-Indian Racial Mixtures in Eastern United States," *Annals of the Association of American Geographers*, 43, No. 2 (1953), 138–55.

7 Figure 4-3, which the reader will need to refer to repeatedly in the pages that follow, is apparently the first attempt ever made to delimit cultural areas for

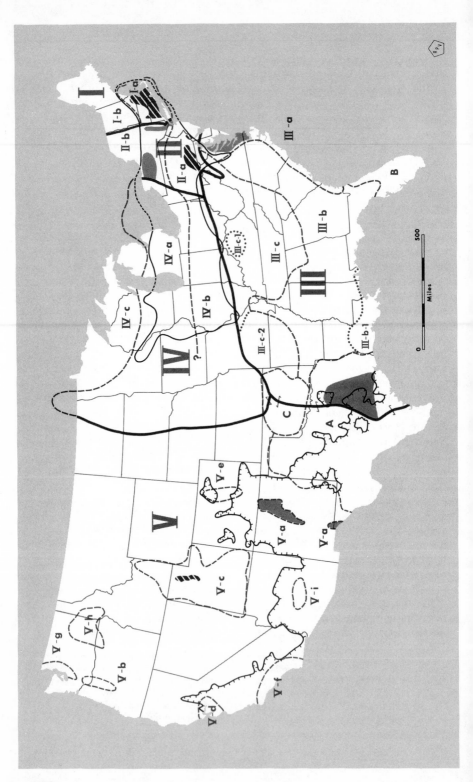

Legend

▬▬▬	First-order cultural boundary
- - -	Second-order cultural boundary
··········	Third-order cultural boundary
▨	Documented core area
▓	Presumed or incipient core area

| ▬▬▬ | Boundary of Socioeconomic Core Region of North America, ca. 1970 |
| - - - | Northern boundary of significant Hispanic-American settlement (after Nostrand) |

REGION	APPROXIMATE DATES OF SETTLEMENT AND FORMATION	MAJOR SOURCES OF CULTURE (listed in order of importance)
I. NEW ENGLAND		
I-a. Nuclear New England	1620-1830	England
I-b. Northern New England	1620-1750	England
	1750-1830	Nuclear New England; England
II. THE MIDLAND		
II-a. Pennsylvanian Region	1682-1850	England & Wales; Rhineland; Ulster; 19th Century Europe
II-b. New York Region, or New England Extended	1624-1830	Great Britain; New England; 19th Century Europe; Netherlands
III. THE SOUTH		
III-a. Early British Colonial South	1607-1750	England; Africa; British West Indies
III-b. Lowland, or Deep South	1700-1850	Great Britain; Africa; Midland; Early British Colonial South; aborigines
III-b-1. French Louisiana	1700-1760	France; Deep South; Africa; French West Indies
III-c. Upland South	1700-1850	Midland; Lowland South; Great Britain
III-c-1. The Bluegrass	1770-1800	Upland South; Lowland South
III-c-2. The Ozarks	1820-1860	Upland South; Lowland South; Lower Middle West
IV. THE MIDDLE WEST		
IV-a. Upper Middle West	1790-1880	New England Extended; New England; 19th Century Europe; British Canada
IV-b. Lower Middle West	1790-1870	Midland; Upland South; New England Extended; 19th Century Europe
IV-c. Cutover Area	1850-1900	Upper Middle West; 19th Century Europe

REGION	APPROXIMATE DATES OF SETTLEMENT AND FORMATION	MAJOR SOURCES OF CULTURE (listed in order of importance)
V. THE WEST		
V-a. Upper Rio Grande Valley	1590-	Mexico; Anglo-America; aborigines
V-b. Willamette Valley	1830-1900	Northeast U.S.
V-c. Mormon Region	1847-1890	Northeast U.S.; 19th Century Europe
V-d. Central California	(1775-1848) 1840-	(Mexico) Eastern U.S.; 19th Century Europe; Mexico; East Asia
V-e. Colorado Piedmont	1860-	Eastern U.S.; Mexico
V-f. Southern California	(1760-1848) 1880-	(Mexico) Eastern U. S.; 19th & 20th Century Europe; Mormon Region; Mexico; East Asia
V-g. Puget Sound	1870-	Eastern U.S.; 19th & 20th Century Europe; East Asia
V-h. Inland Empire	1880-	Eastern U.S.; 19th & 20th Century Europe
V-i. Central Arizona	1900-	Eastern U.S.; Southern California; Mexico
REGIONS OF UNCERTAIN STATUS OR AFFILIATION		
A. Texas	(1690-1836) 1821-	(Mexico) Lowland South; Upland South; Mexico; 19th Century Central Europe
B. Peninsular Florida	1880-	Northeast U.S.; the South; 20th Century Europe; Antilles
C. Oklahoma	1890-	Upland South; Lowland South; aborigines; Middle West

turn, two general comments may be in order. Even though each of the three is basically British in character, their personalities have been and still are quite distinct, thanks to different social and political conditions during the critical period of First Effective Settlement, along with localized physical and economic circumstances. Secondly, the cultural gradients tend to be much steeper and the boundaries between regions more distinct than is true for the remainder of the continent. There is greater variety within a narrower range of space as one approaches the older, inner regions, but greater blurring of cultural traits and confusion of identity in the reverse direction, toward the outer, newer tracts.

NEW ENGLAND.   If we begin our inventory with the New England culture area, it is not because it is the oldest of our major cultural-geographic entities—an honor it shares with the South or perhaps the Hispanic Southwest—but rather because the region was the most clearly dominant during the century of national expansion following the American Revolution. New England may have been strong, if not preeminent, in the fields of manufacturing, commerce, finance, and maritime activity, but it was in the spheres of higher social and cultural life that the area exercised genuine leadership—in education, politics, theology, literature, science, architecture, and the more advanced forms of mechanical and social technology. Thus, if any single section must be nominated as the leading source of ideas and styles for the remainder of the nation from about 1780 to 1880, New England is the logical candidate.[8] Incidentally,

---

the entirety of the conterminous United States. An earlier map of more limited scope is Figure 1, "Rural-Farm Cultural Regions and Sub-Regions," in A. R. Mangus, *Rural Regions of the United States* (Washington, D.C.: Works Progress Administration, 1940), facing p. 1. Also of considerable interest to the cultural geographer is a map depicting the more or less subliminal regionalization of the country on the part of a test group of Ohio State University students, entitled "Locational Classes of Student Schemata of the U.S.A.," in Kevin R. Cox and Georgia Zannaras, "Designative Perceptions of Macro-Spaces: Concepts, a Methodology and Applications," in John Archea and Charles Eastman, eds., *Proceedings of the 2nd Annual Environmental Design Research Association Conference*, October 1970 (Pittsburgh: October 1970), p. 124.

The contention that the three colonial cultural hearths treated in this chapter are pivotal in the evolution of culture areas at the national scale has been advanced by a number of authors in the past, among them Carle C. Zimmerman and R. E. DuWors, *Graphic Regional Sociology (A Study in American Social Organization)* (Cambridge, Mass.: Phillips Book Store, 1952); Conrad Arensberg, "American Communities," *American Anthropologist*, 57, No. 6 (1955) 1143–60; Donald W. Meinig, "The American Colonial Era: A Geographic Commentary," *Proceedings of the Royal Geographical Society, South Australian Branch* (1957–1958), pp. 1–22; Hans Kurath, *A Word Geography of the Eastern United States* (Ann Arbor: University of Michigan Press, 1949); and Henry Glassie, *Pattern in the Material Folk Culture of the Eastern United States* (Philadelphia: University of Pennsylvania Press, 1968).

[8] Or, as de Toqueville wrote perceptively, if a bit floridly, "The two or three main ideas which constituted the basis of the social theory of the United States were first combined in the Northern English colonies, more generally denominated the States of New England. The principles of New England spread at first to the neighboring States; they then passed successively to the more distant ones; and at length they imbued the whole Confederation. They now extend their influence

it also furnishes an impressive example of the capacity of strongly motivated communities for rising above the constraints of a parsimonious
environment.

Relatively small though it is, the territory occupied by the six New
England states may be usefully split into two subregions: the older, more
densely settled, highly urbanized and industrialized southeastern segment; and the newer, rather thinly occupied northern area, taking in
all of Vermont and nearly all of New Hampshire and Maine, an area
colonized mostly after 1770 by settlers from the nuclear zone. It is the
former tract, of course, which has been so potent as a source of people,
ideas, and influences for much of North America. By virtue of location,
wealth, and seniority, the Boston metropolitan area has acted as the
functional hub for all of New England both culturally and economically;
but its sovereignty is shared to some degree with two other old nuclear
nodes: the lower Connecticut Valley and the Narragansett Bay region.

The demographic and ideological expansion of New England began
quite early with the settlement of parts of Long Island, northern New
Jersey, and the Hudson Valley. The thrust westward was so powerful
and persistent that it is justifiable to call New York, northern New Jersey,
northern Pennsylvania, and much of the Upper Middle West "New
England extended." Nonetheless, strong though the New England component may have been in the Hudson Valley and much of upper New
York State, the western political limits of Connecticut, Massachusetts,
and Vermont (or, roughly, the line of the Taconics, Berkshires, and
Lake Champlain-Lake George valley) do neatly demarcate an area that
is not quite New England from one that truly is—that second and last
good example we can muster of interstate boundaries being nearly identi-
cal with cultural zonation. The civil disturbances of the American Revolution stimulated a major exodus of loyalist New Englanders to Nova
Scotia and Upper Canada (later Ontario), as well as to the British West
Indies. The energetic endeavors of New England whalers, merchants,
and missionaries resulted in a perceptible imprinting of population and
culture in Hawaii, various other Pacific isles, and scattered points in the
Caribbean. New Englanders, arriving by sea, were also active in the
Americanization of early Oregon and Washington, with results visible
to this day. Later, the overland diffusion of New England natives and

---

beyond its limits over the whole American world. The civilization of New England
has been like a beacon lit upon a hill, which, after it has diffused its warmth around,
tinges the distant horizon with its glow." Alexis de ˙Toqueville, *Democracy in
America* (New York: Oxford University Press, 1947), p. 33. The primacy of New
England in higher cultural development is also strongly emphasized in Hugo Münster-
berg, *The Americans* (New York: McClure, Phillips & Co., 1905), pp. 347–64 and
Daniel J. Boorstin, *The Americans: The National Experience* (New York: Random
House, Inc., 1965), pp. 3–48. The most useful and convenient general guide to the
social and cultural characteristics of the region is Hans Kurath, *Handbook of the
Linguistic Geography of New England* (Providence, R.I.: Brown University, 1943).
The topic of demographic and cultural expansion is handled in Lois (Kimball)
Mathews Rosenberry, *The Expansion of New England: The Spread of New England
Settlement and Institutions to the Mississippi River, 1920–1865* (Boston: Houghton
Mifflin Company, 1909).

practices meant a recognizable New England flavor not only for the Upper Midwest from Ohio to the Dakotas but also more dilutely in the Pacific Northwest in general. Beyond the immediate impact of business-man and settler, there is the dissemination of less palpable items—ideas, attitudes, and innovations of all sorts—perhaps of greater weight ulti-mately than the economic or demographic factors. In keeping with the basic criterion for defining a culture area, New Englanders have been keenly, happily aware of their identity, though probably more so in the past than at present; and they have usually been readily labeled by outsiders by virtue of pattern of speech, religion, behavior, or thought. The massive immigration of persons from Ireland, Germany, then eastern and southern Europe and Quebec that began in the 1830's has brought about important shifts in the character of New England society, but the sense of its special early individuality lingers on.

THE SOUTH.   The same observation applies with even greater force to natives of the South, by far the largest of the three primordial Anglo-American culture areas and also the most aberrant of any with respect to national norms.[9] Indeed the South has been so distinct from the non-South in almost every observable or quantifiable feature and so fiercely jealous of its peculiarities that for some years the question of whether it could maintain political and social unity with the non-South was in serious doubt. Only during the twentieth century can one argue for a decisive convergence with the rest of the nation, at least in economic behavior and material culture. An early, persistent deviation from the national mainstream probably commenced during the first years of settle-ment. The Caucasoid settlers of the South were almost purely British and not outwardly different from the British, Welsh, or Scotch-Irish who flocked to New England or the Midland; but almost certainly they were different in motives and social values. The immigration of African slaves may have been a factor, as might also a degree of interaction with the aborigines that was missing further north. And certainly the unusual (for Northwest Europeans) pattern of economy, settlement, and social organization, in part a matter of a starkly unfamiliar physical habitat, may have prompted a swerving away from other culture areas.

In both origin and spatial structure, the South has been characterized by diffuseness. If we must narrow the search for a nuclear hearth down to a single tract, the most plausible choice is the Chesapeake Bay area and the northeastern corner of North Carolina, the earliest area of recog-nizably Southern character. Unlike the nodal zones for New England or the Midland, this was, and still is, an emphatically rural area, despite the growth of two large metropolitan districts—Baltimore and the Hamp-ton Roads conurbations—toward either end of the Bay. It was via this corridor and the routes running further inland from the Delaware River ports that the great bulk of the Southern territory was eventually peopled.

9 For general introductions to the cultural geography of the South, consult Rupert B. Vance, *The Human Geography of the South* (Chapel Hill: University of North Carolina, 1935) and J. Fraser Hart, *The Southeastern United States* (New York: Van Nostrand Reinhold Company, 1967).

But early components of Southern population and culture also arrived from other sources via other routes. A narrow coastal strip running from Carolina down to the Georgia-Florida boundary, and including the Sea Islands, decidedly Southern in flavor yet self-consciously standing apart from other parts of the South, was colonized directly from Great Britain. There were also significant direct connections with the West Indies; and it is here that the African cultural contribution is strongest and purest. The cities of Charleston and Savannah, which have nurtured their own quite special civilizations, dominated this subregion in every sense. Similarly, we can demarcate a French Louisiana that received elements of culture and population, to be stirred into the special Creole mixture, not only from a putative Chesapeake Bay hearth area but also directly from France, Acadia (Colonial French Nova Scotia), the French West Indies, and, of course, Africa. In the south central Texas, the Teutonic influx was so heavy that a special subregion can quite properly be designated.

It would seem, then, that the Southern culture area may be an example of convergent or parallel evolution of a variety of elements arriving along several paths, but subject to some single general process that could mold one larger regional consciousness and way of life. This in contrast to the more common experience of colonists and cultural forces radiating outward from a single early source region. The result, in any case, is a very extensive territory without any truly coherent structure, à la the Meinig Model, or any other that can be suggested. Where was the focal center of the Confederacy: Richmond, Montgomery, Atlanta, or somewhere else? Simply to articulate the question is to realize how difficult it is. One can point to the Cotton Belt, an economic region of variable dimensions, stretching in a great crescent from south central Virginia to east Texas, as the "modal South," one that contains in heightened form nearly all the traits regarded as typically Southern; but it is impossible to claim that the South's historic roots lie there or that it ever operated as an organizing center, economically or culturally. The real power and fount of ideas resided elsewhere.

The South can be subdivided into a much greater number of subregions than can any of the other, older traditional regions. Three have already been mentioned; but these are of a lesser order than the two principal Souths, variously called Upper and Lower South, Upland and Lowland South, or Yeoman and Plantation South.[10] The former, which comprises the Southern Appalachians, the upper Appalachian Piedmont,

10 This basic dichotomy is made, verbally and cartographically, in Wilbur Zelinsky, "Where the South Begins: The Northern Limits of the Cis-Appalachian South in Terms of Settlement Landscape," *Social Forces*, 30 (1951), 172–78; Fred Kniffen, "Folk Housing: Key to Diffusion," *Annals of the Association of American Geographers*, 55, No. 4 (1965), 571–73; Terry G. Jordan, "The Imprint of the Upper and Lower South on Mid-Nineteenth Century Texas," *Ibid.*, 57, No. 4 (1967), 667–90; Hart, *The Southeastern United States;* and Glassie, *Pattern in the Material Folk Culture*, p. 39. The most detailed attempt at subdividing the South—or the larger part of it—into cultural (in this instance, dialect) regions is offered in Gordon R. Wood, *Vocabulary Change: A Study of Variation in Regional Words in Eight of the Southern States* (Carbondale: Southern Illinois University Press, 1971), p. 358.

the Cumberland and other low interior plateaus, and the Ozarks and Ouachitas, was occupied, both culturally and demographically, from two sources: the Chesapeake Bay hearth area and the early Midland. The latter area includes the greater part of the South Atlantic and Gulf coastal plains, along with the lower Appalachian Piedmont, and originated principally in the Chesapeake Bay area, with only minor influences from the coastal Carolina and Georgia belt, Louisiana, or elsewhere. The division between the two subregions remains distinct all the way from Virginia to Texas.[11] Within the Upland South, the Ozark segment might legitimately be detached from the Appalachian;[12] and within the latter, the Kentucky Bluegrass region certainly merits special recognition.

It is toward the margins of the South that one encounters the greatest difficulties in delimiting and assigning subregions. The outer limits themselves are a topic of special interest.[13] There seems to be more than an accidental relationship between these limits and various aspects of the North American climate. Thus the northern boundary, a fuzzy gradational zone, but one definitely not related to the conventional Mason and Dixon Line or the Ohio River, seems isothermal in character, the association being with length of frost-free season or with temperature during the winter months. As the Southern cultural complex was carried to the west, it not only retained its strength but became even more intense, in contrast to the experience of New England or the Midland. But the South finally fades away as one approaches the famous 100th Meridian and a critical decline in annual precipitation. The apparent correlation of the cultural South with a humid subtropical climate is a provocative one.

A possible emergent Oklahoman subregion is still too indistinct to present any immediate problem; but the Texas subregion is so large, unmistakable, vigorous, and self-assertive that it presents some vexing taxonomic and cartographic questions. Meinig has expertly discussed the varied outer influences that have helped make Texas the special place culturally that it undoubtedly is;[14] and he has gone further by subdividing it into nine component areas in a suggestive map. (See Figure 4.4.) But he leaves unresolved the larger matter of whether Texas is simply a subordinate fraction of the Greater South or whether it has now acquired so strong and divergent an identity that it can be denoted a new first-order region. We have chosen to equivocate in Figure 4.3 by showing the Texan region as straddling the frontier of the regular South. It is conceivable that we are witnessing the genesis of a major region in a frontier zone where several distinct cultural communities confront each other, as per the hypothesis put forward by Leslie White.[15]

[11] Terry G. Jordan, "The Texas Appalachia," *Annals of the Association of American Geographers*, 60, No. 3 (1970), 409–27.

[12] E. Joan Wilson Miller, "The Ozark Culture Region as Revealed by Traditional Materials," *Annals of the Association of American Geographers*, 58, No. 1 (1968), 51–77.

[13] Zelinsky, "Where the South Begins."

[14] Donald W. Meinig, *Imperial Texas*.

[15] Leslie A. White, *The Science of Culture* (New York: Farrar, Straus & Giroux, 1949).

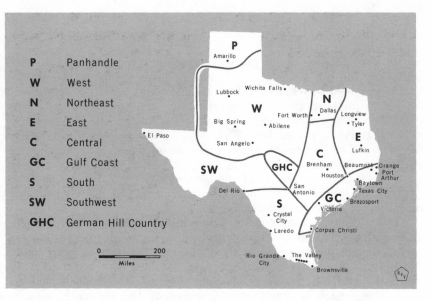

P	Panhandle
W	West
N	Northeast
E	East
C	Central
GC	Gulf Coast
S	South
SW	Southwest
GHC	German Hill Country

FIG. 4.4. The culture areas of Texas in the 1960's. (Adapted from: D. W. Meinig, Imperial Texas *[Austin: University of Texas Press, 1969], p. 93.)*

In a few more decades we may be able to decide. Similarly, peninsular Florida is either within or juxtaposed to the South, but without being unequivocally part of it. In this case, an almost empty territory began to receive significant settlement only after about 1890; and, if like Texas, most of it came from the older South, there were also vigorous infusions from elsewhere. We shall have occasion to return to the identity problems of both peninsular Florida and Texas at a later juncture.

THE MIDLAND. This region has been reserved for last among the major colonial entities not because its significance has been slighter, but because it is the least conspicuous, either to outsiders or to its own inhabitants. And indeed this fact may reflect its centrality to the course of American development. The serious European occupation and development of the Midland began a generation or more after that of the other major cultural nodes, and after several earlier, relatively ineffectual trials by the Dutch, Swedes, Finns, and British. But, once begun late in the seventeenth century by William Penn and associates, the colonization of the area was an instant success. This was especially so in the lower Delaware and Susquehanna valleys; and Philadelphia, the major port of entry, also became preeminent as economic, social, and cultural capital. It was within southeastern Pennsylvania that this culture area first assumed its distinctive form: a prosperous agricultural society, then quite quickly a mixed economy as mercantile and later industrial functions came to the fore. By the middle of the eighteenth century, much of the region has acquired a markedly urban character, resembling in many ways the more advanced portions of the North Sea countries. In this respect at least, the Midland was well ahead of neighboring areas to the north and south.

It also differed in its polyglot ethnicity. From almost the very beginning, the full range of ethnic and religious groups of the British Isles were joined by immigrants from the European mainland. This diversity has, if anything, grown through the years—and promises to persevere indefinitely. The spatial mosaic of colonial ethnic groups has persisted in much of Pennsylvania, New York, New Jersey, and Maryland, as has the remarkable variety of more recent nationalities and churches in coal fields, company towns, cities large and small, and many a rural tract. Much the same sort of ethnic heterogeneity is to be seen in New England, the Middle West, and a few other areas, but the Midland still stands out as our most polyglot region.

If we limit our attention to Pennsylvania and the adjacent tracts of New Jersey, Delaware, and Maryland, a useful distinction can be made (though poorly noted in the literature) between an inner zone, which I call the Pennsylvanian subregion for lack of a better term, in which the Midland culture reached its climactic development, and an outer zone, which is much more nondescript. The former is entirely inland and focused, insofar as it has any core area, upon those sections of the upper Piedmont and the Great Valley lying to the west and north-west of Philadelphia. Although the metropolis is physically separated from the Pennsylvanian subregion, there is every reason to infer a strong umbilical connection during the formative period. It is in the Pennsylvania subregion that such conspicuous diagnostic features as the forebay barn, a localized town morphology, and various house types are located, along with other cultural elements that are less well advertised.[16] The curious fact that the quintessential Midland should have crystallized and flourished well inland rather than within the immediate Philadelphia hinterland is not readily explainable and deserves further study. That this circum-Philadelphia area, in much of Bucks, Montgomery, Chester, and Delaware counties, is sharply set off from the Pennsylvania subregion in terms of ethnic composition, settlement morphology, architecture, and probably other ways is easily established. It is almost totally British, with an especially strong representation of the Welsh and the Quakers. Within the Pennsylvania subregion, the Teutonic element has always been notably strong, accounting for more than 70 per cent of the population of many townships. If it were not for the fact that the Anglo-American culture finally proved supreme, one would indeed be tempted

16 Richard Pillsbury, "The Urban Street Pattern as a Culture Indicator: Pennsylvania, 1682–1815," *Annals of the Association of American Geographers*, 60, No. 3 (1970), 428–46 and Joseph W. Glass, *The Pennsylvania Culture Region: A Geographic Interpretation of Barns and Farmhouses*, doctoral dissertation, Pennsylvania State University, 1971). The best general overview of the Midland is probably still Thomas Jefferson Wertenbaker, *The Founding of American Civilization: The Middle Colonies* (New York: Charles Scribner's Sons, 1938). For an interesting comparison of the regional personality of the Pennsylvania German area with that of New England, see Frank R. Kramer, *Voices in the Valley: Mythmaking and Folk Belief in the Shaping of the Middle West* (Madison: University of Wisconsin Press, 1964), pp. 87–104.

to designate the area as Pennsylvania German. Considerations of land-forms and migrational history have carried the subregion into the Maryland Piedmont; and although its width tapers quickly beyond the Potomac, it does reach into parts of Virginia and West Virginia. As intimated earlier, the demographic and cultural effects of the Midland and the Pennsylvania subregion are legible far down the Appalachian zone and into the South in general. Certain sections of central North Carolina, for example, seem almost like detached fragments of the mother region, as evidenced by a highly un-Southern religious complexion, among other things. Back within Pennsylvania, the areas to the west and north of the two subregions already described are less clearly Midland in character; and much of central and southern New Jersey, except perhaps for a zone within a few miles of Philadelphia, is difficult to classify in any way, and is assigned to the Midland largely by default.

The northern half of the Midland Region, the New York subregion, or New England Extended, presents the cultural geographer with a major classificatory dilemma. Perhaps it is sensible to think of it as a hybrid place formed mainly from two parental strains of almost equal potency: New England and the post-1660 British element moving up the Hudson Valley and beyond. In addition, there has been a persistent, if slight, residue of early Dutch culture and some subtle filtering northward of Pennsylvanian influences. Evidently, it is within the New York subregion that we find the first major *intra*-American blending and fusion of regional cultures, most particularly within the early nineteenth-century Burned-Over District in and near the Finger Lakes and Genesee areas. This locality, another of the many about which we still know much too little, is notable in two respects. It was the seedbed for a number of important innovations;[17] and it was also a major staging area for westward migration and quite possibly a chief source for the people and notions that were to build the Middle Western Region. The boundary between the New York subregion and the (Greater) Pennsylvania subregion in northern Pennsylvania and New Jersey can be delineated rather sharply and in a number of different ways, including language, religion, house types, and town morphology. It also coincides with a significant physiographic barrier, the higher portions of the Allegheny Plateau, and the southern limit of late Wisconsin glaciation. Apparently migrants were deflected from both sides of this border zone by the lay of the land, drainage patterns, and generally poor soil quality.

Toward the west, the Midland or, more specifically, its Pennsylvania subregion, retains its integrity only for a short distance, certainly no further than eastern Ohio, as it pinches out between the South and New England Extended or becomes submerged within the Middle West. Still

17 This is clearly the case for innovations in toponymic practice, as demonstrated in Wilbur Zelinsky, "Classical Town Names in the United States: The Historical Geography of an American Idea," *Geographical Review*, 57, No. 4 (1967), 463–95. The role of west central New York in nineteenth-century religious developments is detailed in Whitney R. Cross, *The Burned-Over District: The Social and Intellectual History of Enthusiastic Religion in Western New York, 1800–1850* (Ithaca, N.Y.: Cornell University Press, 1950).

the significance of the Midland in the genesis of the Middle West or of the national culture must not be belittled. The precise details remain to be worked out, but it is probable that the Midland contribution to overall national patterns will prove to be substantial, just as with the other two colonial hearth areas. Its very success in projecting its image upon so much of the remainder of the country may have rendered the source area less visible. As both the name and location would suggest, the Midland is intermediate in character in many respects between New England and the South. Moreover, its residents are much less concerned with, or conscious of, its existence (excepting the "Pennsylvania Dutch" caricatures) than is true for the other regions, and the Midland also happens to lack their strong political and literary traditions.[18]

THE MIDDLE WEST. There is no such self-effacement in the case of the Middle West, that large triangular region which is justly regarded as the most modal, the section most nearly representative of the national average. Everyone within or outside the Middle West knows of its existence, but no one seems sure where it begins or ends.[19] The older apex of the eastward-pointing equilateral triangle appears to rest in the vicinity of Pittsburgh, and the two western corners melt away somewhere in the Great Plains, possibly southern Manitoba and southern Kansas, respectively. Even though the national sections are distinct enough, this is a clear case of a North American culture area transcending an international boundary.[20] Both southern Ontario and southern Manitoba display an affinity for the adjacent American area that rivals their cultural allegiance to other portions of Canada. The boundary question is irrelevant only along the northeastern side of the Midwest as it gives way to bleak pre-Cambrian country. The eastern terminus and the southern and western borders are obviously broad, indistinct transitional zones.

The historical geography of the Middle West remains largely unstudied, but we can plausibly conjecture that this culture region must be the progeny of all three Colonial regions and that the fertile union took

18 Has Pennsylvania produced any stateman of truly national stature, aside from Benjamin Franklin, that prototypical American, who happens to have been born and reared in Boston? And John O'Hara would seem to be the most eminent author having a strong identification with the Commonwealth. The question of this relatively modest political or literary achievement, at least since Revolutionary days, among a technologically advanced and affluent population, and the contrast in this respect with New England and the South, is a tantalizing one.

19 Apparently the only serious effort thus far to map the limits of the Middle West is that in Joseph W. Brownell, "The Cultural Midwest," *Journal of Geography,* 59 (1960), 43–61.

20 The geometry of Canadian culture areas contrasts strongly with that of the United States. In the latter, the cultural "grain" runs from east to west, while that of Canada would seem to trend from south to north. Moreover, each of the five major Canadian regions—the Maritimes, French Canada, upper Canada (portions of Ontario and southwest Quebec), the Prairie Provinces, and British Columbia—is isolated both culturally and physically from the others, with firmer linkages to the neighboring United States culture area (except for French Canada) than with its Canadian confrères.

place in the upper Ohio Valley.[21] The early routes of travel, employing the Ohio and its tributaries, the Great Lakes, and the low, level corridor along the Mohawk and the Lake Ontario and Lake Erie coastal plains, all converge upon the state of Ohio. It was there that the people and cultural traits from New England, the Midland, and the South were first funneled together. Thence there would seem to have been a fan-like widening westward of the new hybrid area as pioneer settlers worked their way frontierward. Like the South, the Middle West lacks a genuine focal zone or city around which both ideas and commerce were built (although an unconvincing case might be improvised for Chicago). A parallel to the Cotton Belt's role as a climactic zone of development is the central portion of the Corn Belt, or the Cash Grain Region; but it is plainly not a core area in any functional sense.

Two major subregions are readily discerned: the upper and lower Middle West. They are separated by a line roughly approximating the 41st Parallel, one that persists as far west as Colorado in terms of speech patterns[22] and indicates regional differences in ethnic and religious terms as well. Much of the upper Middle West retains a faint New England bouquet, although the Midland is probably equally important as a source of influences. A rich mixture of German, Scandinavian, Slavic, and other non-WASP elements has greatly diversified a stock in which the British element is usually dominant, and the range of church denominations is great and varied. The lower Middle West tends to resemble the South, except for the relative scarcity of Negroes, in its predominantly Protestant and British makeup. There are, of course, many local exceptions, areas of Catholic and non-WASP strength; but on the whole the subregion tends to be more nativistic in inclination than other parts of the nation.

THE PROBLEM OF THE "WEST." The culture areas so far discussed account for roughly the eastern half of the conterminous United States. One faces a genuine dilemma in attempting to arrive at an adequate cultural classification for the remaining half. The concept of an "American West" is strong in the popular imagination and is constantly reinforced by the romanticized images of the cowboy genre. It is tempting to succumb and accept the widespread Western livestock complex as somehow epitomizing the full gamut of Western life, but this would be intellectually dishonest. The cattle industry may have accounted for more than half the active Western *ecumene,* as measured in acres, but it accounts for only a rela-tively small fraction of the total population; and in any case a single sub-culture cannot represent the total regional culture.

Does a genuine, single, grand Western culture region exist? We cannot be certain until the relevant evidence has been rigorously ex-

[21] The question is dealt with, but in tangential fashion, in Kramer, *Voices in the Valley.*

[22] Clyde T. Hankey, *A Colorado Word Geography,* Publication of the American Dialect Society, No. 34 (University, Ala.: University of Alabama Press, 1960); and Roger W. Shuy, *The Northern-Midland Dialect Boundary in Illinois,* Publication of the American Dialect Society, No. 38 (University, Ala.: University of Alabama Press, 1962).

amined. This has not been done to date, nor will it be easy. When suitable measures are devised, it is possible that the cultural distance between, say, San Diego and Fort Worth or Pocatello will appear to be at least as great as that between Kankakee and Harrisburg. Unlike the East, where settlement is virtually continuous through space, and culture areas and subregions abut and overlap in splendid confusion, the west features eight major (and many lesser) nodes of population, separated from each other by wide expanses of nearly uninhabited mountain or arid desert. The only two obvious properties all these isolated clusters have in common is the recent intermixture of several strains of culture, primarily from the East, but with additions from Europe, Mexico, and East Asia as well, and (except for one) a general modernity, having been settled in a serious way no earlier than the 1840's. I should prefer to consider some as inchoate, partially formed cultural entities. The others have acquired definite personalities, but are difficult to classify as first-order or lesser-order culture areas at this time. Their grouping together on Figure 4.3 is a cartographic convenience, not a matter of intellectual conviction.

There are three, and possibly four, major tracts in the western United States that reveal a genuine cultural identity: the upper Rio Grande region; the Mormon region; Southern California; and central California. (To this group one might also add the anomalous Texan and Oklahoman subregions, which may adhere to either the South or the "West," or both). The term upper Rio Grande region has been coined to denote the oldest and strongest of the three sectors of Hispanic-American activity in the American Southwest, the other two having been Southern California and portions of Texas. Although the region is focused upon the valley of the upper Rio Grande, we can also include with it a broader domain taking in segments of Arizona and Colorado as well as other parts of New Mexico. European communities and culture have been present in strength, with only one interruption, since the late sixteenth century. The initial sources were Spain and Mexico, but after 1848 at least three distinct strains of Anglo-American culture have been increasingly well-represented: the Southern, Mormon, and a general un-differentiated northeastern American culture, along with a distinct Texan subcategory.[23] But, for once, all this has occurred without obliterating the aboriginal folk, whose culture endures in various stages of dilution, from the strongly Americanized or Hispanicized down to the almost undisturbed. The general pattern is that of a mosaic, with the aboriginal, Anglo, and Hispanic constituting the main elements. Furthermore, all three major groups, not just the Anglo-American, are complex in character. The aboriginal component embraces the Navaho, Pueblos, and several smaller groups, each of which is quite distinct from the others. The

---

[23] John L. Landgraf, *Land-Use in the Ramah Area of New Mexico: An Anthropological Approach to Areal Study*, Papers of the Peabody Museum of American Archaeology and Ethnology, Vol. 42, No. 1 (Cambridge, Mass.: Harvard University, 1954); and Donald W. Meinig, *Southwest: Three Peoples in Geographical Change, 1600–1970* (New York: Oxford University Press, 1971).

"Hispanic" element is also diverse—modally Mexican Mestizo, that is, Euro-American, but ranging from pure Spanish to nearly pure pre-Spanish aboriginal. Given the strong recent influx of Mexicans and Anglos (many with a cultivated taste for the distinctiveness of the area) and its general economic prosperity, this is one region that appears destined to wax stronger and to nurture zealously its special traits.

The Mormon region also promises to maintain its strength and cultural separateness for many years to come, for it is emphatically expansive in religion and demography, even though it has ceased to expand territorially, as it did so vigorously in the first few decades after establishment.[24] Despite its Great Basin location and an exemplary adaptation to environmental constraints, this cultural complex still appears somewhat non-Western in spirit: The Mormons may be in the West, but they are not entirely of it. The historical derivation from the Middle West and, beyond that, from ultimate sources in New York and New England, is still apparent, along with the generous admixture of European converts. Here again, as in New England, the power of the human will and an intensely cherished abstract design have triumphed over an unfriendly habitat. Despite its relative recency and an unflagging vigor, the region has functioned, at least since the great ingathering of the Latter Day Saints during the past century, as a traditional region—one inhabited by a (religiously defined) tribal group, with a deep natal attachment to a particular tract, and almost ideally structured spatially, as Meinig has shown, in accordance with the principles one would postulate theoretically for an isolated culture area. The Mormon way of life is expressed in many recognizable ways in the settlement landscape and economic activities within a region that is more homogeneous internally than any other American culture area.[25] This is also the only large portion of the United States, aside from the South, whose political allegiance to the federal Union was ever seriously in doubt.

In contrast, the almost precisely coeval Central California region has not yet gained its own strong cultural coloration, except possibly for the city of San Francisco and some of its suburbs. From the first weeks of the great Gold Rush onward, the area drew a thoroughly diverse population from Europe and Asia as well as the older portions of America. Speaking impressionistically, as one must for most Western regions, it is not yet obvious whether the greater part of the Central California region has produced a local culture amounting to more than the averaging out of the contributions brought by in-migrants, early and late. San

24 Donald W. Meinig, "The Mormon Culture Region: Strategies and Patterns in the Geography of the American West, 1847–1964," *Annals of the Association of American Geographers*, 55, No. 2 (1965), 191–220.

25 Joseph E. Spencer, "The Development of Agricultural Villages in Southern Utah," *Agricultural History*, 14 (1940), 181–89 and "House Types of Southern Utah," *Geographical Review*, 35 (1945), 444–57; Lowry Nelson, *The Mormon Village: A Pattern and Technique of Land Settlement* (Salt Lake City: University of Utah Press, 1952); and Richard V. Francaviglia, "The Mormon Landscape: Definition of an Image in the American West," *Proceedings of the Association of American Geographers*, 2 (1970), 59–61.

Francisco, the regional metropolis, may, however, have crossed the qualitative threshold. An unusually cosmopolitan outlook, including an awareness of the Orient stronger than that of any other American city, a fierce self-esteem, and a unique townscape may be symptomatic of a genuinely new, emergent local culture. In any case, the Central California region, along with the Southern Californian and the Upper Rio Grande, has recently acted as a creative zone for the nation as a whole, the springboard for many a fresh innovation.

The Southern California region is the most spectacular of the Western regions, not only in terms of economic and population growth, but also for the luxuriance, regional particularism, and general avante-garde character of its swiftly evolving cultural pattern.[26] Until the coming of a direct transcontinental rail connection in 1885, Southern California was remote, rural, and largely inconsequential. Since then, the invasion by persons from virtually every corner of North America and by the foreign-born has been massive and ceaseless; and a loosely articulated series of conurbations have been encroaching upon what little is left of arable or habitable land in the coast ranges and valleys from Santa Barbara to the Mexican border. Although every significant ethnic and racial group and every other American culture area is amply represented, there is reason to suspect (again largely on subjective grounds) that a process of selection for certain kinds of people, attitudes, and personality traits may have been at work at both source and destination. Certainly the region is aberrant from, or in the vanguard of, the remainder of the nation. One might view Southern California as the super-American region or the outpost of a rapidly approaching postindustrial future; but in any event its cultural distinctiveness, in visible landscape and social behavior, is evident to all. It is also clear that in Southern California we do not behold anything approaching a traditional region, or even the smudged facsimile of such, as is to be found in the eastern United States, but rather the largest, boldest experiment anywhere in creating a voluntary region. In discussing this new variety of geographic phenomenon, we shall shortly return to the Southern California scene.

The remaining Western regions identified in Figure 4.3—the Willamette Valley, Puget Sound, Inland Empire, and Colorado Piedmont—can be treated jointly as potential or emergent culture areas still too close to the national mean to arouse much self-awareness among their inhabitants or special curiosity on the part of the outsider. Conditions may have been propitious for such a regional blossoming in the Inland Empire a century ago or so, according to Meinig, but the unfortunate trisection of the area by Washington, Oregon, and Idaho, through the vagaries of boundary drawing, lessened the chances for such a

---

[26] William L. Thomas, Jr., ed., "Man, Time, and Space in Southern California: A Symposium," *Annals of the Association of American Geographers*, Vol. 49, No. 3, Part 2 (1959); Carey McWilliams, *California: The Great Exception* (Westport, Conn: Greenwood Press, 1949); and Dennis Hale and Jonathan Eisen, eds., *The California Dream* (New York: The MacMillan Company, 1968).

development.[27] In all four regions (and also in the analagous case of British Columbia), one can witness the arrival of a cross-section of the national population and the growth of regional life around one or more major metropolises. A New England element has, however, been noteworthy in the Williamette Valley and Puget Sound regions, whereas a Hispanic-American component appears in the Colorado Piedmont. Only time and further study will reveal whether any of these regions, so distant from the historic sources of American population and culture, can engender the capacity or will for an independent cultural existence.

LESSER-ORDER CULTURE AREAS. Thus far we have scanned the top three levels of the hierarchy of culture areas within the United States: the nation itself; the five or more first-order culture areas; and a number of second-order culture areas. But, contrary to the popular myth of cultural homogeneity, there also exists a multitude of much smaller tracts, each distinctive as to culture. These microregions are both traditional and voluntary in type; and if we have only a sparse scattering of serious descriptions of the former, there is virtually no literature on the latter.

The most conspicuous of these small, culturally distinctive areas are several cities that maintain intimate economic and social connections with their hinterlands, yet have personalities all their own. The case of San Francisco has been noted already, and we can add to it such places as Charleston, Savannah, New Orleans, St. Louis, Philadelphia, Baltimore, Cincinnati, Detroit, Chicago, and New York—each a world unto itself, despite a functional centrality to a much broader area. This uniqueness is attested to by the unique speech patterns, at least in New York City, Boston, Philadelphia, and Chicago;[28] and some observers would testify that linguistic peculiarities are recognizable at the borough or neighborhood level.

The persistence of very minute culture areas in both urban and rural areas has been reported by the few geographers and others who have troubled to search for them. These dwarfish entities are most clearly visible in terms of ethnicity or religion. They have been described in Kalamazoo and Denver,[29] and definitively in Chicago's Near West Side.[30] Within a rural setting, an almost ideal example is to be seen in the Mennonite culture of central Pennsylvania's Kishicoquillas Valley. The distinctive character of yet another small valley, in northern New Jersey,

[27] Donald W. Meinig, *The Great Columbia Plain: A Historical Geography, 1805–1910* (Seattle: University of Washington Press, 1968), pp. 359–64.

[28] Metropolitan New York and Philadelphia are accorded subregional status in a map delimiting "The Speech Areas of the Eastern States," Kurath, *A Word Geography of the Eastern United States,* Figure 3.

[29] John A. Jakle and James O. Wheeler, "The Changing Residential Structure of the Dutch Population in Kalamazoo, Michigan," *Annals of the Association of American Geographers,* 59, No. 3 (1969), 441–60; and Daniel F. Doeppers, "The Globeville Neighborhood in Denver," *Geographical Review,* 57, No. 4 (1967), 506–22.

[30] Gerald D. Suttles, *The Social Order of the Slum: Ethnicity and Territory in the Inner City* (Chicago: University of Chicago Press, 1968).

has been analyzed in detail by Peter Wacker.[31] The great profusion of rural ethnic neighborhoods has been precisely documented for the entire state of Kansas in an exemplary atlas.[32] But clearly there remains an imposing agenda of unfinished business for the cultural and social geographer working at the microscopic level in Anglo-America.

The Voluntary Region

A new geometry of cultural space may have begun to materialize in the United States. The series of traditional spatial parcels, that is, discrete, contiguous patches of real estate, within each of which relative uniformity prevails, may be in the process of being replaced by a multi-layered sandwich (or hyperspace) in which very numerous strata of variable thickness tend to span the entire country. Formerly if one sought cultural diversity, one would move laterally or horizontally along the earth's surface from one place-bound group to another. Now, with minimal physical effort, one may experience this variety by shifting vertically, so to speak, in cultural space, from one layer of the sandwich to another— or by hobnobbing with different subcultures vicariously by means of telecommunications, which have brought about truly revolutionary changes in the physical, social, and mental mobility of individuals. To pursue our metaphor of the recent up-ending of interfaces between cultural groups, a particular layer of the cultural sandwich, (a subculture) may thicken so markedly at one point or another in its transcontinental expanse that that group then dominates the locality. When this occurs, for whatever reason, a voluntary region has come into being. Let us search for a few.

Voluntary regions are so novel and recent that few observers have consciously recognized or described them. Much of this discussion, then, must remain speculative, based on scattered observations, hints, and hunches. The massive American economic, social, and demographic data gathering systems are not yet attuned to their existence. This lag is illustrated by the relative dearth of hard data on tourism, recreation, and leisure time activities. Although these activities are of much concern to the student of voluntary regions and also to many businessmen, we are not yet reconciled to the pagan notion that these are serious items, socially or academically. There is also the matter of scale, whether spatial or temporal. Most of the emergent regions are tiny, fragmentary, or ephemeral. But these are inadequate reasons for ignoring them, for the smallness or spatial irregularity of the voluntary region may simply reflect the new spatial geometry of post-industrial communities, about which very little is yet known. Furthermore, all spatial structures, not just the cultural, are dynamic and evanescent. The spatially coherent cultural group that coheres for five days or five hours is just as real, and perhaps

31 Peter O. Wacker, *The Musconetcong Valley of New Jersey: A Historical Geography* (New Brunswick, N.J.: Rutgers University Press, 1968).
32 J. Neale Carman, *Foreign-Language Units of Kansas. I. Historical Atlas and Statistics* (Lawrence: University of Kansas Press, 1962).

as interesting, as one that persists for five hundred or five thousand years.

There are, however, at least two extensive tracts within the United States that appear to be taking on the character of voluntary regions and show every sign of relative stability: the Southern Californian and the peninsular Florida subregions. (A rather weaker case might also be made out for the upper Rio Grande and one or two other Western subregions.) The former two began, conventionally enough, as agricultural and ranching frontiers, with the regular later accretion of higher economic functions. Then, more recently, it has become evident that the large volume and character of the continuing in-migrations were controlled by factors other than economic. The opportunity to prosper remains important, but more and more of those bound for portions of Southern California and Florida seem to be seeking congenial surroundings and like-minded companions, even though we cannot yet specify the precise ways in which these perceptions, decisions, and migrations have been occurring. The popular impression that the Southern Californian is self-selected for certain personality traits merits careful investigation.

In any case, the basic condition for the voluntary region appears to be met: the replacement of social regions determined by the traditional factors of circumstance of birth and social heredity by self-selected groups of like-minded, mobile, atomistic individuals. The cultural personality of Southern California is decreasingly defined by its nineteenth century infancy; instead, there is constant redefinition with the arrival of more strangers and the formulation of new attitudes and cultural entities, as some still obscure new processes become ascendant. In the case of peninsular Florida, there is virtually no nineteenth-century residue to be expunged. The great influx of settlers—many, of course, from the South, but a large fraction from the non-South (or the Caribbean)—have been continuously improvising a fresh cultural milieu. We still have no clear picture of the emergent regional culture and subcultures of an area with no genuine *raison d'être* except the presence of people; but there is little doubt that the many hundreds of thousands of persons pursuing the varied amenities of Florida and their own self-realization are building something far different from the culture areas of colonial America or premodern Europe.

At the micro level, we can assume a large, diversified array of voluntary regions. Here we shall briefly note only a few categories: those that are conspicuously visible and also adhere, at least partially, to the conventional rules of spatial contiguity and concentration. A number of possibilities are omitted because their existence is still too speculative and their unusual spatial attributes too difficult to specify with the limited means at our command. Let us proceed from traditional examples to the relatively avant-garde.

MILITARY SUBREGIONS. There is, of course, nothing particularly newsworthy in the existence of a professional military population with its own way of life and discrete spatial enclaves. We can readily find analogies in many other countries, some much less advanced in development than the United States. We can also assume a universal tendency for the military subpopulation to be self-selected for certain attitudes or personality traits, over and above purely mercenary considerations. But what tends to be special in the United States is the sheer size, solidity, territorial extent, population size, and local social impact of the larger military establishments. Thus a special subculture suffuses and tends to dominate several sizeable metropolitan areas, for example, San Diego, Colorado Springs, Columbus, Georgia, Norfolk, Annapolis, and Pensacola. This is also true for paramilitary research and development centers at Los Alamos, Oak Ridge, Huntsville, or Cape Kennedy. All these places, along with many a lesser locality, actually constitute one large, discontinuous region, or network of points, whose various interchangeable components are in constant, intimate connection with each other, more so perhaps than with other spatial systems.

EDUCATIONAL SUBREGIONS. The close connection of many widely scattered points is even more obvious when one observes our hundreds of colleges and universities with their faculties, students, and hangers-on, including a growing cohort of the retired. As elsewhere, economic factors are present, but the decision to live or work in a college community, or in which specific one, is increasingly subsidiary to matters of taste and personality. We can also identify analogies abroad and scattered local examples in our own earlier history. But, again, the massiveness of this population, involving some millions of students and faculty members, their rapid growth since 1945, and intense social and cultural development of our many college towns and college ghettos within larger metropolises has meant a new, truly unprecedented order of cultural subregions. Not every colleage automatically generates its own microregion: many are too weak or thoroughly overpowered by the larger society, or are frequented by commuting student bodies and faculties. But if many of our burgeoning institutions of higher learning have acquired and staunchly cling to their own idiosyncratic personalities, the similarities among these places and their people are far closer than those with local traditional regions or with other spatially discontinuous, national subcultures. Like most of the remainder of this discussion, these remarks are impressionistic. The social and cultural geography of college populations is still almost totally *terra incognita.*

THE PLEASURING PLACES. The richest category of voluntary regions includes all those many places and people who, in the wider sense of the terms, are in quest of pleasure, surcease, or self-improvement. Assuredly, no other nation or epoch has spawned such a number or variety of amenity-oriented communities, ephemeral or not. The following subcategories do not begin to exhaust the possibilities. Nor are they mutually exclusive; many localities fall into two or more classes.

In a few years, we can expect to have virtually every physically attractive *amphibious region* thoroughly exploited and seasonally saturated with patrons. As it is, there are few suitable, undeveloped, privately owned tracts remaining along the Atlantic, Pacific, or Great Lakes coasts, and the Gulf Coast is also filling up rapidly. The same story can be told of the glaciated lake country of the Northeast and the lakes and artificial reservoirs in other parts of the country. During a warm season that varies from scarcely two months in the far north to the entire year in the far south, uncounted millions of Americans gravitate to the waterside to swim, fish, boat, surf, beach-comb, sun-bathe, cavort in the sand, or just stare at seascape and shore. Each of these communities, generally stretched out along a beach and only a few hundred yards in width, tends to have its own social characteristics and to foster a peculiar subculture. Certainly as a group the amphibious communities claim a personality all their own; and many, although only seasonally alive, are so vigorous as to dominate the entire annual cycle of their localities.

Many of the *heliotropic* (sun-seeking) *regions* also fall into this category, but others, especially in the relatively warm, cloudless Southwest, are high and dry. In turn, a very large fraction of the *retirement subregions,* notably those in Florida, Arizona, and California, are either heliotropic or amphibious. But a considerable number of these are being deliberately engineered, mainly for commercial gain, in other parts of the country. Such spatial segregation of the aged (on a scale beyond the conventional old people's home) is a novel phenomenon, one still rather neglected by geographer and sociologist.

All those accessible *montane regions* with adequate slopes and natural (or artificial) snow potential within range of large metropolitan populations eager for skiing and other winter sports have undergone rapid development in recent years, especially in New England, New York, and the Sierras. Parallel development also proceeds in sections of Colorado and Idaho, where skiiers arrive mainly by jet. Indeed the elaboration of the ski subculture, along with various summer recreational activities, has been so intense in much of Vermont and nearby states that a genuine transformation of the cultural character of that area may be in progress. The socioeconomic impact of the pleasure-seekers here, as in other pleasuring places, has been quite profound.

The one subcategory of amenity-oriented subregion that seems well-rooted in European antecedents, aside from the dwindling medicinal spas,[33] are the American *equine regions.* They are, or at least have been, markedly and affectedly British in style. There are now a goodly number of such areas, where the breeding and rearing of horses, riding, and hunting literally constitute a whole way of life. The strongest development appears in southern Megalopolis, especially in parts of Piedmont Maryland and Virginia that are suburban to Washington and Baltimore; the Bluegrass; and a tract in northern Florida.

The subcategory that in lieu of a better label is termed the *forbidden fruitlands* is not peculiar to North America; but again there is no development elsewhere comparable in scale. These are the areas where social and economic existence is based upon activities classed as illegal in most states or municipalities—gambling, prostitution, nudism, unrestricted

---

[33] David Lowenthal, "Tourists and Thermalists," *Geographical Review,* 52, No. 1 (1962), 124–27.

liquor consumption, open homosexual behavior, and certain sports. Beyond any question, this is how Reno, Las Vegas, the Lake Tahoe resorts, and the other urban centers of Nevada must be regarded, or the string of international twin cities along the United States-Mexican boundary, and a variety of satellite towns along several of our interstate lines. Again, the disreputable activities may be combined with more wholesome ones in various hunting and fishing or seaside areas. The transient subpopulations who frequent such areas and the service groups who cater to them act to create a special cultural ambience that has yet to be analyzed geographically.

Still within the realm of pleasure, there are many other temporary aggregations of persons of common taste or purpose who may manage to impose more than a fleeting impact upon a considerable locality: the rallies of cyclists or hot-rodders, "wilderness" camping, rock festivals, summer music camps, revival meetings, and the like.

LATTER-DAY BOHEMIAS AND UTOPIAS. The last pair of spatially discrete sets of voluntary regions are unquestionably North American in character, if not in ultimate origin, then certainly in their current full-bodied expression. The first of these is so very recent that scarcely any academic notice has been taken of them (and they still lack a suitable generic term). The "New Bohemias" are those quite distinctive neighborhoods toward the center of our larger cities that have attracted such urban folk as actively relish diversity, unconventional behavior, and a variety of exotic stimuli. They are complex in ethnic, racial, class, and age structure, and (with the possible exceptions of the prototypical Greenwich Village in New York and North Beach in San Francisco) are products of the 1950's and 1960's. They are still emerging, spontaneously or by design. Perhaps the best way to define them is to cite examples. In addition to Greenwich Village and North Beach, there is Chicago's Old Town, the Beacon Hill-Back Bay section of Boston, Atlanta's Peachtree Street, N.E., the French Quarter of New Orleans, Rittenhouse Square in Philadelphia, Georgetown and Dupont Circle in Washington, and Cincinnati's Mount Adams. In many places, such as Berkeley, Seattle, Minneapolis, or Toronto, the special university neighborhood coincides perfectly with the New Bohemia; but in most, the two sections lead quite separate existences. One can anticipate a further proliferation of this novel form of urban life not only in the United States but in other highly advanced nations in the near future.

During the past decade, a great number of *communal colonies* have sprung up in virtually all parts of the country. Examples abound in urban as well as rural settings; they vary considerably in size, mode of organization, style, purpose, and type of membership. By their very nature (many go to some pains to escape detection), they are not readily susceptible to synoptic analysis. Perhaps the only attributes they share are communality of property, a rejection of the regnant values and rules of the greater world, and an adherence to the principles of simple living and decent poverty. What is not clear is whether these latter-day communes are the natural progeny of the numerous utopian experiments, largely religious or political in character, that flourished in large numbers, though briefly, during the past century, or whether they have sprouted spontaneously out of the inner core of American culture. In any event, it remains to be seen what, if anything, they herald of the future shape of the American cultural landscape.

The foregoing sketch is confined to what is known or reasonably assumed to exist and to those entities within the family of voluntary regions that can be readily plotted on the conventional two-dimensional map. Possibly they are only the leading edge, the most visible, mappable forerunners of a large new galaxy of cultural associations that observe an as yet uncharted code of spatial rules. We must be alert to the emergence of unexpected modes of cultural interaction within the American realm. Assuredly we are entering, or are well into, a period of shattering change in the social organization of highly advanced communities, and in the rapid unfolding of technologies and mental worlds still scarcely dreamed of. It is axiomatic that spatial structures and processes are interdependent with the basic social and perceptual attributes of a people. It would be strange indeed if we did not soon find ourselves stumbling across a threshold into radically unfamiliar ways of locating our cultural and other experiences on this fragile earth-shell as we grope our way so painfully toward an undisclosed destination.

Postlude

Anyone who has flipped to the back of this volume to find an answer to the question posed in its first line will be doubly disappointed. There is no valid answer, and there is no real conclusion—only a pause. These closing lines are offered in lieu of a proper introduction: an author is often not fully aware of what he wishes to say until his manuscript tells him; and the reader is seldom primed to appreciate an introduction until he has traversed the main body of a work.

This has been an attempt to organize an important, but previously unorganized subject, the cultural geography of the United States. As the first such effort, it is subject to many hazards. Not the least of these, all too obviously, is the writer's frailties, including major zones of ignorance and many instances of personal bias. No apology is needed, however, for one basic decision, namely to eschew the discursive, encyclopedic recounting of the cultural features of the nation. The materials for such a panoramic treatment, or at least many aspects thereof, are reasonably abundant. The reader in need of factual nourishment is earnestly directed to the selected and annotated references that follow; indeed this list is an integral part of the volume and should be foraged with care.

The design chosen for this essay seeks to interweave the theoretical with the particular so as to shed light on both. This is done in the conviction that serious attempts to combine theory with the regional method have been all too rare or timid in modern geography, and that much is to be gained thereby. But in view of how little is truly known by either anthropologist or geographer about the basic processes that mold the cultures of large nations or ethnic groups, or their constituent regions, this volume is interrogatory in tone. I have settled on four basic questions: Culturally speaking, who are we Americans? What are the sources of our identity? What processes, operating how, when, and where, have molded our cultural patterns? And what spatial configurations have emerged from such activity? In experimental fashion, I have offered one tentative way of seeking answers, but without any illusions that this scheme is either final or impregnable to challenge. Confining an unruly reality within a simple conceptual harness is an impossible chore. But I do hope that this perspective on the American cultural landscape has at least the merit of provoking better, clearer ones. In any event, it seems to accommodate a maximum of fact with minimal mutilation; it illuminates many murky items, and it suggests many new questions. I anticipate better schemata in the near future, and await them with interest. Lasting consensus (or tolerance) is sought from readers, critics, and successors on only four points:

1. The cultural patterns of the United States are exceedingly interesting in themselves. Infatuation with any and all of their details is a commendable form of madness.
2. Such patterns are important not only to Americans but to the contemporary world in general. It is urgent to get at their fundamental structure in the cause of planetary social and physical survival and the fostering of civilized existence.
3. Both the spatial and temporal texture of cultural events must be apprehended before the inner logic or laws of cultural transactions can be spelled out. Where, when, and how form a sacred threesome, triune yet unitary.
4. We live in a period of rapid structural change in terms of ongoing cultural process in the United States and of penetrating the most fundamental questions concerning human thought and behavior, as they are constrained within the cultural matrix. We can also anticipate a period of almost revolutionary insights that will vastly enrich our understanding of what we have been, who we are now, the most likely forms for future cultural dealings among people, places, and things, and even how they can be manipulated so as to give ourselves a fighting chance for survival and salvation.

Selected references

The published literature available to the student of American cultural geography is vast in quantity, immensely broad and diversified as to topic, but quite uneven in quality and depth of coverage. The following list is severely selective, and is intended to suggest to the serious reader only the more notable works, or bibliographic starting points, in 15 topical areas, along with one section for miscellany. The absence of annotation indicates an item of substantial merit whose contents are adequately described by the title.

1. General Bibliography

OSCAR HANDLIN, et al., *Harvard Guide to American History*. Cambridge, Mass.: Harvard University Press, 1954. A massive bibliography covering not simply the usual historical items but virtually every aspect of American life and civilization. Splendid up through the early 1950s, but now badly in need of updating.

GORDON R. LEWTHWAITE, EDWARD T. PRICE, JR., and HAROLD A. WINTERS, eds., *A Geographical Bibliography for American College Libraries*, Commission on College Geography, Publication No. 9 (Washington: Association of American Geographers, 1970). A thoughtful selection of 1,760 titles, briefly annotated. The sections on "General Human and Historical Geography" (pp. 36–42) and "Anglo-America" (pp. 104–23) are especially apposite. Some of the comments are excerpted below, with an attribution to GBACL.

HUGH C. PRINCE, "Three Realms of Historical Geography: Real, Imagined and Abstract Worlds of the Past," *Progress in Geography*, 3 (1971), 4–86. A major review article and a major bibliography, with the bulk of the references dealing with the North American scene.

U.S. LIBRARY OF CONGRESS, *A Guide to the Study of the United States of America: Representative Books Reflecting the Development of American Life and Thought* (Washington, D.C.: Government Printing Office, 1960). "A selection of 6,486 titles, liberally annotated, that afford an excellent introduction to every variety of study related to the United States." (GBACL.)

2. Cultural Geography—General Works

GEORGE F. CARTER, *Man and the Land; a Cultural Geography*, 2nd ed. (New York: Holt, Rinehart & Winston, Inc., 1968). "A well-revised, clearly written text which both places culture-groups in their physical setting and presents a sustained attack on environmental determinism in favor of cultural diffusion." (GBACL.)

SAMUEL N. DICKEN AND FORREST R. PITTS, *Introduction to Cultural Geography* (Waltham, Mass.: Xerox College Publishing, 1971). A revision of the original 1963 edition, one that takes a topical approach to the field. Several of the chapters are highly original in coverage.

ALFRED L. KROEBER, *The Nature of Culture* (Chicago: University of Chicago Press, 1952). As definitive a statement as one could hope for on a profoundly difficult question by one of the foremost leaders in anthropological thought.

JOSEPH E. SPENCER AND WILLIAM L. THOMAS, JR., *Cultural Geography; an Evolutionary Introduction to Our Humanized Earth* (New York: John Wiley & Sons, Inc., 1969). A richly rewarding monograph that is rich in theory, fact, and exceptional maps and photos. The book relies upon a genetic, or evolutionary, approach to cultural process and form.

PHILIP L. WAGNER, *The Human Use of the Earth,* (New York: The Free Press, 1960). "Discusses the elements of cultural geography and proposes a classification of these elements and processes. A broad synthesis of the relevant findings of several disciplines." (GBACL.)

——— and MARVIN W. MIKESELL, eds., *Readings in Cultural Geography* (Chicago: University of Chicago Press, 1962). Even more valuable than the judicious selections from scholars in human geography and related disciplines are the editors' deeply probing introduction and prefatory comments accompanying each section.

3. Atlases

HILDE H. KAGAN, ed., *The American Heritage Pictorial Atlas of United States History* (New York: McGraw-Hill Book Company, 1966). "A colorful popular atlas with many old maps mixed in with the new." (GBACL.) Although this volume supplements rather than replaces the redoubtable Paullin-Wright atlas—and overstresses the gorier aspects of the American past—there is much of interest here for the scholar interested in settlement history, economy, population, and society.

THEODORE R. MILLER, *Graphic History of the Americas* (New York: John Wiley and Sons, Inc., 1969). The 61 black-and-white plates in this atlas provide a great amount of useful, well-arranged information on the historical geography of the Western Hemisphere.

CHARLES O. PAULLIN and JOHN K. WRIGHT, *Atlas of the Historical Geography of the United States* (Washington, D.C. and New York: Carnegie Institution and the American Geographical Society, 1932). The American geographer exiled to a desert island and with a baggage limit of one book should give this item serious consideration despite its antiquity. "One of the truly mighty monuments of American historical and geographic scholarship. . . . Most of the plates—dealing with a broad range of physical, historical, social, political, and economic topics—were painstakingly compiled from multiple sources. Detailed notes on source materials. An indispensable volume" (GBACL).

READER'S DIGEST ASSOCIATION, *These United States: Our Nation's Geography, History and People* (Pleasantville, N.Y.: Readers Digest, 1968). The best approximation of a national atlas until the genuine article arrived two years later. Imaginative design and useful coverage of a broad range of topics at both national and regional scale.

U.S. DEPARTMENT OF THE INTERIOR, GEOLOGICAL SURVEY, *The National Atlas of the United States of America* (Washington, D.C.: Government Printing Office, 1970). Although there are some distressing lacunae in topical coverage (for example, in such areas as ethnic groups or linguistic characteristics), the United States has at long last covered itself with cartographic glory in this handsome volume. The plates and marginal comments on population, settlement, and social structure are executed very well indeed.

4. General Descriptions of the United States

CONRAD M. ARENSBERG and SOLON T. KIMBALL, *Culture and Community* (New York: Harcourt Brace Jovanovich, 1965). A collection of their earlier papers by two social anthropologists dealing with the theory and substance of American community studies. Although often too fuzzy, this is probably the best statement on the topic.

RALPH H. BROWN, *Mirror for Americans: Likeness of the Eastern Seaboard, 1810* (New York: American Geographical Society, 1943). *Sui generis*—a veritable *tour de force* of the geographical imagination. "The regional geography of the United States in 1810, as it might have been written by a contemporary geographer." (GBACL.)

PETER KALM, *Travels in North America; the English Version of 1770*, rev. and ed. by Adolph E. Benson, 2 vols. (New York: Dover Publications, Inc., 1966). Perhaps the most notable and informative of the first-hand accounts of colonial British America, especially the middle and northern Colonies, written by a Swedish natural scientist with a keen eye and a catholic curiosity.

MAX LERNER, *America as a Civilization: Life and Thought in the United States Today* (New York: Simon & Schuster, Inc., 1957). Encyclopedic observations and reflections on the grand theme of the nature and meaning of the American experience by an able scholar and journalist.

FERDINAND LUNDBERG, *The Rich and the Super-Rich: A Study in the Power of Money* (New York: Lyle Stuart, 1968). A massive, acidulous, and important treatise on the social and political implications of the concentration of property and power, with some keen geographic sidelights. Muckraking in the grand manner, with ample documentation.

ANDRE SIEGFRIED, *America at Mid-Century* (New York: Harcourt Brace Jovanovich, Inc., 1955). "A refreshing, deeply perceptive, highly readable view of the nature of the American land and people by a widely travelled French geographer." (GBACL.) Thematically organized, including the ethnic and religious.

GEORGE R. STEWART, *U.S. 40: Cross Section of the United States of America* (Boston: Houghton Mifflin Company, 1953). A magnificent interpretation of the American landscape that is a mixture of travelogue, photograph, caption, and essay. Much more than just a book about a road.

W. LLOYD WARNER, *American Life: Dream and Reality* (Chicago: University of Chicago Press, 1953). Ruminations by a distinguished sociologist, based in large part on his intensive studies of a small New England city. Essentially an anthropological view of some basic attributes of the American social structure and value system.

J. WREFORD WATSON, *North America, its Countries and Regions*, rev. ed. (New York: Frederich A. Praeger, Inc., 1967). Perhaps the only college text on the continent that is sufficiently literate, intellectually nutritious, and up-to-date to be noted without wincing, and the only one according culture and history more than token attention. A useful basic reference designed for the British public.

THOMAS C. WHEELER, ed., *A Vanishing America: The Life and Times of the Small Town* (New York: Holt, Rinehart & Winston, Inc., 1964). Twelve beautifully written essays, each by a gifted author dealing with a place he knows and cherishes. Wallace Stegner's introduction is memorable.

5. National Character

JOHN GILLIN, "National and Regional Cultural Values in the United States," *Social Forces,* 34 (December 1955), 107–13. Every word counts in this pithy essay.

FRANCIS L. K. HSU, *Americans and Chinese: Two Ways of Life* (New York: Henry Schuman, 1953). A truly superb analysis by a "marginal man," an anthropologist deeply rooted in both Chinese and Euro-American life. The theme throughout is the dominant role of mutual dependence within the primary group among the Chinese and its absence among Americans.

HOWARD MUMFORD JONES, *O Strange New World: American Culture: the Formative Years* (New York: The Viking Press, Inc., 1964). This account by a cultural historian of the shaping of our national language, laws, religion, ideals, education, literature, and arts through the interplay of Old World and New World forces is original, insightful, and readable.

MICHAEL MCGIFFERT, *The Character of Americans; a Book of Readings* (Homewood Ill.: Dorsey Press, 1965). An excellent selection of essays, old and new, on the peculiarities of *Homo Americanus.* Opulent bibliography.

PERRY MILLER, *Nature's Nation* (Cambridge, Mass.: Harvard University Press, 1967). A posthumous collection of worthy essays on a variety of American themes by the historian who labored so diligently and productively on the intellectual evolution of New England.

HUGO MUNSTERBERG, *The Americans* (New York: McClure, Phillips & Co., 1905). A compendious interpretation of the American scene for the German public by a German psychologist teaching at Harvard. Well below the level of the greatest items in this genre, but still interesting for its facts and biases.

GEORGE JEAN NATHAN and H. L. MENCKEN, *The American Credo: A Contribution toward the Interpretation of the National Mind* (New York: Alfred A. Knopf, Inc., 1920). Superficially this appears to be nothing more than a string of epigrams by the two reigning wits of the 1920s. In actuality, a great deal of shrewd observation and wisdom lies beneath the glittering surface.

ALEXIS DE TOQUEVILLE, *Democracy in America,* ed. by Henry Steele Commager (New York: Oxford University Press, 1947). The scholarly consensus is correct: This remarkable, enduring work (written in the 1830s) is the most perceptive commentary yet on a distinctively new nation.

6. Historical Geography of Settlement and the Economy

RAY A. BILLINGTON, *Westward Expansion: A History of the American Frontier* (New York: The Macmillan Company, 1967).

RALPH H. BROWN, *Historical Geography of the United States* (New York: Harcourt Brace Jovanovich, Inc., 1948). "A scholarly, well-written narrative and geographic analysis of the settlement and occupation of the major regions of the United States until 1870. Still the best and most comprehensive essay of its sort." (GBACL.)

HERMAN R. FRIIS, *A Series of Population Maps of the Colonies and the United States,* 1625–1790, Mimeographed Publication No. 3 (New York: American Geographical Society, 1940; rev. ed. 1968). Minutely detailed maps, accompanied by extensive documentation. A basic source for the study of early frontiers and of population and settlement patterns.

FRANCIS J. MARSCHNER, *Land Use and Its Patterns in the U.S.,* U.S.D.A. Agriculture Handbook No. 153 (Washington, D.C.: Government Printing Office, 1959). "The first 100 pages treat land use patterns and their development in the United States from a historical perspective. The remainder is a selection of air photos which depict land use patterns...throughout the forty-eight coterminous states." (GBACL.)

DOUGLAS R. MCMANIS, *Historical Geography of the United States: A Bibliography (excluding Alaska and Hawaii)* (Ypsilanti, Mich.: Division of Field Services,

Eastern Michigan University, 1965). An extensive compilation of titles, arranged by region and topic, but without annotation. Concentrates mainly on land settlement and the economy.

RANDALL D. SALE and EDWIN D. KARN, *American Expansion: A Book of Maps* (Homewood, Ill.: Dorsey Press, 1962). Twelve neatly executed maps, accompanied by brief commentary, covering the period 1790–1900. The location of land offices is shown.

NORMAN J. W. THROWER, *Original Survey and Land Subdivision: A Comparative Study of the Form and Effect of Contrasting Cadastral Surveys* (Chicago: Rand McNally & Company, 1966). A detailed analysis of the Ohio material.

FREDERICK JACKSON TURNER, *The Frontier in American History* (Magnolia, Mass.: Peter Smith, 1953). A collection of 13 major essays by Turner. His contention that the frontier experience was central to the development of American life and institutions has had a major impact on scholarly thought and controversy.

DAVID WARD, *Cities and Immigrants: A Geography of Change in Nineteenth-Century America* (New York: Oxford University Press, 1971).

7. The American Landscape, Attitudes Toward the Land

PETER BLAKE, *God's Own Junkyard: The Planned Deterioration of America's Landscape* (New York: Holt, Rinehart & Winston, Inc., 1963). Written "not in anger, but in fury." This combination of photograph, quotation, and brief text is a powerful polemic against those who have raped the American environment for private profit. Intemperate, but instructive.

WOLFGANG BORN, *American Landscape Painting* (New Haven: Yale University Press, 1948). The best survey yet of a subject rich in potential interest for the cultural geographer.

WILSON O. CLOUGH, *The Necessary Earth: Nature and Solitude in American Literature* (Austin: University of Texas Press, 1964). A volume of modest accomplishment. Through sheer persistence, Clough does make his point about the centrality of wild nature as a literary—and thus a basic cultural—theme in American experience.

ARTHUR E. EKIRCH, *Man and Nature in America* (New York: Columbia University Press, 1963).

HANS HUTH, *Nature and the American: Three Centuries of Changing Attitudes* (Berkeley: University of California Press, 1957). A thoughtful, useful survey of the topic, crammed with much detail concerning artists, travelers, conservationists, vacationers, and others.

DAVID LOWENTHAL, "The American Scene," *Geographical Review*, 58, No. 1 (1968), 61–88. Digs deeply into fundamental issues. Highly recommended.

LEO MARX, *The Machine in the Garden: Technology and the Pastoral Ideal in America* (New York: Oxford University Press, 1964). A highly influential volume; indeed a classic. Largely on the basis of literary evidence, the zone of tension among the forces of technology, the wilderness ideal, and the pastoral vision in the American mind is charted most expressively.

IAN NAIRN, *The American Landscape: A Critical View* (New York: Random House, Inc., 1965). A provocative mélange of photo and prose by a British architect that is more than a simple jeremiad. The central argument is that the basic flaw in the visual landscape (and inferentially in American life in general?) is the weakness or absence of genuine relationship and identity—an outgrowth of the essential privatism of Americans.

RODERICK NASH, *Wilderness and the American Mind* (New Haven: Yale University Press, 1967). A sensitive, thoughtful, erudite chronicle of American (and European) attitudes toward wilderness in all their ambiguity. Extensive bibliography.

FORREST R. PITTS, "Japanese and American World-Views and their Landscapes," in *Proceedings of IGU Regional Conference in Japan 1957* (Tokyo, 1957), pp. 447–59. Comparative cultural geography as it should be written. Elegant.

CHARLES L. SANFORD, *The Quest for Paradise: Europe and the American Moral Imagination* (Urbana: University of Illinois Press, 1961). A major work that delves deeply into the origin of the edenic theme and its many outcroppings in American thought and action.

PETER J. SCHMITT, *Back to Nature: The Arcadian Myth in Urban America* (New York: Oxford University Press, 1969). A detailed survey of the subject, as approached from many angles. Strong on detail; deficient in analysis or theory.

HENRY NASH SMITH, *Virgin Land: The American West as Symbol and Myth* (Cambridge, Mass.: Harvard University Press, 1950). The seminal work on the topic.

HARRY SWAIN and COTTON MATHER, *St. Croix Border Country* (Prescott, Wisc.: Trimbelle Press & Pierce County Geographical Society, 1968). A witty dissection of the exurban landscape. "Unlikely as its parochial title and auspices may make it seem, this slim guidebook is an item of wide general interest—for anyone... who is concerned with...the peripheries of American metropolitan regions." (GBACL.)

J. WREFORD WATSON, "Image Geography: The Myth of America in the American Scene," *The Advancement of Science*, 27 (1970–1971), 1–9. A quite basic, eloquent statement on the pivotal role of mental images and myths in the shaping of American ways and landscapes.

8. Ethnic and Racial Groups

LOUIS ADAMIC, *A Nation of Nations* (New York: Harper & Row, Publishers, 1945).

ELAINE M. BJORKLUND, "Ideology and Culture as Exemplified in Southwest Michigan," *Annals of the Association of American Geographers*, 54, No. 2 (1964), 227–41. A detailed analysis of a Dutch-American region.

J. NEALE CARMAN, *Foreign-Language Units of Kansas. I. Historical Atlas and Statistics* (Lawrence: University of Kansas Press, 1962). A historical-cartographic survey, county by county—nay, township by township—of the foreign-language groups of the state, in staggering detail. Large mass of statistics, notes, and graphs included. The basic theme is cultural assimilation. A formidable example unlikely to be emulated by scholars in other states.

HAROLD E. DRIVER, *Indians of North America* (Chicago: University of Chicago Press, 1961). A comprehensive, authoritative description and interpretation that covers a score or more of major topics.

MILTON M. GORDON, *Assimilation in American Life: The Role of Race, Religion, and National Origin* (New York: Oxford University Press, 1964). An extremely useful, stimulating essay that attempts a comprehensive theoretical statement on the changing nature of social groups in the United States. Basic reading.

A. IRVING HALLOWELL, "The Backlash of the Frontier: The Impact of the Indian on American Culture," in *Smithsonian Report for 1958* (Washington, D.C.: Smithsonian Institution, 1959). Probably the best concise statement on the subject.

OSCAR HANDLIN, *The Uprooted: The Epic Story of the Great Migrations that Made the American People* (New York: Grosset & Dunlap, Inc., 1951).

J. FRASER HART, "The Changing Distribution of the American Negro," *Annals of the Association of American Geographers*, 50 (1960), 242–66.

RICHARD HARTSHORNE, "Racial Maps of the United States," *Geographical Review*, 28 (1938), 276–88.

MELVILLE HERSKOVITS, *The Myth of the Negro Past* (New York: Harper & Row, Publishers, 1941). The first serious examination of the nature and extent of African cultural transfers to the United States. An epochal piece of scholarship whose full repercussions have just begun to be felt.

TERRY G. JORDAN, "Population Origin Groups in Rural Texas," (Map, scale 1:1,500,000), *Annals of the Association of American Geographers*, Vol. 60, No. 2 (1970), Map Supplement No. 13. A splendid research effort. Now all we need are 49 maps of similar quality for the remaining states.

ALFRED L. KROEBER, *Cultural and Natural Areas of Native North America*, Publications in American Archaeology and Ethnology, Vol. 38 (Berkeley: University of California Press, 1939). "A masterly synthesis of what is known about the location, population, ecology, and cultural identity of the aboriginal groups inhabiting all of North America during immediate pre-contact time." (GBACL.)

GERALD D. SUTTLES, *The Social Order of the Slum: Ethnicity and Territory in the Inner City* (Chicago: University of Chicago Press, 1968). An important analysis at the micro scale of the social geography and sociology of a few square blocks of Chicago's Near West Side by a participant observer.

9. Settlement Characteristics

KENNETH E. COREY, *A Spatial Analysis of Urban Houses*, doctoral dissertation, University of Cincinnati, 1969. Although mainly concerned with the detailed description of a small Cincinnati neighborhood, this document also includes a comprehensive listing and discussion of the literature on the morphology of urban dwellings.

JAMES MARSTON FITCH, *American Building. I. the Historical Forces that Shaped It*, 2d ed. (Boston: Houghton Mifflin, Company, 1966). A rather curious tract that never really comes to grip with any specific problem, but touches provocatively on many. The most pervasive theme is that basic, unresolved tension (at least since 1850) between the technology of construction and the American socioeconomic system, as expressed in building and civic design.

ALAN GOWANS, *Images of American Living: Four Centuries of Architecture and Furniture as Cultural Expression* (Philadelphia: J. B. Lippincott 1964). A splendid, profound work—the nearest thing yet to a definitive treatment of the meaning of American architecture (and furniture).

J. FRASER HART, "Field Patterns in Indiana," *Geographical Review*, 58 (1968), 450–71. Apparently the only treatment of the topic in the American literature.

FRED KNIFFEN, "The American Agricultural Fair: Time and Place," *Annals of the Association of American Geographers*, 41 (1951), 42–57. Another valuable diffusion study.

———, "The American Covered Bridge," *Geographical Review*, 41 (1951), 114–23. One of the first accounts of the spatial diffusion of an American innovation.

———, "Folk Housing: Key to Diffusion," *Annals of the Association of American Geographers*, 55 (1965), 549–77. The culture areas of the early nineteenth century as discerned through field investigation of rural houses.

———, "Louisiana House Types," *Annals of the Association of American Geographers*, 26 (1936), 179–93. The first major article by an American geographer on house morphology.

PEIRCE F. LEWIS, "The Geography of Old Houses," *Earth and Mineral Sciences* (Pennsylvania State University), 39, No. 5 (February 1970), 33–37. The only thing wrong with this statement on the historical-geographic implications of early houses is that it is too brief.

LEWIS MUMFORD, *Sticks and Stones: A Study of American Architecture and Civilization* (New York: Boni & Liveright, 1924). An attempt to evaluate architecture in America in terms of our civilization.

WILLIAM D. PATTISON, *Beginnings of the American Rectangular Land Survey 1784–1800*, Research Paper No. 50 (Chicago: University of Chicago, Department of Geography, 1957). "A definitive essay on the first formulation of and experiments in Ohio with the system of land survey soon to be adopted for the entire national domain." (GBACL.)

EDWARD T. PRICE, "The Central Courthouse Square in the American County Seat," *Geographical Review*, 58 (1968), 29–60. The historical geography and diffusion of several distinct types of square.

AMOS RAPOPORT, *House Form and Culture* (Englewood Cliffs, N.J.: Prentice-Hall, Inc., 1969). A stimulating, general synthesis dealing with the interaction of social, cultural, and environmental forces in building morphology. The references to the American scene are only incidental.

JOHN W. REPS, *The Making of Urban America: A History of City Planning in the United States* (Princeton, N.J.: Princeton University Press, 1965). "This profusely illustrated, monumental volume is an excellent source for all sorts of material on the beginnings, layouts, and growth of American towns and cities." (GBACL.) A unique, indispensable volume.

JOHN E. RICKERT, "House Facades of the Northeastern United States: A Tool of Geographic Analysis," *Annals of the Association of American Geographers,* 57 (1967), 211–38. Contains a comprehensive bibliography.

ERIC SLOANE, *American Barns and Covered Bridges* (New York: Wilfred Funk, Inc., 1954). Excellent line drawings, along with comments and reflections, by an artist specializing in early Americana.

GLENN T. TREWARTHA, "Some Regional Characteristics of American Farmsteads," *Annals of the Association of American Geographers,* 38 (1948), 196–225. The only substantial effort in this direction thus far by an American geographer, and an interesting experiment.

CHRISTOPHER TUNNARD and HENRY HOPE REED, *American Skyline: The Growth and Form of Our Cities and Towns* (Boston: Houghton Mifflin Company, 1956). "The only well-rounded discussion of the evolution of the American urban landscape yet published—and a good one. Many valuable sidelights on the general historical geography of the nation." (GBACL.)

10. *Language*

MEREDITH F. BURRILL, "Toponymic Generics," *Names,* 4, No. 3 (September 1956), 129–45 and 4, No. 4 (December 1956), 226–40. The cultural and geographic significance of some of the more important generic terms in American place names.

JOSHUA A. FISHMAN, *Yiddish in America: Socio-Linguistic Description and Analysis,* Publication 36 (Bloomington, Ind.: Indiana University Research Center in Anthropology, Folklore, and Linguistics, 1965). An innovative, intriguing treatment of the linguistic geography and sociology of speakers of a dwindling language in both Eastern Europe and the United States.

———, et al., *Language Loyalty in the United States: The Maintenance and Perpetuation of Non-English Mother Tongues by American Ethnic and Religious Groups* (The Hague: Mouton, 1966). A massive, many-sided treatment by a number of contributors in a volume that promises to be the most definitive on the subject.

HANS KURATH, *A Word Geography of the Eastern United States* (Ann Arbor: University of Michigan Press, 1949). "Analysis and interpretation, through texts and maps, of the spatial distribution of selected elements in the American vocabulary, and a tentative postulation of linguistic regions for the Eastern Seaboard." (GBACL.) Absolutely essential for the student of American culture.

HANS KURATH and RAVEN I. MCDAVID, JR., *The Pronunciation of English in the Atlantic States* (Ann Arbor: University of Michigan Press, 1961). A sequel to the preceding item and, like it, rich in cartographic documentation.

CHARLTON LAIRD, *Language in America* (Cleveland: The World Publishing Company, 1970). A large, ambitious work, strong in both fact and theory, that views the entire Western Hemisphere (before and after the European invasion) as a grand experiment in linguistic change through time and space.

RAVEN I. MCDAVID, JR., "The Dialects of American English," in W. Nelson Francis, *The Structure of American English* (New York: The Ronald Press Co., 1958), pp. 480–543.

HENRY L. MENCKEN, *The American Language: An Inquiry into the Development of English in the United States,* 4th ed. (New York: Alfred A. Knopf, Inc., 1936); *Supplement I,* 1945; *Supplement II,* 1948. Everything you ever wanted to know about the language (including the spatial dimension) and much more, by a writer who could never be dull even if he tried. Mencken was an untrained, but ardent, word-watcher—one of the last great amateur scholars in a world of galloping specialization.

CARROLL E. REED, *Dialects of American English* (Cleveland: The World Publishing Company, 1967). A brief, semipopular, but highly serviceable introduction and survey of the subject.

RICHARD B. SEALOCK and PAULINE A. SEELY, *Bibliography of Place-Name Literature: United States and Canada*, 2d ed. (Chicago: American Library Association, 1967). Conscientiously comprehensive. Annual supplements have been appearing in *Names* magazine.

ELSDON C. SMITH, *American Surnames* (Philadelphia: Chilton Company—Book Division, 1969). This is the only truly solid, comprehensive treatment of the subject, one that is somehow both encyclopedic and penetrating. A labor of love by another leisure-time scholar.

GEORGE R. STEWART, *Names on the Land: A Historical Account of Place-Naming in the United States*, rev. ed. (Boston: Houghton Mifflin Company, 1958). This volume still stands in solitary splendor as the only worthwhile work on the subject. Scholarly and highly readable.

WILBUR ZELINSKY, "Some Problems in the Distribution of Generic Terms in the Place-Names of the Northeastern United States," *Annals of the Association of American Geographers*, 45 (1955), 319–49.

———, "Cultural Variation in Personal Name Patterns in the Eastern United States," *Annals of the Association of American Geographers*, 60 (1970), 743–69. Evidently the only geographic analysis of forenames thus far, and one of my favorite pieces of reading.

11. Religion

WHITNEY R. CROSS, *The Burned-Over District: The Social and Intellectual History of Enthusiastic Religion in Western New York, 1800–1850* (Ithaca, N.Y.: Cornell University Press, 1950).

EDWIN S. GAUSTAD, *Historical Atlas of Religion in America* (New York: Harper & Row, Publishers, 1962). "A definitive analysis, in text, map, and graph, of the historical geography of the major American denominations." (GBACL.)

DAVID E. SOPHER, *Geography of Religions* (Englewood Cliffs, N.J.: Prentice-Hall, Inc., 1967). The first monographic treatment of the subject—and an excellent one, original in concept, and rich in ideas and fact. Several pages are devoted to the United States.

WILBUR ZELINSKY, "An Approach to the Religious Geography of the United States; Patterns of Church Membership in 1952," *Annals of the Association of American Geographers*, 51 (1961), 139–93.

12. Political Behavior

If this section seems short, it simply reflects the fact that geographers have been curiously reluctant to examine the domestic politics of the United States in their spatial, historical, and cultural context. All three selections are by political scientists.

V. O. KEY, JR., *Southern Politics* (New York: Alfred A. Knopf, Inc., 1949). "Solid stuff on the not-so-solid South before Brown vs. Topeka. Loaded with maps, graphs, and a vast body of political and geographical savvy. If you want to learn about Southern politics in depth, start here." (P. F. Lewis)

KEVIN P. PHILLIPS, *The Emerging Republican Majority* (Garden City, N.Y.: Doubleday & Co., Inc., 1969). Although instantly obsolete, often superficial, and burdened with a wildly misleading title, this exasperating mish-mash does contain a superfluity of interesting and useful detail, in word and map, not only on political geography but also on the geography of settlement and ethnic groups.

RICHARD L. MERRITT, *Symbols of American Community, 1735–1775* (New Haven, Conn.: Yale University Press, 1966). How feelings of national unity germinated and sprouted during a critical period, as revealed through the content analysis of place references in newspapers in four provincial metropolises. An important contribution to general political theory and quantitative behavioral studies.

13. Diet

The geographic cupboard is almost totally bare when it comes to serious work on what people eat and drink and where within the United States. In fact, the most substantial contributions are imbedded in larger works by two *sub rosa* geographers, George Stewart and Rupert Vance. The items in question are noted elsewhere on this list.

American Heritage Cookbook and Illustrated History of American Eating and Drinking (New York: Simon & Schuster, Inc., 1964). "A trifle folksy in spots and regrettably undocumented, this is nonetheless the only comprehensive attempt I know to paint a broad picture of American culinary history and eating habits." (P. F. Lewis.)

RICHARD O. CUMMINGS, *The American and His Food: A History of Food Habits in the United States*, rev. ed. (Chicago: University of Chicago Press, 1941). A valiant attempt, but, alas, only a beginning.

MARGARET CUSSLER and MARY L. DE GIVE, *'Twixt the Cup and the Lip; Psychological and Socio-Cultural Factors Affecting Food Habits* (New York: Twayne Publishers, 1952).

SAM HILLIARD, "Hog Meat and Cornpone: Food Habits in the Ante-Bellum South," *Proceedings of the American Philosophical Society*, 113 (January 1969), 1–13.

14. Folklore and Handicrafts

JAN HAROLD BRUNVAND, *The Study of American Folklore: An Introduction* (New York: W. W. Norton & Co., Inc., 1968). An excellent survey of the discipline, broad in coverage and overflowing with good bibliographies.

RICHARD M. DORSON, *American Folklore* (Chicago: University of Chicago Press, 1959). A good, general account which includes a generous section on modern folklore. In "Regional Folk Cultures" (pp. 74–134), the Pennsylvania German, Spanish Southwest, Maine coast, and Mormon areas are dealt with.

HENRY GLASSIE, *Pattern in the Material Folk Culture of the Eastern United States* (Philadelphia: University of Pennsylvania Press, 1969). An extraordinary, if eclectic and disorganized, account of an amazing range of phenomena, but mainly houses and other structures, based on extensive reading and field observation. The absence of index and table of contents is maddening. The bibliographic citations are uniquely valuable—if you can find them.

JOHN A. KOUWENHOVEN, *Made in America: The Arts in Modern Civilization* (Garden City, N.Y.: Doubleday & Co., Inc., 1948). A thoughtful essay on the chronic tension in American thought and art between the honest expedience of locally developed vernacular crafts and imported European traditions and standards.

E. JOAN WILSON MILLER, "The Ozark Culture Region as Revealed by Traditional Materials," *Annals of the Association of American Geographers*, 58 (1968), 51–77. Verbal folklore as grist for the geographic mill.

15. Regional Studies

a. GENERAL WORKS

CONRAD M. ARENSBERG, "American Communities," *American Anthropologist*, 57 (1955), 1143–60. A significant treatment of the major sociocultural regions of the country.

OTIS W. COAN and RICHARD G. LILLARD, *American in Fiction: An Annotated List of Novels that Interpret Aspects of Life in the United States, Canada, and Mexico*, 5th ed. (Palo Alto, Calif.: Pacific Press, 1967).

A. R. MANGUS, *Rural Regions of the United States* (Washington, D.C.: Works Progress Administration, 1940). Figure 1 (facing p. 4) is a map entitled "Rural-Farm Cultural Regions and Sub-Regions," one that depicts 32 regions and 218 subregions based upon uniformities in population.

DONALD W. MEINIG, "The American Colonial Era: A Geographic Commentary," *Proceedings of the Royal Geographical Society, South Australian Branch* (1957–58), 1–22. The origins, nature, and significance of the three principal colonial culture hearths stated succinctly and effectively.

CARLE C. ZIMMERMAN and R. E. DU WORS, *Graphic Regional Sociology* (*A Study in American Social Organization*) (Cambridge, Mass.: Phillips Book Store, 1952). A curious mixture of syllabus and essay, cliché and fresh insight. The sociology, economy, and culture of seven regions are presented: the South; Appalachian-Ozark Region; Northeastern-Urban Industrial Region; Corn Belt; Wheat Belt; Arid West; and Pacific Region.

b. NEW ENGLAND

HANS KURATH, *Handbook to the Linguistic Atlas of New England* (Providence, R.I.: Brown University Press, 1943). Ventures well beyond the province of language to offer a sound historical, geographic, social, and cultural introduction to the region.

SUMNER CHILTON POWELL, *Puritan Village: The Formation of a New England Town* (Middletown, Conn.: Wesleyan University Press, 1963). An exemplary analysis of how the social and physical attributes of the town were crystallized from elements imported from Old England.

LOIS (KIMBALL) MATHEWS ROSENBERRY, *The Expansion of New England: The Spread of New England Settlement and Institutions to the Mississippi River, 1620–1865* (Boston: Houghton Mifflin Company, 1909).

WALTER M. WHITEHILL, *Boston: A Topographical History*, 2d ed. (Cambridge, Mass.: Harvard University Press, 1968). "...how Boston became Boston in the growth of its physical layout, building patterns, and landmarks," (GBACL.) Virtually a unique item in the American literature.

c. THE MIDLAND

STEVENSON W. FLETCHER, *Pennsylvania Agriculture and Country Life, 1640–1840* (Harrisburg: Pennsylvania Historical and Museum Commission, 1950). An amazingly detailed and comprehensive book.

JEAN GOTTMANN, *Megalopolis: The Urbanized Northeastern Seaboard of the United States* (New York: Twentieth Century Fund, 1961). "A detailed geographic interpretation of the area between Portland, Maine and Washington, D.C. as the prototype of the super-metropolitan agglomeration..." (GBACL.) Cultural factors are accorded major attention in this influential volume.

JOHN A. HOSTETLER, *Amish Society* (Baltimore: Johns Hopkins Press, 1963). Perhaps no other population of comparable minuteness has stimulated so much general interest or so many publications, good and bad. Hostetler, who writes with the special vision of an insider, provides perhaps the most satisfying general survey of this peculiar community.

JOHN H. THOMPSON, ed., *The Geography of New York State* (Syracuse, N.Y.: Syracuse University Press, 1966). This collaborative work sets a standard not yet rivaled by any other recent publication on local geography in the United States. Of special interest are the three chapters on the state's historical geography by Donald W. Meinig.

THOMAS J. WERTENBAKER, *The Founding of American Civilization: The Middle Colonies* (New York: Charles Scribner's Sons, 1938).

d. THE SOUTH

HARRIETTE L. ARNOW, *Hunter's Horn* (New York: The Macmillan Company, 1949). Good regional fiction is a "must" for the serious student of American cultural geography; and this is the logical choice if a single sample must be cited. This story of a remote community in Kentucky's Cumberland Valley ca. 1941 contains some superlative ethnography, history, regional sociology, physical and cultural geography, all related in first-rate prose and a hypnotically gripping narrative.

JEAN GOTTMANN, *Virginia in Our Century* (Charlottesville: University of Virginia Press, 1969). "A multi-faceted regional study by the noted French geographer. This is almost unique as a full-dimensional geographical monograph on an American region." (GBACL.)

J. FRASER HART, *The Southeastern United States* (New York: Van Nostrand Reinhold, 1967). A capsule regional geography, and one devoting a relatively large share of its attention to matters social and cultural.

TERRY G. JORDAN, *German Seed in Texas Soil: Immigrant Farmers in Nineteenth-Century Texas* (Austin: University of Texas Press, 1966).

———, "The Imprint of the Upper and Lower South on Mid-Nineteenth-Century Texas," *Annals of the Association of American Geographers*, 57 (1967), 667–90. The demographic and cultural contributions of the two principal streams of migration into Texas.

———, "The Texas Appalachia," *Annals of the Association of American Geographers*, 60 (1970), 409–27. How a replica of Appalachia and Ozarkia was created in Texas by bearers of their culture.

DONALD W. MEINIG, *Imperial Texas: An Interpretive Essay in Cultural Geography* (Austin: University of Texas Press, 1968). Another classic. A concise, penetrating, highly original study of how the populations and culture areas of the state have taken shape over time and space.

HARRY ROY MERRENS, *Colonial North Carolina in the Eighteenth Century: A Study in Historical Geography* (Chapel Hill: University of North Carolina Press, 1964). "The settlement, economy, and transport network of North Carolina in the 1770s reconstructed painstakingly from all possible sources in a model study of historico-geographic method." (GBACL.)

FREDERICK LAW OLMSTED, *The Cotton Kingdom: A Traveller's Observations on Cotton and Slavery in the American Slave States*, ed. Arthur M. Schlesinger (New York: Alfred A. Knopf, Inc., 1953). First-hand description and interpretation of the highest order. "The work of this gifted social critic and landscape architect remains a basic source for the historical geography of the South." (GBACL.)

RUPERT B. VANCE, *Human Geography of the South: A Study in Regional Resources and Human Adequacy* (Chapel Hill: University of North Carolina Press, 1935). After more than three decades, this treatment of the region by a sociologist has not been superseded. Contains material on social and cultural items, including diet, not found in the ordinary geography or sociology text.

e. THE MIDDLE WEST

JOSEPH W. BROWNELL, "The Cultural Midwest," *Journal of Geography*, 39 (Feb. 1960), 81–85. Apparently the first attempt to delineate the outer limits of the region.

DAVID GRAHAM HUTTON, *Midwest at Noon* (Chicago: University of Chicago Press, 1946). "...combines historical perspectives, economic analyses, personal observations, psychological characterizations, and social interpretations in about equal measure to make a rich and sympathetic volume which resists summary." (U.S. Library of Congress: *A Guide to the Study of the United States of America.*)

HAROLD M. MAYER and RICHARD C. WADE, *Chicago: Growth of a Metropolis* (Chicago: University of Chicago Press, 1969). A unique, masterly visual-verbal-cartographic study of growth, in form and process, and of a multitude of urban phenomena, including vernacular architecture and ethnic geography, along with the usual economic topics.

THOMAS T. MCAVOY et al., *The Midwest: Myth or Reality?* (Notre Dame, Ind.: University of Notre Dame Press, 1961). A symposial volume of highly uneven quality that must be cited in lieu of anything better.

f. THE WEST

JOHN L. LANDGRAF, *Land-Use in the Ramah Area of New Mexico: An Anthropological Approach to Areal Study,* Papers of the Peabody Museum of American Archaeology and Ethnology, Vol. 42, No. 1 (Cambridge, Mass.: Harvard University, 1954). An excellent study of the area, the various peoples (Anglos, Texans, Mormons, Spanish-Americans, and Navaho), their relations to the land and to one another.

G. MALCOLM LEWIS, "Regional Ideas and Reality in the Cis-Rocky Mountain West," *Transactions and Papers, Institute of British Geographers,* Publication 38 (1966), 135–50. The Great Plains as a mental concept and as a mappable reality.

DONALD W. MEINIG, *The Great Columbia Plain: A Historical Geography, 1805–1910* (Seattle: University of Washington Press, 1968). "An outstanding study of an American region. The Columbia Plain as perceived, conceived, and developed by leading explorers, settlers, promoters, scientists, and officials." (GBACL.)

———, "The Mormon Culture Region: Strategies and Patterns in the Geography of the American West, 1847–1964," *Annals of the Association of American Geographers,* 55 (1965), 191–220. In addition to being a masterly synthesis of the historical geography of Mormon population and culture, this article also proposes an interesting general model for culture areas.

———, *Southwest: Three Peoples in Geographical Change, 1600–1970* (New York: Oxford University Press, 1971). A study of New Mexico and Arizona. Although it stands brilliantly upon its own merits, it is most usefully read in conjunction with Meinig's earlier volume on Texas, which it resembles in both format and quality.

RICHARD L. NOSTRAND, "The Hispanic-American Borderland: Delimitation of an American Culture Region," *Annals of the Association of American Geographers,* 60 (1970), 638–61.

WILLIAM L. THOMAS, JR., ed., "Man, Time, and Space in Southern California," *Annals of the Association of American Geographers,* Vol. 49, No. 3, Part 2 (1959). A symposial effort: five excellent essays, plus critical commentaries.

WALTER PRESCOTT WEBB, *The Great Plains* (Boston: Ginn & Company, 1931). "This is one of the classics, a seminal work on the trials and errors of humid-land settlers in a subhumid environment. Cultural, technological, and physical factors are dealt with in satisfying fashion." (GBACL.)

16. *Miscellaneous and Unclassifiable*

DAVID T. BAZELON, *Power in America: The Politics of the New Class* (New York: New American Library, 1967). As one reviewer noted, this is indeed "a book of subtle contradictions...brilliant, provocative, and self-consciously seductive." It charges off inconclusively in many interesting directions, but the underlying theme is a powerful one: America as a shallow society of confused individualists, lacking in genuine community.

DANIEL J. BOORSTIN, *The Americans: The National Experience* (New York: Random House, Inc., 1965). An assemblage of essays—brilliant and original for the most part—dealing with some major aspects of American life in the early nineteenth century, among them the versatility of New Englanders, transience as a basic theme in American existence, boosterism, "the vagueness of the land" (thas is, the spatial ambiguity of America), language and speech. For sheer refreshment, try the sparkling essay on the American hotel (pp. 134–47).

JAMES H. CASSEDY, *Demography in Early America: Beginnings of the Statistical Mind, 1600–1800* (Cambridge, Mass.: Harvard University Press, 1969). Significant not only for facts and chronicling of demographic thought, knowledge, theory, and programs, but, as the subtitle indicates, as a case study in the budding of the "statistical mind." Transdemographic implications.

ERIC FISCHER, *The Passing of the European Age: A Study of the Transfer of Civilization and its Renewal in Other Continents.* rev. ed. (Cambridge, Mass.: Harvard University Press, 1948).

EDWARD T. HALL, *The Hidden Dimension* (Garden City, N.Y.: Doubleday & Co., Inc., 1966). A stimulating exploration, albeit occasionally fuzzy, of the more intimate spatial-sensory world of human beings. In this pioneering effort in "proxemics," (the perception and culturally conditioned use of personal space), Hall deals only briefly or tangentially with Americans; but this volume holds interest for students of any cultural group.

MARK HOLLOWAY, *Heavens on Earth: Utopian Communities in America, 1680–1880,* 2d ed. (New York: Dover Publications, Inc., 1966).

HANS KOHN, *American Nationalism: An Interpretative Essay* (New York: Crowell-Collier-Macmillan, 1957). A broad-ranging, generally insightful essay on five facets of the origin and character of American nationalism: its roots; the unique familial link with Britain and its culture; sectionalism; the significance of large-scale immigration; and the United States as a world power.

FRANK R. KRAMER, *Voices in the Valley: Mythmaking and Folk Belief in the Shaping of the Middle West* (Madison: University of Wisconsin Press, 1964). The role of myth in the Middle West (and Huronia) and the parental New England, Pennsylvanian, and southern regions. Pretentious, overwritten, and often incoherent, but with occasional flashes of brilliance. The myth of the homestead is one of the central items.

ALLAN I. LUDWIG, *Graven Images: New England Stonecarving and its Symbols, 1650–1815* (Middletown, Conn.: Wesleyan University Press, 1966). A splendidly produced volume that converges on its subject from several angles: the basic theory of visual symbols; Puritan theology; the burial customs of Puritans and English; and the historical-spatial- stylistic analysis of New England gravestones. A rare treatment of the cultural geography of a folk art in North America.

ROBERT O. MEAD, *Atlantic Legacy: Essays in American-European Cultural History* (New York: New York University Press, 1969). An account, roughly chronological, of the continuing trans-Atlantic exchange of influences at the higher cultural and psychological levels.

ROBERT MEREDITH, ed., *American Studies: Essays on Theory and Method* (Columbus, Ohio: Charles E. Merrill Publishing Company, 1968). An excellent, well-edited collection of recent papers dealing with methodological and substantive issues in American Studies.

PERRY MILLER, *The Life of the Mind in America: From the Revolution to the Civil War* (New York: Harcourt Brace Jovanovich, 1965). Two-and-a-fraction parts of Miller's unfinished last opus. Highly erudite, literate prose. Book One deals with evangelism and revivalism; Book Two considers "The Legal Mentality," and the attitude of Americans toward law and lawyers.

LEWIS MUMFORD, *The Myth of the Machine: Technics and Human Development* (New York: Harcourt Brace Jovanovich, 1967) and *The Myth of the Machine: The Pentagon of Power* (Harcourt Brace Jovanovich, 1970). These two volumes climax a scholarly career that in its depth and breadth defies classification or capsule description. This is a most eloquent statement concerning the interplay among myth, technology, and social behavior from prehistoric times to the present, and provides a rich backdrop for any analysis of a contemporary community.

KARL B. RAITZ, and JOHN FRASER HART, eds., *A Preliminary List of Topographic Maps Illustrating Aspects of the Cultural Geography of the United States* (Minneapolis: University of Minnesota, Department of Geography, 1970). Mimeographed. The cultural geographer has at his disposal in the thousands of topographic quadrangles produced by the U.S. Geological Survey an almost infinite store of facts and abundant inspiration. This annotated list is a welcome guide for novice and graybeard alike.

GEORGE R. STEWART, *American Ways of Life* (Garden City, N.Y.: Doubleday & Co., Inc., 1954). "A rare instance of an angel rushing in where fools fear to tread. Stewart writes about all sorts of peculiarly American things (including almost the only decent thing on American diet that I know about) and does it very well. The book is now out of print—a literary and scholarly catastrophe." (P. F. Lewis.)

ALAN TRACHTENBERG, *Brooklyn Bridge: Fact and Symbol* (New York: Oxford University Press, 1965). An eminently satisfying exploration of the history and meaning of one of the most influential artifacts man has wrought upon the American continent. This particular bridge does have a great deal to tell us about ourselves, as some poets and painters have discovered.

EDWARD L. ULLMAN, "Amenities as a Factor in Regional Growth," *Geographical Review*, 44 (1954), 119–32. A manifesto concerning the importance of trans-economic factors in the demographic and social development of the United States, one whose implications are only now beginning to be appreciated.

JOHN K. WRIGHT, *Human Nature in Geography; Fourteen Papers, 1925–1965* (Cambridge, Mass.: Harvard University Press, 1966). "Fourteen imaginative papers... touching on marvels, discoveries, philosophies, and organization, and human awareness of spatial diversity." Deals with American topics, among others. A writer of rare charm, versatility, and erudition of whom every student of the American scene should be aware.

Index